TERMINAL PARADOX

Published by Grove Weidenfeld
A division of Grove Press, Inc.
841 Broadway
New York, NY 10003-4793

Published in Canada by General Publishing Company, Ltd.

Library of Congress Cataloging-in-Publication Data

Banerjee, Maria Němcová.
Terminal paradox : the novels of Milan Kundera / Maria Němcová Banerjee. — 1st ed.
p. cm.
Includes bibliographical references.
1. Kundera, Milan—Criticism and interpretation. I. Title.
PG5039.21.U6Z54 1990
891.8′635—dc20 89-25942
CIP

ISBN 0-8021-1127-0
ISBN 0-8021-3233-2 (pbk.)

Manufactured in the United States of America

Printed on acid-free paper

Designed by Irving Perkins Associates

First Edition 1990
First Evergreen Edition 1992

1 3 5 7 9 10 8 6 4 2

For Ron

CONTENTS

ACKNOWLEDGMENTS

The following publishers have kindly granted permission to use excerpts from Milan Kundera's works: From *Life Is Elsewhere*. English translation by Peter Kussi copyright © 1974 by Alfred A. Knopf, Inc. Translated from *Život je jinde,* copyright © 1973 by Milan Kundera. From *Laughable Loves*. English translation by Suzanne Rappaport copyright © 1974 by Alfred A. Knopf, Inc. Translated from *Směšné lásky,* copyright © 1969, 1987 by Milan Kundera. From *The Farewell Party*. English translation by Peter Kussi copyright © 1976 by Alfred A. Knopf, Inc. Translated from *Valčík na rozloučenou,* copyright © 1973 by Milan Kundera. From *The Book of Laughter and Forgetting*. English translation by Michael Henry Heim copyright © 1980 by Alfred A. Knopf, Inc. Translated from *Kniha smíchu a zapomnění,* copyright © 1978 by Milan Kundera. All reprinted by permission of Alfred A. Knopf, Inc. From *The Joke*. English translation by Michael Henry Heim copyright © 1982 by Harper & Row, Publishers, Inc. Translated from *Žert,* copyright © 1967 by Milan Kundera. From *The Unbearable Lightness of Being*. English translation by Michael Henry Heim copyright © 1984 by Harper & Row, Publishers, Inc. Translated from *Nesnesitelná lehkost bytí,* copyright © 1984 by Milan Kundera. All reprinted by permission of Harper & Row, Publishers, Inc. In direct quotations from Kundera's works in English translation, I have followed throughout his practice of omitting accent marks from Czech words, though I have retained the accents in my own text.

Part of chapter 2 of the present work, "*Laughable Loves;* or, The Impossible Don Juan," appeared in a slightly different version in *The Review of Contemporary Fiction* 9, no. 2 (Summer 1984):37–46.

I wish to thank my editor, Joy Johannessen, for her intelligent and sensitive work.

TERMINAL PARADOX

INTRODUCTION

In his Jerusalem Address (1985), meditating on the European tradition of the novel, Milan Kundera asks:

> But what is that wisdom, what is the novel? There is a fine Jewish proverb: Man thinks, God laughs. Inspired by that adage, I like to imagine that François Rabelais heard God's laughter one day, and thus was born the idea of the first great European novel. It pleases me to think that the art of the novel came into the world as the echo of God's laughter.[1]

This myth of origins, invented at the apex of his maturity by a novelist living in the age he has defined as one of terminal paradoxes, is strangely moving. It moves with the beauty of human reverence, touched by a deeply felt awareness of the radical mortality of all things human. The novel too is mortal, "as mortal as the West of the Modern Era,"[2] says Kundera.

But if one takes a second, more analytical look at Kundera's fable, one discerns the scenario for a comic skit involving two players whose modes of being are in essential contradiction. God, whose nature it is to rejoice in the full knowledge of his being, looks down on earth and catches man in the act of aping him, contorting himself silly in the effort to think out the truth of his own being as it keeps eluding him. Pascal said that man tries to make himself out an angel and makes a beast of himself. The problem, Kundera says, is that "man is never what he thinks he is."[3] Even Rabelais, who played with the Promethean myth of a usurping man capable of scaling Olympus, nevertheless ended his wise book with a parodistic portrayal of the mystery of human apotheosis in the guise of a descent into a wine cave. "*De vin on divin devient*"[4] is the playful gloss handed down to Panurge and his companions during their ritual of enlightenment. We recall that Bacbuc's oracular injunction—to drink—is delivered at the end of a journey of discovery that took the questioners to the outer margins of the physical world, since the wise men cogitating dry in a mock Symposium had failed to heal Panurge's anguish.

Kundera's gloss on the art of novelistic gnosis is permeated by the spirit of generative paradox, just like Bacbuc's formula, which can be instantly translated into a multiplicity of individual meanings by the initiates. Kundera's God would rather be entertained than sit in perpetual judgment over human imperfections. That is why he is moved to laughter by the spectacle of the thinking fool's antics. Man, catching an echo of that merriment and suddenly understanding, joins in to become for a brief instant, not God nor an angel, but the wise fool, a joyous master of his own laughter. Laughter, in Kundera's mind, figures as the locus of mystery where, in a moment of rare congruence, the human and the divine meet on the uncertain ground of creative possibility, never to be captured as a certainty.

During the Renaissance, when the European novel was in its infancy, the art of paradoxy flourished in all the intricacy of its mutually entangled varieties. In her brilliant study of the Renaissance tradition of paradox, *Paradoxia Epidemica,* Rosalie Colie writes, "One element common to all these kinds of paradox [the rhetorical, the logical, and the epistemological] is their exploitation of the fact of relative, or competing, value systems. The paradox is always somehow involved in dialectic; challenging some orthodoxy, the paradox is an oblique criticism of absolute judgment or absolute convention."[5] Like laughter, paradox is a sworn enemy of all absolutes. In its unadulterated humanist form, it used to serve as a corrective to the totalitarian reductionism embedded in the logical operations of reason. A game of reason played at the extreme limits of the rational discourse, paradox became the favorite device in the intellectual arsenal of the Renaissance fool. Erasmus, the fool in God, and Panurge, the secular fool once he had reached the end of his journey, both understood that the highest form of *serio ludere* engages the player in laughing back at himself in the very act of criticizing the world. A true paradoxist unsettles those who take his meaning too seriously, as well as those who do not take it seriously enough.

"I was born on the first of April. That has its metaphysical significance,"[6] Kundera told Antonín Liehm in a February 1967 interview, thus claiming the role of philosophical fool as his birthright. By then he was already the author of two notebooks of *Laughable Loves,* as well as a novel, *The Joke.* Between the first and the last notebooks of *Laughable Loves* falls the shadow of public events marking the time span between 1967 and 1969 as the great matrix of meanings that cut deep into the lives of Czechs of Kundera's generation. The duplicitous year 1968 stamped European consciousness with two superimposed and contradictory images of Prague. First there was the festive show of freedom in the streets of an old Central European city, and then the resident genius of historical irony, well schooled in the art of double exposure, cut that image open to let the Russian tanks roll through those same streets in the dog days of August.

For Kundera, the moment of awakening to the Russian tanks in Prague on the morning of August 21, 1968, no longer belongs to History, which commands the decreative power of time. Instead, it lives with the emotional power of memory in the *anachronistic* imagination he has unleashed in his novels. Here it figures as the moment when death, once again, knocks at the Czech nation's door, this time wearing the smiling mask of a naive young Russian soldier. The messenger from a civilization dominated by the vastness of its physical space beckons the Czechs to step outside their own waking time and join him in the immensity of the Russian night. After years of living in the West, Kundera would describe the experience as the violent death of the West, and of its culture based on the values of Renaissance individualism. But by then he would also understand that this moment of his consciousness was impenetrably Central European, and therefore peripheral to the Western mind.

In the essay "A Kidnapped West; or, Culture Bows Out" (1984), Kundera asks himself why it is so easy for present-day Europe to dispense with its borderlands to the east, which have grown thinkers and artistic innovators of genius, men like Freud and Einstein, Kafka, Husserl, Bartók, and others, without whom it is impossible to conceive of twentieth-century culture. In Prague, during the tragic days of August 1968, he had assumed that culture "existed as a realm in which supreme values were enacted."[7] But now he sees that there is another side to the deadly conundrum in which his country is trapped. Europe itself has changed. No longer a crucible of cultural significance, Europe no longer experiences itself as a value, and thus cannot understand why a small nation at its eastern margins needs it. Kundera concludes that "the real tragedy for Central Europe, then, is not Russia but Europe."[8]

Kundera's vision of contemporary Europe reveals a once brilliantly peopled stage growing bare. Culture is bowing out and the mass media are muscling in to occupy a privileged position at the center of modern life. These quantifiers of human experience serve as a permanently installed Chorus, endlessly purveying images and sounds that have neither depth nor true vitality. In the cultural wasteland of our actuality the mass media have constituted themselves as a formidable system of power, and like other power systems Kundera has observed, they are dedicated to the task of reducing all reality to their own level. The mode of being they propagate is characterized by the rule of minimum diversity over a maximum range.

In "The Depreciated Legacy of Cervantes," which serves as the lead essay in his *Art of the Novel,*[9] Kundera pursues the question of disappearing values in the domain of his artistic predilection. In seeking to illuminate the significance of the novel to the European spirit, he reaches back to the point of origin, when the world of the "Modern Era," and with it the novel, "the image and model of that world," was born.[10] The European adventure, as Kundera conceives it, began when Don Quixote, armed with his semantic certainties, stepped out into a world from which God was already retreating, leaving behind a vast open question. "The key moment of European history,"[11] captured in the inimitable shorthand of this singular novelistic action, is marked by a characteristic ambiguity. It is, as Kundera says, "decline and progress at the same time,"[12] since Don Quixote's engagement with the question of what is real leaves us with a world of expanding possibilities as well as with an inner magnitude of loss.

But the seventeenth century, which saw Don Quixote as an aging man playing the role of an imagined youth, was also the

Europe. The paradoxical effect of that cataclysm is a world increasingly united, offering a leveled global arena for uniform models of humanity, and leaving no space where the remaining individuals can play. Under the condition of terminal paradoxes, all existential categories undergo a fraudulent conversion that changes all values into parodies of themselves. The nature of paradox itself suffers a similar degradation in the process. What had been a play of the mind during the Renaissance, always actively generating improvised meanings, has now passed out of the domain of human freedom to become the terminal form of human entrapment. The reification of paradox is the underlying, unspoken phenomenon of this discourse.[17]

Kundera insists that even at the nadir of the age of terminal paradoxes, the novel retains the capability to create an experimental time and space fit for habitation by free human individuals. But it can only do so if it remains at odds with the prevailing spirit of the times. Kundera is sometimes described as a postmodernist, and it is true, of course, that he has rejected the modernism of the 1920s, with its "glorification of the technical" and its "fascination with the future." Instead, he practices what he calls "antimodern modernism,"[18] combining skepticism about the novelties of our actuality, which usually come down to us preprocessed by the media, with the imperative to "make new," which he applies to both the form and the substance of his novels.

The charge of Europocentrism that has been leveled at Kundera is potentially more misleading. The word comes to literature from the vocabulary of contemporary politics and has the undertaste of a nostalgic imperialism. The label does not fit Kundera. Apart from obscuring his genuine admiration for the American novel (both Latin and North American), it misses completely the idiosyncratic, uniquely personal significance of the category "Europe" in Kundera's novels and essays. While perfectly intelligible to all those who know it as a geographical and historical entity, Kundera's Europe of the Modern Era also functions as a personal metaphor for the metaphysical territory on which the house of his novels is built. And it must be emphasized that for Kundera the term "metaphysical" connotes a dimension of human existence that does not lie *beyond* the physical but vaults *over* it like a fragile luminous bow of many colors overarching the cascading stream of time. Perhaps the best way to understand the value Kundera attaches to his Europe-in-the-mind is to look at it as a reflection glimpsed in the crooked but premonitory mirror of Czech history. That image—of a culture drawing life from an awareness of death standing at its shoulder—is Kundera's Europe, not the new imperium of wealth the politicians promise for the 1990s.

But now, let us *read* Kundera's novels.

1

The Joke

OR

Uneasy Rider

The Joke, Kundera's first novel, has the precise formal articulation and ironic bite of the two cycles of short stories that preceded it, the first two notebooks of *Laughable Loves.*[1] But the imaginative scope here is much vaster, and the complex intellectual resonances sound poignantly lyrical, as seldom again after. "Remorseful nostalgia and remorseless skepticism are the two pans of the scales that give the novel its equilibrium"[2]—thus the author characterizes his book's brilliant discordance.

Though modernist in technique and feeling, *The Joke* accommodates a larger chunk of life and more descriptive detail than the elliptical novels that would follow. Critics have called it a realistic novel[3] because of the way it exemplifies the conditions of Czechoslovak society in the first two decades of the Communist regime. The unmistakable typicality of the characters and their situations afforded the pleasure of instant recognition to Czech and Slovak readers in 1967, when the novel first appeared in print, soon to be turned into a popular film.[4] In the year of the memorable Fourth Congress of Czechoslovak Writers, even a difficult work like *The Joke* soon ran through three large printings. Readers tended to see Kundera's novel in light of the prevailing literary trend, which emphasized criticism of the Stalinist fifties, with their political trials and atmosphere of terror. In works of this kind, the settling of accounts with the recent past could be presented as a family drama built around a rebellious son's challenge to a rigidly authoritarian father.[5] The indictment of Stalinism figures more directly in nonfiction writings, such as Ladislav Mnačko's *The Taste of Power* (1967), as well as in many autobiographical tales of political persecution. One of the paradoxes of this period was that the victims of Communism were often the very devotees who had helped usher it in. However, the point of view of the victim dominated the attention of the Czech public in the sixties.

The Joke also takes on these themes, but after its own original fashion. The action develops around a scheme of revenge: Ludvik Jahn plots to humiliate Pavel Zemanek by sleeping with his wife, Helena, because Zemanek presided over the student tribunal that expelled him from the university and the Party in 1949. But the human sympathy belongs to Ludvik's childhood friend Jaroslav, an ardent Communist dreamer distressed by a loss of communication with his teenage son Vladimir. The questions raised by these mutually entangled fates are of a subtler order than politics, and they bounce off the historical context rather than playing into it.

In the West, *The Joke* first appeared in Paris during the autumn of 1968, under the huge shadow cast by the Soviet tanks in Prague. In his introduction to the first French edition,[6] Louis Aragon, the venerable lyric voice of French Communism, declared it "one of the greatest novels of this century." He also praised it as a piece of true history, preserving the authenticity of the moment of hope that was Prague in 1967–68 against the distortions of the mythographers who, he suspected, would soon begin writing the winners' version of events. Fourteen years later, a Czech citizen no longer, Kundera wrote his own preface to the first integral English text of the novel,[7] using the occasion to reject the bowdlerized version that had been published in England without his permission in 1969.[8] He acknowledged the acuteness of Aragon's insight into the politics of historiography while deriding the poet's short-lived capacity for outrage. "Four years later his legs consented to take him to Moscow to receive a decoration from Brezhnev. . . . And yet the very same Aragon wrote what is probably the most eloquent and penetrating piece anyone has written on the Russian invasion of Czechoslovakia: his foreword to *The Joke*" (p. ix).

Kundera, however, is extremely impatient with those who persist in treating his fiction as the captive of history. "When in 1980, during a television panel discussion devoted to my works, someone called *The Joke* 'a major indictment of Stalinism,' I was quick to interject, 'Spare me your Stalinism, please. *The Joke* is a love story!' " He goes on to explain that "the spark that started me off" on this first novel "was an event in a small Czech town: the arrest of a girl for stealing flowers from a cemetery and offering them to her lover as a gift" (p. vii). In the novel, the same kind of floral tribute is addressed by Lucie to the young Ludvik during his forced service in an army penal battalion. But as the narrative opens fifteen years later, Ludvik is a middle-aged cynic about to exact his revenge upon the man he holds responsible for the ordeal of that captivity. Lucie's forbidden gesture of love, the consecration of Eros by despoiling Thanatos, is about to be obliterated by Ludvik's inversion of the act of love into an expression of "all the hatred he has accumulated during his life" (p. viii).

Kundera has observed that "the paradoxes of history and private life have the same basic properties" (p. viii). In *The*

Joke, sexual love is paradoxical not only because of the ancient discord between body and soul, already recorded in the two notebooks of *Laughable Loves,* but also because the signs and gestures modern men and women use to express it are endowed with an untamable and often perverse ambiguity. The critic Sylvie Richterová, who interprets Kundera's first three novels as meditations on the problem of communication, notes that each verbal message and each gesture in *The Joke* is immediately subjected to a multiplicity of interpretations. "The novel's characters are thrashing around in a vortex where everything can be inverted," she writes.[9] In the same vein, Květoslav Chvatík draws attention to the fact that Kundera's novel, published soon after Michel Foucault's *Les mots et les choses* (1966), also addresses the problematic relation between human experience and its expression in language.[10]

With its seven-part structure and four distinct narrators, three male and one female, *The Joke* has been compared to a musical composition based on a scheme of seven and three.[11] In the first six parts, each narrative sequence is a self-contained unit controlled by a single voice. Ludvik, who initiates the series, is heard three times in this arrangement (Ludvik-Helena-Ludvik-Jaroslav-Ludvik-Kostka). But while he dominates the first two chords of the narrative scale that stops at the problematic seventh step, he shares the last part with Jaroslav and Helena as all three alternate in rapid counterpoint to tell the jarring action that unravels the plot, and with it the eighteen years of personal history evoked earlier.

The time span of the novel, from about 1947 to 1965, encompasses the lead characters' passage from early youth to encroaching middle age. It also corresponds to the first two decades of Communism in Czechoslovakia. Ludvik, Helena, and Pavel, as well as Jaroslav and Kostka, all belong to the postwar generation of university students recruited by the Party to form the intellectual elite of the future. With the exception of Kostka, they all joined shortly before or after the establishment of the Communist regime. Kostka and Ludvik stumbled early in their careers, while Jaroslav and both Zemaneks prospered. But in the spring of 1965, as the five of them converge on that weekend of collisions when all illusions explode, it is difficult to tell the victims from the winners.

The stage is set in the small Moravian town and adjoining village where Ludvik and Jaroslav were born. It is first described in part 1, through Ludvik's eyes, as he arrives on a Friday afternoon from Prague, intent on completing his sexual conquest of Helena.

> Standing in the main square (which I'd crossed countless times in my childhood, boyhood, and youth), I felt no emotion whatsoever; all I could think was that the flat space, with the spire of its town hall (like a soldier in an ancient helmet) rising above the rooftops, looked like a huge parade ground and that the military past of the Moravian town, once a bastion against Magyar and Turk invaders, had engraved a set of irrevocably hideous features on its face. (p. 1)

The abandoned parade ground of history, with its ugly reminders of past significance, pleases Ludvik as an appropriately ironic backdrop to his mission of revenge, which he plans to execute in the combat zone of the bedroom. Helena, his erotic target, is no more to Ludvik than a means to an end. And so also his homecoming serves as a convenient pretext for a project that he himself views as "so cynical and base as to make a mockery of any suspicion that I had come out of any maudlin attachment to things past" (pp. 1–2). As he goes about his methodical preparations, reconnoitering the pitifully inadequate accommodations of his shabby hotel, Ludvik is intensely conscious of the parodistic quality of all his moves and gestures. In his assault on the past, the avenger craves symmetry above all, and a precise symbolic articulation of the grand act of reversal that he hopes will take him back into wholeness. Thus, Ludvik plans to possess Helena in order to compensate himself for the humiliation of having been cast from the royal train of History into a life of triviality. By his act of sexual domination he seeks not only to subdue his enemy Zemanek but also to gain mastery once for all over the power of mockery that has devastated his life.

The hotel room having convinced him of its unworthiness with its thin walls and creaking bed, Ludvik decides to borrow his friend Kostka's bachelor apartment for his appointment with Helena the next day. Dr. Kostka is a virologist at the local hospital, and Ludvik had helped him to secure the job. In his aversion for everything that reminds him of his boyhood, Ludvik avoids seeking Jaroslav's help, and when he meets his childhood companion on the street, he fails to greet him. Still another figure from the past emerges quite unexpectedly in the afternoon's grayness. In a barbershop recommended by Kostka, Ludvik rediscovers his old lost love, Lucie, in the woman who is shaving his face.

He has been leaning back idly against the headrest, abandoning his face to the feminine touch of the razor-wielding hands, allowing his eyes to roam the blotchy ceiling so as to avoid contact with the mirror in front of him. In the intimacy of the anonymous caress, his mind soon invents a game on the edge of eroticism: his disembodied head enjoying the unseen woman's tenderness and simultaneously registering the deadly threat implied in the blade. When he finally meets her face in the mirror, he finds that his "tender assassin" (p. 7) is none other than Lucie, whom he had loved passionately fifteen years before. In spite of the mask time has pressed upon the once girlish features, he knows her true face by the eyes. Then, listening to her voice in casual conversation with another customer, he is shocked by its coarseness, and she is a stranger to him once again.

In this scene of imperfect remembering, the ritual of the lovers' mutual salutation by look and gentle smile is left incomplete and deeply flawed. Though he "felt a chill run up [his] spine" (p. 7) when he first glimpsed Lucie in the mirror, Ludvik's shudder of recognition is only a very distant recall of the love terror that seized Dante in Earthly Paradise, on the summit of Mount Purgatory, when Beatrice unveiled herself for him. Ludvik is a lover who wants "to believe her hands, to recognize her by her hands" (p. 8), and when Lucie fails to grant him the grace of sensual recognition, he leaves the barbershop "oddly frustrated," diminished even in his capacity for knowledge. "All I knew was that I knew nothing and that failing to recognize a face once dearly loved was a sign of great *callousness*" (p. 9).

Yet as he hurries back to the hotel, he deliberately refuses to acknowledge Jaroslav, his oldest friend, when he passes him on the street. This second, distinctly willful moment of non-recognition evens his score against the forces of forgetting. A casual exchange on the phone with Kostka confirms Lucie's name, but instead of answering when Kostka asks how he knows her, he comments vaguely that it was long ago. The question of Lucie is thus left hanging in the darkening air, and Ludvik sets off to wander through town.

The void created in the narrative by the suspension of knowledge about Lucie is filled by Helena, who has the voice in the second part. Her internal monologue, as she lies in her comfortable bed in Prague on the eve of her Moravian adventure with Ludvik, has the same brevity as his exposition, but not its crisp tone. Helena's sentences run on agitatedly, accreting self-pity, defensively self-righteous, as she reviews her faltering marriage to the ever popular, handsome Pavel. While his career in the Party and with women has been one charmed round of successful performances—"he can't live without applause, it's his alcohol and nicotine" (p. 15)—her femininity has been turning sour at the edges. She clings to the Communist doctrine Pavel "never tired of repeating" in the days of their courtship, when they were both students at the university in Prague in 1949, "that the new man differed from the old insofar as he had abolished the distinction between public and private life" (p. 14). She considers herself a new woman, body and soul, forever purposeful and optimistic, resolutely rejecting the "fashionable skepticism" (p. 11) that crept in around "fifty-six when there was all that talk about Stalin's crimes, and people went wild and began rejecting everything." She knows that people call her "a hard-liner, a fanatic, a dogmatist, a Party bloodhound" (p. 15), but she remains loyal to the rhetoric of feeling and the emotional arguments Pavel has taught her. "He was never satisfied with reaching the mind alone, he had to get at the emotions," in those days when she felt so young and attractive around him and life was "like a fairy tale" (p. 12) and they sang together in the Fučík Song and Dance Ensemble.

Helena's complaining voice rises to a singing pitch when she describes the moment in Old Town Square in May 1949, on the anniversary of the liberation of Prague by the Soviet armies, that she considers the historic consecration of her love for Pavel. Standing near him in the dense crowd, she had seized his hand. As he squeezed back, their love mingled with the tidal wave of lyric solidarity that rose from so many young throats toward the rostrum, where the Italian Communist leader Togliatti stood with other dignitaries, Czech and foreign, clapping and chanting slogans.

This poetic flight of memory reads like a set piece, a grotesque parody of the typical propaganda vignette. It sounds excruciatingly false. When Helena whispers into her pillow the heroic, death-defying message the martyr Fučík left to posterity before he was hanged by the Nazis in 1943—"May melancholy never taint my name" (p. 11)—the words sound like a frightened prayer in the mouth of a *fausse dévote*. When she and Pavel got engaged, he had given her "a locket with a picture of the Kremlin on it" (p. 14) as a talisman of their common faith. Pavel says it was a gift from a dying Soviet soldier he nursed in Prague in 1945, but Ludvik in part 5 will reflect bitterly that the symbolic memento of Pavel's Communist baptism is as phony as his Moravian folk costume, a histrionic prop used to good effect by the consummate actor of the Revolution. Pavel Zemanek, like Helena, is of bourgeois origin, but that is not what is wrong here. Helena is the perfect illustration of the easy conviviality between Czech Communism and what used to be labeled the bourgeois spirit. The Kremlin locket, the dying Soviet soldier, Fučík's testament, and Togliatti's song are authentic Communist kitsch, in the sense Kundera gives the term in the essay that forms a part of his novel *The Unbearable Lightness of Being.* Their function is to drape a pleasing, sentimental veil over the anguishing reality of death. Elsewhere Kundera has defined "kitsch" more concretely (and more cruelly, for Helena) as "the absolute denial of shit."[12]

Helena is a blowsy, lustful beauty who lies alone in her matrimonial bed and, like Molly Bloom in Joyce's *Ulysses,* recalls the ecstasy of her first sexual surrender to the man who became her husband. Like Molly, she is all woman in her commitment to the bodily language of love. But when Helena says, "It was love, love of love" (p. 17), she is not talking of a carnal embrace but explaining why she felt compelled to denounce a colleague to the Party. Helena has been properly schooled by Pavel in the fundamental civic lesson of Communism that there is nothing private in life. "I want it to be one from beginning to end" (p. 11), as she says in the self-referential style that dominates all her discourse. Confusing a colleague's marital infidelity with a breach of Party discipline, and mixing private spite with public indignation, she has denounced him to her local committee. "The Party is almost like a living being, I can tell it all my most intimate thoughts now that I have nothing to say to Pavel" (p. 16), she explains, invoking the emotional necessity that rules her under the accommodating cloak of official ideology.

One of the characteristics of Communist consciousness is

that the true believer is never alone within it. Kundera calls this the "violation of solitude" that occurs in the nightmarish world of pseudotheological despotism. It is a state of being he finds described in Kafka's fiction: "The *Kafkan* is not restricted to either the private or the public domain; it encompasses both. The public is the mirror of the private, the private reflects the public."[13] Helena, who takes the Party with her to bed, lives the comic side of Kafka's nightmare without knowing it. Self-delusion is the leitmotif of her life; she believes that the sadness she reads on Ludvik's face signals the beginning of his love for her and that it will be like "seeing my youth return from the shadows" (p. 19). Helena, brazenly claiming for herself a life free of tragedy, is a model of the historical optimism of the victorious class. She will fly to her Moravian rendezvous armed with the paraphernalia of success—the reporter's tape recorder to capture the sounds of the folk festival, the imported Italian raincoat sportily draped on her body. And she will deliver all into the trap of Ludvik's vengeful arms.

When Ludvik's voice is heard again, opening the longest narrative section of the novel, he is walking outside town, through an absent landscape where fields stretch out behind deserted houses, factories, courtyards, and heaps of rubbish. The desolation around him has the color of the memories Lucie has stirred in him. He reflects on the curious interchangeability of life's phenomena as he suddenly sees in his hometown a mirror of Ostrava, the mining center of Moravian Silesia where he met Lucie. The drama of his thwarted life, now reemerging from his memory, really began with the debacle in Prague—a consequence of his "fatal predilection for silly jokes" (p. 22).

Ludvik relates his disasters in a quiet, even tone devoid of self-pity. The experiencing self in his autobiographical narrative is disciplined by an overarching intelligence that keeps directing the storytelling toward the pole of analysis. The result is a brilliant piece of sustained philosophical prose that succeeds in transforming personal remembrance into an essay on the phenomenology of the age. The loss of the distinction between private and public—a convenience for Helena, allowing her to masquerade her most selfish impulses under a grand banner—was a stumbling block in Ludvik's path. His fall from the Party's grace took the form of an essentially comic *quid pro quo* between love and politics.

Ludvik was one of the first in his generation to join the Revolution, welcoming the new age even before the Communists seized full power in February 1948. As Jaroslav remembers him after his first year in Prague, "He had the look all Communists had at the time. He looked as if he'd made a secret pact with the future and thereby acquired the right to act in its name" (p. 120). Because of the seductive arguments Ludvik uses to convert the boys back home to Communism in that first summer of 1948, Jaroslav nicknames him the Pied Piper.

But the next summer Ludvik's other side, that of a twenty-year-old boy entangled in the contradiction between his sexual aggressiveness and his inexperience, rears up in pain. He has been courting Marketa inconclusively for several months. She, an infinitely gullible, pretty girl, has been sending him impersonal letters from her summer training camp, full of the grave enthusiasm the age demands, and woefully lacking even a hint at flirtation. Smarting from the humiliation he feels at her indifference to his passion, Ludvik fires off a postcard inscribed, "Optimism is the opium of the people! A healthy atmosphere stinks of stupidity! Long live Trotsky! Ludvik!" (p. 26). The three exclamation marks in this provocative message are the clues that betray the hurt and rage of the rebuffed lover, concealed under a wise-guy posture. This coded communication is Ludvik's ultimate salvo in a losing game of seduction, a parting shot fired in the air for revenge. It contains all the agonistic bravado of male adolescence, with its cruel vulnerability and its profoundly ambiguous attitude toward the girl addressee. Despite its overt allusion to politics, it is most emphatically *not* a political statement.

Marketa, who takes everything literally, and whose mind, like the society it reflects so perfectly, is entirely humorless, cannot understand Ludvik's verbal game. She considers the card subversive and surrenders it to the camp authorities, who question her about her correspondence. "They knew all about it before talking to you" (p. 34), Ludvik consoles her when they talk again in the fall. Marketa, for her part, wishes him no harm. Inspired by the example of a heroic wife in a then popular Soviet film, *Court of Honor,* and strengthened in her resolve by a conversation with Comrade Zemanek, she offers to stand by Ludvik providing he admits his guilt to the Party. Ludvik knows that everything is possible for him, including the conquest of Marketa at last, if only he will play this deadly serious game of political salvation. Yet he says no to her, accepting his loss in love and the peril of a head-on confrontation with Zemanek.

Sylvie Richterová has pointed out that Ludvik's fall into disgrace, like most of the crucial events in Kundera's first three novels, begins with a single verbal act. She argues that the postcard, once launched, assumes an autonomous existence quite beyond Ludvik's will.[14] That perceptive observation requires some amplification, for the paradigm does not quite fit Ludvik's case. After all, he has the option of taking back his unfortunate joke if he will only allow the Party *agélastes*[15] to reinterpret what he has written in accordance with their pseudotheology, which reduces all texts to the single measure of the Party's authorized speech. The joke, penned by Ludvik in a moment of emotional confusion, has unexpectedly presented him with a clear moral choice. If we momentarily forget the absurdist interpretation that Ludvik's own analysis of his fate presses on us, the situation he confronts when he appears before Zemanek's committee is the archetypal dilemma of a man who must either opt for a convenient lie or suffer the unpleasant consequences of telling the truth as he sees it.

In his address to the Fourth Congress of Czechoslovak Writers, two years after *The Joke* was written, the philosopher Karel Kosík read from a letter that Jan Hus, "the great Czech intellectual of the fifteenth century," wrote from prison on June 18, 1415, describing what happened to him at the Council of Constance.

> One theologian told me: that everything will be allowed and made possible for me, providing I submit to the council, adding: should the council proclaim that you have only one eye, even though you have two, it would be your duty to profess, together with the council, that it is indeed so. I answered him: even if the whole world affirmed this to me, I, possessed of the reason which I now have, could not admit it without resistance of my conscience.[16]

In his commentary on this text, Kosík compared Hus's stand against arbitrary authority with the options of a contemporary intellectual in a similar quandary. Unlike the fifteenth-century religious humanist, Kosík argued, the present-day thinker could not rely on his individual reason and his conscience because the two did not necessarily work together in his world. Yet, Kosík stressed, "only in that unity do they (reason and conscience) become the foundation of human existence." He concluded that the modern mind, which views reason and conscience as two independent, mutually indifferent, or even hostile entities, stands groundless before the problem of truth.

Ludvik not only suffers from such a split between reason and conscience, he no longer even claims his conscience as his own. His conscience belongs to History, which is a creature of the Party that purports to be History's servant. When the accusation of subversion is leveled against Ludvik, he feels guilty even though his reason objects to the analysis behind the charge.

> Because I (like the rest of us) stood before the Revolution and its Party with permanently bowed head, I gradually became reconciled to the idea that my words, though genuinely intended as a joke, were still a transgression of sorts, and torrents of tortured self-criticism started whirling through my head. (p. 37)

Ludvik's reason plays the knave to his captive conscience and begins spinning out the sophistic argument that ultimately reconciles his residual sense of the truth with his overwhelming need to feel guilty. "Looking back on my state of mind at the time," Ludvik the narrator reflects after many years that it was similar to the Christian conscience with its "fundamental and never-ending guilt" (p. 37). But more accurately, Ludvik before the session of the Party division committee is like K. in *The Trial,* a defendant still searching for his guilt. Kundera has described this "Kafkan," "pseudotheological" consciousness as a creation of modern totalitarian society, where power "behaves like God" and "awakens religious feelings toward itself."[17]

Why, then, does Ludvik say no to Marketa and Zemanek's persuasion? For all Ludvik's introspection, the question is left hanging, just as in the more frivolous version of the truth-teller in spite of himself, "Nobody Will Laugh" (*Laughable Loves*), which tells the story of an art historian who refuses to write a dishonest review. Conscience is the unacknowledged ghost in the machine of Kundera's absurd world, situated beyond the limits of inquiry in the consciousness of his characters and narrators.

As Ludvik tells it, Zemanek's performance as inquisitor was so spellbinding as to bring everyone at the session, including Ludvik's friends and teachers, to vote for his expulsion. The actual description of the trial is strategically postponed until part 5, where it surges from Ludvik's vengeful memory in sharply etched detail, to provide a delicious incitement for the equally virtuoso scene he is about to play opposite Helena in bed. Zemanek, a past master of the emotional argument, had read Ludvik's facetious postcard to the investigating committee right after his own pathos-laden recitation from Julius Fučík's *Notes from the Gallows*. "That text, written clandestinely in prison, then published after the war in a million copies, broadcast over the radio, studied in schools as required reading, was the scripture of the age" (p. 166). By contrast, the text of Ludvik's postcard, as Květoslav Chvatík has pointed out, is virtually meaningless outside the existential situation that generated it.[18] Zemanek forces it into the extraneous context of Fučík's testament, and by that semiotic manipulation, he manages to transform a frivolous quip into blasphemy, the most extreme form of unauthorized speech. While Ludvik is thus shamed by his own words, Fučík's "fervent, yet pure" face looks down at him from the poetic portrait in profile done by the painter Švabinský on the basis of an old photograph—a lyric icon that soon obliterates the memory of the real man's more prosaic look. Under that silently eloquent gaze, Ludvik feels crushed by a sense of his own aesthetic unworthiness. But when one of Zemanek's acolytes, "the girl with the pigtail," pipes up to deliver the rhetorical kill—"Tell me, how do you think the Comrades tortured by the Gestapo, tortured to death, would have reacted to your words?" (p. 167)—he suddenly remembers his own father, who did not return from a Nazi camp. He answers, "If they had read my postcard, they might well have laughed" (p. 168). In a flash of ironic insight Ludvik sees the incongruity between the real tragedy of death in a concentration camp and the theatrical performance into which he has been drawn. That moment of truth legitimizes laughter for him, but it also isolates him from "the Comrades." He will be condemned under the category of treasonous skepticism.

Ludvik's stand does not originate in the deliberations of either his reason or his conscience. Rather, it is the spontaneous eruption of an irrepressible comic instinct. It is also an act of courage that momentarily restores the integrity of the word. Yet Ludvik cannot quite believe in the value of his gesture and finds himself in the absurd situation of a martyr of comic courage who persists in looking at himself with the humorless eyes of his executioners. He is a victim rather than a master of his laughter, a man "caught in the trap of a joke" and "condemned to triviality" as Kundera puts it (p. vii). Seen from outside, his personal catastrophe is ludicrous, lacking any moral or aesthetic dignity. In his disgrace, Ludvik self-consciously abandons the stage of history for the humbler pursuit of love in what he calls the "everyday world" (p. 77).

In the penal battalion to which he is assigned to work in the coal mines near Ostrava, he temporarily recovers a lost feeling of solidarity with members of his own generation. This time he and his fellows are on the receiving end of history. His companions, who all wear the black insignia of political prisoners, have been condemned for a variety of offenses, most of them as trivial as his own. The list, which Richterová calls "surrealistic,"[19] ranges from striking a policeman to pissing on a curb while drunk during a May Day demonstration. The politicals are united by their propensity to look at the world from below and their capacity for mockery, the vitriolic power of the powerless. The masterpiece of their collective parodistic spirit is the game they improvise to subvert an athletic competition organized as part of a punishment decreed by their fanatical "boy commander," a potential Saint-Just who illustrates Ludvik's observation that "youth is a terrible thing" (p. 76), particularly when it inherits history for its playground. The type will reappear in the person of the poet Jaromil in Kundera's next novel, *Life Is Elsewhere*. Both adolescents are monsters of inexperience who rampage through life draped in the purple cloak of the tragic stage, mistaking words for feelings and symbols for things.

The inspired clowning of the inmates, temporarily transformed into athletes, disrupts the command performance. By limping, puffing, and stumbling along the racecourse, the runners exaggerate the zeal of extreme athletic effort, simultaneously miming their own hobbled condition as prisoners. Only one competitor among them runs in earnest: Alexej, the son of a highly placed Communist official recently condemned as a Western spy. His inherited guilt, like his Russian-sounding name, sits heavily on his narrow shoulders. He is a character out of Koestler's *Darkness at Noon,* lost in a Central European underworld of Schweiks. Alexej runs in earnest, but his inadequate body, sweating authentic pain, cannot outdistance the clowns. Ironically, he is the one the boy commander singles out for punishment as a saboteur. Irony, in the world of *The Joke,* is the great equalizer whose tentacular web no one can escape. As Richterová has observed, there is a sense that the characters in this novel and the situations they endure are essentially interchangeable.[20] Alexej and the boy commander, who drives him to suicide by an overdose of barbiturates, are really spiritual twins, absurdly separated by an arbitrary barbed-wire fence. Later, contemplating Alexej's rigid body, which looks frail in death, like that of a child, Ludvik is moved to violent pity by the fate of this boy whose virulent faith in the system made him a misfit among his fellow prisoners. "He was trying to tell me that the moment the Party banishes a man from its ranks, that man has no reason to live." Ludvik can no longer share Alexej's conviction, yet his death draws Ludvik back to his old guilt and his nostalgia for the lost paradise of Communism. As a result, he loses his newfound sense of community, reflecting bitterly that "the collective of the black insignia was as capable of bullying a man (making him an outcast, hounding him to death) as the collective in that lecture hall, as any collective" (p. 102).

This new dispossession coincides with the moment when Ludvik discovers that he has lost Lucie, the girl in whose love he had sought compensation for his "exit from history." Lucie figures in his career as a second prize, a consolation for an ambitious youth who has lost the higher privilege of "standing near the *wheel of history*" (p. 61). When he first sees her in front of a cinema in suburban Ostrava, her solitary, strangely idle figure affects him with the force of overpowering revelation. "Lucie had revealed herself to me the way *religious truth* reveals itself to others" (p. 57). But their love, though it begins with a vision, is instantly marred by the manipulations of his intellect. Ludvik argues to himself that this "pitiful girl," whose presence seems to hold the mystery of ordinariness, is "eminently worthy of love" as a figure standing on "the meadow of day-to-day existence," a creature living far from history, "*beneath* it," who can open to him the lyric realm of a long-lost pastoral (p. 61). Ludvik's imagination casts a myth of love over Lucie, like a net or a veil, a myth he has fashioned by turning the fabric of his humiliation inside out. Even before Lucie becomes an erotic object for his inflamed senses, she is the plaything of his imagination in its frustrated longing for aesthetic dignity.

The high romance of Lucie is preceded by the episode of the blonde on a tractor, a shabby sexual encounter that inspires in Ludvik a cruel recoil from the realities of his life. During an evening furlough in town, Ludvik and his friends manage to persuade a prostitute to abandon the legitimate soldiers monopolizing her attention in a cheap bar and join their gang instead. They go to a back alley, where they take turns making love to her while she is enthroned on the seat of "a tractor-like contraption" (p. 51). When his moment comes, Ludvik's body performs adequately, releasing him from his "raging lust for a woman; any woman" (p. 52), while his mind scrambles desperately for some illusion of personal uniqueness. Once the alcoholic glamor is stripped from the event, it shows itself in all the bleakness of a serialized mechanical transaction. Ludvik feels his soul contracting in the aftermath of this collective cockcrow, even as he recognizes the experience as "*the norm* of my existence" (p. 53).

In the early, disembodied phase of their love, Lucie's gentle responsiveness is profoundly healing for Ludvik. It restores in him a lost spontaneity of feeling, and in the haze of his tenderness, her body, as yet untouched by his vociferous desire, has a brief moment of transparency that allows their souls a silent communion—"More than beauty more than anything / A festival of understanding" (p. 64). Ludvik reads Lucie these words from a poem by František Halas[21] in a voice without false pathos or emphasis, as if this poetry were the natural language of their days together.

But the disarmed state of their love is soon disrupted by "*the revelation of her body*" (p. 70), which Ludvik experiences as he watches her try on an elegant new dress he is buying for her. That black evening gown, concealing and revealing her form, becomes the metonym of the new sexual identity she has acquired with it. She puts it on to receive him alone in her dormitory room. All the props of the ritual of sexual consummation are in place for the occasion, but the ceremony is interrupted by Lucie's sudden and unexpected physical resistance. Ludvik interprets her fierce struggle as an excessive defense of her virginity. She leaves him with that illusion intact, merely promising to surrender the next time. In a novel full of the clamor of voices about her, Lucie's own voice is never raised in explanation of her baffling conduct.

For Ludvik, the period that follows the first scene of Lucie's denial is the most romantic phase of his love. With the intensity of a Fabrizio del Dongo in his high tower, keeping passionate watch over Clelia in Stendhal's *Charterhouse of Parma,* Ludvik lives for Lucie's brief visits at the camp fence. Instead of writing to him, Lucie comes, bringing bunches of flowers. At first Ludvik is embarrassed by what he sees as a reversal of the male/female roles in courtship, but gradually he accepts her offerings as "a form of speech" quite unlike "the heavy-handed imagery of conventional flower symbolism," intuiting "an older, vaguer, more instinctive *precursor of language*" in her gesture (p. 68). Like Stendhal's hero, Ludvik is a lover contemplating the object of his desire through the barrier of a prison. But his imagination, unlike Fabrizio's, is also a captive of the barbed wire behind which this age of anonymity herds its rebels, inventing other, obfuscating names for the flat, arbitrary places thus circumscribed. His is not the age of exalted individualism.

> So when Lucie came up to the fence, I wasn't the only one looking at her; I was joined by ten or so of my fellow soldiers, who knew precisely what she was like when she made love (what she said, how she moaned) and who would make all kinds of innuendos about the black heels she had on again, and picture her parading naked in them around her tiny room. (p. 92)

That image of a provocative and compliant Lucie, which Ludvik offers as the price of his admission to the collective of the black insignia, is a sham, but it is sufficient to relieve the men's sexual hunger. For Ludvik's part, his willingness to share his most intimate moments is the impulse of a dubious charity, carrying the trademark of the age that has abolished privacy. The essence of romantic love, as Fabrizio or Henry Brulard understood it, and as Ludvik himself briefly sensed it when he read Halas to Lucie, rises from the sexual act elevated above the body's cockcrow. It exists only within the pathos, which is a blessing, of agonistic individuation. For all his suffering, Ludvik's norm as lover remains that of a gang rapist, however much he tries to escape from the surrounding world of triviality where values have lost their *arche*.[22]

Pursuing his own parody of romance, Ludvik resolves to brave the danger of crossing the barrier that separates him from Lucie. Disguised in a borrowed suit, he makes his way past the guards to a bare room in a house outside the camp, where Lucie is waiting for him. The much-desired scene of intimacy that follows unravels all his hopes by cruelly inverting the symbols of sexual domination he had conjured up during his long anticipation.

> I realized that everything had turned out the opposite of what I'd dreamed: instead of a naked girl serving wine to a fully dressed man, a naked man was lying in the lap of a fully dressed woman. I saw myself as the naked Christ taken down from the cross and placed in the arms of a grieving Mary, and I was horrified, because I hadn't come to Lucie for compassion and consolation, I'd come for something entirely different. (pp. 97–98)

Like all of Kundera's young men, Ludvik abhors any suggestion of the maternal in the woman he desires, as if it contained the negation of his manhood. Lucie's compassionate lap forces him "to eat the humble pie of [his] immaturity." In a rage of humiliation, he starts tearing off her clothes, unconsciously debasing the ceremony of erotic disrobement into the brutal impersonality of a rape. "Possessed by the same blind force" (p. 98) that tragically divides them, Ludvik and Lucie struggle until their love duel climaxes with his slap across her face. By now he has lost all sense of her individuality, just like the boyfriend in the story "The Hitchhiking Game" (*Laughable Loves*), who experiences the same loss at the height of sexual mastery.

Lucie flees from Ludvik, leaving him to face alone the additional ordeal of Alexej's suicide. In the cynical hangover from those two events, his mind takes bitter satisfaction in noting, without self-pity but also without forgiveness, that "I was more the object than the subject of my story" (p. 104).

This awareness of his own indignity, an incurable falling-short of the tragic norm his imagination craves, has followed Ludvik from the playground of history into the world of the tarnished pastoral.

But in this polyphonic novel, no statement is allowed to stand without being confronted with the possibility of its opposite. In part 4, Jaroslav sketches a retrospect of Ludvik's life that might very well fit the tragic mold. We learn that Ludvik is the son of a village bricklayer who died in a Nazi camp and that he had to endure the ostentatious charity of his rich relatives, the Kouteckys. As Jaroslav sees it, that boyhood humiliation is the key to Ludvik's ardent Communism, a commitment Ludvik himself prefers to discuss in more philosophical terms. Jaroslav's own life is bound together by a deep loyalty to his roots, and he naturally interprets Ludvik's enforced absence from his mother's funeral, which took place while he was in jail for desertion, as an event of prime significance. The Kouteckys, left to dispose of the dead woman's body as they pleased, ensconced it in a monument of marble "guarded by a white angel with curly hair and a sprig of flowers." For Jaroslav, that angel is the emblem of petty bourgeois kitsch, for which he and Ludvik hold a shared aversion. "I'll never forget that angel, soaring above the ravaged life of a friend whose parents' corpses had been snatched from him along with everything else. It was an angel of devastation" (p. 132). Impervious to the historical irony lurking in that statement, Jaroslav, who is still a sincere Communist, lumps together under the hated aegis of the Kouteckys both the Nazi occupation and the more recent depredation of which Ludvik is a victim.

Jaroslav's voice shifts the narrative from bitter irony to a warm tone of a deeply felt nostalgia. He is a six-foot-two giant constitutionally unable to resist anyone he perceives to be weaker than himself. In his mouth, the adjective "poor" is more a term of endearment than a label of class warfare. His is the Communism of the heart, open to all generous illusions.

Like his schoolteacher father, who was also Ludvik's mentor, Jaroslav is deeply attached to the folklore of his native Moravia. Ludvik, the Pied Piper of Revolution, had persuaded him that Communism, in abolishing private property, would by the same stroke reawaken the "languorous Sleeping Beauty of the past" (p. 121) in popular music and ritual, and so he had joined the Party while studying at the university in Brno. In the fall of 1949, Jaroslav had returned home to be near his father, who was in frail health after a stroke. This sacrifice of a university career unexpectedly leads to undreamt-of success on the home ground of his village. Under the watchful eyes of the Party, the cimbalom ensemble he organizes to play songs ancient and new soon catapults him to national fame. His group's repertoire includes hymns to Stalin and songs about the collectivization of agriculture, as well as lyrics about love and death.

As Jaroslav's voice surfaces in the novel, he is on the verge of seeing an old dream fulfilled. It is a Friday night in June 1965, and that Sunday his son Vladimir is to play the role of king in a folk ritual known as the Ride of the Kings, which his native village has celebrated from time immemorial. The exact origin and meaning of this seasonal rite is veiled in obscurity, a subject of learned dispute among ethnographers. But for Jaroslav, it speaks with the intensity of a cherished personal memory, consecrating his filial bond to his dead father. In 1944, when the Ride took on secret meaning as a national demonstration against the Nazi occupation, the villagers had selected him to play the lead role, seeking thus to honor the spirit of his patriotic father. In the coded language of the ceremony, which the Germans did not trouble to decipher, the village was acting out its "pilgrimage to our sources" (p. 111), articulating the great lesson of survival through remembrance, a lesson the nation had retrieved from its long history of dispossession. The figure of the beggar-king riding with his retinue through the village, silent and veiled, while his heralds ask the people for alms, was intuitively perceived as a symbol of the humiliated majesty that belonged to a threatened Czech culture communicating in a language always on the verge of extinction but so dearly loved that nothing could erase it from memory.

When we first hear Jaroslav's voice, he is shown as a lonely figure in the Moravian landscape, lying on a grassy verge among small fields. To the alert Czech reader of 1967, this tiny descriptive detail would immediately have brought home the anachronistic character of the setting. These grassy verges (*meze*), which marked the borders of individually owned farming plots, had been forcibly ploughed over in the collectivization process of the early 1950s. In 1965, when Jaroslav is lying there, such *meze* had long disappeared from the Moravian landscape, if not from Jaroslav's personal memory. His questions at the outset—"Do these lands I cross belong to another age? What lands are they?" (p. 105)—signal the mind's flight from historical actuality that informs his entire reverie. Jaroslav is trying to escape the oppression of present success and the anxiety about his son by turning to the dream world of the old myth that is the matrix of all his reverence. Private tenderness and public passion merge harmoniously within his meditation, making music together, not ideology. "I believe things have a meaning, Vladimir," he tells his son in an imaginary colloquy. "I want to hand my kingdom over to you. And I want you to accept it from me" (p. 112). Jaroslav knows that his son is reluctant to play the king; moreover, he is not sure about his wife's attitude. In his dream vision, as he relives his wedding to Vlasta, the images of the Moravian nuptial feast keep flowing into scenes from the Ride, now strangely transformed into a drama of defeat and desertion. The central characters of both pageants, the bride and the beggar-king, are concealed figures, and the effectiveness of the event hinges on their quasimagical power to compel recognition. Jaroslav the bridegroom, guided by the patriarch as the ritual demands, reads the signs flawlessly, rejecting the sham bride first offered under the mask of a kerchief in a playful mimicry of courtship. He still knows his Vlasta in her poetic essence, as "a poor man's daughter" (p. 107), whoever her father might be, because he looks at life with the second sight of a *voyant* who sees by not seeing as other people do. "Vlasta calls me a dreamer. She says I don't see things as they are. Well, she's wrong. I do see things as they are, but in addition to the visible I see the invisible" (p. 124).

For Jaroslav, folk song and folk ritual are the *arche* of experience. He calls them "a tunnel beneath history" (p. 116), because through them his imagination enters the lives and emotions of men and women long dead, whose names do not figure in official history's record of battles and political deals, with their dubious gains and losses. Jaroslav believes that unlike modern man, who "cheats," his ancestors, for all their passionate hereditary attachment to growing things, had the ability to come to terms with death as "the fact of no return." When he experiences folk ritual, it is a homecoming into the real life modern man has lost, a sinking down as peaceful as when a child goes to sleep. "I felt the inexorable order of it all," he says (p. 129), reflecting on his wedding feast. "Then Vlasta and I climbed into the bed piled high with quilts, and it was as though all mankind in its never-ending wisdom had taken us into its gentle arms" (p. 130).

Part 5, where Ludvik's voice returns for the third time, functions somewhat deceptively, like the dominant step in a major scale, as if to conclude the assertive chord of the theme of revenge announced by the tonic. While the avenger deliberately fuses his description of the bedroom scene with Helena and his memory of Zemanek's triumph at the trial, another echo is overheard by the attentive reader. The *Pietà* scene with Lucie reverberates through the sadism of Ludvik's lovemaking with Helena, an unwanted replay that is all the more disturbing because it seems to creep in on the telling in spite of the narrator's intellectual control. Underlining the Lucie connection, part 5 is framed by Ludvik's reflections on the paradoxical nature of sexual love. These thoughts, whose philosophical pessimism recalls the observations of Schopenhauer or the maxims of Georges Bataille, dwell on the essential loneliness of the lover, which persists into the most intimate fulfillment of his body's desire. In Ludvik's formulation of the problem, the agonistic self-enclosure of the lover is doubled by the egotism of the poet-actor who teams up with him for the duration of the erotic game, thus converting his experiencing self into an aesthetic object of his own making that rivals the beloved for passionate attention. Lucie's reappearance in the barbershop seems to have given a rough jolt to the poetic text of Ludvik's life, where she has figured as "a kind of legend or myth, inscribed on parchment and laid in a metal casket at the very foundation of my life" (p. 140). Unlike the Byronic lover whose predatory imagination he shares, Ludvik feels himself void of the charisma to generate from within an aesthetically compelling myth of his self. He needs Lucie as a talisman against his loss of individuation.

As he walks through town on Saturday morning, killing time before Helena's arrival, he notices a Baroque monument to victims of plague, which stands as a reminder of the town's once fervently Catholic past.

> There was a saint on the pedestal, a cloud on the saint, an angel on the cloud, and on that angel's cloud another angel, the last. I took a long look at the poignant pyramid of saints, clouds, and angels masquerading in stone as heaven, then at the real heaven—a pale (morning) blue hopelessly removed from that dusty stretch of earth. (p. 142)

In this description of the statuary grouping, Ludvik's not so innocent eye opens the way for the mind's demystification. By reading the monument upside down and by insisting on the pull of gravity that binds all the figures to earth, he has transformed the angels and the clouds and the saints into mere pedestals to support the vain illusion of soaring weightlessness, which no longer holds. Contemplating this monument to an ancient faith that has lost all power to compel belief, Ludvik experiences a feeling of very personal loss. It has become too easy to deconstruct all systems of meaning, and the price to be paid for such sophistication is a perception of reality deprived of any sense of authenticity. This *acedia,* as the medieval monks might have called it, turns the world around Ludvik into a sham, always a parody of something else, like the grotesque ceremony of the "welcoming of new citizens to life" (p. 148), a travesty of Christian baptism that he witnesses soon after passing the monument.

Ludvik the narrator chooses to depict this rite of civic initiation by means of the device of *ostranenie* (estrangement), made famous by Tolstoy's description of an opera performance through the eyes of a countrified Natasha in book 8 of *War and Peace.* Kundera wields the same device in the intellectual manner of an eighteenth-century *philosophe.* Young Pioneers march with military precision to form a guard of Communist angels around the newborns while the mothers look on in embarrassment, uncertain about what to do with the precious bundles that are now being claimed by the State.

Several pages later, after Ludvik has picked Helena up at the bus station, the motif of the monument returns: it "jutted up above the square like a piece of broken-off sky that couldn't find its way back" (p. 155). This time Ludvik's commentary characterizes it as an emblem of the age he lives in, with its relentlessly downward pull of inherent baseness. The availability of Helena's body at his side fills him with bitter recognition of his own lack of nobility, so he complicates his game by teasing her mind a bit, since that mind also belongs to Zemanek. When they pass the monument again, after having a drink, he points to the statuary, and Helena, conforming to his expectations, delivers herself of a small pearl of Communist kitsch. "Why do they keep them anyway, those holy statues? Why don't they build something to celebrate life instead of all that mysticism?" (p. 159) she pipes in a perfect falsetto that recalls the naive enthusiasm of Marketa.

Having executed "without a hitch" (p. 154) the intellectual foreplay to this pathetically unequal sexual duel, Ludvik feels himself master of irony at last. In Dr. Kostka's borrowed apartment, just before the kill, as he places his hands on Helena's legs—"the very legs whose opening and closing have provided the rhythm, the pulsations for a decade of Zemanek's life" (pp. 168–69)—his intellect is firmly focused on his target. But Helena as erotic victim, a nothing in herself, is also a stand-in for Lucie's body, whose pulsations he could never master. And in the sadistic ribaldry of possessing Helena, whom he orders to undress for him while denying her the intimacy of a kiss, he also debases Lucie's image. The middle-aged seducer executes his scenario of sexual subjugation with routine skill, but in the process he senses his mind wandering. "I was to be a man guarding his fugitive prey with total vigilance," he muses, leaving unsaid the fact that the fugitive prey in contention is Lucie, not the ever-willing Helena. His abstracted mind proceeds to develop its conceit about love while Helena beckons him with shameless abandon. "Physical love only rarely merges with spiritual love," the narrator cuts into the action.

> What does the spirit actually do when the body unites (in its age-old, universal, immutable motion) with another body? Think of the wonderful ideas it comes up with during those times, proving as they inevitably do its superiority over the never-ending monotony of the life of the body! Think of the scorn it has for the body. . . . Or conversely: think of the joy it takes in disparaging the body by leaving it to its push-pull game and giving free rein to its own wide-ranging thoughts. (p. 170)

In the Czech original of the text, Ludvik uses the feminine noun *duše* (soul)[23] instead of "spirit." It is a word Kundera always uses to denote the spiritual aspect of love, which he so often pits against the opposing concept of the body, in a perennial discord his lovers cannot resolve. Michael Heim's translation, the only one that sounds natural in English, does not alter the substance of Ludvik's statement, but it carries a faint allusion to Shakespeare's "The expense of spirit in a waste of shame / Is lust in action" (Sonnet 129), which has the effect of tempering the mind's arrogance crowing from Ludvik's aside. For the *spirit* (or the soul) is held in the same scorn as the poor body in a scene of cruel lovemaking under the watchful gaze of a sadistic *intellect* that enjoys the comic *quid pro quo* inflicted on Helena, a foolish woman who mistakes brutality for passion and a slap in the face for a lover's extreme caress.

When he finally confronts his own face in the mirror as he washes up, Ludvik bursts into a peal of laughter and takes this reaction as a token of his victory. For her part, Helena is exultant in her pleasure, boasting of the infallible instinct of her body, which, she says, has recognized in him from the start "a mysterious *élan vital*, . . . the joy of youth eternal" (p. 175). In her new effusiveness, she confesses the secret of her collapsing marriage, a revelation that "made [his] flesh creep" (p. 176). His scheme of revenge is suddenly devalued into a joke at his own expense, and Helena's body looms before him as the ugly reality of a virulently comic contrappasso. When she finally leaves him alone with himself, he seeks to escape into the thought of Lucie, the incorporeal one, his "goddess of vain pursuit" (p. 178). Momentarily, his own longing for abstract purity masks the guilt he feels for the violation he has just inflicted on Lucie's image.

The penultimate narrative section introduces an "outside person" whose function is to open "a secret window through the novel's wall."[24] In the solitude of his apartment, which has now recovered its ascetic character, Dr. Kostka reviews the themes of his conversation with Ludvik, who has asked him about Lucie. The meditations of this medical scientist, who reads Jan Hus, Luther, and Pascal, have the probing introspective quality of a rigorous examination of conscience. In Kostka's exposition of events and characters, the narrative matter is subject to the imperative of self-judgment, in the confessional mode as interpreted by a Christian. His ultimate interlocutor, even when he appears to address Ludvik or Lucie, is the unseen God, as in Augustine's *Confessions*.

Kostka is an anguished evangelical Christian who dreams of realizing the promise of brotherly love contained in the Gospels. It was this hope for humankind, for this world but not of it, that determined his relation to Communism. At the university in 1947, before the Party seized absolute control, he had sided with the Communists in all the debates, thus scandalizing his fellow Christians. Soon after the February coup, he fell under suspicion as an internal dissenter who moreover "took the side of several students due to be expelled for the political stance of their parents" (p. 181). At a Party hearing, a student named Ludvik Jahn stood up for him, arguing that the Party owed him respect for his support before the coup and that his Christianity was no doubt a mere phase. The friendship between the two men dates from this gesture by Ludvik and the private exchange of views that followed, in which Kostka felt bound to declare that he did not expect to outgrow his faith in God and Ludvik responded that religious faith was "of no concern to anyone but the individual" (p. 182).

That first meeting set the tone for their continuing friendship, which is characterized by what Kostka terms "external sympathies" and "internal conflicts" (p. 179). Each time they talk, they return to their fundamental disagreement about the origins and meaning of Communism. While Ludvik sees socialism as the culmination of the secular, antireligious spirit of European skepticism, stemming from Renaissance rationalism, Kostka argues that socialism is religious in its essence, a significant but passing phase in the long history of humanity's quest for the kingdom of God on this earth.[25] For Kostka, the atheism professed by the Communists dooms them to transience. But he assigns a religious meaning even to their apostasy, interpreting it as still another chapter in mankind's unending dialogue with God, "a sign that mortals cannot sit on His throne with impunity and that without His participation even the most equitable order of worldly affairs is doomed to failure and corruption" (p. 181).

In Kostka's world, everything, including absence and failure, has a meaning that hinges on its relation to the absolute good of human redemption. It is from this perspective that he views his own relationship with Lucie, whom he met in the fall of 1951, after she fled from Ludvik to the Cheb region of western Bohemia, where she was born. Kostka was then working as a technical adviser at a collective farm, having resigned his position at Prague University. Lucie first crops up in Kostka's pastoral as a mysterious runaway who hides in the hills, begging bread and milk from the shepherds. She is like Dorotea in *Don Quixote,* a girl fleeing love's madness in disguise, or, closer to home, like Viktorka in Božena Němcová's much-loved nineteenth-century novel *Babička* (*The Grandmother*), half woman and half *víla* (a spirit of the woods), who lives on the extreme margins of the domesticated lands of a Czech village. Even before meeting the girl, Kostka is deeply moved by her power to evoke the protective instinct of the local people, especially the children, who call her the "wandering fairy" (p. 186).

This sentimental idyll of spontaneous Christian feeling is soon interrupted when the police find Lucie and identify her as a girl with a morals charge and a theft on her record. She is nevertheless given a job at the state farm, where Kostka, who sees her as a symbol of an age of defilement, takes her on as his assistant and becomes her protector. Throughout the winter, Kostka the healer nurtures Lucie's trust with infinite patience and gentleness, until she tells him about the two mysteries of her past, each of them linked to a social transgression. At sixteen, she had been the only girl in a gang of six young hoodlums, who subjected her to a collective rape as a ritual of initiation. The boys were arrested for stealing, and she spent a year in the reformatory for having given them "everything a young girl could give" (p. 197). From there she went to faraway Ostrava, where she was a model worker until she was again arrested, this time for taking flowers from a cemetery.

As Kostka contemplates Lucie's fate, with its perpetual running away—from Cheb to Ostrava and back again, from a loveless home into the brutal embrace of the gang, from there into the rough arms of an "insistent soldier" (p. 198), and finally into his own soothing presence—it assumes the keenness of an instinctive, not fully understood quest for the sacred meaning of life. Lucie is for him the child-victim of the age of religious emptiness. Under his prompting, the gang rape and the struggle with Ludvik emerge as a confession of two experiences of violation, ordeals enacted against the background of the religious pictures hanging on the walls of the bare rooms in which the two events took place. The image of the *Madonna lactans* presided over Lucie's humiliating sexual baptism, and the Christ of Gethsemane was the privileged witness of Ludvik's attempt to rape her. Kostka's retelling of Lucie's life has all the inner coherence but also the oppressiveness of a religious allegory. The human figures are reduced to their proper scale as illustrations of the perennially moving sacred drama of the birth and killing of the Man-God. It is quite obvious that Kostka does not know that the "insistent soldier" is his friend Ludvik, to whom he confides the tale of Lucie's past, and Ludvik fails to enlighten him. As a result of this withholding of facts, the two legends of Lucie, Ludvik's and Kostka's, are made to stand side by side in the novel in unmediated confrontation.

At the end of the long winter, the deadening grip of shame is finally unclasped from Lucie's soul, and she responds to Kostka with the passionate flowering of "the great female springtime." Their lovemaking on a hilltop is a fulfillment of the pastoral promise of beauty that eluded Ludvik's grasp. As Kostka tells it, the scene of sexual consummation is ushered in by a spiritual epiphany in a landscape suddenly transfigured into the temple of God. But his severe, almost Jansenist conscience also weighs in, casting the bitter seeds of guilt on that triumph of the spirit over the body. He blames himself for being "a seducer in priest's robes" (p. 200), at the same time acknowledging that this scruple, which prompts him to resign from the farm and separate himself from Lucie, is also a great wrong done to her love for him, an abandonment and a human betrayal.

Kostka lives with an internal tribunal sitting in permanent session in his conscience. Unlike the Communist believer, whose propensity for self-accusation he shares, the judgments to which he subjects himself are not open to external manipulation, and they rarely accommodate anyone's convenience. Kostka is not afraid of the truth, wherever it may lead him, yet for all its agonized honesty, his voice is burdened by too much certainty and grates unpleasantly against Ludvik's equally relentless but much lighter skepticism. Kostka's discourse, dominated by the vocative mode, is obtrusively insistent, even though it is gentle when directed at Lucie and stern mostly in dialogue with himself. Like the voice of the priest in the Cathedral scene of *The Trial,* it seems to come from a vast empty distance, and it resonates with a strangely inhuman sound.

The final part of the novel hinges on two near-death scenes that produce first a comic and then a tragic catharsis. Both events, Helena's overdose and Jaroslav's heart attack, are preceded by a shattering of illusions, a leitmotif that connects the two characters to Ludvik, who is the third narrator of this part. As the three voices alternate in telling the action, the tempo varies from the staccato of the minimal sections to the more leisurely and even pace of the longer narrative passages.

On Sunday morning, three spectators converge upon the Ride of the Kings, which takes place on the main street of the suburban village. Jaroslav has followed the preparations with anxious trepidation, even while giving perfunctory answers to the routine questions with which Helena, armed with a tape recorder, plies him. Ludvik, who is longing to leave the events of the past day behind him and return to Prague, stumbles into the din of the festival in a mood of cynical indifference. Kostka's revelations the evening before have destroyed his legend about Lucie's innocence, and with it, his own pathos as the unfulfilled lover. He now sees himself as the dupe in a laughable, somewhat obscene anecdote about a child-whore.

In the yard of Jaroslav's house, the veiled beggar-king, dressed in a woman's costume as custom demands, and guarded by two pages also disguised as women, sits astride his festive horse. Deeply moved, Jaroslav forgets his exhaustion, approaches the figure, and whispers his son's name. Blinded by his will to believe that Vladimir has at last accepted the precious legacy he himself had received from his father, he is quite unaware that the real Vladimir has absconded to the motorcycle races in Brno with the active collusion of his mother. For the first time in his life, Jaroslav's second sight has failed him. He will follow the performance of insincere actors with true emotion, until his illusion is punctured by old man Koutecky, who tells him with a bit of malice that Vladimir has gone off with his grandson Milos.

By contrast, Ludvik enters the spectacle in the middle, with a mind forewarned against a ritual debased into mass entertainment. The shabbiness of it all, the noise of the loudspeakers and the inattentiveness of the crowd, which keeps interfering with the cortege as it winds its way through a traffic jam, exceeds even his expectations. But then, making an effort to filter out the vulgar noise that surrounds him,

Ludvik begins to listen to the strange music of the heralds, gradually discovering an island of pure sound, "a construct on the border of speech and song." His musician's ear distinguishes each individual note in the "richly variegated canon" (p. 221) of this primitive polyphony, whose incantatory power suggests to him the recitation of Greek tragedy. The formal beauty of the archaic verse he hears moves him as sublime poetry, precisely because he can read no particular meaning into it. His imagination, worn down by a perpetual wandering in a maze of symbols of his own making, which have all been inverted into parodies, takes in the healing power of chaste sound. Ludvik knows that the Ride of the Kings has been interpreted as a stylized commemoration of a historical event, perhaps the flight of defeated Hungarian king Matthias or, as some say (though Ludvik doesn't mention it), the escape from captivity of Prince Viktorín, son of the popular fifteenth-century Czech king Jiří Poděbrady. He also knows about speculations that the Ride may be a survival of pagan rites of passage from boyhood to manhood. But he finds both readings redundant. As he lets himself sink into the vortex of rhythmic utterance, he momentarily experiences the vertigo of eternal forgetting. Twenty years earlier, when he had played one of the heralds to Jaroslav's king, he "hadn't seen a thing," because he had experienced the Ride "*from within*" (p. 222). But as the coded speech works its deeper life-in-death magic upon him, it finally releases its hidden thaumaturgic gift of vision, without which all poetry, no matter how beautiful its inner articulation, would be a dead letter. "Looking at the veiled king, I saw Lucie riding (unknown and unknowable) majestically (and mockingly) through my life" (p. 223).

The Ride of the Kings, Kundera says in his preface, "frames the action of the novel; it is a frame of forgetting" (p. viii). But it also connotes the very opposite of the act of forgetting, a ceremony of mnemonic empowering. Performed yearly on Whitsunday, the seventh Sunday after Easter, this seasonal ritual conceals in its pagan heart an allusion to the Pentecostal mystery of spiritual initiation. The beggar who hides the king, and the young man about to reach the first peak of virility disguised as a woman, are oxymoronic symbols of dignity masked in humility, of great power about to be released from constraint. In this ironic novel about the modern distemper between words and the things they signify, poetry suddenly flares out with its ancient tongue of flame. At last disabused of his deadening cynicism, Ludvik comes to the verge of addressing Lucie in the rediscovered language of love, the language in which she had courted him when she gave him those flowers picked from the cemetery. Freed from the narrow confines of Kostka's allegory—a tale that "mixed truth with fiction and produced a new legend (closer to the truth, perhaps, more beautiful, more profound) to superimpose on the old" (p. 223)—Lucie, the dispossessed figure of innocence, is finally reinstated by Ludvik to the intimate dignity of the beloved.

The vision of Lucie rediscovered is abruptly dispelled by the sound of a male voice calling out to Ludvik. It is Pavel Zemanek, smilingly advancing with outstretched hand. Ludvik takes that hand just before the scene cuts to Jaroslav and his no less dumbfounding encounter with old Koutecky, the expropriated rich man who tells him the truth about his son Vladimir.

Old hatreds are like old loves. One day they die, leaving in their fiery wake something like a budding nostalgia for shared memories. So Ludvik, in the next scene, hearing Pavel's attractive young girlfriend praise the former Stalinist as a liberal of the mid-sixties, one of the most popular lecturers at the university, registers a sneaking sympathy for his old enemy. Once again, Zemanek is successfully pointing his rhetoric in the same direction the whole country is headed.

Sensing that "the dishonorable truce" (p. 236) with Zemanek is imminent, Ludvik is prepared to submit, only to be bested once again. His inveterate tormentor reduces the dreaded ceremony of reconciliation to a casual glance at his watch before departing with his beautiful young girlfriend on his arm. Ludvik then proceeds to tell Helena that he does not love her and will not see her again, in full awareness that "she was quite innocent with respect to me" (p. 237). Under that blow, Helena's bloated world collapses instantly. But she is a woman of appetite, with little talent for despair. While her distracted mind toys with the temptation of eternal oblivion, she feels driven to indulge herself one more time by allowing Jindra, the young sound technician who dogs her footsteps with adolescent devotion, to kiss her on the mouth. Jindra is the source of the pills she has just ingested in a dangerously exaggerated quantity, in order to still the ache that racks her head.

The consequences of Helena's halfhearted suicide attempt are described suspensefully from the perspective of a terrified Ludvik. He fears the worst once he has scanned Helena's melodramatic farewell message, which Jindra delivers to him by hand, in an envelope bearing the official letterhead of the Party District Council. The two men conduct a frantic search that finally leads them to the bolted door of a country outhouse. Forced open, the latrine yields a vision of comic anguish that more than matches in its extremity the dreaded image of a dead or dying Helena. Jindra's pills were not analgesics, as Helena had thought, but laxatives mislabeled in a gesture of self-protective prudery by an adolescent ashamed of the unpoetic character of his digestive tract.

Helena, perched on the wooden seat of the primitive toilet with her skirt pulled up, is an outrageous sight that underlines the cruelty of laughter with a sadism that has shocked some of Kundera's readers. In 1967, when *The Joke* first appeared, the Czechs laughed freely, because they saw the Party being humiliated through Helena. But if we heed Kundera's counsel against a political interpretation of the novel, we are faced with the revolting spectacle of woman's body shamed through its "place of excrement," without even a pornographic trace of anything that might remind us of Yeats' paradox about love's mansion. Panurge's obscene trick, which turns the pious lady who rejected his sexual advances into an object of unseemly attention for excited dogs right in the middle of a religious service,[26] seems like a prank compared with the treatment Kundera reserves as Helena's reward for excessive complacency. Jindra, maddened by pity, turns upon the mortally embarrassed Ludvik. "She doesn't need you for anything!" he yells. "She doesn't give a shit!" (p. 254). In Czech, the throwaway phrase has a directed concreteness impossible to reproduce in English. The expression "*Sere na Vás*" ("She shits on you"),[27] which Jindra repeats twice without fully realizing what he is saying, turns the offensive noun "shit" into an active verb with Helena as its ruling grammatical subject. In this way, Czech speech manages to retrieve something for Helena from this agonizing scene, by endowing her body with the mimetic power of a Schweik. She suddenly escapes from the humiliating trap of her concrete position into the realm of verbal abstraction, where the words generate a vivid metaphor for the state of mind of a whole nation that has overdosed on so many lies for so many years. There is a measure of justice for Ludvik as well in this fully realized trope. He is, after all, the mirror as well as the victim of the age whose ill humors are thus purged. In the process, Helena's body is freed at last of the phony-noble rhetoric that has draped it, and it becomes pure *physis* once more, the Rabelaisian touchstone of truth, as when the child Gargantua demonstrates the empirical method of philosophical inquiry by testing for the best possible asswipe.[28] Jindra's words release laughter from the grip of cruelty and bring merciful comic relief to Ludvik and to the narrative as well.

Jaroslav's release from illusion follows immediately after. In a confrontation with Vlasta in their kitchen, he taxes her with complicity in Vladimir's betrayal, and when she retaliates, the exchange heats into a quarrel between the Communist and the kulak's daughter. She sullenly keeps her thin back turned to him as she stands at her stove, pretending to be busy with her cooking. The rage inside him keeps mounting, until he starts breaking the dishes on the floor. After this uncharacteristic bout of violence, he steps over the rubble in his home, where he had "borne the tender yoke of the poor man's daughter" (p. 257), conscious of stepping out of his dream world forever.

In his anger at Vlasta, who has been filling his house with the tasteless bibelots of neo-bourgeois consumerism, Jaroslav would like to think that he is hitting out against the Koutecky element. But Ludvik, whom he meets outdoors, knows better, having understood that "they" and "we," terms once pitted against each other in the ideological discourse of 1948, are hopelessly ambiguous whenever applied to real experience. History, with its lure of eternal memory, is really a very ironic jade. "All rectification (both vengeance and forgiveness) will be taken over by oblivion" (p. 245). This maxim belongs to Ludvik, mulling over his encounter with Zemanek, but it applies equally to the aftertaste of Jaroslav's confrontation with Vlasta, when he is like "an abandoned king past his prime" (p. 258), a man deprived of his sense of the future by the sudden loss of his legitimate heir.

In the last, poignant scene of the novel, Ludvik sits down to play with Jaroslav's cimbalom ensemble in the same restaurant where Jindra had sounded his false alarm that afternoon. The two old friends, when they acknowledge each other at last, at the end of the harrowing weekend, seem to have exchanged roles. Jaroslav, still the masterful fiddler, plays with the passion born of despair, as if trying to hold the melody one more time against the growing tide of indifference about to engulf him. Ludvik, chastened by what he has been through, picks up his clarinet with the authentic tenderness of a long-delayed homecoming. As they concentrate on playing, life appears to Ludvik bathed in the gentle light of forgiveness. From within the "glass cabin" of an ancient love song, the values he and Jaroslav shared in their youth, which circulated in words like "comrade," "Fučík," and "the future," revealing a sinister underside in the process, appear to him again in their original innocence, like Lucie come back to him in the "magic circle of music" (p. 264) to plead "on behalf of a devastated world." Moved by an irresistible wave of understanding compassion, Ludvik accepts her lyric persuasion. "The blame lay elsewhere and was so great that its shadow had fallen over a vast area, over the world of innocent things (and words), and was devastating them" (p. 262).

This statement, rising with the insistence that only final conclusions can muster in any discourse, seems to beg for a commentary transcending the immediacy of the moment of grace that inspired it. *The Joke* was written in 1965, when Czech culture was experiencing the gathering momentum of hope. It is characteristic of Kundera's temper that he ends his novel against the grain of optimism and the righteous clamor for retribution that filled the Czech air at the time. One may well ask how much hope there should have been about the liberalizing trend in Communism whose representative is the opportunistic Zemanek. Rather than looking forward to a time when "Communism with a human face" would be the slogan meant to legitimize an outburst of radical skepticism to Russian ears, Kundera's nostalgic coda contemplates the meaning of 1948 and the things long gone, which people like Zemanek were busily forgetting. But even in relation to Zemanek, Ludvik's mind, purged of all venom, leans toward an understanding that has the poignantly personal quality of generational sympathy.

As the music swells, Jaroslav, the defeated dreamer, suffers a heart attack that will doom him to live out the rest of his life without passion, "under the watchful eye of death." He is the image of a man of true feeling whom the age has played false. But it is inside the skeptical mind of Ludvik that Jaroslav's lost faith flares up one last time, with a tragic incandescence that lingers with the reader as the novel's culminating effect. Looking down at his stricken friend, Ludvik pictures himself "holding him in my arms, holding him and carrying him, carrying him, big and heavy as he was, carrying my own obscure guilt; I could picture myself carrying him through the indifferent mob, weeping as I went" (p. 266). The repetition of the word "carrying," with its rhythmic insistence on the burdensome assumption of guilty responsibility in an act of purely gratuitous love, becomes a dirge for a past never more loved than at this moment of its passing into a dreamlike state of being.

While Zemanek the timeserver elbows his way back to the helm of unfolding events, Ludvik chooses to stay behind with Jaroslav, who is making his sad exit from history. The skeptic mourns the death of the idealist in an experience of guilt that is the other side of tenderness, a purely private emotion that has nothing to do with the dubious rights or wrongs human beings persist in attaching to public events. Ludvik has surrendered the realm of historical meaning and imperatives to Zemanek, the inveterate actor who exists for and within the eyes of his public. We expect Pavel to be highly effective at the rostrum and in the lively streets during the festive months of the Prague Spring. If he is like his real-life brothers within the movement for Czech socialist renewal (like Pavel Kohout,[29] whom he resembles), Pavel Zemanek will not make his peace with Moscow after the events of August 1968 (unlike Aragon). But these are questions of the future, outside the purview of this novel, which persists in looking back, first in anger and ultimately in forgiveness. The emotional resolution of ideological conflicts that brings together the winners and losers of the historical game is the beginning of Kundera's protracted farewell to the idea of History.

2

Laughable Loves OR The Impossible Don Juan

Laughable Loves was the first of Milan Kundera's works to reach American readers. It was published in New York in 1974,[1] with an introduction by Philip Roth, while its author was still living in Czechoslovakia. But all seven stories that make up the volume were written much earlier, between 1959 and 1969, during that marvelous decade of Czech culture which was also a time of great artistic ferment for Kundera. Originally, the title *Směšné lásky* (*Laughable Loves*) linked a series of ten short stories issued in three separate "notebooks,"[2] the last of which saw print in 1969, during the final gasp of Czech literary freedom. In the definitive form achieved after several authorial interventions,[3] stripped down to seven entries rearranged in a sequence that highlights the emotional counterpoint between laughter and pathos, *Laughable Loves* prefigures the structural archetype of Kundera's later, elliptical novels.[4]

In his dialogue with Christian Salmon, Kundera offers his quintessential definition of the novel as "a meditation on existence as seen through the medium of imaginary characters." And when his interlocutor objects that by so broad a definition even *The Decameron* could be called a novel, Kundera retorts, "I won't be so provocative as to call *The Decameron* a novel. Still, that book is one of the first efforts in modern Europe to create a large-scale composition in narrative prose, and as such it has a place in the history of the novel *at least* as its source and forerunner."[5] Granting Kundera the same latitude he himself gives Boccaccio, we may discuss *Laughable Loves* as an experimental link in the sequence of his novels and a source of some of his important themes.

Though *Laughable Loves* obviously lacks unity of action and has independent sets of characters (the single exception being Dr. Havel, who connects the fourth and sixth stories), the series achieves internal coherence as a reflection on the paradoxical entanglements of three major themes. These themes, first raised in the opening trio of stories to be more fully developed in the remaining four (all of which date from the last stage of composition), are: the uneasy nature of truth in an age of easy certainties; modern Don Juanism; and the discord between body and soul in erotic situations. While the book employs a diversity of narrators, the perspective on the action throughout is one of irony, which Kundera considers "consubstantial" with the spirit of the European novel.[6]

The laughter resounding in these tales of erotic debacle is never quite free of the admixture of sadness that turns it into a grimace.[7] But the narrative tempo is *allegro con brio,* and the resourceful narrators manage to maintain a posture of playful brightness even when the action explodes in their faces. This is particularly true of the opening entry, "Nobody Will Laugh," which is told by an unlucky jester caught in a society where laughter has been suspended. At the beginning of the story, he is a successful university lecturer in art history who finds himself comfortably in possession of a beautiful mistress named Klara. By the end, she has turned against him and left him "because a man who lies can't be respected by any woman" (p. 38).

This reversal originates in the narrator's unfortunate attempt to evade the truth, an instinctive, dubiously motivated reaction that might even be construed as a sudden access of kindness. As a professional art historian, he is being badgered for a critical appraisal by an amateur scholar who has written an utterly worthless, derivative article about a well-known nineteenth-century Czech painter. Since he is at core a man of strict intellectual standards, the narrator cannot praise Mr. Zaturetsky's pedantic drivel, but there is something within him that rebels against the thought of playing executioner of the little man's plodding hopes and ambitions. Unfortunately for both of them, Zaturetsky is relentless in his pursuit of the punishing truth, and he finally manages to corner his unwilling critic, who has been playing an elaborate game of escape from his would-be victim. Zaturetsky even tracks down our hero's private retreat, a bachelor flat where he keeps Klara under wraps. When this carefully preserved separation between public obligations and secret pleasures crumbles, indulgence gives way to spite, and he falsely accuses the little man of trying to seduce Klara. The situation becomes grave when Zaturetsky's personal outrage escalates into an accusation of slander that is instantly submitted for investigation and eventual judgment by the neighborhood committee of comrades, which keeps a tight watch over socialist morals.

The inventive fibster soon discovers that all around him expected laughter has frozen into rigid indignation. He cannot even persuade his mistress that a personal code of integrity lies concealed under the elaborate structure of deception he has erected. Klara will not understand the distinction between the lie in the heart and the lie on the lips, and she urges him to get everyone out of trouble by satisfying Zaturetsky's craving for scholarly approval. Even though he feels himself driven to a fall by the laughable lie of his own creation, our hero resists her expedient advice and instead proceeds to tell Zaturetsky's wife what he really thinks of her husband's article. But that long-suffering woman harbors a pathetic faith in her partner's vocation that makes her utterly impervious to the truth at hand, and in the end the liar turned truthteller *in extremis* finds himself surrounded by distrust. To cap it all, his mistress accuses him of being a "stereotyped cynic" to justify dropping him. In the "chilly silence" (p. 38) that descends on him after that parting shot, the newly self-aware narrator consoles himself with the thought that he is a lonely comic spirit stranded in a world of banished laughter.

In this overture to a cycle of tales where, as Philip Roth tells us, "*erotic* play and power are the subjects frequently at the center,"[8] the love interest stays in the background. It is a losing stake, thrown almost casually into a game of make-believe played at the extreme edges of the problem of truth. In positing a disjunction between intellectual truth and the pleasures of Eros, which are the chosen domain of the nonserious spirit, this story, the only one Kundera preserved from the first notebook (1963), anticipates the masterly "Symposium" (1969).

In the book's definitive sequence, "Nobody Will Laugh" and "Symposium" frame two stories about the pursuit of sexual love, both published originally in 1965. "The Hitchhiking Game," the third of the series of seven, places a physically confident young man of twenty-eight opposite a woman six years younger who is only just discovering her body's potential to give and receive pleasure. The two have been lovers for a year, but she is still anguished about her lack of sexual ease. Imagining her reserve to be an obstacle for her lover, whom she adores with a jealous passion, she never suspects that he cherishes her shyness as a sign of innocence. While driving together on the first day of a holiday trip to the mountains, they inadvertently stumble into an adventure of erotic exploration, a dangerous game of masks that will throw their love off course. Attempting to imitate the kind of sophisticated flirtation she thinks he enjoys when he is away from her, the young woman pretends to be a hitchhiker and assumes the suggestive manner of an easy pickup. At first reluctantly, then with mounting ferocity, the young man responds to her provocative double-talk by escalating the verbal game into gesture. At the end of the road down which imagination leads them, they stand opposite each other in a hotel room, two faceless bodies topped by masks. Their lovemaking is a grappling in the dark, neither of them knowing the other who lies in this harsh embrace while the body's pleasure feeds the pain it inflicts on the exiled soul.

Roth writes that this "confusion of identities, and the heightened eroticism [it] provokes in the lovers, with its scary sado-masochistic edge, is not so catastrophic to either of them as his joke turns out to be for Ludvik Jahn."[9] Perhaps so. It is true that the private catastrophe that results from this brutal *marivaudage* remains locked behind a bedroom door. But it seems to me that Roth, who sees the grimness of these tales in the long shadow society casts over the erotic game, misses the metaphysical dimension of Kundera's dark vision of the comedy of the sexes.

The theme of Don Juanism makes its first appearance in "The Golden Apple of Eternal Desire," the second of the seven tales. Here Kundera's Don Juan is Martin, a man who has just crossed the threshold of forty, and is married and in love with his wife. His chronicler is a younger friend, a scholar by profession, and by predilection a student of the discipline of the erotic chase that Martin exemplifies and teaches. This unnamed narrator casts a reflective eye on the action as it unfolds within the time span of a single Saturday afternoon. The master, with his disciple in tow, embarks on the road of sexual adventure that will take them from their starting point in Prague, from village to village, to their appointed goal at a small-town hospital where two nurses are awaiting them.

Behind the wheel of a rented Fiat, the obliging pupil drives along, compelled by the imperious desire for adventure that resides within the older man sitting in the passenger seat beside him. The undivided quality of his master's will fascinates him like a force of nature. For his part, he knows he has been tricked into joining the action: the preceding Monday, when they met one of the nurses in Prague, Martin had managed to snatch a rare book about Etruscan culture from his hands and slip it into her bag while negotiating the weekend rendezvous. The prospect of reclaiming that book taints his own motivation with a distinctly scholarly duplicity. He admits to himself that unlike Martin, he is a mere "dilettante," a man "*playing* at something which Martin *lives*." "Sometimes," he reflects, "I have the feeling that the whole of my polygamous life is a consequence of nothing but my imitation of other men" (p. 48). Yet he also acknowledges that playful imitation has been the controlling value of his life, an imperative of sorts, to which he has consistently subordinated all his personal interests and desires.

Martin and his narrator/companion represent Kundera's first variation on that mythical pair of sexual adventurers, Don Juan and his servant, whose name keeps changing with each new version of the story while his master's remains fixed forever. Don Juan's man is called Catalinón in Tirso de Molina's *The Playboy of Seville; or, Supper with a Statue* (1616?), becoming Sganarelle in Molière's *Dom Juan* (1665), and thereafter Leporello in Lorenzo Da Ponte's libretto to Mozart's opera *Don Giovanni* (1787). Kierkegaard, in an essay on Mozart's tragicomic opera, observed that "there is also something erotic in Leporello's relationship to Don Juan, there is a power by which Don Juan captivates him, even against his will."[10] This brilliant perception sheds indirect light on the bond that unites Martin and his friend. They are attached to each other by something that approximates but does not quite match the power of erotic seduction. Rather, they are inseparable as two game players are, who need each other to carry on with the game. Martin, whom his companion posits as the natural Don Juan, serves as a talismanic figure in whose living presence the illusion of physical authenticity is preserved, and he in turn uses his friend, always so obedient to the call of his master's unquestionable desire for women, as the mirror that will return a reassuring image of his own fabulous potency. Both are caught in a shared delusion of a perennially conquering male sexuality.

Kierkegaard heard in Mozart's opera the "opulent moment"[11] of sensuousness rising above the dread to which Christian spirituality had consigned it. He interpreted *Don Giovanni* as the supreme classical expression of the Don Juan myth, capturing in all its ideality, as only music could, the "daemonic joy of life"[12] that is Don Juan's gift to women. Kundera's treatment of the myth in *Laughable Loves* is essentially antimusical, charting an aggressively intellectual territory at the opposite pole from the Mozartian spirit of immediacy as Kierkegaard defined it. In Da Ponte's libretto, it is the servant Leporello who recites the famous catalogue of Don Giovanni's conquests, an "epic survey of his master's life,"[13] Kierkegaard calls it, whose tantalizingly incomplete tally of 1,003 invites the imagination to lose itself in an ever-expanding prospect of seductions to come. Kierkegaard conceived Mozart's Don Giovanni as "handsome, not very young," and placed his age at thirty-three, "the length of a generation."[14] Martin, at forty, falls well within that span, in our contemporary reckoning. But Kundera's variation on Leporello clearly breaks away from the original mold. In the opera, Don Giovanni's power over Leporello is such that the servant can almost be assimilated to his master, even becoming "a voice for Don Juan."[15] In the first scene of the second act, Don Giovanni and Leporello exchange costumes; the servant, instructed by his master, dons the mythical hat with white feathers, the broad cloak, and the sword of the sexual conquistador to woo the discarded Elvira, while the real Don Juan borrows his servant's clothes to seduce Elvira's maid.

The type of the great aristocrat slumming, *le grand seigneur qui s'encanaille,* was familiar to Parisian playgoers in the waning decades of the eighteenth century. Beaumarchais, whose comedy *The Marriage of Figaro* Da Ponte had adapted for Mozart a year earlier, in 1786, used the type *con brio,* provoking dangerously ambiguous laughter in the urbanized aristocratic audience. Don Juan also takes advantage of his servant one time too many, since for him too, it is growing late for such tricks. In his socialist Bohemia, Kundera's Don Juan retains no servant to compile the record of his amorous exploits. He is reduced to being his own accountant, but he requires a secondary male presence at his heels to witness the actuarial function that rivals and ultimately overwhelms the primary activity for which Don Juan's sword once stood as guarantor and metonymic emblem.

Martin is a highly theoretical quantifier of women. He has invented an elaborate verbal technique for targeting and pinning down his prey, and this is the essence of the art of seduction he teaches his disciple. In describing the two initial stages of his strictly codified, systematic approach to women, he deliberately uses the abstract, latinate words *registráž* (registration) and *kontaktáž* (contact),[16] words a pollster might use in preparing a survey. Martin's erotic foreplay is a cerebral activity that imitates the precision of a laboratory experiment, within a time frame arbitrarily limited as in a bureaucratic schedule. The adventure of the high road to sexual conquest starts in Prague at 2:00 P.M. and ends there before the stroke of 9:00 so that Martin, a devoted husband, can play a promised game of cards with his wife. The interval thus circumscribed is spacious enough for the two men to duly register and contact a number of new women on the way to the predetermined assignation with the nurses. The sexual consummation is postponed to a hypothetical future as the new contacts are carefully tucked away in Don Juan's impressive file.

Philip Roth has compared the Don Juanism in this story to "a sport played by a man against a team of women, oftentimes without body contact"—a witty metaphor that effectively expresses Roth's sense of the tale as a "mild satire" on Don Juanism.[17] Martin's intellectual invention compares favorably with the typical spectator sport that middle-aged men commonly indulge in on Saturday afternoons, in New York as in Prague, seated before their television screens. But it seems to me that Kundera's tale has a deeper bottom than mild satire can fathom. The reflective narrator who watches Martin's game while also participating in it is contemplated from an even greater distance by the all-seeing yet unseen author. It was Kundera, after all, who gave the tale an epigraph from Pascal's Pensée 139, on *divertissement:* ". . . ils ne savent pas que ce n'est que la chasse, et non pas la prise qu'ils recherchent" (". . . they do not know that they seek only the chase and not the quarry"). The hunt, that quintessentially aristocratic sport of the seventeenth century, is Pascal's elected metaphor for the concept of *divertissement,* which he defines as "une occupation violente et impétueuse qui les détourne de penser à soi" ("a violent and impetuous activity that deflects men from thinking about themselves").[18] In Kundera's fiction, sex, not sport, is the privileged trope for the obsessive chase after nothingness that drives human beings away from the thought of death, which seems unbearable when all sense of God has been voided in the head. But Kundera insists on retaining the original, nonmetaphoric meaning of the word *divertissement,* which denotes a frivolous kind of entertainment. Frivolity assumes the value of a philosophical concept in Kundera's world. It functions as a snare for the spirit of gravity, or as an acid test for questions of the order Pascal raises in his meditation on the misery of the human condition in the absence of God.

By the end of the mock-epic narrative, Martin's reflective companion will have understood the illusory nature of his master's activity. At bottom, Martin is a mere imitator, just like his pupil, even though his game may be constructed from a real memory of his younger self. The narrator voices off abruptly at the moment when his cameralike eye has trained its lens on Martin, and himself at his side, traveling the road of return, suspended in futile animation within an ephemeral present quickened by elusive anticipation. Stoically faithful to the obligation of frivolity that Kundera likes to impose on his most conscious male characters, the disingenuous companion of borrowed adventure cuts off the inconclusive action with a fine verbal flourish, pinning down the forever receding object by naming it The Golden Apple of Eternal Desire. The sexual connotation of the symbolic apple lingers on within the word like a precious essence, even though Eve herself has become the vanishing point of an illusionistic prospect. The allusion to the primal sin in the lost garden, whose grave echo was heard in the Pascal epigraph, dissipates in the advancing twilight.

Kundera's Don Juans are haunted by the pathos of imitation and the consciousness of living a parodistic derivative of a once charismatic identity. In *Laughable Loves,* the perfection of the type is the intellectual and sexually practiced Dr. Havel, a man of wit who figures as the lead character in two of the stories. The first of these, "Symposium," takes the form of a miniature drama in five acts, built around the twin questions of love and death. Like the Platonic dialogue from which it takes off, it is primarily a drama of ideas. Talk occupies the foreground while a single event, Alzhbeta's questionable suicide attempt, occurs in the background and is brought forward for commentary, somewhat like Alcibiades' failed seduction of Socrates in

Plato's text. The conversation, which engages three men and two women, plays itself out during an improvised party in a hospital staff room. Dr. Havel and the sex-starved nurse Alzhbeta are both on duty, and they are joined by three colleagues: the chief physician, a bald, aging, happily married philanderer; his attractive younger mistress, who is also a doctor; and the handsome young intern Flaishman.

The atmosphere inside the room is licentious and charged with crisscrossing currents of sexual tension. Alzhbeta, a mature woman whose beautiful body is topped by a repulsive face, desires Dr. Havel in particular and all men in general, only to be rebuffed by the three who are present. Flaishman, the would-be romantic, is drawn to the woman doctor and believes he has read the signals of his imminent success in her vaguely flirtatious manner. But she, whom her lover the chief physician has dubbed Diana, "cold, sportive, and spiteful" (p. 110), in the second act, will take sexual aim at her lover's friend Dr. Havel in the fourth act. The chief physician, also ranked as the senior libertine of the group, delivers himself of a tongue-in-cheek panegyric to Platonic love in the first act (p. 98), having earlier expressed the opinion that "eroticism is not only a desire for the body, but to an equal extent a desire for honor. The partner, whom you've won, who cares about you and loves you, is your mirror, the measure of what you are and what you stand for. In eroticism we seek the image of our own significance and importance" (p. 94).

In postulating a solipsistic Eros, the chief physician has undermined the basic assumption behind the doctrine of philosophical love Diotima once taught Socrates. Plato's Eros is a force that unites two selves in the pursuit of a good higher than either of them can contain or muster in isolation. Diotima taught that the function of Eros was "that of procreation in what is beautiful, and such procreation can be either physical or spiritual."[19] Before bidding the physical realm of being farewell, the woman of Mantinea restored its essential dignity to the human body, by appropriating it as a central symbol of vitality in her myth of the philosopher's quest for truth and beauty. By contrast, Alzhbeta's body is held in contempt by the assembled sophists, whose practice of love is mired in mockery and whose discourse never rises above the level of *doxa*.

Alzhbeta is reduced to making imaginary love to herself in a sad mock striptease, which she performs fully clothed in the second act, to the embarrassment of those present. She leaves the room an offended woman, having unwittingly swallowed a dose of sleeping pills administered by Havel instead of the pep pill she had asked for. The truth about Alzhbeta's ensuing brush with death by gas inhalation is never established in the text. The chief physician calls it a fake suicide attempt staged to attract Havel's attention. Flaishman considers Alzhbeta's unrequited love for him the cause of a real suicide attempt that fans the flame of his erotic conceit. The woman doctor argues that it was a mishap: Alzhbeta's coffee water boiled over and extinguished the gas burner after she fell asleep. Dr. Havel affirms that Alzhbeta's intent was to offer her body to death since the living would have no part of it.

Death as the substitute lover is an image from Dr. Havel's myth about himself. In the first act, referring to his friend's sexual omnivorousness, the chief physician says, "You're like death; you take everything" (p. 93), and urges Alzhbeta's body upon him. In the second act, he reiterates that definition—"Havel is death"—contradicting the woman doctor, who says that "Havel is Don Juan. He's not old, but he's getting old" (p. 110). This exchange prompts Dr. Havel to deliver a brief discourse on "the end of the Don Juans."

> "If I should pass judgment on whether I'm Don Juan or death, I must incline, albeit unhappily, toward the chief physician's opinion," said Havel, taking a long drink. "Don Juan. He, after all, was a conqueror. Rather in capital letters. A Great Conqueror. But I ask you, how can you be a conqueror in a domain

where no one refuses you, where everything is possible and everything is permitted? Don Juan's era has come to an end. Today, Don Juan's descendant no longer *conquers*, but only *collects*. The figure of the Great Collector has taken the place of the Great Conqueror, only the Collector is no longer really Don Juan at all. Don Juan was a tragic figure. He was burdened by his guilt. He sinned gaily and laughed at God. He was a blasphemer and ended up in hell." (p. 110)

In quite another context, Kundera has called Prague the city of endings.[20] It is the same city that had turned festive for Mozart when it saw and heard the world premiere of his *Don Giovanni* in 1787. With an uncanny sense of time and place, Kundera has brought the mythical playboy from Seville to die of exhaustion in an anonymous hospital not far from the old imperial town that was once the stage of his most refined triumph. Almost two centuries after Mozart, Kundera sees the defiance of death (in the form of the Commander's statue), and the subsequent descent into hell, as a verbal metaphor that evokes nostalgia rather than dread. He ushers his Don Juan to extinction with a flourish of talk aimed at chasing away a yawn, and not, like Tirso de Molina, with one last stab of the fabled blade into the empty air.[21]

Like Don Quixote and Sancho Panza, the tragicomic myth of Don Juan is a legacy from the crepuscular glory of Spain's Golden Age. In the original play, Tirso portrayed Don Juan as a trickster, a feckless young man without a thought for death. "Plenty of time for that" is his refrainlike retort to all sermons. The fatal shaking of hands with the statue of the dead Commander is more a gesture of bravado than of blasphemy. It is above all an instinctive expression of the caste value of physical courage, the only virtue this aristocratic clown honors. But though his appetites may enjoy complete license, his mind is not yet libertine. "Let me send for a priest at least; I want to confess and be absolved" he cries on his way to hell.[22]

It was Molière who first developed the intellectual potential of the type in his comedy *Dom Juan*. His hero believes in nothing save his own reason. "I believe two and two make four, Sganarelle, and four and four make eight," he declares, mocking his superstitious servant.[23] He is the ideal *grand seigneur* after the Fronde, untrammeled by feudal obligations and chafing at the tightening grip of authority. Molière endows him with a pursuing wife, Elvira, a woman no sooner wed than abandoned. Dom Juan argues the case for his boundless appetite for women and his need for variety on the basis of a convenient definition of Nature. He does not wait to be challenged to supper with the statue but initiates the invitation himself. Before going down under the Commander, he has one final chance to reject Elvira, when she enters as a veiled figure of Repentance, soon to be changed into the image of Time the Reaper, with scythe in hand. Arrogant to the end, the aristocratic libertine defies the moral connotation of death twice, once in the form of Repentance, the temporal worm, and then as Damnation, the eternal one.

In Mozart's music for Da Ponte's libretto of *Don Giovanni*, Don Juan emerges in his fullest incarnation, brilliantly modulating the tension between the tragic and comic modes that was inherent in the myth from the start. Don Giovanni is the lyric embodiment of the phallic illusion that death can be conquered in the repetition *ad infinitum* of the small death of sexual consummation, when time, in its relentless thrust, is seized and held fast against the vertiginous beat of a woman's heart. If Mozart's Don Juan blasphemes, it is with the conviction of his loins, and not, like Molière's libertine, with his head.

Dr. Havel's postmortem invocation of the Don Juan myth alludes to all three classical versions of the hero—the conquistador turned playboy, the licentious blasphemer, and the genius of seduction—only to negate them in the type of the Great Collector. On Havel's argument, Don Juanism is a practical and philosophical impossibility. The Great Collector, the image of a Don Juan defeated by the absence of resistance, is contaminated by death long before his term on earth is up. Once his heroic antagonism with death has been demystified, the Great Conqueror assumes the attributes of his hated enemy. Dr. Havel admits to being "at most a figure of comedy," but it is a comedy corroded by sadness, without the expansive vitality of the Spanish archetype. "Only against the historical background of his tragic gaiety can you to some extent perceive the comic sadness of my womanizing existence" (p. 112), says Havel, admitting an awareness of his own lack of authenticity.

It is revealing that Havel, whose body is at its sexual apex in "Symposium" even as his mind sounds the death knell of the Don Juan myth, should be almost frantic to resurrect that myth when we meet him again in "Dr. Havel After Twenty Years."[24] At this late stage in his career, he is a married man who has just developed gallbladder trouble. He finds himself wifeless on the tiny stage of a provincial spa, where he has gone to take the waters, and where he discovers to his dismay that his reputation as a Don Juan has preceded his anatomy down the road to decay. In his new vulnerability, he must endure the humiliation of being handled with businesslike indifference by a young masseuse administering water therapy. Even though he has long known that Don Juanism has lost its epic status, he now experiences a pathetic need to practice it again. This longing is not quite a desire for women but rather a violently childish caprice for something of himself that now seems gone forever. In his hour of need, the two subordinate characters from the old myth come to the rescue of the aging Don Juan: Leporello, in the familiar form of a younger disciple, and Elvira, the pursuing wife. In Kundera's variation, the wife is a glamorous movie star whose devotion to Havel is fed by a smoldering jealousy of his philandering. When she makes her appearance in the town, the provincial public is mesmerized by her unquestionable beauty and the magnitude of her fame. Riding the comet tail of that mirage,

Havel slips back into the highest orbit of his former identity. Once again, all women are accessible to him, and he happily harnesses his verbal technique to his derivative charisma as the man in possession of a mysterious and beautiful wife.

Feeling reinstated in his mastery, Havel turns playfully malicious. His young friend and admirer, a local journalist, has succumbed to the seduction of his Don Juan reputation and has solicited his expert opinion on the worth of his current erotic interest, a young woman with whom he is starting to fall in love. In a *tour de force* of verbal mystification, Havel succeeds in redirecting his friend's attention to the frankly middle-aged Dr. Frantishka, whose expressive legs and manner of walking, he claims, possess a beauty far superior to "ready-made prettiness" (p. 186). The kindly woman doctor is in reality the embodiment of everything maternal, a category of femininity that stands at the opposite pole from the erotic in Kundera's world. She will keep on babbling about her grown son even as the baffled young journalist is making love to her. When the obedient disciple reports back to his master on this experience, Havel launches into a discourse on the role of words in making the most casual sexual encounter uniquely memorable. "They say of me that I'm a collector of women," explains the *ci-devant* Don Juan turned erotic sophist. "In reality, I'm far more a collector of words" (p. 199).

Its essential physicality infected by words, the Don Juan myth in *Laughable Loves* is also touched by a corresponding erosion of gender privilege. Woman, after all, no less than man, can play at being the Great Collector, and "death" (*smrt*) is female in Czech, as in the Romance languages. In the two remaining stories of the cycle, Kundera shows two mature women exercising a highly contemporary equality with men in the matter of sexual adventurism. In Kundera's fiction, supremacy in that domain belongs to technique, which goes with age and experience. But his erotic women seem to have a greater capacity than the men for slipping into blasphemy.

In "Let the Old Dead Make Room for the Young Dead," a story that belongs to the same 1969 cycle as the Havel diptych, a woman of dignity, a widow of ten years well into her fifties, surrenders herself to a man twenty years her junior. The event occurs during her trip to a small town to visit her husband's grave. But when the widow arrives at the cemetery, whose path she knows so well, she finds that "where the gray sandstone monument with the name of her husband in gold lettering used to be, precisely on that spot (she confidently recognized the two neighboring graves) now stood a black marble headstone with a quite different name in gilt" (p. 138). The cemetery administration explains that her ten-year lease on the grave has expired and was canceled automatically, without notice, because of overcrowding. The operative rule, they say, is that "*the old dead ought to make room for the young dead*" (p. 139). This statement of necessity, couched as an upbeat slogan in the style of a mass society with futuristic ambitions, offends her spirit of reverence. Yet before the day is over, she herself will fling memory and self-respect to the winds for the sake of one last moment of sexual pleasure. She will give herself to the younger man who made love to her inexpertly once before, fifteen years earlier, when she still wore the halo of sexual grace.

The widow's conscious choice of sex above honor, the stepping over sacred memorials to the past and to the dead, recalls the blasphemous wooing in the cemetery that Pushkin imagined as the scene of Don Juan's greatest triumph. Kierkegaard, having postulated a reflective seducer, a master of "the beguiling, systematic, continuous seduction," as the romantic counterpart to the classical Don Juan, ruled Byron's Don Juan a failure because his seduction "extends itself epically."[25] Writing in 1843, he did not know Pushkin's one-act play *The Stone Guest* (1830), where the romantic type of Don Juan achieves its ideal expression. In that drama, Doña Anna is the widow, not the daughter, of the Commander Don Juan has slain, apparently without any particular intent: "When hard by the Escurial we met, / He ran upon my sword-point and expired, / Just like a dragon-fly upon a pin."[26] Don Juan first courts Doña Anna disguised as a monk, while she is at her devotions in front of her dead husband's monument. But the erotic will of this intensive seducer requires that he snatch the widow from the embrace of death and possess her in his own name, with his true identity unmasked. In the culminating fourth scene of the drama, which fuses the adventure of seduction and the confrontation with the statue, Don Juan and Doña Anna are both supremely conscious of the shadow of death at their shoulders, and they end by sinking into the ground in a mutual embrace. "Ah, what is death? For one sweet moment's tryst / I'd give my life without a murmur," Don Juan whispers to Doña Anna, who hesitates on the brink of surrender.[27] He throws his defiance of death at her feet as his ultimate forfeit in a game where she hazards her feminine honor. But his victory over her, anticipated in the kiss she allows him just when the statue knocks at the door, is as much an expression of her tender pity for him ("And so you are concerned about the life / Of poor Juan!")[28] as of her pride at having secured such a pledge of passion.

In Kundera's treatment of the wooing-over-the-grave motif, the woman's surrender also represents a collapse from the maternal into the erotic, but it is accomplished in a psychic atmosphere tainted by cynicism and vindictiveness. Kundera's fifty-five-year-old widow, who is also the mother of a demanding adolescent, harbors no illusions about the sexual moment she is about to share with this man from her distant past, almost a stranger to her now, but in whose memory she is enshrined as an elusively beautiful image. "She knew men and their approach to the female body. She was aware that in love even the most passionate idealism will not rid the body's surface of its terrible, basic importance." Neither of them really believes his tempting assurance that "she was still beautiful, that in fact nothing had changed, that a human being always remains the same" (pp. 156–57). She, in particular, is painfully lucid about her body's inadequacy for the task to which their mutual greed for a taste of the past compels her. Like Pushkin's Doña Anna, she must choose between the moment's seduction and her honor, though in this case the memorial she is about to betray is more "her memorial, which this man beside her had honored for fifteen years in his thoughts" (p. 159), than her husband's. She suddenly visualizes her "son-enemy" (p. 157) as a monster of youthful egotism denying her the last vestiges of sexuality and pushing her closer to her grave. It is he, the living ghost, rather than her buried husband, who stands at her shoulder with a forbidding *memento mori* countenance while she hesitates. When she finally gives in to her insistent seducer, she inwardly hisses at her invisible son the blasphemous words "*The old dead must make room for the young dead, my boy!*" (p. 158), and with that profane thought, she turns to her last joyless lovemaking. Kundera, like Pushkin before him, interrupts the erotic scene at the moment of her yielding, but not before he has changed the embracing lovers into an obscene vision of carrion flesh mating over an open grave.

The last of the stories, "Edward and God," is the adventure of a seducer who, entangled in an irresistible combination of social necessity and his own hypocrisy, becomes a blasphemer in spite of himself. Edward begins by courting Alice, a young woman whose anachronistic religiosity forbids sexual consummation outside marriage. In order to achieve his end, he feigns a vague yearning for Alice's God, which immediately heightens her interest in their relationship. He goes with her to church, carefully mimicking her pious gestures with the studied mien of a Tartuffe. But soon his devotion is duly noted by the powers that be, and since this is a small town in the late fifties, he is hauled before a committee of socialist inquisitors at the school where he teaches.

The school directress is a fanatical Communist who was the cause of Edward's older brother's expulsion from the university years earlier, when he made light of her extravagant display of grief over Stalin's death. Now she is an ugly spinster "with the greasy black hair of a gypsy, black eyes, and black down under her nose" (p. 204), and with a secret penchant for young men. In imminent danger of being driven out of his job, Edward summons his powers of hypocrisy. This time he plays the other side of the coin of his putative faith in God, reinterpreting the theology of doubt with which he had courted the reluctant Alice as a crisis of a convinced Communist assailed by irrational religious belief. He explains to the committee that in spite of all the arguments his well-trained reason may advance, he cannot get rid of his faith in God. "You see, comrades, I'm telling it to you the way it is. It's better that I confess to you, because I don't want to be a hypocrite. I want you to know what I'm really like," he tells them, hanging his head. (p. 217).

This ostentatious demonstration of sincerity touches a responsive chord in the directress's gypsy heart. She takes Edward under her wing as her special pedagogic project, and he soon realizes that the game has slipped out of his control and that he is now a pawn in her erotic power play. The stage is thus set for the grotesque scene in the bachelorette flat where the directress has lured him for the kill. Entangled in the strings of his virtuoso lies, Edward is forced to confront the consequences of his words, and when the moment of truth ripens to the point where rhetoric must yield to action, Edward fears that "his body would sabotage his assiduous will" (p. 231). The anguish of physical impotence is holding him in a deadly grip when in a sudden inspiration he seizes upon the power of blasphemy to stiffen his faltering desire. Acting out the role of a religious man about to overstep the barrier of mortal sin, Edward commands the atheist woman to assume a kneeling posture and pray, "so that God may forgive us."

> As she uttered the words of the prayer, she glanced up at him as if he were God Himself. He watched her with growing pleasure: in front of him was kneeling the directress, being humiliated by a subordinate; in front of him a naked revolutionary was being humiliated by prayer; in front of him a praying lady was being humiliated by her nakedness. (pp. 232–33)

Edward, master of the easy lie, who has devised this farcical scene of make-believe blasphemy out of extreme expediency, is suddenly transformed into a master of erotic sadism. Intoxicated by "this threefold image of degradation" (p. 233), he finds that he can now command his body at will. The double-edged blasphemy performed at cross-purposes by the believing Communist and the assumed Christian acts like a magic philter to release Edward's sexual drive.

The conquest of Alice, which follows in the next section, is almost a letdown for Edward after the satanic high he has reached with the directress. Alice gives herself to him because she sees him as a martyr suffering at the hands of the Communist system she hates. But Edward, who knows better, is disappointed in the second prize his hypocrisy has won for him. He secretly reproaches Alice for so easily betraying her once all-powerful God of chastity.

Edward's story is told by a discursive narrator whose ironic manner recalls the narrator/participant of "The Golden Apple of Eternal Desire." This time, the final click of the camera delivers a double exposure of Edward: as he sits alone in an empty church, "tormented with sorrow, because God does not exist," the shadow of a smile is superimposed on his face, with its solemn mask, for the grieving hypocrite senses "the genuine *living* face of God" emerging from the depths of that sorrow. The narrator treats Edward's sad face as a photographic pentimento and begs his readers, "Please, keep him in your memory with this smile," having already implicated us all in Edward's condition with a dramatic sigh in the manner of

Gogol: "Ah, ladies and gentlemen, a man lives a sad life when he cannot take anything or anyone seriously!" (p. 240).

The world of Edward, which he shares with Martin and Dr. Havel and all the other sophistic lovers and their victims, is a small socialist country with sealed borders, where a man can travel from the center to the periphery and back again in the space of a single afternoon. On that radically reduced *theatrum mundi*, men and women pursue each other, striving to recapture a sense of their own centrality by escaping the dull anonymity of their social condition into the illusion of a privileged sexual moment. But in the place of sensuality they find only a phantom freedom, a verbal artifact that functions as the dialectical negation of a ubiquitous external power that has posited itself as the only permissible image of God.

3

Life Is Elsewhere OR Poetry and Revolution

If the last pages of *The Joke* read like a lyric farewell to the revolutionary dream of Kundera's youth, *Life Is Elsewhere*[1] dismisses the lyricism of European revolutions with a well-aimed parting kick. Kundera began writing his second novel before the Russian invasion of 1968 and completed it in 1970, during the hard times of the Husák regime. In the fall of 1968, when he was in Paris for the French publication of *The Joke,* his "eyes were still seeing Russian tanks parked on Prague's streets," as he has written.[2] Josef Škvorecký, who met Kundera then, offers another recollection of the mood of that moment.

> I remember Paris in 1968. We were standing in front of Les Deux Magots like poor relations whose house had just burned down and Milan Kundera said, "I only hope I die soon. There's been too much of everything. How much longer do you think we can last?"[3]

There is a tendency in the West to interpret *The Joke* in light of the events of August 1968. After all, the novel burst upon the consciousness of European readers just as images of tanks on the streets of Prague were vanishing from their television screens. But the association of the two is misleading, like an optical illusion. Kundera's first novel was written in the relatively benign atmosphere of the Czech mid-sixties and was published in 1967, when, as he recalls, "it was a joy to be alive."[4] In those few years, the gap between the hopes of Kundera's generation and the reality around them seemed to have narrowed. Read without the interference of historical hindsight, *The Joke* reveals its essentially temperate, conciliatory spirit; its ironic thrust is directed at the fanaticism of revenge, and its lingering lyricism is that of forgiveness. Rising above his customary cynicism in the book's last meditation, Ludvik declares from the "glass cabin" of Jaroslav's song that the values of 1948 are innocent of blame. By contrast, in part 6 of *Life Is Elsewhere,* the narrator, who has made the same mental journey as Ludvik to the origins of the Czech Communist regime, casts a cold eye on the murderous innocence that then ruled hearts and minds with the help of lyrical blindness.

> What actually remains of that distant time? Today, people regard those days as an era of political trials, persecutions, forbidden books, and legalized murder. But we who remember must bear witness: it was not only an epoch of terror, but also an epoch of lyricism, ruled hand in hand by the hangman and the poet.
>
> The wall behind which people were imprisoned was made of verse. There was dancing in front of it. No, not a danse macabre! A dance of innocence. Innocence with a bloody smile. (p. 270)

Elsewhere Kundera has remarked that "to rewrite history even in Orwell's sense is not an inhuman activity. On the contrary, it is very human."[5] In *Life Is Elsewhere,* the human need to reclaim the past for the present manifests itself in a groping toward a painful integrity of personal and public remembrance.

With his awareness of the inescapable ambivalence of all human endeavors, Kundera has translated the serious impulse to tell the truth about the year 1948, as he lived it, into a comic fiction plotted by an exceptionally wakeful intellect.

At the center of the novel is Jaromil, the only son of a bourgeois Prague family, who becomes a boy wonder of surrealism and then, still in his his teens, a successful poet of revolution shortly after 1948. The meteoric career of this holy monster of lyricism is subjected to relentless sardonic probing. Kundera takes Jaromil from the moment of conception in his mother's womb through his triumphs as child prodigy and his adolescent erotic fumbling to his premature death at the peak of his literary celebrity. Laughter acts as executioner in this irreverent *vita,* in which Kundera attempts to do much more than liquidate his own past as a young poet and young Communist. In desecrating the icon of Jaromil, he aims to dismantle the formidable triad of values—youth, poetry, revolution—under whose banner European modernism has marched for so long. At the core of *Life Is Elsewhere* is a polemical novelistic essay that interrogates the powerful irrationality of the lyric impulse and demystifies the peculiarly agonistic twentieth-century relationship between the artistic avant-garde and revolutionary power.

In *The Joke* Kundera deployed a plurality of narrative perspectives crisscrossing in a carefully delimited time and space to create a polyphonic effect. His second novel uses a single narrator whose voice is heard persistently questioning and thinking about the fictional matter at hand. He acts as an ironic master of ceremonies who can summon or dismiss at will the two central characters, Jaromil and his mother, as well as a host of subordinates. Jaromil's own voice is not allowed free play; he is spoken about rather than speaking, and even his poems are instantly dissected by the intrusive narrator in the very act of their making. Jaromil serves as the concrete universal embodiment of the idea of the adolescent poet of genius, a cherished figure of European cultural mythology with deep roots in nineteenth-century romanticism. The novel treats Jaromil with radical skepticism, subjecting him to a forensic examination like the aberrant phenomenon he is.

To contemplate Jaromil, the narrator anchors his observatory at a privileged moment in the flow of human time, and from this vantage point he dominates a vast expanse of European history. He moves his searchlight back and forth from the near to the farther view, carefully examining his takes, and comparing, evaluating, judging all the while. His intellectual method calls to mind the grand manner of Hegel or Marx, neither of whom is remembered for his sense of ambiguity. But Kundera deliberately spoils the game of philosophical historicism by infiltrating it with his own game of masks and mirrors. At various sensitive points in the narrative, he cuts into the linear exposition of Jaromil's life with anachronistic flashes from the lives of historically eminent poets. By allowing Jaromil to run portions of his fated course with the consecrated features of a Rimbaud, Shelley, Lermontov, or Wolker superimposed on his face, Kundera sets up a double-edged parodistic relationship between the poet of flesh and the poet of myth. Imagination and reality chase after each other in the playground of this novel, in a constant dialogue of mutual negation that ends by diminishing both. With this technique of narrative collage Kundera jumbles temporal planes and blurs the border between the real and the ideal. Pitting a subversive device from the formal arsenal of twentieth-century avant-gardism against a distinctly nineteenth-century ground plan, he thumbs his nose at the incongruous alliance between poetic rebellion and revolutionary dogmatism that Jaromil exemplifies. With this narrative gesture Kundera destabilizes the historical construction of European modernism.

Life Is Elsewhere, whose hero never sets foot outside his native land, is a truly European novel, not only in the deliberate outreach of its allusions, but more importantly in the scope of its implications. Writing at a time when he had little hope of seeing his work published at home, Kundera directed his words beyond the Czech border and specifically to his French readers, whose minds he knew he could reach. "My books were banned at the time of the Russian invasion, but I continued to live in Prague afterwards. I was fortunate in already having a contract with the French publisher Gallimard so I knew that what I was writing would be published," he said in an interview.[6] Rimbaud's presence in the novel is so pervasive that a French critic has entertained the possibility of reading it as a twentieth-century parody of the case of Rimbaud.[7] Claude Roy, whose review of *Life Is Elsewhere*[8] greeted Kundera as a writer of world stature, noted that the projection of Rimbaud into the role of double for a character like Jaromil, who is often treated as a figure from the vulgar vaudeville, amounts to a provocation of the mandarins of the Parisian cultural left. Worse still, Rimbaud figures not just as a mask for Jaromil but as the mirror in which the genius of lyricism, stripped down by irony, shows the pathetic likeness of an escapist burdened with an immense power drive. And Jaromil on his own is much more than a mere caricature of someone who plays at being the poet. As François Ricard has observed,[9] the final sting of this novel is felt only when one understands that Jaromil's poetry is good and that he himself, as lyric genius, is the real thing.

When Kundera's book reached Paris, the name of Rimbaud signified more than a valued piece of French cultural property. He was of course the crown prince of the dark succession of late-nineteenth-century *poètes maudits,* the prodigious child-seer whom the surrealists had installed at the center of their imaginary pantheon in the 1920s. But now there was a fresher magic of actuality around that hallowed name. In May 1968, the rebellious Parisian students had breathed a new and incandescent life into the aging myth by raising Rimbaud's message about the primacy of poetry in the revolutionary enterprise as their battle cry: "*L'imagination au pouvoir!*" In 1971, for the centennial of the Paris Commune, Gallimard published a pamphlet by Pierre Gascar, *Rimbaud et la Commune,* celebrating that doomed revolt as a festival of the popular imagination, and linking Rimbaud to it as the poet who first understood that revolution is history raised to the power of a child's dreaming.[10]

In *Life Is Elsewhere* Kundera sees Rimbaud's adventure during the terrible year 1870–71 quite differently. The disagreement is not about the facts, but over what to make of them. Rimbaud had run off to Paris from his native Charleville in February 1871, but he was back home again on May 13, when he wrote to his former teacher Izambard,[11] who had urged him to finish his baccalaureate, "Insane rage drives me toward the battle of Paris—where so many workers are dying while I write to you! Schoolwork now, never, never, never, I'm on strike."[12] But instead of rushing off to Paris to fight side by side with the workers, Rimbaud stayed in his mother's house and strove to remake himself into the poet-seer ("Je travaille à me rendre *Voyant*").[13] The poetic manifesto of this enterprise, known as *Lettre du voyant,* would follow two days later, no longer addressed to the uncomprehending Izambard, but to another literary friend, Paul Demeny. It stakes a claim for the imagination so absolute that nothing that happened in Paris could match it.[14]

In the core section of the novel (part 4, "The Poet on the Run"), where the narrative substance is argued out in the form of a visually suggestive essay, the image of the seventeen-year-old Rimbaud escaping from Charleville and his mother's harsh possessiveness initiates a whole sequence of vignettes showing poets "on the run": "But Arthur Rimbaud keeps running away, again and again, a collar securely fastened around his neck, writing poetry on the run" (p. 161). The colloquial English expression "on the run" does nicely in this sentence, but the Czech phrase it aims to translate, *básník utíká,* carries an ambiguity impossible to reproduce in a short phrase. Standing by itself, apart from any particular verbal context, as in the title of part 4, *básník utíká* can refer both to the repeated, habitual action of running and to a single act in the quick of the moment. More important, it is impossible to tell from the verb *utíká* in this usage whether the subject, *básník* (the poet), is running away from or toward something. That crucial ambiguity pervades the entire sequence of images of poets on the run. Kundera's take on Rimbaud and his great adventure tells only the first part of the story: "The year was 1870, and the guns of the Franco-Prussian War echoed through Charleville. That was an especially favorable situation for escape; lyrical poets are nostalgically drawn to the sound of battle" (p. 161). The second part unfolds when he runs back again to Charleville, there to write the letter that would ignite the poetic rebellions of surrealism in the 1920s and after. That portion of Rimbaud's course is left dark by Kundera's narrative searchlight, but its meaning is implied in all that the novel tells us about Jaromil.

Kundera's Czech revision of the case of Rimbaud can serve as a key to unlock the complicated historical perspective contained in this novel. I like to imagine that the real-life equivalent of the privileged vantage point from which the narrator views the Czech year 1948 is located with the two writers who stood before a Left Bank cafe, Les Deux Magots, one day in September 1968. As the two forty-year-old Czechs looked toward Saint Germain-des-Prés, the crunch of armored wheels over Prague's distant cobblestones was a barely distinguishable interference overheard through the ordinary din of the prosperous Western city. Yet it was there, peremptorily overriding the last verbal debris from the spring clamor at the nearby Sorbonne or Nanterre, and even the raucous sounds of the summer riot in Chicago. The observatory thus perched, close upon the last cruel twist of that unruly year, is equipped with a two-headed telescope. One barrel fixes Prague, the problematic gateway to the European theater, while the other aims at the Paris of modern revolutions, "la cité sainte assise à l'Occident."[15] From the purely Czech point of view, Kundera's words—"There's been too much of everything"—express the loathing of a pattern of repetition that is also a process of degradation, something far worse than a mere treading in place. For Czechs of Kundera and Škvorecký's generation, who woke up on the morning of August 21 to find Russian tanks under their windows ravaging their hard-won cultural heritage, 1968 came to mean that they were being forced back to 1948, stripped of all their old as well as their newer illusions, revisited by the ghost of the Munich surrender in 1938. On the French side, the grand revolt of the Parisian students assumed the appearance of a sham carnival, a staged event postponed from late winter to the sensuous complacency of May and reserved for the children of the bourgeoisie. The show might play again, after a decent interval, but it would change nothing.

> A mile away, on the other bank of the Seine, the present owners of the world continue to live their normal lives and think of the turmoil in the Latin Quarter as something happening far away. *Dream is reality,* the students wrote on the walls, but it seems that the opposite was true: their reality (the barricades, the overturned cars [the original Czech has felled trees instead of cars], the red flags) was a dream. (p. 175)

Elsewhere, in an essay comparing the revolt of the Parisian youth in May 1968 to the spirit of the Prague Spring, Kundera has written:

> May in Paris was an explosion of revolutionary lyricism. The Prague Spring was the explosion of post-revolutionary scepticism. That's why the Parisian students looked towards Prague with mistrust (or rather, with indifference), and the man in Prague could only smile at Parisian illusions which (rightly or wrongly) he thought discredited, comic or dangerous.[16]

In the novel, Jaromil keeps marching under his triple banner, impervious to the reflective narrator, who has just had his say about the lyrical dream of a youthful revolution. "The students marched through the streets with Jaromil at their side; he was responsible for the slogans on the banners and for the declamation of his colleagues" (p. 176). With its double telescopic vision, the novel collapses the Paris of 1968 into the Prague of 1948–49, and Jaromil marches in step with the "thousands of Rimbauds [who] have their own barricades" in the Latin Quarter (p. 175). So while Paris in 1968 was discordant noise to the men of Prague, who listened to it with one ear only, in Kundera's novel it is the song of their own city as it was in 1948. But the ironic narrator is quick to point out that "for Czech students the year 1949 marked that interesting transition when a dream is no longer just a dream. Their jubilation was still voluntary and yet it was already compulsory as well" (p. 176). In accordance with the mood of that transition, Jaromil discards the imaginative slogans he has dictated to his classmates to paint on festive May Day banners—lyrical imperatives meant to rend the air of Prague (or is it Paris?), annihilating the past and opening the floodgates of the future: "*No churches. . . . No freedom for the enemies of freedom! . . . Power to the imagination! . . . Revolution in politics, in the family, in love!*" (p. 174). It seems that the more workmanlike acclamations copied from the official daily of the victorious Czech Communist Party—"*Long live socialism, long live the socialist family!*" (p. 175)—are better suited to a revolution already into its second year of power.

When Karl Marx wrote the opening sentences of his pamphlet *The Eighteenth Brumaire of Louis Bonaparte* (1852)—"Hegel remarks somewhere that all great world historical facts and personages occur, as it were, twice. He has forgotten to add: the first time as tragedy, the second as farce"[17]—he was aiming his sarcasm at the defeat of his revolutionary hopes in 1848, in the June days in Paris and their aftermath. He did not imagine that his words would also apply to his posthumous victory in Prague a hundred years later, in February 1948. "It's easy to pull off a revolution when you've got the army behind you and the police and a certain big country besides" (p. 127), Jaromil's uncle had taunted him on the day when Communist premier Klement Gottwald[18] addressed a throng in Old Town Square to demand that all power should pass into the hands of the Party. Jaromil's uncle may be a reactionary and an ignoramus "who considered Voltaire the father of volts" (p. 128), but he knows as well as Marx did that a putsch is not a revolution, and that Gottwald is no more a Lenin than Louis Bonaparte was a Napoleon. But for Jaromil, February 1948 signaled the beginning of a great new era in history, and that is why, a year later, he is willing to acquiesce to the Party's realistic slogans. In private he celebrates this interesting transition from dream to reality by winning his sexual manhood at last, in the arms of a young proletarian redhead. "He slid off her body. As he lay stretched out next to her, tired and content, it occurred to him that he was not resting after two bouts of love but after a long, long run" (p. 181). In that moment of ease, captured at the ego's crest just before the sexual redolence begins to recede, Jaromil for the first time touches the forever receding shore of the promised "real world."

The question of what is real is the pivot around which Jaromil's life whirls. His problem is encapsulated in the novel's title, *Life Is Elsewhere,* an utterance mentioned in the text as one of the slogans written on the Sorbonne walls by the rebellious students of 1968. The phrase echoes the declaration "*L'existence est ailleurs,*" with which André Breton closed his first *Surrealist Manifesto* (1924). Like all avant-garde proclamations, this one does much more than outline a new artistic program. In his first sentences, Breton heralds a revolution in the mind that will emancipate man from his ancient bondage to reason and sequential time. Man, the "definitive dreamer" (*ce rêveur définitif*), will no longer passively accept the reality of those everyday objects and ideas that his reason endlessly manipulates and his senescent society condemns him to use. Taking his cue from Rimbaud's doctrine of *voyance,* Breton decrees that this transformation of all aspects of life will be accomplished in the crucible of a new language empowered by dreaming. Armed with Freud's myth of the unconscious, the surrealist gnosis weds the alchemy of words to the release of previously suppressed psychic energies. It celebrates childhood, the dream, and all forms of associative, alogical thinking. In a soaring peroration Breton sums up his message of freedom in a chain of provocative dicta: "This summer roses are blue; the wood is glass. Earth draped in its greenery affects me no more than a ghost. To live and to cease living are imaginary solutions. Existence is elsewhere."[19]

This passage, which begins by canceling our ordinary sensory perceptions through two peremptory image-definitions, proceeds to deny the reality of human time, whether conceived as a natural cycle or as an experiential sequence punctuated by death. In each of the aphorisms, the copula signifies a leap out of logic into free association, a method of articulation that opens up a new world where the here and now of actuality is charged with the ideal absolute of something hitherto unknown—what Rimbaud called *l'inconnu.* The closing formula of the manifesto, "*L'existence est ailleurs,*" projects the moment of fullness of the imagination, when it feels itself big with a fabulously free and rich new life. But when Kundera weaves the slogan "Life is elsewhere" into the novel's action, it functions inversely as a formula of defeat, an acknowledgment of a radical void at the core of imagination's fiat. As Jaromil marches on under his obligatory banners, it seems to him that these "festive parades are only pale imitations of great revolutionary demonstrations, that they have no substance, and vanish like smoke in the air" (p. 177). He reaches a temporary plateau in the spiraling irony that functions as the destabilizing axis of his life when his revolutionary exaltation finds compensatory consummation in bed. By that time, Jaromil is a first-year university student in the faculty of political science and a full-blown poet whose existential praxis is marked by an awareness of inadequacy, as if contaminated by the pain that issues from Rimbaud's sigh "What a life! Real life is elsewhere. We are not in the world" (in *Une saison en enfer,* the last great prose poem he would ever write before giving up the poetic magic for good).[20]

Kundera's interpretation of the making of the adolescent poet occupies the first part of the novel. "The Poet Is Born" examines Jaromil's progress from his mother's womb to the moment of lyrical empowerment at age thirteen when his first fully conscious act of poetic creation is consecrated by his mother's tearful embrace. In placing the mother/son couple at the center of his investigation of lyricism, Kundera pursues his indictment of the phenomenon down to its roots as a disorder of nature. The Freudian notion of sexual causality is brought into play to counterpoint and subvert the controlling historicism of the narrative perspective. But though he toys with the Oedipal paradigm constantly, Kundera's version of the archetypal disorder of the sexes differs from Freud's. In Kundera's scheme, it is the mother who presides over the generational conflict, which is not a battle for authority, with the son/rival playing the dynamic role of challenger, but a struggle over autonomy in which the son's very existence as a separate individual is at stake. Kundera's Jocasta and the adolescent Oedipus confront each other in the conspicuous absence of an Abraham-like father figure. Jaromil's tragedy, like that of the original Oedipus, does of course hinge on his failure to escape from the maternal trap. But Jaromil's lame foot, or in Kundera's terms the dog collar he must wear while he runs—"Alas, dear Jaromil . . . You will walk the world like a dog on a long leash! Even when you are far away you will still feel the collar around your neck!" (pp. 120–21)—is a crippling wound inflicted upon him long before he was even born. He is the child of an offended womb, the victim of a distemper of the sexes far more radical than the one Freud diagnosed. Kundera's phenomenology of Eros postulates a basic dissociation of sexual excitement, in the woman as much as in the man, from its natural significance within the generative act. The erotic embrace that locks together two solipsists of sexual desire opens up the vast realm of postcoital imagination as a new arena for the age-old battle of the sexes.

The moment of Jaromil's illegitimate conception during a premarital affair is marked by a typical Kunderesque misunderstanding. His mother, the bookish second daughter of a prosperous Prague pharmacist, seizes upon the event as a symbolic blessing upon her romantic rebellion, a token of success in her quest for the mythical "great love." His father, a footloose young engineer, treats the pregnancy as a personal calamity, an early stumble in a promising career of sexual libertinage. The marriage that follows normalizes the imaginative divide between them into a permanent state of sexual hostility, characterized by self-pity on her side and obstinate nonengagement on his. Jaromil inherits nothing of his father's autonomous maleness. But in his mother's milk the juices of nonbeing ferment into a subtle poison. He is the dream child of her feminine revenge, whom she consecrates to the kitschy, effeminate statuette of Apollo that stands in a corner of the conjugal bedroom and comes alive in her fantasies.

Kundera offers a striking formulation of the Oedipal situation between Jaromil and his mother: "What a remarkable sight, mother and son, in their tug-of-war! She is pulling him into his diapers, he is pulling her into her shroud. Ah, what a lovely sight!" (p. 246). It is a grotesque vignette, with its suggestion of a domestic combat no less deadly for being essentially sham. The narrator's mockery aims beyond this Jocasta and her Oedipus into the sentimental heart of the motherhood myth. In the second chapter of part 1, Kundera analyzes in great detail the meaning of the pleasures Jaromil's mother savors in the fullness of her pregnant womb, and the "*paradisiac* state" (p. 11) she experiences in intimacy with the body of her newborn child. Her ego, humiliated by her lover's offer to arrange an abortion, is now triumphant in the discovery of her body's autonomous capacity for pleasure, and she revels in the feeling, the touch, even the taste of its creative swell. Passionate though it may be, her bond to Jaromil is not that of a mother who has enthroned a longed-for child at the center of her thoughts. For Jaromil's mother, the maternal vocation is a by-product of an autistic love affair between her conscious self and her body. She embraces motherhood in an emotional recoil from romantic defeat, revamping the traditional Madonna myth to console her for the enforced retreat from a rebellion undertaken in the name of untrammeled, unconventional passion.

She is not the typical authoritarian single parent who chastises her son for the defection of a husband. Jaromil's father disappears inside a Nazi concentration camp, and only after the war is over does the widow discover that the hero-husband had been unfaithful to her with a Jewish woman. Jaromil's case is one of masked emotions, and in that respect it differs markedly from Rimbaud's, whose rebellion pitted him against the stone wall of a grasping, vindictive woman of peasant stock, newly installed in bourgeois respectability and contemptuous of literature. Jaromil's mother has little in common with Madame Vitalie Rimbaud, née Cuif, whom the novel will show in part 7 ("The Poet Dies") as "that severe old lady in the black dress," in the act of "examining the dark, damp vault, making sure that the coffin [where her son Arthur has been lying for nine years] is in the right place and properly closed" (p. 306). In her attitude toward her son the poet, Jaromil's mother more closely resembles Paní Wolkerová, the proudly doting mother of the Czech poet Jiří Wolker,[21] who also figures in the novel alongside her son.

Jiří Wolker was born in 1900 into a family of undeniable bourgeois respectability, and grew up surrounded by the affectionate care of his mother and her equally fond parents. The artistically well-rounded Jiří experimented with painting (like

Jaromil) and even musical composition before settling down to poetry at age sixteen. At nineteen, Wolker left his native Moravia to study law in Prague, where he associated with the avant-garde group Devětsil and joined the Communist Party. After his premature death from tuberculosis, Paní Wolkerová self-consciously cultivated his myth as the foremost Czech proletarian poet. She wrote a memoir[22] that Kundera burlesques in the script narrated by Jaromil's mother in part 5 ("The Poet Is Jealous") to accompany a documentary about her son, the young poet of revolution. This mythical film biography, prepared by a beautiful young woman cinematographer in collaboration with the poet's mother, consists of a series of romantic clichés revamped to serve the interests and tastes of the victorious proletariat. In the psychological tug-of-war between Jaromil and his mother, the making of the film signals his defeat. She has always fantasized the moment of Jaromil's conception against a rural landscape dotted with boulders, and now she insists that this landscape serve as the natural backdrop for a mood-setting outdoor scene. Posed against a protruding rock, pinned to it by the camera in this fiction of his life for a mass audience, Jaromil clumsily recites a poem. His mother's scenario forces Jaromil, who is in fact an accomplished avant-garde poet, back into the matrix of romantic kitsch. The irony is that this bourgeois style fits the spirit of post-1948 Prague as if expressly created for it.

In part 7, Kundera shows Paní Wolkerová walking behind the funeral cart of her beloved Jiří. "A corner of a white cushion is sticking out from under the black lid. It sticks out like a reproach that the final resting place of her boy (he was twenty-four years old) was badly made up. She feels an enormous urge to rearrange the cushion under his head" (p. 302). The poet Jaroslav Seifert, who was present at Jiří Wolker's burial, described in his memoirs the real-life scene in the Wolker family home just after the return from the cemetery. In the middle of the funeral meal, Mrs. Wolker rose from her seat and "in a slightly raised voice" solemnly asked her son's last girlfriend (Seifert calls her "the black bride"), in the name of Jiří's love and his memory, to give up the world and enter a nunnery.[23] *Life Is Elsewhere,* unhampered by Seifert's deeply ingrained reluctance to speak ill of a woman, savages every display of maternal possessiveness, conflating Madame Rimbaud's proprietary inspection of her son's coffin with Paní Wolkerová's desperate tenderness as she takes her boy to his last sleep. In a particularly unkind scene, Jaromil's mother interrupts her son's lovemaking with the redhead by bursting into his bedroom to offer medicinal relief on the pretext of being alarmed by the young woman's intermittent moaning. Kundera's unforgiving vision reveals the cunningly indirect aggression of the weak as no less vicious for its essential masochism. The same holds for Jaromil as a child, when he joins his only school friend, the janitor's son, to torment a "well-scrubbed and neatly dressed" boy they mock as "Mama's little darling" (p. 23). In that scene lies the psychological seed of the poet's future attraction to the rough-and-ready proletarian justice of the Party.

As a poet, Jaromil is born twice, first in his mother's imagination and then in his own. Each time the moment of genesis is a staged event in which the mother plays a dominant role either as director or as mediatrix. In the opening chapter of the novel she is shown manipulating her memory of "a particular sunny summer morning behind a huge boulder picturesquely silhouetted against a green valley" (p. 3), in order to idealize the commonplace event of her son's conception. Jaromil's brief but exemplary career as twentieth-century poet-rebel is marked by two major attempts to break loose from the congenital dog collar of romantic kitsch, which Kundera posits as the stylistic signature of bourgeois inauthenticity. First he turns from his mother's definition of what is poetic to surrealism, and then he veers to proletarian lyricism, only to find the romantic leash still firmly attached. Renato Poggioli observes in *The Theory of the Avant-Garde* that those critics who are most hostile to artistic modernism usually link it to "what they call the 'disease of romanticism.' "[24] Until recently, this polemical approach has been the hallmark of conservative critics like Irving Babbitt in America or Julien Benda in France. Kundera comes from the opposite end of the cultural spectrum, but his ironic treatment of the dialectics of Jaromil's poetic rebellion only confirms Poggioli's insight.

Jaromil's initiation into the doctrines of surrealism is a side benefit of his mother's brief adultery with the wildly original painter they meet at a spa shortly after the outbreak of the war. The painter, who wears a leather coat and is accompanied by a magnificent black dog, like André Breton, practices all the varieties of the surrealist quest for the miraculous, which can only be discovered in the epiphany of chance associations. His studio in Prague, where he spends the years of the Nazi occupation painting what his inward eye sees, with his back turned on History, is a sanctuary of the forbidden artistic avant-garde, a magic space full of books about poetry and art, half-finished canvases, and strange, exotic objects. Jaromil becomes a regular visitor after his mother, gratified by the painter's admiration for the boy's sketches of human beings with dogs' heads, decides that the child prodigy needs drawing lessons. It is here that Jaromil imbibes two major precepts of artistic modernism: that the word "bourgeois" is an insult applicable to "the person who wants pictures to look like real life" (p. 35), and that the avant-garde is an exclusive sect of uniquely gifted individuals destined to transform the world radically. As Jaromil grapples with these new ideas, his mother submits her body to the painter, who treats it as a temporary object of his artistic and erotic interest. He first possesses her under a canvas showing ravaged landscape into which he has scratched a female figure in white that "seemed to be floating rather than walking, shimmering at a distance rather than actually present" (p. 39).

Under that vision of Woman rising from and above the savagery of modern war, the painter's lovemaking is as peremptory and passionate as his maxims about art. "Love is either madness or nothing at all" (p. 41),[25] he whispers to her as she registers the auditory evidence of Jaromil's arrival for his lesson. This incongruous occurrence acts as a spark igniting the painter's imagination, which seizes upon it as if it were the chance bolt cracking the surface of reality to let the dream-stuff surge through. He takes command of the surrealistic happening and treats the terrified woman in the studio-alcove and the boy acolyte in the antechamber as twin communicating vessels of his alchemy. Out of their forbidden association he creates a new lovemaking fashioned of the thrill of her terror, which has all the violent beauty of "the random meeting of an umbrella and a sewing machine on an operating-room table,"[26] in Lautréamont's famous phrase. When the painter quotes that magic formula of sadomasochistic ecstasy to Jaromil, the pupil surmises from his teacher's emotion that the mystery contained in these words he does not understand is sexual as well as poetic, and that he himself is somehow its stimulus. His mother, unseen by him, figures on the other side of the partition as the all-important sacrificial genitrix who must die in agony to give birth to a new and violently free poetic beauty.

A short time later Jaromil writes his first surrealistic poem, which, like the painter's staged lovemaking, originates in an erotic situation intertwined with a verbal formula. Magda, the family maid, has been weeping over her lover, recently executed by the Gestapo, and Jaromil, enraptured by her lovely expression of pain, associates her with a line from a poem by Paul Éluard. "Éluard had become the poet of Magda's calm body and of her eyes bathed by a sea of tears. He saw his entire life locked in the spell of a single line: *sorrow-lovely face*. Yes, that was Magda: sorrow-lovely face" (p. 55).[27] He peeps at Magda through the keyhole when she is undressing for her bath, but once she gets into the tub, all he can see is her face floating above the water's surface. In the visual absence of the naked body he has just glimpsed, which now remains submerged and can only be imagined, the boy feels a stab of desire for the complex mystery of a woman's face "*illumined by the body's nakedness*" (p. 56). In the latest sketches he has been showing the painter, Jaromil had drawn women's bodies without heads, in all kinds of positions suggesting humiliation or torture. He now understands that the sword of Eros can be cruel to him who wields it as well as to his victim. This first sexual adventure fills him with self-contempt, for he has played the part of voyeur while wanting to be much more than that. He knows that the bathroom door was not locked and that he and Magda were all alone in the house. Jaromil at age thirteen has the precocious arrogance of the adolescent genius, and he feels a sense of defeat no less cutting for being the result of a fantasy. To escape from the indignity suffered at the keyhole, he writes a poem in which he addresses his "aquatic love" in the commandingly rhythmic voice of a true master.

Out of this experience Jaromil, the failed lover empowered by the compensatory magic of verse, creates his new surrealistic persona, Xavier. The Spanish name is a code word for his estrangement from his everyday life, hinting at the exotically sadistic masculinity of a Lautréamont or of a Spanish bullfighter, which his imagination has absorbed in the painter's studio. In the second part of the novel, Xavier walks through a Prague liberated from its wartime enthrallment. Crossing the Charles Bridge toward Hradčany Castle, he sees an open window, and through it a rococo birdcage hanging in a room that recesses into semidarkness, half revealing the silhouette of a woman. It is the spring of 1946, Kundera tells us, but the calendar date does not matter, because the instant Xavier boldly leaps into that room with a briefcase full of schoolbooks, he abolishes the tyranny of sequential time, to live his freedom inside the surrealistic dream from which he wakes only to enter another dream. Xavier's Prague is less the real city than that place of endless wonder whose "mysterious order" (*tajemné uspořádání*) the poet Nezval revealed in his cycle *Praha s prsty deště* (*Prague with Fingers of Rain*, 1936).[28]

Xavier is the masterful lover who experiences his domination of the Madonna of Sorrows with a sadism lyrically blurred by psychological ambivalence. He requires the death of the beloved as the supreme token of her love, but he also merges with her by assimilating the delight of her pain. His triumph comes when he saves her from the brutality of her usual master, imagined as a booted policeman. But if all the rooms Xavier enters turn into bedrooms, they also have an open window through which the sounds of shooting and men marching come softly floating in, like the cooing of a bird from infinite distance. While he is with the woman, Xavier knows that the greater beauty is in that uncomplicated male violence out there, and that he must sacrifice the beloved if he is to mount the barricades. His revolutionary lyricism comes rising on the wings of erotic betrayal.

Xavier's dream adventures set the stage for part 3 ("The Poet Masturbates"), in which the actual event of the Communist seizure of power on February 24, 1948, catches Jaromil unprepared, even though he has been arguing for it in various student circles, defining it as a leap from prehistory into history, "from the realm of necessity into that of freedom" (p. 115). At this point in his life, he is struggling to leave behind his own prehistory of sexual virginity, but that moment of radical transformation keeps eluding him. On the morning when Klement Gottwald addresses the huge crowd in Old Town Square, Jaromil is at home nursing a bad cold. His participation in the pivotal day of the Czech revolution is therefore limited to a shouting match with his reactionary uncle, who also lives in the family villa. In a paroxysm of excitement Jaromil shrills, "And I always knew that the working class would sweep capitalist parasites like you into the dust bin of history!" (p. 127). Until now, he has always avoided what seemed to him vulgar in

Communist jargon, but suddenly he feels it liberating to give up his own form of expression and merge linguistically with the thousand-headed dragon of the militant masses out in the square. This change of speech marks the emergence of Jaromil as poet of proletarian revolution.

In this novel, which laughs so cruelly at the presumption of the imaginative act to leap ahead of reality, it is imagination itself that predicts and even engineers its own dethronement from power. The surrealists had long held the view that the violently oppositionist stance of poetry in a bourgeois society would perforce give way to something else once the social structure of tyranny had been dismantled. André Breton, addressing the intellectuals of the Left Front against Fascism in Prague on April 1, 1935, at a meeting organized by Nezval, said that while artists in the bourgeois West were living in open conflict with the immediate world around them ("nous vivons en conflit ouvert avec le monde immédiat qui nous entoure"), it was a different matter for "our Russian comrades," who had the privilege of participating in the building of a new world "whose becoming opens a limitless field for human hope."[29] That old argument and the same rhetoric are being heard once again in Prague after 1948, and nowhere is the question debated more intensely than in the painter's studio.

As the eighteen-year-old Jaromil sits with his mentor and his circle of friends, a woman with an alto voice remarks casually that he reminds her of "Rimbaud surrounded by Verlaine and his gang, in that painting by La Tour. A child among men" (pp. 145–46). By now Jaromil understands that in this context, to be a child means to possess the supreme dignity of the poet-seer. The painter praises his unpublished verse as "the remarkably finished and mature poems of this quite unfinished and virginal young man" (p. 146). But Jaromil longs to be a man at last, like those workers in Old Town Square, and besides, the famous avant-garde poet to whom he had sent his work with a humbly respectful letter has not yet answered him. Even Rimbaud gave up on the alchemy of the word before he was twenty years old, going off to North Africa to trade with real men. The question of betrayal hangs in the air. "That's our dilemma," says one of the guests. "Should we betray the art we grew up with, or the revolution we admire?" The painter, decisive as ever, declares, "A revolution that wants to dig up dead academic art and that manufactures busts of statesmen on an assembly line betrays not only modern art, but itself" (p. 148). With forceful malice, Jaromil returns the thrust: "Revolution is violence, . . . that's a well-known fact. Surrealism above all other movements realized that old clowns have to be brutally kicked off the stage, but it didn't have the sense to know that it had turned old and useless itself" (p. 149). It does not matter that he can still hear the echo of his mentor's peremptory voice in his own words; for once Jaromil has turned his youth to his advantage in this *coup de main* and paid the painter back in his own coin.

That same year, after passing his final examinations at the gymnasium, while the taste of that sweet rebellion against the painter still lingers in his mouth, Jaromil sends a "surrealistic object" to the famous poet, in a desperate attempt to compel a response to the samples of his own poetry. He mails him a package containing twenty severed telephone receivers, a symbolic plea for the poet's voice in reply. But on his way out of the post office, he is accosted by his old school friend, the janitor's son, who invites him to his apartment. "They sat down and Jaromil saw there was a crib with a small baby on the other side of the room. He realized his friend was a paterfamilias, while he was an onanist" (p. 154). In addition to being a family man, Jaromil's childhood playmate is also a policeman, a bona fide member of the brotherhood of those whose duty it is to guard the revolution against its enemies. This encounter proves decisive for Jaromil. Sensing in his friend's attitude that he is welcome to join the virile ranks of men—composed of boys of his own generation—Jaromil is able to complete his revolt against the painter's authority. His artistic mentor being the only approximate father figure in Jaromil's experience, the filial rebellion assumes the character of a literary *clinamen*[30] at one remove. Jaromil confirms his apostasy from the church of the avant-garde by mentally reinterpreting his coded message to the famous poet as a gesture of defiant rejection, as if the telephone receivers were "the severed heads of his loyalty" and he was "derisively sending them back, like a Turkish sultan sending the heads of captured crusaders to the Christian commander" (p. 156). Armed with this epic simile, Jaromil steps from the myth of his boyhood into the myth of his maturity.

At last reality seems infinitely obliging, as if the changing world of Czech society were determined to accommodate Jaromil. The proletarian redhead relieves him of the embarrassing burden of his virginity even as the janitor's son draws him deeper into the "real life" of physical maleness, symbolized by the revolver he wears on his backside. In a moment of comradely intimacy, when Jaromil visits the janitor's son at the headquarters of the political police, the poet finds out that in the aftermath of the Communist revolution even policemen read poetry. Not that they have become effeminate, the janitor's son explains, but precisely for the opposite reason. "We're in a tough trade—let me tell you, my friend, how tough it can be—but we enjoy something delicate once in a while," as he puts it (p. 217). For Jaromil, the association of a policeman with poetry is every bit as beautiful as the random meeting of an umbrella and a sewing machine on an operating table.

In the "romantic" era of Czech Stalinism—the period when Jaromil becomes a public figure—the police and the poets in fact courted each other. Poetry readings were organized inside the recreational villas reserved for the security elite, just like the one in chapter 7 of part 5, where Jaromil achieves instant stardom. That event, complete with refreshments, is filmed on the spot by a seductive young woman cinematographer with large, dark eyes. The satirical high point of the proceedings is reached during the discussion period, which brings the eleven performing poets back to the podium for questioning by a radically thinned-down public of ten proletarian aristocrats, among them the janitor's son. In keeping with the spirit of the times, the classic requirement that men of letters pay their respects to men of power, which was once acknowledged straightforwardly in the form of an author's preface or dedication, is now a public spectacle, like an exhibition soccer match between two friendly teams, or an American talk show where a writer might share the stage with a diet expert, a reborn felon, or any other salesman. But here the poets are a collective, and as the novice Jaromil soon discovers, they know their script well.[31]

Jaromil jumps in when the questioning turns to the subject of love. How can one tell from a love poem whether it was written by a socialist poet? Jaromil asserts that "only the new era, by sweeping away the power of money and influence of prejudice, would enable man to be fully human and restore love to its glory. Socialist love poetry is the voice of this great, liberated emotion." While these words "flowed from his mouth like brave ships sailing into the harbor of those big, dark eyes," one of his fellow poets stabs him in the back by asking sarcastically, "You really think that there is more feeling in your lines than in the poems of Heinrich Heine? Do the loves of Victor Hugo seem too petty to you?" (pp. 233–34). While Jaromil spars with his sardonic colleague over the definition of the new beauty of socialist love, a middle-aged woman in the audience keeps asking, with a touch of real-life desperation in her voice, "How is love today any different from love in the old days?" Her question is left hanging as "the man with the wooden leg," who "had been following the debate carefully, but with evident impatience" (p. 235), cuts in to demand that the bus stop be moved back to its old place in front of the villa, where it used to be in the days before the building belonged to the working people. The poetry evening disintegrates on contact with this rocklike *vox populi*.

In the immediate afterglow of his sexual empowerment at the end of part 4, Jaromil had rested briefly on the plateau of his contentment. But in part 5, the initial ease of his socialist love for the redheaded shopgirl soon gives way to insatiable jealousy. Worse still, Jaromil admits to himself, just after the poetry reading, that his beloved comes nowhere near the norm of physical beauty exemplified by the dark-eyed woman who had fixed her camera on him, and he begins punishing her for it. Yet when the ecstatic silver-maned poet who befriended him at the reading goads him to pursue his chance with the filmmaker before the night is over, Jaromil declines, explaining that he has staked everything on a single great love and that his girl is worth more to him than a thousand petty affairs. Jaromil's rejection of libertinism is nothing but a rhetorical lie and a cover-up. The reason for his erotic retreat is much more mundane. Jaromil is ashamed to undress for fear of revealing the extremely wide, long underpants he wears, with their "comical open wedge over the belly" (p. 239). In the Spartan days of Czech Stalinism, before a credit-based consumerism hit the countries of the Eastern bloc, this particularly hideous form of male intimate apparel was standard. The more hip members of Jaromil's generation resorted to the shorter, sporty-looking "trainers" that were being sold as gym wear. But in Jaromil's case, the selection of underwear is strictly controlled by his mother. After the redhead's entrance into his life, he had learned to circumvent maternal vigilance, but the unexpected opportunity with the filmmaker catches him unprepared. Somewhat like Ludvik's facetious postcard in *The Joke,* the interfering underpants become the comic vehicle of his fate. Installed at the hard core of the novel's laughter, this symbolic object—the phenomenological locus where the Marxist and Freudian lines of causality meet—seems endowed with a powerful negative magic, setting off a chain of events that will drag Jaromil from the pinnacle of success down to an ignominious death.

Awed by the youthful intransigence of Jaromil's fine words, the old poet goes down on his knees to signify his homage to the new socialist love. But Jaromil knows better, and his inner humiliation rankles. One day the redhead has the misfortune of being late for a rendezvous, and Jaromil turns on her with a fierce proprietary anger. As he revels in the irresistible downward pull of articulating this emotion, it takes on the intoxicating charm of real hatred. In her desperation the young woman tells him that the reason for her delay is her brother, who has just decided to leave the country illegally and wanted to see her one last time. "Love means all or nothing," decrees Jaromil (p. 255). He demands to know if she loves him enough to sacrifice all her other attachments, and she swears that she could not live without him. For the first time, Jaromil experiences the possibility of real danger in his lovemaking. Deeply moved, he returns the pledge and embraces her with a passion magnified by a poetic intimation of death. When she dissolves tearfully in his arms, he feels he is holding his "aquatic love" at last—only to experience a terrible sense of betrayal moments later, when she says she would be lonely and sad (but alive) without him. Then he knows that soon after they leave off kissing he will sacrifice her to the Revolution.

The next day, climbing the stairs to police headquarters, Jaromil is conscious of a new firmness in his step. The janitor's son receives his information about the redhead's brother with extreme interest. "We've got to get those bugs under a magnifying glass," he says cheerfully, intensifying Jaromil's excitement. The knowledge that his girl is "now in the hands of strange men" (p. 264), exposed to their cruelty, only inflates his feeling that he is a lover of great lyric pathos. He assures himself that "he did not expose his girl to danger because love meant little to him—quite the contrary" (p. 265). Back at home in his room, Jaromil/Xavier the police informer is strangely gentle when he asks his mother not to disturb him because he is writing the greatest poem of his life.

From this point on, the narrator treats Jaromil with increasing high-handedness, exposing him to the machinations of a savagely farcical dramatic irony. In part 6, "The Middle-Aged Man," Jaromil is set aside altogether, yielding the stage to a new character. When Jaromil is retrieved once more in the last movement (part 7, "The Poet Dies"), it is to be rushed, *prestissimo,* to an ignominious death in the company of other "poets on the run." Kundera has explained that the writing of part 6 was an afterthought, begun only when the novel was completed.

> The book was almost done, and it had six parts. I wasn't satisfied with it. The story seemed flat. Suddenly it occurred to me to put in a story that would take place three years after the hero's death (that is, beyond the time frame of the novel. It became the next-to-last part, the sixth, "The Middle-aged Man." Instantly the whole thing seemed right.[32]

The outside character who "opens a secret window through the novel's wall" is not only an escape vehicle for a narrator who resembles Cide Hamete Benengeli in part 2 of *Don Quixote,* with his complaints about being confined to a single cast of characters. Like Cervantes' digressions, Kundera's interpolated tale stands "in about the same relationship to the rest of the story as does a small guesthouse to a country manor" (p. 271). It serves to open another perspective on the central action, showing romantic love humbled by libertinism and youth deflated by middle age. The man in his forties—"of all my characters the one closest to me,"[33] Kundera has said in one of his rare confessional asides—is a master of irony who lives "outside the drama of his own life" (p. 280). He had fought the war from England as a pilot and had lost his wife in a London air raid. Considered unreliable by the Czech Communist regime because of his Western contacts, he has turned his back on History and now works as a laborer, spending his evenings in the enjoyment of his books (mostly the classics) and women. His bachelor flat is the refuge of a stoic in whose mind the idea of his own death keeps a quiet vigil over all his pleasures, a man who reasons serenely with life's shadows. We learn that Jaromil's redhead was once his mistress, a special favorite for her sexual obligingness during a protracted casual affair that overlapped with the poet's "great love." The middle-aged lover, not the brother, was the man she saw just before her last fatal rendezvous with Jaromil; it was a farewell visit, since she had resolved to give up the affair for Jaromil's sake. Now, three years later, she comes back to her old friend after her release from prison because she has nowhere else to go. Knowing that her brother has yet to be released, she is too crushed by shame to see her family. The news of Jaromil's death, dropped casually by the middle-aged man, rings with a hollow sound against the pain of her guilt as a guiltless victim. The man is moved by her speechless suffering, and as the evening proceeds, his sympathy grows as powerful as the most passionate sexual arousal, even as her body lies unresponsive in his arms, closed against pleasure by her moral humiliation. The silent couple in the small guesthouse sink gently into sleep while the distant sound of Jaromil's death "impatiently stamping its feet" is heard through the window that opens on the main story. "He listened to her breathing, her troubled tossing and turning, and when he thought she had fallen asleep he lightly caressed her arm, happy that he was able to provide her a first night of rest in the new era of her mournful freedom" (p. 286). This is the only scene in the novel where tenderness is allowed to flow unchecked by the narrator's irony, and the only one in which a character experiences emotion untainted by the mind's secret cunning.

Speaking to youth about youth, André Breton said in a speech to Yale University students in 1942, as they were about to go off to the great war, "surrealism was born of the limitless affirmation of faith in the *genius* of youth."[34] In 1968, when youth believed in its own generosity, the cry on campus was "Don't trust anyone over thirty!" Kundera's answer to all that is his middle-aged man, who can only offer a night's rest in a moment of vivid sympathy for a young woman robbed of her sense of self by Jaromil's lyric genius. *Life Is Elsewhere* is a novel in which none of the characters, with the exception of Jaromil and his historical masks, have proper names. Jaromil's beloved is consistently referred to as the "redhead," a word that has a slightly demeaning connotation in the Czech original (*zrzka*). In the middle-aged man's story she figures as *dívka* (young girl),[35] a word graced with echoes of the great tradition of Czech love poetry, from Mácha to Seifert.

With the first sentence of the last narrative movement, the essay takes over once more, in a meditation on the death of poets. "Only a real poet knows how lonely it is inside the mirrored house of poetry," Kundera writes (p. 289). That is why a poet will always be lured by the distant sound of gunfire. But as we have already seen, Kundera interprets the magic formula "Life is elsewhere" as a conundrum about the romantic temper, forever thwarted by the escapism that gnaws at its power drive. In tune with the rest of the book, his version of the tragic tale of the poet dead before his time becomes a metaphysical farce about a clown hoist by his own petard. Jaromil runs his last lap in the company of a great Russian poet of the nineteenth century. Like Lermontov (and Pushkin before him), he makes "a false move and steps outside his mirrored domain" by provoking a duel in which he will die. But as Kundera's narrator remarks, "The act of dying has its own semantics" (pp. 289–90), and the Czech poet gives a characteristically laughable twist to the event.

The scene of Jaromil's challenge to a deadly foe occurs at a party given by the seductive filmmaker, where the poet repairs in suit and tie one freezing winter night, determined to recoup the opportunity lost for lack of proper underwear. He tries to summon the confident step of Xavier, but once inside the villa, confronted with a casually dressed, sophisticated crowd of guests from the world of cinema and theater, he suffers a relapse into his old sense of inadequacy. In the hostess's room he is approached by "a man about thirty years old" (p. 295), who asks him sarcastically why he has not been to see his old mentor, the painter, now reduced to working as a construction laborer because he will not recant his beliefs about modern art. Jaromil rises to the bait and retorts that "objectively speaking," it matters little whether the painter is painting at all since "the whole world of his pictures has been dead for years." Carried away by his own rhetoric, he concludes with the disdainful valediction "I have nothing against the dead. May the earth cover them gently. And I say the same to you. . . . May the earth cover you gently. You're dead and don't even know it." The thirty-year-old man rises to his feet and challenges Jaromil to "try a contest between a poet and a corpse" (p. 297). Then, with a sharp jerk, he grabs the poet by the collar and the seat of his pants, carries him to the balcony door "thrashing in the air like some desperate, gentle fish," and sends him flying into the cold with a kick. "O land of the Czechs! O land where the glory of a pistol shot turns into the joke of a kick in the pants!" apostrophizes the mock-epic narrator (p. 298).

The act of defenestration figures almost emblematically in the tragicomic history of the Czech nation. On May 23, 1618, two royal governors of Bohemia and their secretary were thrown out of a seventy-foot-high window in Hradčany Castle by a group of Prague inhabitants angry at the curtailment of their chartered political and religious rights. The three men landed safely on a heap of manure, but in the Thirty Years War that followed, the Czechs and the Moravians lost their kingdom and their autonomy, for a period that would last exactly three hundred years.

> Jan Masaryk ended his life in nineteen-forty-eight with a fall into the courtyard of a Prague palace, after having seen his fate shattered against the hard keel of destiny. Three years later, the poet Konstantin Biebl—hounded by people he had considered his comrades—jumped from a fifth floor to a pavement of the same city. Like Icarus, the element he was crushed by was earth, his death symbolizing the tragic conflict between space and mass, dream and awakening. (p. 290)

Jaromil's drop to the concrete floor of the balcony is much shorter than either of these falls. And unlike Masaryk's[36] or Biebl's flight to the Prague cobblestones, the defenestration of this grotesque Icarus partakes of the comic disgrace of the three functionaries whose landing on a dunghill opened a major chapter in the long history of European intolerance. For Jaromil too, the farce is a prologue to death. His teeth chattering from cold, he endures a mortifying vigil on the other side of the shut window, through whose frozen pane he vaguely discerns that inside the warm room someone else is making love to his filmmaker. As Xavier, he had dreamed of another such room in a cottage high in the mountains in winter. From that dream window he could see endless snowdrifts, and in the midst of that whiteness, the frail blonde girl who had been following him all night, desperate with unrequited love and slowly dying in the cold grip of the frost as he made love to someone else. Her death had evoked in him a passionately tender cruelty that was supremely beautiful. A poet's dreaming is always prophetic, even though real life has a knack of confusing characters and turning images upside down. Thus Jaromil on the balcony, having clumsily urinated into the yard below, dreams of dying as an act of revenge against the two lovers inside the warm room even as his body catches its death of pneumonia.

Jaromil, not yet twenty years old, lies dying in his childhood room. His delirium is the last sequence of dreams he will ever see, and within it Xavier appears, addressing him as a woman:

"You are very beautiful, but I must betray you" (p. 304). As the flames of high fever lick Jaromil's face, his mother gently nurses her martyred child. She has removed his father's photograph from the wall, and when he asks her why in an interval of lucidity, she tells him that his father never wanted him to be born. Mother and son are alone with each other now, like Rimbaud on his deathbed in Marseilles, attended by his sister Isabelle, whose work would only be completed in the act of handing the poet over to the priest. Jaromil's mother too has won her tug of war with her rebellious, forever escaping boy. Before dying, Jaromil confesses to her that she is the only woman he has ever loved.

Bathed as he is in his mother's tears, Jaromil will not perish in the flames of his fever. Death by fire, says Kundera, belongs to those who, like Jan Hus or Giordano Bruno or Jan Palach, died for their truth, and whose "lives were thus converted into signal lights, beacons, torches that shine far into the ages, for the body is temporal and thought is eternal and the shimmering essence of flame is an image of thought." The image of Jaromil's death is fashioned of water, "for the watery depths are closely related to human depths" (p. 290). The watery realm of his mother's womb was Jaromil's fatal cradle, and the only kingdom he was predestined to rule as a poet. Now, as he gazes into her weeping eyes, Jaromil's surrender to the powers of oblivion carries the erotic shiver of Narcissus bending over a still pond. Then, suddenly, a great shudder of fear passes over his mother's face, and in that unpurged image of terror, death leaves its fleeting but definitive imprint on Jaromil's and the reader's consciousness.

4

The Farewell Party

OR

Black Farce with Angel

"To bring together the extreme gravity of the question and the extreme lightness of the form—that has always been my ambition," said Kundera in a 1984 interview.[1] This aspiration is brilliantly fulfilled in the last novel he wrote before leaving his country. *The Farewell Party* had been completed in 1970–71 but could be published only five years later in France, after Kundera had moved there.[2]

The Farewell Party is an antirealistic novel with a well-made plot that turns on the idea of theoretical murder. The fast-paced action, condensed into five consecutive days at a spa town near the western border of Bohemia, swings between the polar opposites of birth and death in discordant moods of frivolity and graveness, always pushing the reader to the outer edge of meanings, where they either turn back upon themselves or collapse into meaninglessness. The novelist has staged a provocative game of misunderstandings, strange encounters, and accidents, which he uses as a crucible of absurdity for testing major ideas, in the manner of the philosophical fools of the Renaissance.

Like Panurge, who disputes with Thaumaste by signs in Rabelais' good-humored parody of debates between humanists, Kundera parries the intense interrogation lying barely concealed under the artifice of his plot with a dumb show of ribald gestures in which body mocks the portentous intent of the mind's query. Thaumaste never discloses the exact nature of the question that is burning his tongue. The words "And if Mercury . . . ," which slip out of his mouth shortly after the proceedings commence, and the exclamation "Ha, gentlemen, 'the great secret!' He has put his hand in up to the elbow,"[3] heard near the climax, together hint at the abyss above the human and the abyss within, as if to demarcate the extreme limits of the inquiry under pursuit. Rabelais caps the unvoiced argument between the learned Englishman and the fool with another mystification:

> As for the significance of the propositions set out by Thaumaste, and the meaning of the signs which they used in argument, I would have expounded them to you, but I am told that Thaumaste has made a great book of them, printed in London, in which he explains everything without exception. Therefore, I refrain for the present.[4]

Not so Kundera, who values clarity of intellectual articulation no less than laughter. He himself defines the question posed in his novel thus: "*The Farewell Party* asks: Does man deserve to live on this earth, shouldn't the 'planet be freed from man's clutches'?"[5]

The harmonious correspondence between the little world of man and the cosmic sphere he inhabits, which Thaumaste and Panurge could take for granted as the shared assumption on which to base their natural language, was disrupted long before the ebb of the twentieth century, when Kundera wrote what he believed might be the last of his novels.[6] Here, the lust to know "the great secret" of being has turned into an anxiety about human existence in history. Man, no longer at ease in his cosmic playground, feels compelled to ask about himself the kind of questions the tribunes of a roused humanity used to throw at the effigy of God in the ripeness of the Modern Era of Europe. The Supreme Father had been put on trial so many times and in so many ways during the two hundred years prior to Kundera's novel that the passion has gone out of the proceedings. Ivan Karamazov had already pointed the way beyond such arguments by raising the formula "Everything is allowed" as his banner of action. When philosophical reason slumbers, sham priests of many varieties take over and tend to their obedient flocks.

Theodicy, an intellectual discipline that strives to justify the ways of God to man, has been relegated to the doghouse of philosophy since the serene days of Leibniz, when it still occupied the *piano nobile*. In *The Farewell Party* Kundera turns the tables on man, playing with the inversion of the established categories of our anthropocentric universe. He mocks the Judeo-Christian assumption of the supremacy of man over all other living creatures, and more pointedly, the degeneration of that idea in contemporary Marxist-Leninist praxis, by positing as its emblem the old men of the "Citizens' Corps for Civil Order," who patrol the streets sporting red armbands and brandishing "long poles equipped with wire loops at one end" (p. 45) in a relentless war of canine extermination. This grotesque vignette also serves to link the novel's action to recent Czech history by suggesting that it takes place not long after the Russian invasion, when such a crusade against dogs was in fact launched, as Kundera has told us elsewhere.[7]

Kundera's first question—"Does man deserve to live on this earth?"—raises the necessity of justifying man's legitimacy on the planet. It is a metaphysical problem wrapped inside an interrogation whose form calls for an answer in moral or even judicial terms. Yet the second question—"Shouldn't the 'planet be freed from man's clutches'?"—assumes that the moral accounts between human beings and the universe from which they lease and borrow have already been closed, with man showing heavily in the red. Kundera's questioning opens the way to the paradoxical proposition of a metaphysically sanctioned genocide, an idea couched in the form of a hypothetical imperative.

The philosophical time of *The Farewell Party* is the time of epilogues, that is, a time beyond the formal narrative sequence. In order of composition this novel overlaps with the play *Jacques and His Master* (1970–71), an original variation on Diderot's novel *Jacques le fataliste* (1773), which Kundera wrote as a private gesture of homage to a work and a writer he loves. Ten years later in Paris he recalled that the sense of endings that had prompted him to create a stage version of that old French comic novel encompassed a much greater magnitude of loss than the personal deprivation of his freedom to publish what he wrote.

> Faced with the eternity of the Russian night, I had experienced in Prague the violent end of Western culture such as it was conceived at the dawn of the modern age, based on the individual and his reason, on pluralism of thought, and on tolerance. In a small Western country I experienced the end of the West. That was the grand farewell.[8]

In spite of this, *Jacques and His Master* is a bright play, festive and elegant, with just a touch of pathos, like one last flourish of a plumed hat before parting. By putting Diderot's pair of picaresque characters on an empty stage, Kundera invents a theatrical metaphor for his own conception of the great adventure of European humanism. He takes up that road already past the middle of its historical course and translates it into a running dialogue between highly individualized voices. An eighteenth-century French aristocrat down on his luck, having played out his inborn privilege of physical libertinism, is now led on his way by his servant Jacques, whose far more exhilarating libertinism of mind is a spiritual resource painfully acquired through years of hard experience. Together, the presumed master and the irrepressibly encroaching valet engage in a perpetual give-and-take of words, part storytelling and part a battle of wits and wills, but always, in essence, a dynamic game of verbal invention between the straight man and the clever fool. The primary dialogue is augmented by exchanges with a small cast of secondary narrators, and the whole performance is cadenced by laughter.

The Farewell Party counterpoints the play, in spirit as well as in form. Kundera himself advises us that the novel is "a farce in five acts" built in just the same way as "The Symposium" in *Laughable Loves*.[9] But it is also possible to read it as a companion piece to *Jacques and His Master,* a black farce coming on the heels of the bright one, offering a not so fond farewell to that future which lay waiting like a trap at the end of the open road traveled by the play's two libertines. Taken together, the novel as play and the play as novel show Kundera at his best in ambidextrous command of the twin possibilities of fiction making, once it has been cut loose from its nineteenth-century mooring in realistic mimesis. One of the chief characteristics of the farce as Kundera defines it is a sharply accelerated tempo. In *Jacques and His Master* the dizzying pace of progression has an invigorating effect, inducing a laughter of perpetual surprise that is profoundly tonic. In the novel that same acceleration has the relentless downward pull of a machine-made catastrophe. The laughter it provokes is mechanical as well, infected with a distinctly contemporary chill. As Kundera has said, commenting on the progressive degradation of the comic mode in modern European literature, "Rabelais' merry epic has turned into the despairing comedy of Ionesco, who says, 'There's only a thin line between the horrible and the comic.' The European history of laughter comes to an end."[10]

The existential here and now of *The Farewell Party* is the dead end where man knows he is going nowhere. It is situated beyond the asking of the big questions, whose answers are no longer felt to be a mystery by the querent. In this context one can grasp the full import of Kundera's desire to unite "the extreme gravity of the question and the extreme lightness of the form."

> The union of a frivolous form and a serious subject lays bare our dramas (those that occur in our beds as well as those we play out on the great stage of History) in all their terrible insignificance.[11]

The Farewell Party, like the festive farce that precedes it, is constructed around the axis of a journey. But the central metaphor of the open road is replaced here by that of the closed border, a fictitious line drawn in real space and guarded by an arbitrary government. In the course of the first four days, three characters travel separately from Prague to the spa town at the western periphery of Bohemia. Klima, a pop-star trumpeter, undertakes the trip in order to persuade Ruzena, a local nurse he slept with one night on an earlier visit to town, to abort the pregnancy for which she holds him responsible. His jealous wife Kamila follows after him, driven by the need to put an end to her tormenting suspicions. Jakub, a disillusioned intellectual, is on his way out of the country, having been granted a long-awaited permission to emigrate. He stops in the town to take his leave of Dr. Skreta, an old friend, and of Olga, the young woman he had placed under his care. On the fifth day, Ruzena's death interrupts the ongoing sexual games with the suddenness if not the romantic bravura of Stendhal's famed pistol shot fired in the middle of a concert.

The question of abortion is raised on the first day, a Monday afternoon, in a telephone call from Ruzena to Klima in Prague. Their conversation initiates the action and provides the outer frame for the intricate design of life and death motifs at the core of the novel. Neither one of them wants to call "the thing" by its proper name as they talk at cross-purposes. The woman, determined to cling to her accidental pregnancy, uses the pronoun "that" (*to*) or its equivalent, "thing," to designate the abortion she resists: "I know what you're thinking, and you'd better get that idea right out of your head. I'd never do such a thing, they'd have to kill me first" (p. 5). Klima also uses the banal abstraction of that all-purpose pronoun in his attempt to deny the unwanted paternity: "I couldn't have done anything like that, it's simply physiologically impossible" (p. 4). Their verbal reticence has nothing of a traditional scruple or reverence before the option of being or nonbeing, which they are deciding on behalf of an unknown third. The periphrasis is rather a function of the moral vacuum in which the issue is raised, a condition that the novel postulates not as an exception but as the norm. The word *to,* pointing as it does in opposite directions at once, signals the beginning of the oxymoronic discourse about life and death, the act of genesis and the act of murder, that will go on in the rest of the novel. Its occult meaning, quite beyond the ken of the two people who make use of it, is to hint at the formula of *coincidentia oppositorum* in a verbal gesture that gropes for some unseen locus on the mystical circle of significance, where the farthest point traveled on the circumference merges with the point of departure.

Between Ruzena and Klima the uncomfortable exchange of evasive phrases works as the launching pad for a typical Kunderesque battle of the sexes. For the philandering male an accidental pregnancy is like the worm hidden inside the rose. Ruzena's announcement threatens Klima with the whip of sexual necessity, the libertine's *contrappasso* that all Don Juans dread. For her it is an unexpected boon that she hopes to parlay into a ticket out of the boredom of her dreary provincial life. It is not motherhood as such or the respectability of marriage she craves. When her local boyfriend and sometime lover Franta, who keeps pestering her with his insistent devotion, offers to marry her on the third day of the action, she rejects him with a violence that matches Klima's odium for her pregnancy: "I don't want a family. . . . I'd kill myself before I'd have a baby!" (p. 74). But a pregnancy by a bona fide celebrity from Prague fills her with "a new sense of power" (p. 39).

The sexual square-off between Ruzena and Klima is not unlike the conflict that divided Jaromil's parents in *Life Is Elsewhere*. But here the private skirmish between two individuals is played out as a public event that pits two sexual collectives against each other. The jazz musician, whose glamorous image stares down from ubiquitous posters, has become "the common property of the nursing staff" (p. 6), and all the women join forces to egg Ruzena on. The male team constituted by Klima's band is equally partisan. Its youngest member, a guitarist, carried away by enthusiasm, proposes to "entice the nurse out on the highway, and run her over with his car. 'Nobody could prove it wasn't an accident.' " This is the first premonitory sounding of the motif of "the killing of the mandarin," which will be worked out more fully later. Klima treats this hyperbolic expression of misogyny as a touchingly impractical offer of friendship, calling the guitarist "an awfully decent fellow" (p. 11).

Nothing is quite as it seems in Kundera's world, and nowhere is the gap between appearance and reality more pronounced than in the realm of emotions and feelings. So it is with Klima's womanizing. In his heart of hearts this compulsive Don Juan is really his Elvira's slave. Kamila, for her part, may torment herself with a very real and painful jealousy, but she also uses her suffering to keep her passionately devoted husband under her sway. "Kamila soon came to realize that her sorrow contained an unsuspected power to attract and to move. Not surprisingly, she began to exploit this accidentally discovered advantage (perhaps unconsciously, but no less frequently)" (pp. 13–14). At the end of the first day, as the wedded pair of self-enclosed but mutually obsessed lovers lie in bed in Prague, it is hard to say who is the victim and who the victimizer.

Between Klima and Ruzena the common denominator is not tenderness but a ruthlessly exploitive power drive. Even though neither of them commands the reader's sympathy, they too, in a very real sense, are each other's victims. Elizabeth Pochoda, who reads this novel somewhat restrictively as a brutal political farce about the "internalization of social oppression" (p. xii), is nonetheless right in stressing that the victims are also willing victimizers who use sexual conquest as "the swing on which [they] try to move beyond their limited destiny" (p. x).

Sexual love, whether of the passionately tender or the libertine variety, is preeminently the domain of masked feelings in Kundera's fiction. Having discarded the guitarist's plan for getting rid of the woman altogether by main force, Klima, like a good Czech, opts for the safer method of quiet diplomacy. Since he puts little trust in Ruzena's compassion or her common sense, he decides to outwit her sexually by simulating a romantic love so demanding as to brook no interference from premature parenthood. Ironically, that big lie is an accurate description of his actual state of feeling, but transposed from his wife to his one-night paramour.

On Tuesday morning, the false Don Juan from Prague returns to the scene of the fateful seduction, determined to execute an enforced repeat performance. But before knocking at the door of Ruzena's room in Karl Marx House, he takes time out to revisit a certain Bartleff, at whose party he originally met her. The hospitable foreigner occupies a fine apartment on the second floor of Richmond House, just across the street from the more modest building that bears the legendary name of the bearded man who used to take the waters at the spa in the days of its bourgeois prehistory. Currently the resort's medical specialty is the treatment of female infertility.

Bartleff welcomes Klima in his pajamas, immediately proceeding to order a full breakfast for two. A man in his early fifties, with thinning hair, this stranger who seems so much at ease in this place is one of the most puzzling of Kundera's creations. His conspicuous American accent, the outgoing manner, the gesture of reaching for an open cigar box filled with silver half-dollars any time a waiter appears, fit him for the part of the "rich American" in some long-forgotten prewar vaudeville where his interventions might figure as an updated, Yankee-efficient version of the *deus ex machina*. After hearing Klima's confession, Bartleff promises to enlist the help of his old friend Skreta, the chairman of the local medical committee responsible for approving abortions.

The apparition of Bartleff in a cast otherwise composed of characters with recognizable roots in Czech society has something absurdly fantastic about it, as if deliberately made up to provoke the reader's disbelief. The intent of such a provocation cuts much deeper than politics in a farce that may be the most metaphysical piece Kundera has written. Bartleff begins by telling Klima that he loves "those morning hours of inactivity, which are like a beautiful sculpture-lined bridge across which I stroll from night into day, from dream into reality. During those hours, how I long for a miracle!" (p. 22). This familiarity with the miraculous, and Bartleff's sense of the festive pulse of life beating under the everyday gray skin, might belong to a surrealist dreamer. But it soon becomes apparent that the American with the Russian-sounding name dwells on a spiritual rather than a poetic level of consciousness. He has the gift of delving into matters of the spirit with the intense immediacy and childlike innocence of Prince Myshkin about to step out into Petersburg. Like Dostoevsky's holy fool, Bartleff is a mysterious stranger who appears in the midst of a society given to corrupt deals and power plays, having emerged from a foreign land more mythical than real, burdened only with the slight psychological bundle of a nebulous personal history to which he alludes in the form of parables. One of these is the story he tells Klima about the promiscuous girl who taxed him falsely with being the father of her unborn child after a single night of lovemaking. Bartleff's solution was to reach out in sympathy to the loving woman he knew was concealed under the defensive cynicism. This approach is strikingly reminiscent of the "method" Myshkin uses to rehabilitate the Swiss girl Marie, which, however, fails him when he tries to apply it to Nastasia Filipovna in Petersburg, where the state of childhood seems to have been abolished. To Klima, Bartleff's words sound like "a chapter out of some modern version of the Gospel. He felt like bowing down before him" (p. 27). That emotional gesture is expressive of a moment of recognition that echoes Rogozhin's wonder before Myshkin and his exclamation in the carriage of the Warsaw train: "Then you are a regular holy fool, Prince, and such as you God loves."[12]

Kundera has told us that when he was given the opportunity to adapt *The Idiot* for the Czech stage at a difficult moment in his literary career, he was unable to surmount his distaste for what he calls "Dostoyevsky's universe of overblown gestures, murky depths, and aggressive sentimentality."[13] He found his ease instead inside the open, playful world of Diderot's old novel. But the echoes of Kundera's psychomachy with Dostoevsky can be heard in *The Farewell Party,* whose plot takes aim at Raskolnikov's tragedy and deflates it. The allusions to *The Idiot* are more submerged and more difficult to interpret. In the figure of Bartleff, Kundera has managed to create an anti-Dostoevskian variation on Myshkin without giving a hostile portrait of the fool of God. It is true that in the passage just cited, the author throws the acid of his skepticism on Klima's access of reverence for Bartleff by commenting parenthetically, "Let's remember that he was under emotional tension, and subject to exaggerated gestures" (p. 27). But it is Klima's need to bow down and not Bartleff's evangelical lesson that is at issue here.

Bartleff is a Christian mystic whose joy in swimming in the deep sea of being is the paradoxical gift of a spirit that dwells fearlessly in the nearness of death. Just as Myshkin's consciousness hovers precariously on the edge of imminent epileptic collapse, Bartleff's life, as Dr. Skreta reveals, "hangs by a thread" because of a severe heart condition that makes the act of love dangerous to him. "And he knows it," adds Skreta (p. 103). In spite of this, Bartleff is a sensually complete human being, quite the obverse in this respect of the imperfectly incarnated Myshkin, who remains an impossible bridegroom throughout his two simultaneous love relations with Aglaya and Nastasia Filipovna. Bartleff's sexuality is expansive and many-sided. He is a married man with a young wife and a new son he adores, yet he is also known for his numerous affairs with other women. In the long series of Kundera's philanderers, he stands out as the one lover of women whose eroticism is not alienated from procreation. That is why his sexuality is comic in the sublime sense Rabelais attached to it. When he tells Klima, "What I am trying to say is that total acceptance of life means acceptance of the unforeseen. And a child is the essence of the unforeseen, it is the unforeseen itself" (p. 26), one almost hears the tone of Friar John's joyous advice to Panurge, who is caught in the dilemma of wanting with equal fervor a lusty wife and a guarantee that she will never cuckold him. "Call the banns and make the bed creak this very evening," exclaims the monk. "What are you saving yourself for, in God's name? Don't you know that the end of the world's drawing near?"[14]

Bartleff's evangelism is of the serene Erasmian variety rather than the strained Dostoevskian kind. In an exchange with Jakub, he reminds the intellectual of the etymological meaning of the word "evangel," which is "glad tidings," before stating that "the enjoyment of life is the most fundamental legacy of Jesus" (p. 96). He has neither the excessive meekness Prince Myshkin generally displays nor the capacity for sudden intellectual violence that the Russian Christ-bearer demonstrates in his outburst against Catholicism during his engagement party at Aglaya's house. Bartleff's chosen patron saint is the ninth-century Byzantine monk Lazarus, who persisted in painting divine images as his individual way of praising God, in spite of persecutions by his rigidly ascetic brethren. The quality of Bartleff's mind is as open and generous as his sexuality. His question "Do you think people have the right to kill an unborn child?" (p. 25), which alarms Klima at first, does not proceed from the sphere of social and moral conventions, where arguments in favor of unborn life often smell of the hangman's noose, but from the domain of *joyeuseté,* where intellect consorts freely with nature. Bartleff can praise an unconditional acceptance of paternity without losing his sympathy for the plight of a man whose disrespect of all women other than his wife, which Bartleff calls "great blasphemy" (p. 25), originates in the very excess of that one great love. Bartleff's way with paradoxes has a touch of the miraculous, turning their discordance from virulence to blessedness as if by virtue of some mysterious *tertium quid* that no one else in the novel can name or even recognize.

The third day is pivotal to the philosophical meaning of the novel, as it weaves the two superficially divergent themes of paternity and murder more tightly together. Klima, having extracted from Ruzena a promise to appear with him at an abortion hearing on Friday, goes back to Kamila in Prague. In his temporary absence major new characters are brought forward. Action gives way to talk, beginning with a sequence of dialogues and culminating in a mini-symposium in Bartleff's room, where three men (Bartleff, Skreta, Jakub) and a woman

(Olga) reflect on the death option of humanity. In between, we are introduced to Jakub's blue pill and witness his foiling of the dog chase, two motifs that function as harbingers of the deadly denouement in the fifth act.

Jakub, who drives in from Prague on Wednesday morning, is a timeworn, cynical intellectual of the Ludvik Jahn variety. History has nothing more to teach this disillusioned Communist, who has served at the cutting edge of the Party in both an active and a passive capacity. When Olga, the daughter of an old comrade of his who was liquidated in the early purges, asks him, "Was my father the same kind of person as those who condemned him to death?" he replies evasively, "Perhaps." Then he immediately veers in the direction of theory.

> There isn't a person on this planet who is not capable of sending a fellow human being to death without any great pangs of conscience. At least I have never found anyone like that. If humanity ever changes in that regard, it will lose one of its most basic characteristics. Those will no longer be human beings, but creatures of some other type. (p. 68)

Jakub's definition of what it means to be human in effect reduces several centuries of brave discourse about the emancipation of man from nature to one dismal common denominator: a propensity for killing one's own kind, postulated as the distinguishing mark of the species. The measure of man proposed here is captured in the image of Eichmann sitting in the glass cage in Jerusalem, which displayed not so much the monster of violence as a specimen of ordinary human indifference.

The idea of testing the limits of conscience outside the controlling framework of societal laws is the nucleus of Dostoevsky's *Crime and Punishment* (1866). But it had cropped up in European literature earlier, in Balzac's novel *Le Père Goriot* (1834–35), in the formula of the "killing of the mandarin," which the young and ambitious Eugène de Rastignac proposes to his friend, the medical student Bianchon. The conversation takes place in Paris in the Luxembourg Gardens. Rastignac asks Bianchon, "Do you remember the passage where he [Rousseau] asks the reader what he would do if he could make a fortune by killing an old mandarin in China by simply exerting his will, without stirring from Paris?" Bianchon plays along with the idea for a while, inquiring, "Is your mandarin well stricken in years?," but ends by saying a categorical no to the whole scheme.[15] In Rastignac's proposition, the killing of a human being, anonymous behind his social rank, by a simple nod of one's head across an enormous distance and with judicial impunity guaranteed, is framed as an act of extreme license to be undertaken for the *cause majeure* of a gifted individual's self-realization. On either side of the equation, the minus side of moral cost and the plus side of worldly gain, the burden of meaning is heavy. The idea presents itself as a temptation ("*une mauvaise idée*"), a question to be debated internally, weighed, and possibly rejected, as in Bianchon's case. By contrast, Jakub's idea is a theorem born of a mind that has already answered such questions on behalf of everyone else, and that postulates the killing of the mandarin as the norm rather than the exception in human conduct. The form of Jakub's statement, three peremptory negative assertions about humanity in general framing a tentative empirical reservation couched in the first-person singular—"At least I have never found anyone like that"—reveals the quality of his philosophical experience and temper. Here is a man who has eliminated the dimension of the unforeseen from his life and who is in the habit of articulating the future in terms of a logic derived from a tainted past. Jakub has lived with History, reduced to the birdcage dimension of his native Bohemia, for so long that his sense of human possibilities is rigidly circumscribed by his experience. Even now, on his way to cross the border, he is not free from the mental oppression his country and his time have instilled in him. Jakub's moment of consciousness is later than Ludvik Jahn's. It is the unreal quiet after August 1968, beyond History's futile dreams of revenge and restoration, and even beyond the making of distinctions between victims and their oppressors. "I'll tell you the saddest discovery of my life," Jakub says to Olga at the end of their conversation. "The victims are no better than their oppressors. I can easily imagine the roles reversed." The Jerusalem glass cage has grown outsized in Jakub's imagination, large enough to contain us all. "And that, my dear, is a definition of *hell,*" he concludes (p. 70).

Jakub is an unattached man who has had many women in his life. His relationship with Olga, whom he jokingly calls his ward, has been his one emotional indulgence. He has held on to his "obligation-free fatherhood" (p. 67) because it gives him an intimacy with a young woman that on his side, at least, is entirely free of eroticism, and because it secretly heightens his self-esteem. Olga's father, who was executed when she was seven, was one of those responsible for Jakub's arrest, but Olga only knows that the two men were friends.

Apart from saying goodbye to Olga, Jakub has another reason for stopping at the spa. He wants to return a suicide capsule disguised as a commonly used sedative, which Dr. Skreta made for him years ago. "The pill is really the property of this country," he says with an intellectual's double-entendre when his medical friend suggests that "a pill like that might come in handy anywhere" (p. 60). To Olga, Jakub explains that the poison capsule was an idea conceived during his year in prison. "A prisoner needs at least this one certainty—that he is master of his own death, capable of choosing its time and manner" (p. 76). The Roman Stoics taught that the freedom to exit from life when circumstances make it impossible to continue in dignity is the ultimate option reserved for great souls. Jakub, himself an instinctive aristocrat condemned to live in an age of spiritual decadence, is obsessed with this idea of a negative freedom. But the blue pill in his hands, created to serve as the vehicle of a private escape from all contingencies outside the control of human will, is a technological artifact, a thing of power with the potential to instrument its own kind of necessity.

The return of the poison pill to the hands of its maker, which Jakub intended as a gesture marked with a special significance, does not conform to the prepared script. Dr. Skreta, the spa's chief gynecologist, receives his friend at work, immediately ushers him into the inner room where a woman lies ready on the examination table, and hands him a crisply starched white coat. Mumbling a few Latin phrases, he proceeds to initiate the visitor into the mysteries of his office. When Jakub tries to engage him in the ceremony of divestment of the deadly pill, Skreta answers mechanically. With a face of absolute concentration he scrutinizes and palpates the body of a second patient, whose "nice long legs, a well-structured pelvis, a solid rib cage, and very pleasant features" merit his full approbation. "We'll have to perform a little operation," he says (p. 59). Taking a syringe with a short plastic nozzle out of a glass cabinet, he plunges it between the woman's upraised legs. The entire scene has a repellent quality. Two men in white coats looming above an open woman, the one handling her inside out while the other discusses the technology of death, project an image that insinuates dread memories of unmentionable experiments performed not so long ago in the Central European laboratory of History. What we have here is a comic replay of the nightmare, without coercion and without pain, a playful parody that returns the horror as a joke.

Skreta's project, as he will later explain it to Jakub, is inspired by altruistic concern for humanity, not by sadism. His patented method for curing female infertility is to inject his own semen into the wombs of those of his patients he finds anatomically suitable for motherhood. With this technique, which is really a bawdy parody of the scientific method, the universal father has achieved two goals that have eluded humanity so far: he has isolated procreation from love, and he is bringing about "a world where a man would be born not among strangers but among brothers" (p. 104). The first of the two goals Jakub can appreciate as the emancipation of Eros from its ancient servitude to nature, and in the second, that of universal fraternity, he recognizes the touch of the "incorrigible dreamer" (p. 105), a quality in his friend that still retains the capacity to move him.

Dr. Skreta, the rogue scientist, is a figure as fantastic as Bartleff, to whom he is linked by a double bond of paternity. He has made Bartleff a father by curing the infertility of his young wife, and now he is scheming to make himself the rich American's adopted son so that he can get U.S. citizenship, and with it the right to travel freely outside his country. " 'And I'm dying to visit Iceland.' 'Why Iceland of all places?' 'Because that's the best place for catching salmon,' " runs the absurdist exchange in which he explains his newest fantasy to Jakub (p. 87). With the magic tricks he works at both ends of the birth-death spectrum, Skreta reminds us of Panurge and the miraculous powers vested in his fabulous codpiece. But this particular lord of misrule, whose career in the arts of procreation began with a get-rich-quick scheme to breed terriers, is very much a Czech character. Like Schweik, whose hyperbolic mimicry of obedience helped undermine an empire, Skreta is a subversive, and his parody of the scientific method also aims at the political import of human emancipation and brotherhood, ideas that have grown to weeds when transplanted from the mind to the soil of modern history.

> Politics is the dirty foam on the surface, while real life takes place in the depths. Research on female fertility has been going on for thousands of years. It is a history which is solid, reliable. And it doesn't make a particle of difference which government happens to be in power at the moment. When I

> put on my rubber glove and touch a woman's womb, I am much closer to the center of life than you, who have almost lost your own life in your concern for human happiness. (p. 92)

Skreta's statement, intended as a defense of human procreation against Jakub's damning judgment, is eloquent and touching as an expression of man's hereditary attachment to growing things. Insofar as it tilts with politics, it carries the day easily, as Jakub himself is quick to agree that "art and science are the real arenas of history, while politics is actually a closed laboratory for performing novel experiments with human beings" (p. 92).

But the center of life? Our look over Jakub's shoulder into the private garden where Dr. Skreta officiates has revealed a place as barren and arbitrary as the closed laboratory of politics, on which the two friends have turned their backs. His examination room resembles Faust's study in the second part of Goethe's drama: a workshop where Wagner labors to make Homunculus while Faust, the former master of the precincts, lies behind a curtain dreaming of the fabulous mating between a god in the shape of a bird and a mortal woman who will give birth to Helena. It is a playground of nature contaminated by *techne,* and the horror it exudes when we enter with Jakub stems from the absence of all mystery. Skreta's face may wear the mask of the true acolyte, but Jakub's indifferent gaze changes the ritual into an invasive procedure of the intellect, raised to the power of two, ferreting out the vital center of life. Jakub's tunnel vision is our entrance into the meaning of this scene, and the death-obsessed odium it inspires in him changes the woman's body into a chasm of vacancy.

The experience recollects the sense and emotion conveyed by František Halas's poem "Nikde" ("Nowhere"), from his prewar cycle *Dokořán* (*Wide Open,* 1936).[16] It is a blasphemous litany built on the hypnotic repetition of the anaphora *nikde.* In the opening line, the apostrophe "Nikde nebytí o nikde ty má zemi" ("Nowhere of nonbeing O nowhere my land") stakes out the speaker's lyric intimacy with the philosophical theme of nothingness, which most critics take to be the core statement of the poem. For the duration of eleven eight-line stanzas arranged in couplets, the virtuoso voice presses on with the bleak statement, working its abstraction into brilliantly precise metaphors that percuss off the pain of life in harsh but gaudy sonorities and colors. Consonant clusters ride over the long luring vowels until the final couplet, which releases the essence of Halas's metaphysical wit.

> Nikde červotočů stálá vrtby směno
> Nikde velká nahá otevřená ženo.
>
> (Nowhere the screwworm's steady work shift
> Nowhere a great naked open woman.)

In this repellent climax, the violence of the generative act works its irresistible way, demystified of all ennobling illusions desire might have summoned, into a gaping nothingness. Halas has wrecked the magic sexual oxymoron contained in the verb "to die," a word poets have conjured with from Shakespeare to Mácha, erecting in its place a new catachrestic conceit more suitable for the times in which he lived.

The gist of Halas's poetic act of demystification becomes apparent only when the lead word, *nikde,* is divorced from the common level of Czech speech and translated back into the usage it has acquired in its learned Greek form, *outopos.* Thomas More's *Utopia* may or may not be the great book Rabelais alludes to after Panurge's debate with the wise Englishman Thaumaste. We know that Rabelais loved that text and the man who wrote it, even though he poked affectionate fun at them. It is in a quite different spirit that Kundera's inspection scene and Halas's poem reverberate with each other, in common disillusionment with all forms of utopian ambition. Writing in 1936 after being in Spain, Halas already tasted the bitterness of poison on his tongue, and Kundera, in his time, drinks it to the dregs. Skreta is the fool of a secular world that has pitched its desire for transcendence in a hypothetical future to be hammered out by a multitude of human hands obeying an organizing political intelligence. He is good when parodying the tricks and capers of those in control, but when he tries to play it straight and guide Jakub to the "center of life," his magic fails. Then again, with Jakub peering over Skreta's shoulder, even Thélème might seem like a hellhole.

In the evening of the third day a party of four assembles at Bartleff's for a round of drinking and conversation, which soon develops into a debate about the legitimacy of human survival on earth. Speaking for the defense are Bartleff and Skreta, the two married men and fathers. Jakub, the unattached intellectual, is on the attack, and Olga remains silent. Bartleff immediately assumes the high ground of theological realism, an observation deck that can only be reached by an act of faith. He explains that he painted Saint Lazarus' halo blue "because in reality halos are blue" (p. 88), the color of the divine joy of the soul radiating outward. Gold, he suggests, became the heraldic color of sanctity only in the Gothic era, when the Church was at the peak of its secular power. Skreta turns the discussion to the earthly pleasures of fatherhood. His praise of human procreation is based on his idea of nature, circumscribed by strict eugenics and salted with a pinch of self-interest. Once Bartleff leaves the room, Skreta explains that his paean to filiation contained a petty plea on behalf of his desire to have himself adopted as the rich American's son.

Bartleff's affirmation of life is unconditionally inclusive, just like Jakub's radical doubt. Both men proceed from their experience at the limits of the human condition and from knowledge acquired in the "laboratory of politics." Bartleff reveals that he was imprisoned in Nazi Germany after being denounced by the woman he loved, who acted from a jealousy as passionate as the strongest hatred. "Is it not marvelous to find oneself in the hands of the Gestapo and to realize that this fate is actually the privilege of a passionately loved man?" he wonders aloud. Jakub is the quintessential intellectual, and as such, he prefers to talk of his own wounds in a roundabout philosophical fashion. He counters Bartleff's paradox with one of his own, in the form of a retelling of the scriptural story of King Herod and the Massacre of the Innocents, which heralded the birth of Jesus. In Jakub's variation Herod is "an educated, wise, and noble king, who had spent a long apprenticeship in the laboratory of politics and had learned much about the world and man" (p. 93). Herod ordered the slaughter of the children not out of base fear for his power, as tradition has it, but because he was "animated by the noblest longing to liberate the world from the clutches of mankind" (p. 94). Bartleff is in sympathy with Jakub's revision of the image of the mass murderer, whom we remember mainly as the historical antagonist of the Christ. Perhaps Bartleff intuits that this Herod is a mask for Jakub's despair, just as the Grand Inquisitor was for Ivan Karamazov's. His sympathy for Jakub notwithstanding, Bartleff cannot accept the deadly paradox that would legitimize genocide, any more than the silent Christ in Ivan's legend could accept the old Jesuit's casuistry of compassion. Bartleff vaults over Jakub's meaning like a spiritual athlete buoyed by a mighty surge of the heart.[17]

> Jesus loved his Father so much that he could not bear to see His handiwork turn out badly. He was led by love, not by reason. That's why the dispute between Herod and Jesus can be decided only within our hearts. Is it worthwhile to be a human being or not? I have no proof, but I believe with Jesus that the answer is yes. (p. 94)

In the traditional Christian teaching of redemption, divine grace flows from God to man by way of the heavenly son. Bartleff's parable about a son who is moved to compassion for a father deeply humiliated by his flawed act of creation appears to stand this doctrine on its head. But quite unlike Jakub's rewriting of the Gospel, which perpetrates an inversion of its spirit, Bartleff's variation is genuinely evangelical in inspiration, as befits the Erasmian fool in Christ.

Bartleff dwells in his own space high above the intellectual drama of interpretation, like that other saint he admires, Simeon Stylites, who spent forty years perched on a narrow platform atop a pillar some fifty feet high.[18] Bartleff's appearances and disappearances are sudden and marked by a mystifying quality of the inexplicable. He departs from this symposium at the summons of a little girl in a white dress with a huge double bow at the back, like the wings of an angel. Bartleff beckons her in with the words "Don't be afraid, my angel, come on in," and when she tenders him the large dahlia she is holding, he accepts it in the devotional posture of "one of the baroque statues of saints which adorn the squares of provincial towns" (p. 100). Jakub, bemused by this play of shadows, comments, "She really did look like a little angel" (p. 101), and Skreta confirms the strangeness of the child, whom he cannot identify even though he professes to know everyone in town. Olga, who represents the conventional aspect of reason, and whose analytical skepticism moves deftly on the surface of things, breaks her silence to voice her antipathy to the Bartleff phenomenon. "Religious people have a great talent for staging miraculous scenes," she observes (p. 102).

Jakub likes Bartleff, and besides, he is tolerant of eccentricity. That is why he is willing to concede the American his "personal angel" (p. 101) as a go-between who may lead him to God or, if he so prefers, to a woman. And Jakub too is a man who welcomes messengers from beyond the human sphere. His own personal angel comes from the other end of the great chain of being in the affectionate yet to him unfathomable likeness of a dog. Jakub's love for dogs, "these trusting, merry ambassadors from the strange, incomprehensible world of nature" (p. 84), is the reverse side of his misanthropy. It expresses his secret desire to break out of the condition of being human. This, along with his instinctive compassion, is what prompts him to intervene in the street chase organized by the volunteer dogcatchers of the Citizens' Corps for Civil Order, thus saving the life of the runaway bulldog Bobis. Ruzena, whose father is one of the men of the squad, has been watching the scene from the park, noting the ironic expression on the solitary man's face and seeing it soften as he calls to the dog. A flash of recognition lets loose within her a tribal loyalty that swells like the pride of her ripening belly. She moves to bar Jakub's way as he carries Bobis up the stairs of Richmond House cradled in his arms. "I'll bet you're the type that fills baby carriages with dogs!" she shouts at him. The confrontation between this man and this woman whose eyes meet briefly "with the clash of sudden, naked hatred" (p. 84) plunges us into the quick heart of the plot, with all its philosophical implications.

To put it simply, Jakub will kill Ruzena by placing his poison pill inside her tube of medicine. The substitution trick occurs in chapter 10, "Fourth Day," and Ruzena dies in chapter 14, "Fifth Day." Between the inception of the idea of murder and his departure from the spa, Jakub mentally constructs a complicated allegorical drama of motives and choices that runs in tandem with the fast-paced external action. In all, the story of the experiment with death occupies only eighteen hours of the five-day-long farce. It is executed under the comic sign of confusion, just like the last two laps in the course circled by the paternity plot, which Ruzena's demise brings to a screeching stop. The time calculation comes from Jakub, who computes the hours he has put in as the putative murderer once he has reason to believe that the poison pill was a sham with no consequences outside the walls of his own consciousness. Yet he insists on calling himself a murderer. "For it was not important whether the pale blue pill contained real poison or not; what mattered was that he had been convinced of its lethal power and yet had handed it to a stranger without making any real attempt to save her" (pp. 192–93).

The evening before, when he still believes that the poison is real, Jakub finds himself sitting next to his victim at Klima's concert. But even as he mulls over the thought of alerting her, Ruzena figures as no more than a pawn in a drama of temptation staged "for the sole purpose of showing him his true self," by "the God in whose existence he did not believe" (p. 148). Whatever Jakub does or fails to do is for himself alone, echoing Raskolnikov, who tells Sonya, "I murdered for myself, for myself alone."[19]

The Dostoevskian subplot is brought forward in Jakub's meditation on the meaning of his experiment with murder as he finally drives out of town. Comparing himself with Raskolnikov, he focuses on what he perceives to be the main difference between them. "Raskolnikov was asking whether an outstanding person had the right to sacrifice an inferior existence for the sake of his own advantage" (p. 193), he says, reducing the complex casuistry of the Petersburg idea to the simple clarity of Rastignac's question about killing the mandarin.[20] Of course, Raskolnikov was not so much concerned with the asking of questions as he was curious about testing his will in the crucible of a theoretical imperative. In *Crime and Punishment,* the Balzacian crime of appetite has grown into an almost unfathomable passion of the mind, with such swollen objectives that Raskolnikov himself, for all his intellectual sharpness, cannot pin them down by analysis. At the climax of his confession to Sonya he whispers ecstatically, "I only wanted to dare, Sonya, that was the only reason." In that tautological formula, all questions and theories collapse into the abyss of a will with nothing but itself for its object.

In his experiment Jakub exhibits the same monstrous subjectivism but not the feverish activism of his Russian counterpart. Raskolnikov wants to be a Napoleon while living in the anonymously industrious age of the great man's nephew. Born in the wrong country, too late for the siege of Toulon but still too early to play the commissar, he suffers from the romantic malaise of a century that entertained extravagant illusions about History. Jakub's moment is very different, and he knows his time only too well. Though convinced that nobody has the right to sacrifice the life of another, he is conscious of living "in a world where human lives were readily being destroyed for the sake of abstract ideas," and he loathes the "militant innocence" (p. 193) of the mass-produced killers of mandarins. Raskolnikov is a soloist of murder, who pieces together his personal justification, defines for himself the particularities of his victim, and slips inside his courtyard to pick up the axe. Contemporary man, as Jakub sees him, is the hypocritical *semblable* of the shadow inside the Jerusalem glass cage, a being dependent on others to provide him with what he needs in order to kill. Murder and even genocide have become problems of means and liabilities rather than questions left open for the individual will to resolve. "Jakub knew that if every person on earth had the power to murder secretly and at long range, humanity would die out within a few minutes. He therefore considered Raskolnikov's experiment totally unnecessary" (p. 194).

Viewed in this light, Jakub's own experiment with the pill seems metaphysically redundant, simply another accident in a world ruled by malevolent chance. But as he focuses his mind on it, his gesture of passing the contaminated tube to the nurse becomes "like a crevice where all his past life, all his disgust with people, could be lodged and gain leverage" (p. 194). The substitution trick may have been a gratuitous act and a game, but in the matter of defining the victim, his intellect has proceeded with deliberate concentration, with a precision of aim to equal Raskolnikov's. Alëna Ivanovna, the usurious pawnbroker with a neck like a hen's leg, who, moreover, was known to persecute her gentle sister Lizaveta viciously, stood as a perfectly adequate symbol for all that Raskolnikov found abhorrent in the world of Petersburg. Similarly, Jakub hits his target when he recognizes in Ruzena "the people's ambassador," one of those who "would always gladly deliver him into the hands of men with snare-tipped poles" (p. 85), during their confrontation over the dog. But even before that flare-up, from the moment he laid eyes on her, the woman has repelled and fascinated him. "Her whole face is concentrated on her mouth," he observes to Olga as he watches the nurse busily chewing her food and talking loudly all the while at a nearby table in the patients' dining room. "I must say she's quite attractive," he muses, adding quickly, "But I'd be scared of that mouth. I'd be scared it might gobble me up" (p. 66). His intellect riding that sudden phobia to the limit of abstraction, he endows Ruzena's mouth with a threatening being of its own, quite independent of the woman it is meant to symbolize. Jakub condemns its sensuality by citing Hegel's reflections on the Grecian profile, whose intellectual and spiritual beauty, according to the philosopher, resides in the emphasis it lends to the upper part of the head. Unknown to Jakub, his disquisition reads like an intellectual gloss on the kiss recorded in the novel the previous day. Klima, leaning over to press his lips to Ruzena's pretty, youthful mouth, found that her tongue, which had once appeared to him "like a flame," was now "a distasteful morsel that he could neither swallow nor spit out" (p. 47). Ruzena as a sensual woman stands on the borderline between attractiveness and repulsiveness, caught in a crossfire between sex as necessity and the mind's *acedia*. Her mouth, and that other cavity Jakub inspected with Skreta, figure in the novel as signs of devaluation posted at the two openings of the human body by an intelligence profoundly disloyal to life.

No action remains gratuitous once it is duly registered by human consciousness. Even the instant of arbitrary violence that sends a quiet stranger tumbling to his death through the open door of a speeding train is meaningful when read in the continuum of a life, as André Gide presents it in *Lafcadio's Adventures* (*Les caves du Vatican*, 1914). Lafcadio Wluiki is a youth of nineteen when he enters the novel under the label "Roumanian subject—orphan."[21] He kills his mandarin single-handedly, in direct contact, with one brutal lurch of his strong young body and without moral deliberations or definable objectives. Lafcadio is the natural son of a French nobleman and a Roumanian courtesan. "No civil act, no document, attest to your identity," his father tells him when he grants him an inheritance of forty thousand livres a year, even while withholding public recognition of his paternity.[22] The footloose young man values above all else his sense of unbounded disponibility for both good and evil and his opportunities for manifesting the autarchy of his will. On the most obvious level of meaning, his murder of Amédée Fleurissoire is an anarchic act aimed at the established order of a society that has failed to register his singular being. It is also a challenge from a masterful predator to the police pack to join the game of pursuit. But beyond all such reasons, Lafcadio kills for himself alone, just like Raskolnikov before him and Jakub after, having set up the murder situation as a private experiment with his own possibilities. As the train speeds through the night,[23] Lafcadio begins counting slowly, having resolved that the stranger's life falls forfeit if he spots a light in the landscape outside before reaching twelve. The mandarin's luck runs out at the count of ten.

Lafcadio is a child of fortune, and he plays into chance as if it were identical with his will, ruthlessly self-absorbed like a Homeric god. He is driven by curiosity about that instant of indetermination between the idea and the act, a desire to test himself within that brief gap where all the unforeseen possibilities of life flow freely and intensely before they are trapped and tamed by consciousness. Jakub's trick with the poison pill is also a game of chance that draws an unsuspecting stranger into its calculated risk. But instead of a sudden spurt of violence, his gesture of placing the suicide capsule inside Ruzena's medicine tube, on top of her own pills, is a careful manipulation that will protract the lethal moment into an indefinite future. Throughout the operation Jakub maintains the composure of the detached observer with his finger steady on his own pulse, never achieving the momentary self-abandon of Lafcadio. Jakub has been watching Klima plead with Ruzena at the window table of a restaurant where he is waiting for Olga. He cannot hear their words, but he recognizes the nurse and reads their dumb show in accordance with his own preconceptions. "He still regarded the blonde as the bystander obligingly helping to pin down a victim for the executioner, and he did not doubt for one moment that the young man was on the side of life and that she was on the side of death" (p. 122). After the couple leave, Jakub finds a tube of medication lying on the tabletop. He picks it up and, examining the pills inside, notes that they are blue, only slightly lighter and larger than the pill he carries in his own pocket. The substitution trick hangs on this chance resemblance between the poison and the healing drug. "He dropped both pills into the tube. Now they looked so similar that a quick glance would not show the difference. The topmost of the pills, probably intended for a trivial medicinal purpose, now couched death" (p. 126). The juxtaposition of death and triviality carries the signature of the historical moment in which Jakub finds himself trapped. Surrendering to its odious fascination, he tampers with Ruzena's medicine apparently for no better reason than because it can be done so easily. Here the instrumentality of death has its own momentum, which pushes Jakub's will to the periphery as his hands deftly perform the deed with the skill of a technician.

While the lethal opportunity is thus arranged with workmanlike objectivity, in a perfectly sterile emotional environment, the hate animus flows into the situation the instant

Ruzena reappears to retrieve her tube. She and Jakub wrangle briefly over it, as in their spat over Bobis. But this time he lets her win. "Jakub stared into her eyes, and then slowly, ceremoniously, he opened his hand" (p. 126). His gesture is a mock ritual eloquent with the cunning of irony. Its secret code bespeaks Jakub's vindictiveness toward "the people," whose chosen ambassador he sees in the foolish woman returning to demand her own death with the same self-righteous obstinacy she had summoned to ratify the destruction of a stray dog. Jakub's ceremony of justice is highly personalized, but with his little bow he also signals that he has relinquished his own responsibility for the act and is playing the role of executioner for someone or something higher than himself.

The fulfillment of Nemesis is administered by Chance, since it hinges on whether or not the zigzagging graph of the woman's untutored will intersects with the linear necessity of the pill. Having set up the hazardous game, Jakub immediately withdraws to sit the event out, watching from the sidelines. During the next eighteen hours the unforeseen dimension of life resides precariously in Ruzena's luck or caprice. Jakub, meanwhile, is mesmerized by his own invincible passivity as he keeps resisting the pinpricks of his submerged conscience. "A voice was constantly reminding him that the nurse had poison in her handbag and that he was responsible for her life or death. This voice was obtrusively incessant and yet at the same time remarkably weak, as if coming from abysmal depths" (p. 130). Jakub, who has eliminated the unforeseen from his philosophical mind, now enters into a secret pact of collusion with the pill that once symbolized his only chance to free himself from the trap his life had become. At end game, when he believes the pill has played him false, he is revealed to himself in all his awful insignificance, as neither the superman nor yet the full-fledged criminal (identities still struggling within Raskolnikov as he goes to Siberia) but as a collaborator like everyone else. Real or fake, the suicide pill does its job in the laboratory of Jakub's mind. It works to change the last philosophical value to which he had clung during his bad years in the birdcage of Bohemia from an idea of some nobility into a thing of power that pulls him down into the vertigo of nothingness.

> Raskolnikov experienced his act of murder as a tragedy, and staggered under the weight of his deed. Jakub was amazed to find that his deed was weightless, easy to bear, light as air. And he wondered whether there was not more horror in this lightness than in all the dark agonies and contortions of the Russian hero. (pp. 194–95)

Lafcadio Wluiki thinks of himself as an adventurer rather than a criminal. He improvises with his life by playing aggressively into his chance and ends by being caught at his own game. Instead of proceeding from Naples to Brindisi and from there to the Orient, far away from tired old Europe, he is compelled to retrace his steps back to Rome, where the consequences of his act have preceded him. The puny stranger had managed to grab at his assailant's hat and pull it down with him in his fall. Lafcadio's hat, which slips into the gap of opportunity between imagination and enactment, thus implanting his signature on the crime, functions as the vehicle for Gide's irony. For although *Lafcadio's Adventures* is a satirical farce[24] that parodies *Crime and Punishment,* Gide has retained the moral framework of the Dostoevskian paradigm he admires. Lafcadio's crime, undertaken as an assertion of autonomy, recoils on him by forcing him to depend on other characters who now control the strings of his destiny.

Kundera's irony works inversely by allowing the criminal to escape the objective consequences of his action. Jakub will cross the border still convinced that Ruzena is alive, an illusion the novel has already dispelled. Ruzena has collapsed earlier that day near a swimming pool full of splashing, naked women, into a death that has every appearance of suicide. Franta, her unlucky boyfriend, will go through life thinking he killed her, since he knows it was his importunate pleading that drove her to pop the pill into her mouth. Only two people in town are aware that Jakub had been the owner of the blue capsule. Skreta is sure to cover up for his friend, and Olga, who has spent the night before Ruzena's death in bed with Jakub, is determined to nurture the secret knowledge in silence, as an exotic grace mark indelibly etched on the memory of her singular erotic triumph. Even Bartleff, who arrives on the scene angrily affirming his conviction that Ruzena is innocent of the spiritual crime of despair, will prove helpless before the plausible circumstantial evidence to the contrary.

In outward appearance, the matter of Ruzena's exit from life is surrounded by the same unresolved questions as the matter of her abortion. Klima will never know what she might have done in the last instance, since she changed her mind several times between Monday afternoon and Friday morning, when he went with her to the medical hearing. Nor will the reader find out who was the real father of her baby, the reluctant Klima or the willing Franta. Ruzena's sexually inviting body remains a slippery mire of uncertainties even in death, and an obdurate obstacle to truth of any kind. At any rate, Klima, like the police, is happy to close the book on her case.

In the formal design of the novel, which is strictly governed by the rule of frivolity, Ruzena's death and the corresponding theme of theoretical murder are reduced to an episode within a comedy of sexual imbroglios and misunderstandings. Thursday night, when the nurse's life is trembling in the balance, three couples are brought to bed in Richmond House. Two of them are caught in the pain of Kundera's variation on the "cross-eyed Cupid" situation, which finds body and soul working relentlessly against each other as the paired lovers embrace. Klima's passionate tenderness for his wife paralyzes his sexual appetite in an excess of guilt and anxiety, causing an erotic fiasco that the jealous Kamila interprets as a sign of his infatuation with another woman. Jakub's flawless performance in another bedroom shatters his idyllic vision of himself. Olga, for her part, exults in his soulless desire even as his mind drifts away from her to imagine the humiliating circumstances that attended his own birth. "He imagined his tiny body sliding through a narrow, damp tunnel, his nose and mouth full of slime" (p. 161).

The third couple is Bartleff and Ruzena. He has approached her that afternoon when she is drinking in the garden of a rundown inn with Kamila and three filmmakers. The improvised party is shrill with sexual promise, offering easy seduction to the men and a brief release from anxiety to the two women. When the stranger materializes in their midst, the shabby occasion turns into a feast in the sun, ennobled by a bottle of excellent wine of 1922 vintage that the innkeeper produces at the American's bidding. Bartleff raises his glass to Ruzena's beauty, celebrating it with the taste of the ancient sweetness. Their lovemaking that same night is recorded exclusively as it feels to Ruzena, who wakes up from it as if from a profoundly healing dream. "Then she woke and it seemed to her that the whole room was bathed by a peculiar bluish light" (p. 163). Ruzena's vision appears to confirm the reality of Bartleff's mysterious aura, which Klima also noted earlier in the week. But this halo, which her embittered soul registers in the gratitude of a body that has recovered its loveliness in the gift of Bartleff's desire, belongs to the magical seeming of eroticism that progressing daylight may dispel. That is perhaps why Ruzena closes her eyes when her lover leans over her caressing her face.

The next day, Jakub too is granted a revelation of sorts, just before crossing the border. Having stopped his car in one of the last Czech villages, he sees in the window of a house a boy of about five looking out at him through thick-lensed glasses that almost cover his whole face. The image of the child, whose vision remains encased within this frame, "as if he were looking out through the bars of a prison to which he had been given a life sentence," looses a wave of pity inside Jakub, "like the sudden rush of water after the collapse of a dam" (p. 204). The exchange of looks between them is a recognition scene resonant with great emotions from the past. Like Achilles gazing at Priam, who has come to his tent to reclaim the butchered body of Hector, and like Pierre Bezukhov, returning the feeble smile of the dying man whose leonine head rests helplessly on the pillow, Jakub in his epiphany, so rich in self-recognition, also experiences a secret initiation into the mystery of human filiation. Bartleff spoke of the divine drama of compassion, when Jesus acknowledged his father's disfigured act of genesis. Jakub's identification with the little boy tells the other, purely human side of the same story, with the charisma of pity flowing back from a corrupted father to a suffering and corruptible son. Jakub's mind has played out the death option of humanity with the dice loaded against the idea of survival, and the game has compromised his own selfhood. He now knows himself to be "a brother of all those sorry killers" (p. 204) for whom he had felt such contempt. The ceremony of human filiation, which endows the future with the incalculable dimension of hope, requires an act of spiritual divestment from the self and its arrogant ambitions. At the end of his journey to the limits, Jakub surrenders his intellectual hatred for humankind and for the sorry land he is leaving behind. That hatred has been the last refuge of his mind's disappointed demand for perfection and purity.

Elizabeth Pochoda writes that the moment of illumination, obligatory in a comedy of manners, which "brings each person's foolishness home to him with the implication that now he may, if he chooses, behave more wisely" (p. xiv), does not take place in *The Farewell Party.* I read the ending differently. The scene with the little boy shows Jakub, who has denied the tragic meaning of his experience with death, visited by a flicker of something like the time-dimmed glow of illumination that comes at the end of a Greek tragedy. In the light of it, I see Kundera's Bohemia as if in one backward glance of love, an abandoned place haunted by great ghosts.

The formal exit scene, by contrast, is willfully comic again, bringing together two happy couples on the platform of a train station. Bartleff kisses his stylishly dressed young wife, who carries their little boy in her arms, while Skreta greets his newly wed and already pregnant wife with the news of his adoption by the rich American. Together, this grouping presents a grotesque image of the human family entrusted with the burden of its improbable future. Mrs. Skreta looks at Bartleff's son, drawing attention to a birthmark he has on his upper lip, "in exactly the same spot as you," she notes, turning to Skreta. Bartleff instantly dubs the genetic imprint a miracle and praises the good doctor, now his *de jure* son, who has procured the joys of fatherhood for him. "Dr. Skreta, who confers health on women, is an angel, and he leaves his angelic sign on the children he has helped bring into the world. It is therefore not an ordinary birthmark but an angelmark" (p. 209).

The laughter that follows this speech by Bartleff is of the outrageous kind that used to be allowed only in vaudevilles. Here it seems to register the cynic's response to the fact that the holy fool has been duped once more by the clown of the secular world. Yet Kundera describes it as "good-natured laughter," and Bartleff himself takes the lead in the merriment. In a black farce where nothing is quite as it seems and where the same celestial hue denotes both death by poison and a beatific vision, all signs remain open to the most contradictory simultaneous interpretations. The mystifying angelmark on the child's face may also point beyond Skreta to Bartleff, whose laughter from the highest platform of his spirit is a parting gift tossed at our presumptive disbelief.

5

The Book of Laughter and Forgetting

OR

Between Memory and Desire

The experience of losing a dearly loved human being is the intimate heart of *The Book of Laughter and Forgetting,*[1] livening the theme of forgetting by which all seven of its seemingly so disparate parts are held together. In the penultimate movement of this discursive novel, the staccato articulation yields at last to the flow of a more sustained narrative line. Kundera achieves intense emotional coherence by counterpointing the autobiographical account of his father's dying with the fiction of Tamina's dream journey to the island of children.

Poised on the verge of a double descent into death, where the book he is writing will reach its philosophical climax, the self-conscious narrator pauses to meditate on the motion that carries him irresistibly forward.

> This entire book is a novel in the form of variations. The individual parts follow each other like individual stretches of a journey leading toward a theme, a thought, a single situation, the sense of which fades into the distance.
>
> It is a novel about Tamina, and whenever Tamina is absent, it is a novel for Tamina. She is its main character and main audience, and all the other stories are variations on her story and come together in her life as in a mirror. (p. 165)

From the opening page of this text, questions of interpretation have been chasing after every bit of the action. But in this privileged moment of consciousness, the narrator seems to have overtaken his heroine as she is about to stand on the riverbank inclining toward the muddy current she must cross to arrive at the island where all pain of memory is abolished. The narrator's voice, rising reflectively above the lusterless waters of the dream Lethe, has a strangely incantatory tone. At the core of the passage lies the small phrase that joins Tamina's name with the name of the book that has become her home. Cadenced by the mnemonic repetition of the two linked words—"Tamina" and "novel"—this formula of definition suggests the arcane potency of a verbal discipline wedded to the task of creating the music of human recollection. The act of definition is also a naming ceremony of sorts that dubs the book a *novel,* thus investing it with the formal dignity that its binary title, *The Book of Laughter and Forgetting,* deliberately conceals.[2]

The book in question, Kundera's first to be written in exile, is at once the most personal and the most hermetic of his fictions. The narrative gesture at the origin of this multilayered creation is briefly illumined within the text, in part 5, as we are led from anecdotal invention to a drinking party involving real Czech poets and taking place in Prague sometime in the early sixties.

> I watch them from a distance of two thousand kilometers. It is now the autumn of 1977. For eight years my country has been

> drowsing in the sweet, strong embrace of the Russian empire, Voltaire has been thrown out of the university, and my books are banned from all public libraries, locked away in the cellars of the state. I held out a few years and then got into my car and drove as far west as I could, to the Breton town of Rennes, where the very first day I found an apartment on the top floor of the tallest high-rise. When the sun woke me the next morning, I realized that its large picture windows faced east, toward Prague. (p. 128)

The situation of exile, as captured in this vignette, instigates a dramatic reversal of mental perspectives. As the Prague of lived experience disappears in the recessional of memory, distance creates an inner intensity that abolishes the borderline between the fantastic and the real, muddles time. From the watchtower raised at the western limit of Europe, it is possible to observe Franz Kafka climbing the stairs of the baroque palace in Old Town Square where his German gymnasium used to be, and to see him take his place on the balcony with Klement Gottwald, who has just proclaimed the start of the Communist era of Czech history.

There were snow flurries in the air on that crucial day in February 1948, and Clementis, the Slovak leader who stood shoulder to shoulder with Gottwald, took off his fur cap and set it on his comrade's head in a gesture of concern. Kundera's novel opens with that balcony scene. The narrator points out that the moment was photographed and the picture reproduced on a mass scale to serve as the inaugural icon of the dawning age of harmony and innocence. "Four years later," he continues,

> Clementis was charged with treason and hanged. The propaganda section immediately airbrushed him out of history and, obviously, out of all the photographs as well. Ever since, Gottwald has stood on that balcony alone. Where Clementis once stood, there is only bare palace wall. All that remains of Clementis is the cap on Gottwald's head. (p. 3)

On the first page of the novel, Clementis's hat stuck on Gottwald's head sounds the leitmotif of organized forgetting mocked by playful chance. It comes to us *fortissimo,* laden with all the pathos and laughter that the polyphonic narrative will soon proceed to develop. But in the echo chamber of Mirek's mind, that same motif rings like a call to heroic action. Mirek, the first in a series of male "experimental egos" that people this book, is an intellectual and a former Communist who has become a passionate dissident after the Soviet invasion: "It is 1971, and Mirek says that the struggle of man against power is the struggle of memory against forgetting" (p. 3). Yet Mirek is himself busily trying to forget his past, rewriting his personal history in order to make it worthy of his new heroic identity. He is ashamed of his former mistress Zdena, whose ridiculous loyalty to the Party, and more grievously, her physical ugliness, remind him of the aesthetic inadequacy of his youth. In a futile attempt to retrieve his incriminating love letters, he drives off to see her in the small town where she lives, while back in Prague the police are ransacking his apartment for his political papers. "The only reason people want to be masters of the future is to change the past," comments the narrator (p. 22).

When the motif of Clementis's fur cap returns at the beginning of the sixth movement, it has a more hollow, muted sound. The historic scene in Old Town Square, which was witnessed by a roused crowd of more than a hundred thousand Czechs, is now passing under the review of a pair of eyes that belong to Kafka's hero Joseph K., a man who walks an anonymous city of unfathomable evil, a city without memory, where his eyes can connect nothing with nothing. But Kundera knows how the future devours the present relentlessly in the sequential time Europe has preserved into its senility, when only timelessness is real. As Kundera, in Rennes, was writing the words "Gottwald, Clementis, and all the others did not know about Kafka, and Kafka knew they did not know" (p.

157), Prague was completing the eighth year of the Husák presidency, steadily forgetting about Mirek and the Russian tanks, just as earlier it had forgotten about Clementis standing on the balcony with Gottwald. Once Kundera's novel was published in France, anonymous hands, acting on behalf of Husák's power, immediately went to work on the author, airbrushing him out of Czech cultural history. Kundera was officially written off, deprived of his Czech citizenship by order of Husák, "the president of forgetting" (p. 181), who himself figures as a sidekick in the offending novel. Even in the age of terminal paradoxes, the novel retains command over a debased reality, and a secondary figure like Gustav Husák can be drawn into its game of irony, just like the Duke and the Duchess who enter Don Quixote's play-world in the second part of Cervantes' novel. Here again, mockery counters the toils of organized forgetting. Tamina's home may be encircled by the forces of oblivion, but on the inside it is guarded by the occult power of laughter.

But who is Tamina, and what is the meaning of her double privilege as the main character and the main audience of this novel? Her own story is told only in two of the seven narrative movements, binding together part 4 ("Lost Letters") and part 6 ("The Angels"). There, at the core of the book, she is the reigning subject, while everywhere else she is the designated addressee. When she first emerges into being, at the beginning of the fourth part, her name, in its lovely singularity, precedes a minimal description of her physical person. "I am giving her a name no woman has ever had before: Tamina. I picture her as tall and beautiful, thirty-three, and a native of Prague." The act of naming is deliberately brought into relief against the ordinariness of Tamina's situation. She works as a waitress in a cafe "in a provincial town in the west of Europe," whose name is withheld. Tamina's essence proceeds from her name, like that of Don Quixote, who created himself by fiat of language, "in a certain village in La Mancha," which his author did not wish to name. Kundera heightens the Cervantesque echo by declaring that "my heroine belongs to me and me alone" (p. 79), thus reproducing the gesture of identification with which the Spaniard closed his novel: "For me alone Don Quixote was born, and I for him. His was the power of action, mine of writing."[3] In Kundera's text, the invocation of that ancient novelistic magic comes precisely at the moment when Tamina is launched into action. She is the experimental self Kundera invented as he stood at the window of his high-rise in Rennes, looking back at a Prague made larger by love. "I picture Tamina's present (which consists of serving coffee and lending an ear) as a raft drifting on the water, with her sitting on it and looking back, looking only back" (p. 83). Tamina's quest to restore the past by the faithful exercise of disciplined memory represents the quixotic journey turned inward. Her project, like Don Quixote's, is predicated on an ingenuous belief that words and images in the mind possess the power to resurrect the past; and she too sets forth on an adventure in which the highest pathos consorts daily with all the varieties of laughter.

Tamina had left Czechoslovakia illegally with her husband, but about a year after they settled abroad, he fell ill and died. In the immediate aftermath of her loss, she tried to kill herself by swallowing a vial of tranquilizers and swimming out to sea. But the cold water braced her against the sweet drowsiness of death, and she swam back to shore. Since then, she has lived "in silence and for silence" (p. 97), a widow and an exile. "The sum total of her being is no more than what she sees in the distance, behind her." During the twelve years of their marriage, Tamina's husband gave her dozens pet names,[4] but now, in spite of her concerted efforts to remember, she is losing some of them, just as she has already lost the chronology of their life together. She thinks she could "reconstruct the lost link between a pet name and the rhythm of time" if she could only recover the notebooks in which she kept a private record of her marriage. She is desperately looking for a messenger to go to Prague and bring back the notebooks, which she left behind with her husband's love letters. Unlike Mirek[5] in the first narrative movement, who wanted to lend his past a beauty it did not possess, Tamina "is not compelled by a desire for beauty, she is compelled by a desire for life" (p. 86). After her husband's death, she had his body cremated and the ashes scattered. In life, Tamina's husband had been the stronger of the two: "It had always seemed to her she couldn't hurt him if she tried" (p. 88). Now she feels the urge to cradle him against his nothingness as if he were a child, just as he had held her safe within his polynomial tenderness. Tamina has developed a special technique for breathing life into her husband's image: a piece-by-piece mental remodeling of the faces of men she meets into a likeness of the features and texture of his face. Like Ignatius of Loyola, the Spanish soldier turned saint who exercised his faith in daily contemplation of all the images of Christ's passion, Tamina is a spiritual athlete in her devotion to memory.

In a world filled with the incessant racket of the entertainment and news media, Tamina stands out as the lonely musician of silence. While everyone around her is determined to pour out his or her confessional self into every available ear, or failing that, into the writing of a book no one will read, she is a good listener who keeps her own lips tightly sealed. "She had a golden ring in her mouth, and she feared for its safety" (p. 102), explains the narrator. The image of the golden ring instantly summons the distant echo of the motif of consecrated love.

Once, walking to a restaurant with Hugo, the young man she wants to send to Prague for her papers, Tamina observes a cluster of ostriches pushing against the wire fence of a country zoo. They are stretching their necks toward her, opening and closing their beaks soundlessly. Bewitched by their mute speech, she stares back at them, unable to to figure out what they want to tell her. The image of the ostriches, first described in chapter 10 of part 4, returns to haunt Tamina like a recurrent nightmare. In chapter 17, Kundera demystifies the strange language of the ostriches by identifying it as the common verbal mode of contemporary Western life. This imitation speech, like the spreading graphomania, is an act of empty self-assertion whose net effect is to negate the fortuitous and superfluous addressee.

Tamina's love-beyond-the-grave motif sounds a note of unreal enchantment when it enters, discordantly beautiful against the bit of noise heard immediately before. "What we need is a revolution," says Bibi. "Something's just got to happen around here." Bibi, a regular customer at Tamina's cafe, has just come in, complaining loudly about her husband Dédé, who, she says, "can't seem to get it through his head that fucking means nothing to me" (pp. 101–2). To Kundera, recording from his high-rise in Rennes, Bibi's cry of boredom and frustration is the sound of Western Europe in its post-cultural phase. Hers is the motif of sex without desire, and its explosive vacancy speaks for all those lives spent under the hypnosis of television screens, where instant history, with its gallop of accelerated forgetting, parades by in images of magnified but quickly fading violence.

But the narrator, as if stunned by Tamina's motif, strikes off into an interrogative digression: "Why do I picture her with a golden ring in her mouth?" Thinking associatively, with the triple metaphoric power of sight, hearing, and remembering, he proceeds to weave a fragment from another text into Tamina's story. It is an early tale by Thomas Mann about a mortally ill young man who travels to an unknown town and takes a room in the house of an old woman whose forehead is covered with eczema. From that story, a single brief passage is lifted and transplanted to Tamina's book: "In between the sounds made by his footsteps he heard another sound in the rooms on either side—a soft, clear, metallic tone—but perhaps it was only an illusion. Like a golden ring falling into a silver basin, he thought. . . ." (p. 103).[6] This "minor acoustic event," Kundera says, has only one function, which is to create silence.

Within that silence Mann's Albrecht van der Qualen, a youth absorbed in dreaming of his soon to be real dying, can hear "*beauty-death*"[7] speaking to him. Similarly, Tamina's golden ring is "that tuning fork" which measures the minimal degree of silence she needs to hear her memory speak. That is why she dreads the ostriches clamoring at her from the other side of the wire fence.

We recall that Tamina's devotion to memory is motivated by a desire not for beauty but for life. Yet beauty appears to be all that memory can give her. Her own name, if we listen to it carefully, is also a singular acoustic event. The three syllables that compose it have a soft, clear, metallic tone that invites musical articulation. "Tamina" rhymes perfectly with "Pamina," the name of the Queen of the Night's daughter in Mozart's opera *The Magic Flute* (1791). In the libretto, Pamina is the object of a love quest by Prince Tamino, who wields the magic flute as protection on his journey to rescue her from Sarastro, a magician deemed evil by those who are not initiated into the meaning of his secret nature.[8] In Kundera's variation, it is the woman and not the man who undertakes the rescue of the beloved. The apparent gender reversal is really a fusion of the two into one, since all that now remains of Tamino's body is the image held tight inside his Pamina's mind. The first part of Tamina's name, *tam,* signifies "over there" in Czech. Twice this daughter of the Queen of the Night has traveled to the threshold of death, once with her husband and then on her own, but her love quest takes the road of return to life. Yet she proceeds along it with head averted, against the flow of time, intent on a spiritual act of recovery rather than spurred forward by desire.

Kundera has said that "the erotic scene is the focus where all the themes of the story converge and where its deepest secrets are located" (Afterword, p. 236). The observation is applicable to all his works, but it holds particularly true of this novel and its articulation of the master theme of memory. At the periphery, the theme is formulated as an ironic statement about the public and private politics of forgetting, but at the vital center, it turns into an open-ended meditation on the endless play between memory and sexual desire. Two major erotic scenes, one in part 4, the other in part 2, reflect back on each other like opposing mirrors, creating a complicated image of the contradictory possibilities of that entanglement. Memory annihilates desire when Tamina submits her body to Hugo as the price to be paid for his promise to retrieve her notebooks and love letters from Prague. In the other scene, the cruel disjunction between memory and desire yields to a mutually intensifying congruence as a man (Karel) makes love to two women (his wife Marketa and his mistress Eva) on the momentum of arousal yoked to a childhood recollection.

Tamina endures Hugo's sexual passion as an ordeal of necessity. "She accepted it the way one accepts the inevitable." Throughout the event she turns away from the young man's excited face, her eyes riveted by the mental image of her husband, which follows her around the room wherever she looks. "It was a giant image of a grotesquely giant husband, a husband much larger than life, yet just what she had imagined for three years" (p. 109). This petrifying image of memory looms hugely over the sex scene like the statue of the dead Commander, which finally stalled the insatiable Don Juan. It blights the vital moisture inside the woman,[9] but the unseeing man, deeply roused by her averted head, keeps laboring on. "A glance at Tamina's backside (at the open eye of her handsome, mature backside, an eye staring out pitilessly at him)" (p. 110), so transfixes him that he has to close his eyes. In darkness he rides that headless woman's body as if to tame the animal half of the wooing Sphinx. The narrator describes the mating scene by alternating the male and the female perspectives on the action. The philosophical overview that emerges reveals two suffering solipsists, each locked into a psychomachy with the ghost of the other—he with her soul, she with his body.

The third presence, the one that holds the woman's eyes under its sway, is death disguised as memory.

Hugo, offended by Tamina's evident indifference, aborts his mission to Prague in a postcoital venting of resentment passed off as a matter of political import. He alleges that the article he has published in a small journal, dealing with "the problem of power" (p. 113), is bound to have been noticed by the Czech police. He also explains to Tamina that he wants to write a book—"a political story about love and a love story about politics" (p. 112). Earlier in this narrative section Kundera has observed that "by writing books, the individual becomes a universe" (p. 105). In a society where the private self is devalued, the act of going public about it in the form of a book is simultaneously a desperate bid for significance and an assault on everyone else's uniqueness. Hugo's book serves him as a pretext to cover up his callous betrayal of Tamina's trust, but it is being written only because she is denying him the illusion of his consequence. Tamina, having gambled her body to recover the written record of her love, is left with nothing but an ugly imprint on her senses. She had asked for life rather than for beauty, but now, walking away from Hugo with her mouth full of the sour smell of his breath, she knows that the loss of beauty has robbed the discipline of memory of its meaning.

Memory and its capacity for creating beauty are explored in the second narrative part, "Mother," which is set in a Czech town sometime in the early 1970s. A married couple, Karel and Marketa, prepare for a night of three-way lovemaking with their weekend guest Eva. Like Klima in *The Farewell Party,* Karel is a compulsive womanizer caught in the trap of his love for a long-suffering wife. Marketa has always tried to disguise her jealousy under a mask of playful indulgence, and in her desperation to get a grip on the tormenting situation, she takes to staging occasional sex parties for three, deliberately seeking out the women Karel finds attractive. But in spite of Marketa's stratagems, their marriage remains mired in anxiety and guilt. It does not take long for Karel to understand that Marketa's extraordinary ventures into debauchery are in reality a painful exercise in self-denial. "When he saw her in the arms of another woman, he felt like falling to his knees and begging her forgiveness" (p. 40). After a few times, these penitential sex games no longer provide an escape from their erotic impasse.

Eva is a carefree sensualist who pursues sex for its own sake, utterly unmindful of the long shadow love casts. When she first came to Karel, with that quick body like the body of a boy hunter, so keen on its pleasure, he knew that he had found his perfect partner at last. She has now been his mistress for ten years. But since Eva is as generous in friendship as she is predatory in her sexual instincts, she agreed to a game plan Karel hatched in order to break the deadlock. With that in mind, she had seduced Marketa six years ago, after feigning a chance encounter with her in a sauna at a spa. Marketa, believing that Eva was her own discovery, was thrilled by the younger woman's enthusiasm for her body, which so far had been the sad locus of her love's misery. Buoyed by a new erotic self-confidence, she happily offered to share Eva with Karel in bed, and that has been their arrangement ever since.

But now, after supper, when the two women withdraw to prepare for the night's entertainment, Karel's heart is not in the game. He finds himself contemplating their little domestic orgy like Sisyphus about to begin another uphill roll. He is almost relieved when his mother, who also happens to be visiting this weekend, unexpectedly enters the room where he is waiting. The image of a mother interrupting her son's erotic play brings to mind the grotesque scene where Jaromil's mother bursts in on her son and the redhead in *Life Is Elsewhere*. Indeed, Karel's mother has always been an unwelcome guest in his household: when she was younger, she wielded her mother-power like a general, and later, in widowhood, like an expert manipulator of guilt. But during this visit everything has turned out differently. When Karel and Marketa take her out for a walk, she seems unsteady on her feet, feels light as a feather leaning on their arms. For the first time in his life, Karel sees a vulnerable Mother, a being radically reduced in size and consequence. When he notices that her sight has declined as well, he registers a powerful upsurge of pity.

All through the weekend Karel has been trying to make sense of these shifting emotional perspectives. But if perspectivism prevails in the sphere of emotions, he finds that it permeates the realm of memory as well. Take Mother's reaction to the Russian invasion of 1968. When everybody else was thinking about the tanks, she kept harping on some pears in her garden that had gone to waste because the local pharmacist, having promised to come and pick them, failed to show up. At the time, Mother's insistence on her private peeve had struck Karel and Marketa in its pettiness; it even figured as a major item on their list of grievances against her. Now that four years have passed since the Russian tanks rolled through Czech streets, Karel finds himself sympathizing with Mother's distorted vision: "A big pear in the foreground and somewhere off in the distance a tank, tiny as a ladybug, ready at any moment to take wing and disappear from sight. So Mother was right after all," he concludes to himself, "tanks are mortal, pears eternal" (p. 29).

Karel's newfound maxim would be quite at home in Tolstoy's *War and Peace*. There, in book 10, chapter 5, as Napoleon is driving the Russian army into retreat past Smolensk, Prince Andrew Bolkonsky, who commands a regiment, rides into the abandoned garden of the Bald Hill estate his family has evacuated. Amidst the desolation, he suddenly comes upon "two little girls, running out from the hot house carrying in their skirts plums they had plucked from the trees." This sight fills him with "a new sensation of comfort and relief" as he realizes that the little girls' mission—to pick the plums from the master's trees without getting caught—is as real and legitimate as his own preoccupation with the war.[10] Tolstoy's vantage point on history—from the bottom up—commands a view that is dizzying in its moral steepness. If Kundera, more than a hundred years later, revives the debate between the needs of Nature and the necessities of History, it is not to favor one at the expense of the other. Karel, whose intellect toys briefly with his Tolstoyan maxim about pears and tanks, seems much more interested in the discovery he has made about the changeability of his own mind than in the axiomatic conclusion.

Karel's mother is not exactly a touchstone of naturalness when it comes to remembrance of the past. Like most old people, she likes to reminisce, and it seems perfectly normal that her memory should have developed some holes. Afflicted as it is by mental osteoporosis, Mother's memory is not impervious to the cunning of history. She keeps insisting that in 1918 she recited a patriotic poem in school, at a special ceremony celebrating the proclamation of the Czechoslovak Republic. Karel's precise reconstruction may prove to her that she was already out of school in 1918, yet she will not let go of the glamorous image of herself on the platform, a young girl in braids, bright and hopeful as her country at its new beginning. The public meaning of the year 1918 seems to have been lost in the Czech nation's enforced march toward forgetting, but the old date remains a red marker of personal significance on the tattered reel of Mother's memory. Like Mirek in part 1, Mother has retouched her past to give it a greater beauty, but in her case a manipulative memory performs shifts of chronology rather than displacements of people, and she herself appears to be honestly deceived.

During this visit, Karel grows to envy his mother her perspective, free of the constraints imposed by sequential time and objective spatial relations. And then, unexpectedly that night, she becomes the catalyst for an epiphany of memory that causes him to understand that "beauty is a clean sweep of chronology, a rebellion against time" (p. 52). Intent on resuming the discussion about her past, she rushes out of her room and surprises the embarrassed trio just as they are on the point of going to bed. Karel, who is pleased by this erotic suspense, launches into another round of detailed questioning. After a while, Mother looks at Eva and says, "You know who [she] reminds me of, Karel? Nora!" (p. 45). At Karel's bidding, Eva uneasily begins to parade before them in her night gear. The name "Nora," which has popped out of Mother's capricious memory, has the instant power to make the long-submerged image of that tall, strikingly beautiful woman float up to the surface of Karel's mind. He had once seen Nora naked, with her back turned to him, as a four-year-old boy stranded in a ladies' changing room.

> The image of that taut, naked body seen from behind had never left him. A small boy at the time, he had looked up at her from below. For that kind of distortion, given his present height, he would have to look up at a fifteen-foot statue. He was so near the body and yet so remote. Doubly remote. Remote in space and in time. It towered over him far into the heights and was cut off from him by a countless number of years. That double distance had brought on a dizzy spell in the four-year-old. He was having another one now, an extremely intense one. (p. 46)

Mother returns to her room consoled by the small victory she has just won over old age and the forces of oblivion. Karel then turns to his double lovemaking with an imagination renewed by his magic leap into an instant of pure arousal, when his desire for a woman's body, unfulfilled and as yet unfulfillable, had the intensity of a child's capacity for wonder. In the vertigo created by his memory, Karel's mind records the simple pendulum motion of the male sexual act in which he is engaged, "that movement, usually measuring six inches at most" (p. 47), as an immense parabola vaulting over the familiar contours of the two women in his grasp. This erotic happening has a magnitude of beauty Kundera usually reserves for dream sequences. It matches Jaroslav's visionary reenactment of his wedding night, which is also a descent into the vortex of memory. Karel's experience offers a stark contrast to Tamina's odious copulation with Hugo, also a threesome, with the ghost of the dead husband occupying the place of the shadowy Nora.

Yet even at the apex of fulfillment, when sexuality freely rejoices in itself, Kundera shows the minds of the three pleasure-takers cloistered in self-absorption while their three bodies mingle and play. Karel, feeling "like a grandmaster who has just finished off two opponents on adjoining chessboards," shouts, "I'm Bobby Fischer!" (p. 47). The analogy between sex and chess, once voiced, makes him laugh out loud. But that happy male laughter exulting in its deliverance sounds "incredibly ridiculous" to Marketa. She is also experiencing a blissful release from her usual sexual self, with her mind not on Karel but on Eva, who has given her a sudden revelation of the possibilities of a purely physical love. To enter Eva's sensual Eden, Marketa has had to leave her "overvigilant soul" (p. 49) behind, and with it the memory of her love for Karel. She imagines Karel as a headless male body making love to her efficiently and in perfect anonymity, like an ancillary sexual motor priming her senses for the sweetness of the young female body lying at her side. Eva, the mysterious messenger from a lost world of live bodies unencumbered by anxiety or guilt, is the only one of the three partners whose consciousness is left unexplored. Perhaps her pleasure contains nothing that can be refracted into thought.

Karel's "beautiful night" (p. 50) is cast in the form of a masquerade party choreographed to the motif of a double inconstancy. His own mental infidelity to wife and mistress in favor of Nora is paired with Marketa's first betrayal of her husband's body, which until now has had exclusive possession of her erotic imagination. A realignment of the triangular relationship has occurred, as Marketa promises to reciprocate Eva's visit, but next time without Karel. In this intimate revolution, the sexual primacy has passed from the dominant male to the two women. Kundera, the dark Marivaux of our current erotic distemper, does not allow the light of day to repair the breach between the sexes that the night has opened. Instead, he focuses on Karel and his mother.

In the morning, the fulfilled lover becomes a tender son, lavishing the excess of the night's abundance on the frail, aging woman who gave him birth. Once so forbidding when she ruled him by guilt, she is now obedient and grateful on the receiving end of his emotions, accepting the hundred-crown note he presses into her hand at parting like "a little girl going on a long, long journey." What a marvelous thing is the game of perspectives, which can effect such reversals in relations and such shifts of intensity! That night Karel had experienced a man's highest sexual potency from the point of view of a little boy's boundless dream of desire. In the morning, he discovers within himself a feeling for his distant mother like that of a parent aching for a helpless child. "And the thought went through his mind that beauty is a spark which flares up when two ages meet across the distance of time" (p. 52). Growing old, after all, is a process of gradual diminution of being that begins the instant we reach full size; we are moving points on that trajectory along which death drives us, until we reach the predestined end where all human dimensions disappear.

From the tender *legato* ending of the second part, the next narrative movement opens without transition, loud and harsh. The action is broken into two anecdotes placed back to back without an obvious connecting link. The first is a fictional vignette of a classroom report on Ionesco's absurdist play *Rhinoceros,* set in a small town in the south of France just like the town in the play. From there Kundera takes us back to Prague to recall, in a frankly autobiographical manner, his fall from the Party's grace and the two seasons in hell that followed, one in June 1950, the other in December 1972. The splintered narrative is dominated by philosophical reflection, proceeding from the famed "essay on laughter" (chapter 4), which takes the form of a mock fable about angels and their rivalry with the Devil.

Kundera's tone in this mini-essay is amusingly cynical and sardonic, as befits a tale told from the Devil's point of view.

> World domination, as everyone knows, is divided between demons and angels. But the good of the world does not require the latter to gain precedence over the former (as I thought when I was young); all it needs is a certain equilibrium of power. If there is too much uncontested meaning on earth (the reign of the angels), man collapses under the burden; if the world loses all its meaning (the reign of the demons), life is every bit as impossible. (p. 61)

Rabelais believed that laughter was man's proper lot because it had something of the divine in it. But Kundera's fable says that laughter is "initially . . . the province of the Devil," who invented it the first time he noticed that things had "turned out differently from the way they tried to seem" (p. 61). This redefinition of laughter derives from a fundamentally ironic perspective on the world; the emotional effect it seeks is disjunctive, even contradictory—made up of both pleasure and pain. The Devil's laughter, as Kundera hears it, is an explosion of malice at the discovery of an imperfection at the core of being, but tempered by a distinct sense of relief. The way the Devil tells it, there could have been no laughter in Paradise. Laughter comes only after the Fall; it is a manifestation of human individuation that carries the Devil's mark.

In Kundera's formulation, the Devil is one while the angels are many, just as in the Prologue in Heaven of *Faust,* where Mephisto steps out alone to contest with Der Alte, who sits surrounded by his angelic courtiers. Kundera takes the inversion of the Judeo-Christian paradigm one step further than

Goethe, by showing the choric laughter of the angels to be a secondary, reactive phenomenon, a defensive ploy against the Devil's destabilizing volley. Because the angels' laughter is nothing more than a bad imitation of true laughter, their high-pitched, partisan yea-saying sounds false, like an unconscious parody of the original. Kundera's subversive essay presents us with a dialectical scheme of opposites, proceeding in a dynamic thrust from a primordial act of contradiction. The third term of the Devil's dialectic is "laughable laughter" (*smích, který je k smíchu*),[11] which emerges when the Devil laughs back at the laughing angel: "Devil and angel, face to face, mouths open, both making more or less the same sound, but each expressing himself in a unique timbre—absolute opposites" (p. 62). That scene of confrontation, a cacophonous substitute for Hegel's idea of a final synthesis, is a dramatic performance that encapsulates the notion of the anthropological scandal, a phenomenon that Kundera's novels explore relentlessly, in a variety of situations and combinations.

A scandal is a flawed epiphany of sorts, producing a partial unveiling of reality tinged with all manner of emotional impurity. As Kundera sets up the confrontation between the opposing varieties of laughter, the Devil is the honest party while the angel is a phony. Man, in trying to interpret the scene by uniting the irreconcilable under the single semantic label "laughter," has allowed his language to slip into the lure of angelic conmanship. But *The Book of Laughter and Forgetting* consistently avoids the seduction of an easy harmony. If there is a privileged point of view hidden in this novel's dazzling perspectivism, it is that of a man who has chosen to side with the Devil's honesty in contemplating the irreconcilable dichotomies of human existence. The man with the laughing Devil's mask on his sensitive face sees an endless round of mutually encroaching binary oppositions[12]—memory and desire, desire and laughter—turning malignant by reciprocal contagion. Sometimes, as in the case of Tamina's quest, where memory turns into a journey toward forgetting, a well-defined category of being may lose all its substance in the process of living, or convert into its exact opposite in a trick of consummate perversion.

Part 3 ("The Angels"), which is ostensibly devoted to the theme of laughter, is also an examination of the problem of interpretation. The anecdote about the classroom report delivered by two "angelic" American girls, Gabrielle and Michelle, is a miniature absurdist farce that imitates the style of the text in question. It is also a lesson, administered by a devilish prankster, on how *not* to read a literary text, or for that matter, any other unique manifestation of human complexity. The girls are puzzled by the meaning of "all those people turning into rhinoceroses" in Ionesco's play, and they want to know what the rhinoceros stands for. Their question carries with it the unspoken assumption that there is a single authorized reading of the image. The particular authority they wish to satisfy by solving the rhinoceros puzzle is their favorite teacher, Madame Raphael, who has always treated both of them as her special pets. The questioning moves between the following parameters: Is the rhinoceros a symbol, and if so, what does it represent, or is it *just* a sign, in which case it represents nothing but itself as a sign? "Literature is a system of signs," Gabrielle recites somewhat pedantically (p. 55)—the great truism of the semiotic school of criticism. Either way, as the girls go about it, the act of reading will be stalled by the braking mechanism of reductionist thinking. The rhinoceros can be read "up" allegorically or "down" tautologically, but the procedure is essentially similar in that it leaves out the metaphoric dimension of the image, which can only be sprung loose by an imaginative act that holds a multiplicity of meanings in the same grasp. In the girls' dilemma we recognize the Manichean division between too much uncontested meaning and a void of all meaning, with which the Devil began his fable.

Ionesco has revealed that the source for his play was an

account by Denis de Rougemont of a Nazi rally he witnessed in Nuremberg in 1938.[13] When Hitler materialized and the crowd broke into a frenzy of enthusiasm, Rougemont felt himself sucked into the vortex of mass hysteria, as if by the power of sacred horror. Ionesco was particularly struck by Rougemont's observation that his successful resistance to the collective fanaticism came from the same irrational depth of being as the seduction, and not from his intellect. From this autobiographical sketch, Ionesco drew his conception of "rhinoceritis"—an ideological epidemic of fanatical conformism that suddenly and universally spreads—as a fundamental defect of the imagination that takes cover under the illusion of logic.

The image of Bérenger at the end of Ionesco's last act, standing alone in a room whose walls are crumbling under the butting horns of the beasts, trying to speak with a human voice over the roar of their trumpeting, finds a match in Kundera's text in the autobiographical segment of the movement. The novel shows Kundera in his youth, a lonely dissenter roaming the festive streets of Prague on a particular day in June 1950, when the Communist government has just hanged the Czech surrealist Záviš Kalandra. All around Kundera, the angelic members of his generation are celebrating the victory of their murderous innocence by holding hands and dancing in a ring. The historical moment and the atmosphere of lyric ecstasy belong to the world evoked in *Life Is Elsewhere*. In place of the fictional figure of Jaromil, Kundera now summons the real French poet Paul Éluard as grand master of the revels. And indeed, as Kundera tells us, it is a fact of Éluard's biography that he published a statement in the French journal *Action* on June 19, 1950, in which he refused to join André Breton's open protest against the false accusation that would destroy their friend Kalandra, a comrade from prewar days. Instead, the aging poet preferred to join hands symbolically with the dancing youth of Prague. Kundera shows him reciting "in a metallic voice" (p. 66) those inimitable incantations of his, about the strength of innocence and a future laden with dreams, winged words extolling the smile of peace and love with a touch of modernist elegance. The imaginary poetry reading[14] culminates in a fantastic scene of levitation above Wenceslaus Square in the center of Prague, whence Éluard and his ring of young acolytes are lifted ever higher by the pneumatic power of revolutionary lyricism. We last catch a glimpse of them as they disappear in the clouds, like "a giant wreath taking flight" (p. 68).

The young Kundera, looking up from the pavement alone and wingless, experiences an anguish that has the same origin as the mysterious pull of gravity Rougemont felt at the Nazi rally, or Bérenger's secret shame at being human when everyone else has turned into a rhinoceros. "And just as one extreme may at any moment turn into its opposite" (p. 188),[15] so that lyrical lightness (whose emblem is the dove in flight Picasso painted for the pamphlet of Éluard's poems to which Kundera alludes) can be converted into an image of heaviness, like the trampling rhinoceros symbolizing fascist brutality. Lest we fail to make the connection, Kundera reminds us of the deadly potential of Éluard-inspired lightness by noting that "the smoke climbed to the heavens like a good omen" from the crematorium where they were just finishing off Kalandra (p. 68), and leaves us watching, spellbound, as the giant wreath of dancers disappears in the clouds.

Michelle, Gabrielle, and their teacher, Madame Raphael, are three militant angels, as their names indicate. They also have their scene of levitation, no less fantastic than Éluard's ascent to heaven, but their upward flight is provoked by a devilish kick in the pants, administered with uncanny timing by their classmate Sarah. The two girls, having finally settled on the conclusion that "the symbol of the rhinoceros is meant to create a comic effect" (p. 56), proceed to reenact their discovery in a classroom demonstration for which they don cardboard masks with horns. Their pathetic mimicry reads like a dramatization of the Devil's lesson about laughter, but upside down. The embarrassed class is treated to an unwitting display of laughable laughter, which suddenly unravels into tears when Sarah steps out to deliver her corrective kick. Madame Raphael, misinterpreting her pets' writhing as part of their performance, a sign of comic delight, responds by joining hands with them. As the class watches in mute horror, the angelic trio begins to circle on stamping feet, faster and faster, until their spiraling hysteria lifts them off the floor.

This grotesque levitation scene packs a lot of malice that might seem gratuitous but for the context Kundera has created around it, by framing it with two autobiographical chapters where the sharp edge of laughter is turned against himself. In the second season of his private hell, Kundera's fictional self belongs to a blacklisted writer who earns his living in post-invasion Prague by penning an astrological column under an assumed name. He thoroughly enjoys the put-on, delighting in the irony of "the existence of a man erased from history, literary reference books, even the telephone book, a corpse brought back to life in the amazing reincarnation of a preacher sermonizing hundreds of thousands of young socialists on the great truths of astrology" (p. 60). But when his identity is discovered and the sympathetic editor who gave him this cover is hauled in for interrogation, the laughter stalls.

Chapters 7 and 9, placed on either side of the classroom levitation scene, describe Kundera's meeting with the editor, a young woman he calls R. It takes place on the sly in a borrowed apartment so as to elude surveillance, but the instant she opens the door, he detects panic in her eyes. The sound of flushing water from the bathroom betrays the condition of her terror-stricken bowels, which she, a woman of dignity and intelligence, tries desperately to conceal from him. Their friendship has always been free of sexual tension, but now her altered face and the contradiction he reads on it—"her shit and her ineffable soul" (p. 75)—suddenly rip her wide open, like a gaping wound. He finds himself roused to the edge of rape by a woman whose vulnerability commands his deepest respect. In this singular moment, the quality of his desire has all the flamboyant sadism and despair of the male Eros when pushed to the border of blasphemy. In short, he experiences something akin to sin, a category of spiritual life now disgraced, which once described the very essence of demonism. Confronted with the evidence of that absurd phenomenon within himself, Kundera's authorial self turns to the old metaphor of the Fall in an attempt to account for it.

> Perhaps that wild desire to rape R. was merely a desperate attempt to grab at something during the fall. Because from the day they excluded me from the circle, I have not stopped falling, I am still falling, all they have done is give me another push to make me fall farther, deeper, away from my country and into the void of a world resounding with the terrifying laughter of the angels that covers my every word with its din. (p. 76)

The pathos of the falling Lucifer suffers an unexpected degradation in the act of being translated into a late-twentieth-century novel, where it must share our attention with the bathos of the three angels headed in the opposite direction. A process of mutual contamination has occurred between the two opposing categories of laughter, which the Devil has defined for us with such dazzling clarity. By the time we come to the end of the third movement, ambiguity has crept into the paradigm, and even the Devil's laughter is somewhat suspect.

Intertextual dialogue has been part of the novel's perspectivism since Cervantes, who interpolated several tales of diverse genres and points of view into the main narrative of *Don Quixote*. Practicing the same art, Kundera inserts a short passage about laughter from a contemporary feminist book into the third movement of his novel. The quotation from Annie Leclerc's *Parole de femme*[16] comes at the beginning of chapter 2, just after we have heard the shrill sounds of Gabrielle and Michelle's joy over their discovery about comic effect of the rhinoceros. Instantly, Leclerc's words transport us into a sisterly alcove where two women, stretched side by side on a bed, "play laughter together." At first their laughter is forced and "so laughable [it] made us laugh." But soon, in the consecrated enclosure their two bodies make, another sound explodes: "total" and effusive laughter, "sumptuous and wild" (p. 56), expressing an unbounded delight in being that represents the zenith of the liberated female consciousness, Leclerc argues in her book. Her philosophy of laughter interprets the phenomenon as a wordless epithalamium celebrating the merging of conscious becoming with the eternal instance of being. From the vantage point of this primordial laughter, the Devil's guffaws of contradiction appear tinged with the vindictive resentment of male consciousness at the failure of reason to subjugate all life unto itself. Reason, Leclerc expostulates, is as much a male invention as the linear time of History or the myth of the superiority of the phallus to the womb. Leclerc's feminist sermon is a manifesto of delight proceeding from her discovery of the sensuous capabilities of the female body once it has been uncoupled from its millennial bondage to the desperate desire that lurks inside the male body and the male mind, darkened by the immanent presence of death. In place of the being-for-death consciousness that dominates all male-centered cultures, spawning anguish and violence, Leclerc offers the regained paradise of female bounty, where life turns festive again as all humankind is swept back into the great lap of the earth, to the common rhythm of primordial, eternally harmonious laughter.

Parole de femme is the word of a militant angel who aspires to convert her iconoclastic brainstorming into the gospel of the future. Yet it would be a mistake to interpret Kundera's sudden incursion into Leclerc's territory as an act of hostility. He himself makes it plain that the adventure is undertaken in a spirit free of mockery. "I quote this text from a book called

'Woman's Word.' It was written in 1974 by one of those passionate feminists who have made their mark on our times." A bit later he warns, "Only an imbecile could make fun of this manifesto of delight," and then proceeds to call Leclerc a mystic, like Saint Theresa, in her vaulting effort "to push all the way to the limits" of her idea (pp. 56–57). Starting from an antipodal position, Kundera shares with Leclerc that sense of hovering at the borderline where a thought or situation, stretched to maximum intensity, teeters on the brink of collapse into the ridiculous or the absurd. By opening the pages of his novel to the subversion of Leclerc's tract, which calls into question his main theme, Kundera is staking a high wager on that "wisdom of uncertainty" he considers the essence of the novelistic art.[17]

Leclerc's analysis is particularly acute in its treatment of Don Juanism as a tragic flirtation between death and the illusion of the eternal, enacted in the repeated pursuit of an evanescent sexual fullness.[18] We are reminded of Dr. Havel, Kundera's impossible Don Juan, and his cooption by death. But that process of assimilation is presented in *Laughable Loves* as the historical end game of the type, the ultimate travesty after a long career of brilliant adventures in a variety of social disguises. Leclerc, who thinks *contra* history, places Don Juan's terminal obsession with death at the very origin of the cult of the male desire for woman.

Kundera has pointed out that Tamina occupies the same position in *The Book of Laughter and Forgetting* that Dr. Havel holds in *Laughable Loves*.[19] They both figure in parts 4 and 6 of the books in which they are the main protagonists, acting as formal links that unify the entire composition. Tamina is undoubtedly the vital presence at the core of this novel. She is surrounded by the poetry of suffering, just like Lucie in *The Joke*, who precedes her as the other great feminine figure in Kundera's fiction. The aura of pathos that radiates from her, even after she has been deprived of the music of memory at the end of part 4, would make her a stranger and a misfit in the world Leclerc dreams of. And yet Tamina is not the same woman Don Juan has been pursuing throughout the ages. That woman is Lucie, "goddess of escape," the voiceless and unknowable figure of veiled beauty created by male desire. Tamina may not possess a narrative voice in the novel she inhabits, but she is the reigning subject of her own love story, a woman with full jurisdiction over the entire psychic realm that Eros claims as its domain. Tamina commands the intelligence of love in the service of an absent beloved whose problematic being hangs precariously on the single thread of her taut memory. Unlike the fabulous woman of feminist predication, who is pregnant with the radiant future of humanity, Tamina is wedded to the past. Midwife of memory, she presides over a painful labor whose outcome is derision.

Even as Tamina's defeat is settling at the bottom of the reader's mind, Kundera opens the next narrative sequence. Part 5 proceeds from the question "What is *litost*?" He uses the Czech word as the title of the movement and in the text because, as he explains, it has "no exact translation into any other language" (p. 121). Let me suggest a situational equivalent for Kundera's meaning from English literature. "But yet the pity of it, Iago! O Iago, the pity of it!" cries Othello in act 4, scene 1, of Shakespeare's play, after he has been made to see Desdemona's handkerchief in the hand of a whore. The twice-repeated exclamation expresses a passion of loss that is about to stiffen into cruel violence. Shortly afterward, when Desdemona enters, Othello strikes her in the face, and in the next act he murders her. Othello's savage cry of pain and regret—"the pity of it!" is at the opposite end of the emotional spectrum from the "upsurge of pity" Karel experiences when he realizes how much his mother's sight has deteriorated ("Karla zachvátila *lítost nad tím*, jak se mamince zhoršil zrak"[20]). A single word—*lítost*—designates two contrary reactions to the sudden awareness of a fall from a state of perfection or fullness. Othello's access of *lítost* ruptures his love for Desdemona by darkening his mind, whereas Karel's emotional upsurge reconciles him to his mother in a flash of illumination. It turns out that *lítost,* just like laughter, is a binary phenomenon masquerading under a single name.

One can imagine the Janus head of *lítost* rearing up within Adam's heart as he first stood with his Eve at the locked gate of Paradise, looking back at all he had lost.[21] The word "designates a feeling as infinite as an open accordion, a feeling that is the synthesis of many others: grief, sympathy, remorse, and an indefinable longing. The first syllable, which is long and stressed, sounds like the wail of an abandoned dog" (p. 121).[22] The pain heard in this "wail of an abandoned dog" is the unmediated sound of nature after Adam's fatal interference. It stirs up an ancient, deeply haunting echo of shared misery inside the human heart. But the "open accordion," with its artful amplification, changes the sound of creaturely loss into something complacent and impure, exuding the self-deceitful lyricism of kitsch. *Lítost,* as Kundera defines it, is a veritable Pandora's box of feelings charged with explosive contradictions. Whenever the lid blows open, we see a fascinating display of sadomasochistic effects. "Should our counterpart prove weaker than ourselves, we merely insult him under false pretenses," explains Kundera. "Should our counterpart prove stronger, we are forced to choose a circuitous route—the backhanded slap, murder by means of suicide" (p. 149).

It is no accident, Kundera continues, that the category of *lítost* converted into spite should have been born in the living heart of Bohemia, a small country surrounded by more powerful neighbors, whose history is a series of "glorious defeats setting the course of world history in motion but causing the downfall of its own people" (p. 150). Kundera's paradigm holds true if we transpose it to the tragic situation created by Shakespeare in *Othello.* It is also no accident that the murderous lover who kills Desdemona in a frenzy of aggravated *lítost* is a

Moor caught up in emotional recoil from his entanglement with the patrician society of Venice.

The fifth section of the novel serves as a bright intermezzo between the two larger and darker Tamina movements. It moves with the quickened pace of farce, working out the ambivalent motif of *lítost* within a narrative that is frankly and broadly comic. Once again, as in *The Farewell Party,* an inherently serious question—What is the nature of Eros, and does it alleviate the human condition after the fall?—is treated with deliberate frivolity. To illustrate the existential category of *lítost,* Kundera focuses on two young lovers, a student swimming side by side with his girlfriend. The young man is a weak swimmer, not on par with his devoted but, alas, athletically superior beloved. In spite of the girl's effort to hold herself in check, physical impulse prevails over self-sacrificial intent, and she sprints ahead, beating her lover to the other shore. The humiliated student, undergoing the spiteful backlash of his feeling of inadequacy, harangues her about his concern for her safety and then slaps her. Dissolving into tears, she accepts his vindictiveness as a token of erotic intensity, and they are brought back together on the common ground of the double lie that equalizes them. "The absolute quality of love is actually a desire for absolute identification," says the narrator (p. 122). That redefinition of love recalls Aristophanes' etiological fable in Plato's *Symposium,*[23] which traces Eros back to a longing for completeness shared by two parts of the same human being cut into two by Zeus ("just like fruit which is to be dried and preserved") as a punishment for hubris. Aristophanes' representation of the idea of human perfection in the form of rounded bodies "with four hands and an equal number of legs," propelling themselves forward or backward "like tumblers who perform a cart-wheel and return to an upright position," is the invention of a great comic artist, intended to inspire laughter. Kundera's portrayal of the young pair of lovers, reunited in hypocrisy and happily sharing tears of masked emotion, is no less laughable. Both images are rooted in an understanding of sexual love as a self-centered passion, the complex desire of a mind that seeks nothing but its own good. Later in *The Symposium,* speaking with the voice of Diotima, Socrates refashions Aristophanes' comic fable into a new myth about the birth of Eros as the child of the desperate coupling of Poverty and Contrivance, which took place in the garden of Zeus on the day they were both locked out of the feast honoring newborn Aphrodite. At the conclusion of that dialogue, Socrates, seated between Aristophanes and Agathon, is shown compelling them to admit that "the man who knew how to write a comedy could also write a tragedy."[24] And indeed, on the question of love's humble parentage and the grotesque circumstances of its birth, the sacred word of Diotima's tragic mystery confirms the comic insight Kundera shares with Aristophanes.

Love is a child of human need, and not being beautiful, it is relentless in its pursuit of beauty wherever it may find it. Love and *lítost* are siblings, issuing from the same matrix, since both represent a response to the awareness of a radical lack at the core of human existence after the fall into history. *Lítost* is the older and more foolish of the two sisters (in Czech, both words—*lítost* and *láska*—are feminine nouns). Love came later—perhaps conceived as a remedy for the torment caused by the firstborn—and she was intended to rise higher. But as Kundera has shown, love and *lítost* enjoy playing together like twins, and whenever they do so, they use the comic and tragic masks interchangeably.

Kundera builds the fifth narrative sequence around the laughable figure of the lovesick student, who "represents *lítost* incarnate" (p. 123). When he is finally abandoned by his swimming partner, he seeks to console himself in the arms of a thirty-year-old married woman he meets while vacationing outside Prague. Kristyna, a butcher's wife, is deeply roused by the student's talk of poetry, but try as he may, she will not let him enter her. The narrator explains her reticence as a strange mixture of physical and spiritual dread. Kristyna fears accidental conception, having been warned after her first child that another pregnancy will kill her, and yet she is loath to ask her exotic lover to take the necessary precautions. The narrative makes it plain that the setting is the early 1960s, when Bohemia was still in the pre-Pill phase of its history.

In spite of a futile summer, the frustrated but persistent student invites Kristyna for an overnight visit to Prague. But on the eve of her arrival, he receives a prestigious invitation to a gathering of famous poets that conflicts with the targeted evening of seduction. Always the brilliant opportunist, our literary lover plans for a double-feature night—first the poets at the Writers' Club, and then Kristyna, alone with him in bed. Apart from everything else, she strikes him as too provincial to be shown around when he observes her during dinner at a restaurant. Kristyna herself is so bedazzled by her lover's proximity to those mysterious beings whose poems she once studied in school that she accedes to his every wish. She settles down in his attic to wait for his return with an expectancy that has the arcane charm of high romance.

Following on the heels of the student, we enter into a rollicking conclave of contemporary Czech poets. Kundera's description of their drinking party reads like a lighthearted variation on his mock symposium in *Laughable Loves,* which featured Don Juan transformed into Death. Here the mood is joyous rather than cynical, as befits an affectionate retrospect from the point of view of an exile. Though he does not wish to be recognized, Kundera himself belongs to the party, masked as Boccaccio, the ironic odd man out in the brotherhood of drunken lyricists. Real poets known to Kundera are introduced to us, speaking with their characteristic Czech voices from behind the code names he has borrowed from the European gallery of poetic types.

> I see them against the night lights of Prague the way it was fifteen years ago, before their books had been locked away in the cellars of the state, when they could all have a happy, raucous time together around a large table laden with bottles. I like them all and wouldn't feel right picking random names for them from the telephone book. If I do have to hide their faces behind the masks of assumed names, I might as well make them a gift of it, a decoration, an honor. (p. 128)

Under the mask of Goethe, we recognize the face of Jaroslav Seifert, the poet as an old man, sensuous and tender, grown wise in the many ways of devotion to women. He presides benignly over an assembly of men at least thirty years younger than he is, as a representative of a dwindling generation of great fathers, a surviving member of the legendary galaxy of Czech lyric poets who emerged from the avant-garde movements of the 1920s. The moment captured in the drinking scene is 1962, to be exact (following Kundera's indications in the text: "I write this in 1977," and then, "fifteen years ago"), a time of buoyancy and hope, when freedom was crescent in Czech culture and Kundera was writing his first stories about laughable love.

The boisterous conversation soon turns to the subject of sex and love, which evolves into a dispute about the erotic characteristics and attainments of the two genders. Petrarch is expansive in his praise of women, mixing anecdote with doctrine in order to illustrate his belief in the inherent superiority of womanliness to maleness in all matters of love. Boccaccio, a self-proclaimed misogynist, defends his position by arguing that men like him make the best lovers, because they alone treat each woman as a unique individual and not as a representative of a fixed paradigm. The poet-idolizers instantly raise an outcry against Boccaccio's heresy. The drunken Yesenin treats the paradox of misogyny as a personal insult directed at his mother, and Lermontov, the poet of *lítost,* broods biliously upon all those present. Goethe-Seifert tries to conciliate, revealing himself as a supreme appreciator of women in his triple capacity as poet, lover, and eternal child. At evening's end the aging poet, overcome by too much wine, lies on the floor, his tired body all ache and bulk, moaning piteously that he wants to be allowed to die there. His disciples, lifting him awkwardly, transport him to a taxi, to be ferried home into the safekeeping of his scolding wife. Meanwhile, the suddenly alert Lermontov gets hold of the student and begins explaining the idea of a poem that has just cropped up in his mind. "The Poet Descending," Lermontov says, will be a "grim, but honest" poem (p. 142), charged with all the pathos of real life, as reflected in the fantastic scene just witnessed. In Kundera's text, the image of "the poet descending," with its hidden allusion to Calvary, functions as the near-perfect inversion of the figure of the "poet ascending," which another member of Seifert's generation, the Frenchman Paul Éluard, had executed a decade earlier over the same city.

During the symposium, the lovesick student instinctively identifies with Petrarch against Boccaccio and his subversive laughter. But the short-legged Lermontov, rhetorician of a harsh but fervent honesty, is the one who strikes the most responsive chord in his heart. Inflated by his adventure, Kristyna's wooer returns to his attic bearing two special gifts that only the poets could have conferred upon his love. The first is a dedication from Goethe to Kristyna on the title page of a book of his poems; the old lyricist has told the student that the butcher's wife is the perfect woman for a poet. The second gift, etched in his own memory, is Petrarch's admonition that "Love is poetry, poetry is love" (p. 144). The winged words of poetry float above the lovers' bed as they return to their labors, exalted by a shared awareness of the lyrical magic. But alas, the power of poetic metaphor, which can work havoc with a woman's mind, proves unequal to the task of unlocking Kristyna's thighs. The night of passion, inspired by the combined lyricism of three poets—Petrarch, Goethe, and

Lermontov—is a physical fiasco. "Women always get the better of us," Petrarch had said as he launched into his lecture on the primacy of women in love (p. 129). The butcher's wife and her student bring Petrarch's compliment to womankind down to earth as they are compelled to act out its literal meaning in bodily gestures that are embarrassingly real. "It would kill me," Kristyna tells her lover (p. 146), resisting penetration. He instantly interprets her words to mean that she fears being undone by the intensity of the consummation because her desire for him is beyond her body's capacity. "We'll die together! Let's die together!" he whispers, pursuing what he takes to be her metaphor. Her response, inspired by his extreme flight of lyricism, strikes a posture of unconscious parody. "Instantly she seized the scepter of his love, upright in her honor, and squeezed it with all her splendid honesty: strongly, sincerely, fervently, like a mother, like a sister, like a friend—and passionately" (p. 147). This grotesque image of sexual desire exulting in the denial of its natural issue implicates both sexes in its double-edged mockery. The transformation of the phallic sword of male dominance into the scepter of woman's queenship deconstructs the Petrarchan model of courtly love by showing it as a duping of the strong by the weak through flattery. But the same image, interpreted by a feminist like Annie Leclerc, can be read to signify the ultimate degradation of femaleness. The upraised but futile phallus also mimes the emblem of male power worshiping itself as it stands guard over its idea of woman, like a nuclear missile armed with a full payload of death. But beyond all interpretation, Kundera's vignette of the deluded couple, so imperfectly joined in body and soul, is laughable and pitiable at the same time.

While observing the comic possibilities of Eros in its entanglement with *lítost,* the narrator maintains an amused detachment. The mood shifts radically in the pivotal sixth movement, which brings Tamina back to center stage. It is Tamina's motif of tragic love that is heard now, working its suffering way through the multilayered narrative about the unequal struggle between being and death. Death, as Kundera sees it, has two faces: "One is nonbeing; the other is the terrifying material being that is the corpse." Death with the face of the corpse confronts human consciousness with the certainty that every act of dying, no matter how beautiful or heroic, ends in the same indignity. The individual human body, even one that has been inscribed all over with the private hieroglyphs of significance that love invents, will surely turn into a thing of horror, or worse still, an impersonal object to be manipulated with indifference. Tamina, returning to the hospital room where her husband had died the night before, hears an old man lying on the other bed tell her with fear in his eyes, "They took him by the legs and dragged him along the floor. They thought I was asleep. I saw his head bump against the threshold" (p. 171). Tamina, like the old man, is terrified of becoming a corpse. She orders her husband's body cremated and his ashes thrown to the winds because she does "not want to torture herself over the thought of what might become of his dearly beloved body" (p. 172).

The other face of death, veiled by forgetting, speaks more softly of the constant slippage of being into nothingness. That language is easy on us, since the flow of disappearance within our consciousness is inextricable from the dynamic force that moves it ever forward. When the angel of forgetting comes to claim Tamina at last, to transport her in his red sports car to the clay riverbank from which she will be ferried to the island of children, he tells her "that what she calls remembering is in fact something different, that in fact she is under a spell and watching herself forget." In Czech the verbal noun *vzpomínání* (the act of remembering) and its apparent opposite, *zapomínání* (the act of forgetting)—or in its perfective aspect, *zapomnění* (forgetting as a completed process)—reveal their congruence by sharing a common verbal root. Remembrance turns into forgetting with a simple flip of a prefix (*za-* instead of *vz-*) as Tamina's spiritual labor of *raising* memory up is inverted into a *sinking,* as when the sun goes down (*slunce zapadá*) or a body goes under in the drowning waters. No wonder Tamina accepts the inevitability contained in her messenger's hermetic invitation to undertake the great crossing of Lethe (p. 163): "But what can I do?' asks Tamina. 'Forget your forgetting,' says the young man" (" 'A co mám tedy dělat?' ptá se Tamina. 'Zapomenout své zapomnění,' říká mladík"[25]).

In this movement of the novel, which is anchored in two death scenes—Tamina's own and Kundera's father's—the all-pervasive phenomenon of human forgetting is presented as the lesser twin of death. Forgetting plays death down, but if the event of dying is the tragic zenith of the category of human loss, forgetting is too flat and prolonged to figure as its nadir. In death, banality increases the horror, making it more insidious instead of taming it. That is a lesson Kundera learned from Kafka, and it is therefore fitting that he should begin the sixth narrative part by placing the ghost of young Kafka in the vacancy created beside Klement Gottwald by the airbrushing of Clementis. From that inaugural image, the contrapuntal action unfolds, deliberately intertwining dream and reality, mixing private meanings and public significance, matching imaginative vision with personal retrospect. Kundera's father lies dying in a hospital bed on a particular day in May. Simultaneously, at Hradčany Castle, Gustav Husák—"the president of forgetting"—is receiving the red kerchief of the Honorary Pioneer in a festive ritual that initiates the grown man into the organization of militant Communist children. And at the same moment of novelistic time, somewhere beyond the measurable borders of East and West, Tamina journeys to an island inhabited by children, where the pain of memory and desire is abolished in favor of the eternal instant of the senses.

The death of a much-loved father is presented from the perspective of the grieving son, who must remain alone on this side of Lethe, watching helplessly with wakeful eyes. It is left for Tamina to undertake the great crossing, in an adventure that carries her beyond the limits of her waking self. Afterward, she will die by drowning in a doomed attempt to swim back into living time. In explaining the connection between Tamina's dream voyage to the island and the story of his father's dying, Kundera has said that it is like the random meeting of an umbrella and a sewing machine on an operating table, a congruence of two incongruent realities that can only be grasped by a roused imagination.[26] The allusion to Lautréamont's definition of beauty-terror draws attention to the aura of cruelty emanating from both journeys into death. It is the cruelty of the ripping asunder of the body and its soul, which loans the body its unique significance during the brief vigil of consciousness that constitutes the sum of the human life on earth. For Tamina the severance precedes her physical death, taking the form of surrender to the children's communal sexuality, which turns her nakedness into something "drab, mute, dead" (p. 176).

In the third book of *De rerum natura,* Lucretius argues against the superstitious dread of death by expounding the Epicurean teaching about a mortal soul within a mortal body. Death is a nothing, Lucretius reasons, since we can know it neither while alive nor after we are dead. Kundera, working with the same Epicurean hypothesis, shows what dreams may come when imagination is sucked into the void created by reason around the reality of death. In the absence of a transcending vision, death spawns lower dreams. During the age of youthful lyricism, death may visit the mind clothed in the bluish veil of nonbeing, but in our maturity it confronts us with "the terrifying material being that is the corpse." In part 4, Kundera has invoked the image of *beauty-death* in the sound of "a golden ring falling into a silver basin" (p. 103). Tamina was still possessed of the music of memory then, and could hear love speak in the silence her husband's death had created around her, just as Albrecht van der Qualen, the dying youth of Thomas Mann's tale, could hear death in the form of a beautiful young woman stepping from a closed wardrobe and speaking to him in a strange room in an unknown city. Tamina's love-beyond-death motif sounds once more in the sixth movement, but only faintly, from a great distance. It is instantly overtaken by mockery, in the repetition of the Mann allusion: "Granted, the nonbeing of Mann's young hero was beautiful, but what happened to his body? Did they drag him by the legs over the threshold?" (p. 172).

And now Tamina, bereft of her golden ring, has entered the circle of dancing children on the island of forgetting. There is no silence in this enforced Eden, and no solitude either, only the constant, repeated pulsation of sex, which rocks the children's immature bodies to the beat of a loud rhythmic monotone that cannot sustain the articulation of human speech. "The idiocy of music," Kundera's father had pronounced suddenly, with painstaking slowness, just about a year before dying, when his illness made it difficult for him to put into words all that was in his mind. The novelist-son, interpreting the meaning of the musicologist-father's utterance, attaches a mini-essay about music to the death narrative. The sound of the children's island, we learn, reveals music in its primordial state, expressing "the simple sense of communion with life" by the repetition of the jubilant assertion "Here I am!" (p. 180). This music, void of thought, knows nothing of the ideological divide between East and West. Gustav Husák, "the president of forgetting," acknowledged its power when he wrote a letter to Karel Gott, the Czech pop musician and youth idol, begging him to return home from abroad, at the same time that his regime was driving out hundreds of writers, professors, and artists. "The president of forgetting and the idiot of music deserve one another," writes Kundera. "They are working for the same cause" (p. 181).

In contrast to the eternity of the primordial rhythmic shout, European music, whose history is wedded to human speech, is mortal. Kundera, meditating on the phenomenon in retrospect, says, "It took a monumental effort of heart and mind for music to rise up over this inherent idiocy, and it was this glorious vault arching over centuries of European history that died out at the peak of its flight like a rocket in a fireworks display" (p. 180). In this explosive image of a festive and sudden death, Kundera seems to suggest that like everything else that bears the Devil's mark of human individuation, the course undertaken by European music was predestined to imitate the formal design of tragedy, which traces a rigorous parabola of significance over our common darkness, making good the inevitable fall of its hero in one last flash of incandescence. Classical tragedy itself vaulted and arched over Athens for no more than a single century. But when Euripides brought the chorus on stage and thus redefined the meaning of tragic pity, or when in his time Schönberg invented a new musical vocabulary, they could easily assume that the history of the art they practiced would continue long after them. Kundera, on the other hand, speaks from the posthistorical perspective of a thinker who was once caught in, and then discarded, the most extravagant claims ever made by man about the possibility of cultural progress. Kundera now speaks like the grown son of a small nation that "in moments of clairvoyance . . . can glimpse its own death at close range" (p. 159). Now he can always hear "the lascivious voice of death urging us to make haste," piercing through the joyous "onward and upward" slogans of his youth (p. 179).

On the most obvious level of interpretation, the island of Tamina's dreaming recalls a Pioneer camp in the heyday of the Communist idyll, with its categorical innocence and its strict regimen of communal intimacy. Kundera himself provides the clue to such a reading: "Why is Tamina on a children's island? Why is that where I imagine her? I don't know. Maybe it's because on the day my father died the air was full of joyful songs sung by children's voices" (p. 173). The songs reaching the hospital bed wafted in from the castle, where President Husák was being made an Honorary Pioneer. The cruel incongruity of that stab of angelic joy in the midst of the pain of dying is the emotional nexus linking the autobiographical vignette to the nightmarish fantasy. With this narrative counterpoint, Kundera achieves that "seamless fusion of dream and reality" he so admires in Kafka's stories and novels.[27] The illusion of reality is as palpable in the dream as in the scene recorded from actual experience, and yet in both narratives, imagination soars above the real. We clearly sense that the island of orgasmic children gyrating to the sounds of electric guitars is also the image of Western Europe in its posthistorical phase, where the reigning idiot of music is worth a dozen Schönbergs because he can hold a mass audience spellbound and twelve-tone music cannot.

The fundamentally ambivalent symbolism of Tamina's dream refracts yet other meanings if tested against the entire context. The descent of an adult into the realm of children, whether enacted in a public ritual or experienced in the imaginative enclosure of a dream, can also be read as a parodistic mimesis of Annie Leclerc's feminist utopia, with its promise of a return to the lap of the earth, beyond the reach of the pain caused by memory or desire. Leclerc asks, "What do men, those fanatics of desire," who know nothing of birth, "what do they know of death apart from the horror and fascination of the dead body?"[28] Kundera acknowledges the thrust of Leclerc's questions by placing her sacred word of mystical delight face to face with his irreverent fable about laughter. Furthermore, he writes, "St. Theresa smiled through her agony, and St. Annie Leclerc (for that is the name of the author whose book I have been quoting) claims that death is an integral part of joy that only men are afraid of" (p. 57). But while opening up his text to the subversion of Leclerc's feminist interrogation, Kundera refuses to follow her into the comforting answer.

In the two death scenes contained in part 6, the act of dying is observed from a position firmly anchored on *this* side of Lethe. Even when the experience is told from within, as in Tamina's death, no emotional boon and no transcending vision are offered. Tamina's first crossing, on her way to the island, is easy once she yields to the seduction of lightness. But that passage is not yet her death, only a painless metaphor for it. "It *is* a fairy tale, it *is* a dream!" the narrator reminds us (p. 164). Real death, Kundera tells us from the bedside of his dying father, is hard work. "Death is terrible drudgery. It took my father several days of high fever to die, and from the way he was sweating I could see he was working hard. Death took all his concentration; it seemed almost beyond his powers. He couldn't even tell I was sitting at his bedside; he had no time to notice" (p. 172). Tamina's terminal *agon* comes when she tries to escape from the burden of angelic buoyancy by swimming back to the familiar shore where things have their own weight. Unlike the suicide swim she took in the immediate grief of her husband's loss, this is a return journey, motivated by "a great desire for life" (p. 189). Her disciplined effort is doomed to failure, just like her quest of memory before that, yet she pushes herself to the limit of her strength, until the sun begins to sink. The image of a lone woman struggling to maintain her direction on the darkened waters has a heroic quality that evokes the feel of the miniature epic in canto 26 of the *Inferno*. But unlike Dante's Ulysses, who does not fathom his true antagonist even as his boat crashes against the rock of Mount Purgatory, Tamina has the lucidity to size up her death at the point of reaching her limit. She sees a little boat carrying five children who peer down eagerly at her, and she knows that she has been carried back to the island shore. One last time her soul, which had kept a vigil over her body while it was still inhabited by memory, flickers with life in the desire to keep its charge from the children's hands: "All she could think of now was how she would die, and she wanted to die somewhere in the midst of the waters, removed from all contact, alone with the fish" (p. 190).

The act of dying, as Kundera shows it, is the most absurd of human adventures. It is an arduous journey that must be undertaken alone and in full knowledge of the predetermined end. "Man has an infinite desire to go off and hide his body. But the journey is in vain. When his ride is done, they find him in bed and bang his head on the threshold" (p. 173). This is Kundera's epic fable about dying. With its cavalier image of the desperate ride and its suggestion of an inverted treasure hunt, it tackles what Lucretius decreed to be the *unthinkable* reality of death in all its irreducible physicality. Tolstoy, whose mind seemed to turn androgynous in the nearness of death, summoned the imagery of parturition whenever he wanted to tame his horror of the corpse. Ivan Ilyich, in the last second of his excruciating ordeal, feels himself loosen all over as he breaks through the black sack into which he had resisted being pulled. The most reflective of Tolstoy's heroes, Prince Andrew Bolkonsky, is granted a mental rehearsal of his death in the act of giving birth to a new consciousness, one capable of translating his exit from life into the simple event of a door being opened. By contrast, Kundera's imagination, projected into the shadowy terror of death, is unalterably male and worldly, gracing the philosophical posture of a stoic endowed with comic courage.

At the borderline between life and death, father and son share a moment of laughter. "Hear that? What a joke! Husak is being named an Honorary Pioneer!" Kundera says to his father, thus undercutting with a single stroke of irony the cruel sentence—"His brain is decomposing"—that the doctor had pronounced over the helpless body lying in the bed. The understanding laughter that vaults over the great divide is charged with the same heroic tenor as Tamina's unequal swim strokes contesting the engulfing stream. The mutual gift of laughter is the last flourish of gallantry, a parting salvo for the desperate journey ahead, fired by a passionately grieving son-companion. "Several hours later his fever shot up again. He mounted his horse and rode it hard the next few days. He never saw me again" (p. 174). Tamina likewise experiences a loving farewell at the inception of her death adventure. Standing above the clay riverbank where the sports car takes her, she suddenly recognizes, in one quick stab of unrehearsed memory, a landscape from her past in Bohemia where she and her husband once walked together, "alone in the world" and full of "desperate concern for each other" (p. 166).

The expression of human tenderness at the line of death—the woman looking over her shoulder to see the beloved at her side one last time, or the son sharing a coded message with a dying father—moves us to an overarching pity. The effect brings to mind some of the great exit scenes in Euripides, after the gods have withdrawn from the stage, leaving the humans to suffer through the last of the *agon* by themselves. But Kundera's distinctly modern variation on the Euripidean situation presents us with the sight of *humans* imitating the immortals in their casual indifference. In Tamina's drowning scene, the five children in the boat observe her agony in close-up, but without lifting a hand to help her, and the doctor at Kundera's father's bedside speaks of him with professional detachment, as if he were already a corpse. These impenetrable witnesses add a Kafkan touch to the death scenes, stamping both the dream vision and the real life vignette with the cruel seal of this century. Yet in both narratives, the event of death blows open the book of laughter to allow us an unobstructed view of *lítost* in full epiphany, wearing the mask of tragedy.

Like all expressions of the religious spirit, tragic art strives for metaphysical healing. If Kundera's novel had stopped just after the high note reached in the sixth movement, the effect would have been truly tragic in this sense of the term. The emotion generated by the father's death casts a spell that binds together several strands of meaning. We mourn the public passing of the generation of the great fathers of modern Czech culture in the intimacy of the son's grief. On a more private level, it is possible to read the death scene as a ceremony of initiation that countermands the futuristic thrust of the phony ritual staged for Husák at Hradčany Castle.

As he is approaching his line of death, Kundera's father utters the words "Now I know!" (p. 161), in an attempt to tell his son that he has just discovered the secret significance of the variation form Beethoven created in his last sonatas. Much later, after his death, the writer-son understands the father's message.

> Let me try to explain it by means of an analogy. The symphony is a musical epic. We might compare it to a journey leading through the boundless reaches of the external world, on and on, farther and farther. Variations also constitute a journey, but not through the external world. . . . The journey of the variation form leads to that *second* infinity, the infinity of internal variety concealed in all things. (p. 164)

This insight into musical form, translated into Kundera's favorite literary metaphor of a journey-adventure, is the bridge that leads into the heart of the revelation signaled by the formula of self-definition: "This entire book is a novel in the form of variations" (p. 165). In this privileged moment, Kundera's creative act, becoming fully conscious of itself, rejoices at giving birth to a new novelistic form based on the art of variation. It is particularly apt that the discovery of an internal infinity within a finite theme should come to the European novel as a postmortem legacy from a small country in Central Europe, a region whose cultural genius consists in the cultivation of maximum diversity within minimum space.[29] As in the pivotal sixth canto of the *Aeneid*, where Aeneas meets his father Anchises in the underworld, in order to receive from him the initiation that cancels his identity as an exile, the vision of artistic renewal contained in Kundera's sixth movement has been reached by an arduous inner journey inspired by *pietas*.

But that is not where Kundera's novel ends. The action, shifting back into comic gear, is protracted long past Tamina's death. The final movement, played with a completely new cast of characters, strikes a note of callous indifference. Without transition, we have moved from the creation of intense meanings to their disintegration. Socrates, arguing soberly at the conclusion of a drinking party, had pressed the paradoxical idea that comedy and tragedy are kindred forms, rather like two faces of the same coin. And indeed, in the highest practice of the art, comic action often comes to the very edge of tragedy before proceeding to put all the things it has been busy unsettling back in their places. In *The Farewell Party,* Kundera gave an absurdist twist to the comedic exit scene by placing two sets of incongruously interlocking parents and children on a stage that had just shown the murder of a pregnant woman. In *The Book of Laughter and Forgetting,* the comedy of the last act unsettles our emotions by compelling us to watch the games played by brand-new characters in whom we have invested very little feeling. Yet all the emotional power of the novel is concentrated in this jarring contrast between the sixth and seventh movements. The best way to understand this is to consider a musical analogy Kundera draws in *The Art of the Novel,* where he praises the formal boldness of Chopin's Piano Sonata Opus 35 in b-flat minor, whose third movement is made up of the celebrated *marche funèbre:*

> What more is there to say after that great farewell? Finish the sonata in the usual way with a lively rondo? Not even Beethoven in his Sonata Opus 26 avoids the stereotype—he follows a funeral march (the third movement there too) with a cheerful finale. But the fourth movement in the Chopin sonata is altogether strange: *pianissimo,* fast and short, with no melody, absolutely unsentimental: a distant gust, a muffled sound

> that heralds the ultimate forgetting. The juxtaposition of these two movements (sentimental-unsentimental) makes you gasp. It is absolutely original. I mention it to show that to compose a novel is to set different emotional spaces side by side—and that, to me, is the writer's subtlest craft.[30]

Likewise, the final movement of Kundera's novel is subdued and lacking in emotional cohesion. It is nonmelodic, definitely not *cantabile* in its jagged phrasing, like a piece of modern music that resists being matched to human speech.

The main character in this section is Jan, the last of the novel's male experimental egos. He seems to be a Czech expatriate in the West, perhaps in France. We are told that he is on the verge of emigrating to the United States, and that he is living in "the perfect solidarity of perfect mutual misunderstanding" with his mistress Edwige (p. 227). In Edwige's world, where Jan figures as an exotic outsider, we recognize the lotus-eating Europe of the posthistorical phase. Its condition of being is reminiscent of the children's island, but it comes to us in images such as we might see on the TV screen or read about in the newspapers. Here is Papa Clevis with his brood of tamed progressives, mouthing ideas that are a happy blend of watered-down revolutionary futurism laced with mass acceptance. The talk on the beaches full of braless women is of the long-awaited end of the Judeo-Christian era. Liberated Amazonian women like Barbara have redefined the rules of the sexual game, so that the old male sport of chasing after female quarry will be no more. Instead, there is a notion going around of sex as an athletic performance, a team effort at best, or at worst a drill routine with the woman holding the whip.

Jan, though functioning adequately in this world, finds himself haunted by a recurrent anguish. It is a sense of having crossed "an intangible and immaterial border," beyond which everything loses its meaning. "Human life—and herein lies its secret—takes place in the immediate proximity of that border, even in direct contact with it; it is not miles away, but a fraction of an inch," he reflects (pp. 206–7). Jan's category of "the border" was already implicit in part 6, where it figured as the tragic *moira* of human mortality. The two death scenes we as readers have witnessed lend dramatic substance to Jan's meditation, even though he himself has not been privy to them. In Jan's situation of living "beyond the border," if death perchance should tangle with laughter, the result would be a loss of significance for both.

Passer, an old friend of Jan's, is dying of cancer. Still, his vitality is so great that even at "the border of life and death" (p. 215) he falls passionately in love with the beautiful actress Jeanne. During a visit to the sanatorium, Jan tries to paint the world gray for the sake of the condemned man, but Passer defiantly overrides his carping. Passer's funeral is described two chapters later. It is a discomfiting scene, as we watch the ceremony of death being wrecked by laughter. On a raw and muddy day, the coffin is slowly descending into the pit while the nervous eulogist flounders, his words vainly seeking the disappearing addressee. Suddenly, an intemperate gust of wind blows the hat from Papa Clevis's head, and bouncing lightly across the narrow space separating the mourners from the open grave, the frolicsome object ends up falling in. A silent but irresistible wave of laughter rolls over the assembly, drowning the parting gesture of the hapless orator and the sobbing of Passer's young son. The narrator suggests that "it was as though the indomitably vital and optimistic Passer had stuck his head out for one last look" (p. 221). But we suspect him of speaking tongue in cheek, because the effect created by this laughter issuing from the grave to attack the living has very little about it that is life-affirming. Indeed, this laughter dismantles the human meaning achieved in the other instant of laughter shared by father and son in the preceding movement. Passer, as we know him, cannot be the culprit, nor can the Devil of Kundera's fable, who invented the sound of mirth to articulate the quintessentially human point of view of irony. In this instance, nothing that humankind can muster is being articulated, nothing but that absolute incongruity between the reality of the living and the physical reality of death. Only the Olympian gods could have laughed like this from their distance, with such playful indifference to mortals caught up in their fate.

Clevis's truant hat repeats the motif of Clementis's intractable cap, but once again the terms of the situation are inverted. In the graveside scene playful chance, that latter-day Olympian, mocks the grief of memory in its fragile vigil, not the forces of organized forgetting. Moreover, the shadow of a tragic Hamlet leaping into Ophelia's grave, which hovers grotesquely over the incident, also constitutes an assault on Tamina's love-beyond-the-grave theme.

In the next chapter, we see Jan at Barbara's group sex party. The mistress of the revels monitors the collective exercise like a sergeant major at a drill, moving from couple to couple to quash any sign of the forbidden intimacy of communication. This lugubrious orgy is really a solemn collegium of *agélastes*. When Jan, sensing an explosion of laughter building inside him, shares a look of comic complicity with a balding young man, Barbara ejects him with the words "Don't think you can pull another Passer's funeral on me!" (p. 225). The mirth-in-funeral and dirge-in-marriage effect reveals a world out of joint, where even the Devil cannot find a fitting nook for his laughter.

Jan's private erotic life is also blighted by the specter of misplaced laughter, which threatens to reduce the gestures of physical love to a mere sequence of ridiculous motions. Whenever he makes love to a woman, "laughter was like an enormous trap waiting patiently in the room with them, but hidden behind a thin wall. There was only a fraction of an inch separating intercourse from laughter, and he was terrified of overstepping it; there was only a fraction of an inch separating him from the border, and across the border things no longer had any meaning" (pp. 213–14). Jan, like the sexual adventurer of Kundera's early tale "The Golden Apple of Eternal Desire," is a fanatic of desire rather than an enjoyer of its consummation. But now he senses the nearness of his erotic limit, as if he were Dr. Havel after twenty years of collecting women. Being of a philosophical temper, Jan asks himself if it is the world around him that has changed so radically, or if he is just growing old at the erotic game. "Every time something is repeated, it loses a part of its meaning. . . . For Jan, therefore, the border is the greatest possible degree of admissible repetition" (p. 216). But the ironic narrator at his back is quick to remind Jan that repetition alone is not the cause of his sexual *acedia*. Even as a boy of thirteen, poised at the starting line of his erotic course, Jan had already registered the incongruity between his limitless desire for woman's body and the limited field of possibilities that body offers, circumscribed by the triangle of breasts and genitalia. In that precocious flash of awareness, Jan had discovered the law of sexual incompatibility between the soul's demand and the body' ability to deliver, which governs the tragicomic adventure of Kundera's Don Juan. Since the imaginative reverberation occasioned by the instant of arousal exceeds the intensity of the most complete orgasm, the mind tends to register a deficiency in every act of sexual consummation. Consequently, it is arousal, not the pleasure of fulfillment, that appears to be the prime erotic category for Kundera's male figures.

Dr. Havel, the terminal Don Juan coopted by Death, ultimately acknowledges that he has been a collector of words rather than women. But Jan, in his present state, is not even that. His personal Don Juan's list consists of the cherished names of women who have eluded his grasp altogether. Some of them fall into the class of Lucie—"the goddess of escape"—but lately he has begun to notice the growing number of women who stand "*on the other side of the border*" (p. 207) from him and from his desire. In some of his recent encounters, he has been playing the role of the impossible Don Juan meeting the impossible woman-object. That new breed of woman stares down the man's erotic will, when he pins her with his glance, by simply refusing to undergo the cosmic motion "up from object to being" and "down from being to object" (p. 209), which used to be the essence of her erotic thrill in the old world Jan has lost. The consciousness of being rhythmically in command of that up-and-down motion of a woman's psychic being is what makes it possible to transform the impersonal phallic oscillation into the illusion of an individual erotic event, thereby creating an artful *pas de deux* on the basis of the ancient mating dance.

Jan's mistress Edwige is happily installed in the new world, where the sexist fashions and disguises of the superannuated Don Juan, his cape and his sword, are laughably out of place. To his surprise, Jan finds out one day that for Edwige physical love is a token of convenience, a pure sign, easily convertible into more weighty meanings, such as comradely harmony, good health, or psychic normalcy. Whenever they make love, Edwige's face remains a blank screen, registering nothing. And even Jan loses his power of speech when their two bodies intertwine in perfect contentment.

The novel's last scene places the blissfully mismatched couple on a nudist beach that seems to be somewhere in northern France.[31] For Edwige, nudity represents an ideological statement announcing her release from the oppression of social conventions. Jan, looking at the dismal parade of unveiled human bodies of all ages, is seized by an aggravated attack of his border anguish. He reflects that "the Jews had filed into Hitler's gas chambers naked and en masse." This nightmarish thought prompts him to coin a new definition of nudity, to match the fashion of the age of terminal paradoxes: "Nudity is the uniform of the other side. . . . nudity is a shroud" (p. 226).

The verbal exchange between Jan and Edwige on the beach

assumes the form of an absurdist dialogue between two clowns. He plays the knowing fool to her unknowingly foolish straight woman, secretly but deftly inverting each voiced statement into its opposite inside the registering chamber of his mind. As they walk hand in hand in the sand, they suddenly hear the bleating of a ram, which blends into the roaring of the sea. That pastoral moment moves Jan with an echo of the ancient idyll about Daphnis, the Sicilian shepherd Aphrodite condemned to die of unrequited desire for Chloe, the green one, whose name recalls Demeter, goddess of young, sun-ripe crops. Seized by the nostalgia of origins, yearning for his lost power of desire, Jan says aloud, "Daphnis!" In a typical misreading of his meaning, Edwige decodes the word to suit her own mind's need for authorized innocence and renames the arbitrary place of nakedness where they find themselves—half-Eden and half-concentration camp—"Daphnis Island."

Edwige introduces Jan to a group of naked people on the beach, and "a man with an extraordinary paunch" begins lecturing the small circle of living dead about the impending demise of Judeo-Christian culture. His enthusiastic oratory, which has the effect of transforming the beach into the enclosed space of a university auditorium, is cut off abruptly by the novelist. In the absence of sound, the recording lens focuses sharply on the exposed genitals of the listeners, "their naked genitals staring dully, sadly, listlessly at the yellow sand" (p. 228). On the other side of the coastline from those mute human bodies, one senses the cruel expectancy of the graying ocean from whose foam no Aphrodite will ever rise again, a great waste of waters unstirred by either memory or desire.

6

The Unbearable Lightness of Being

OR

Epicurus Contemplates Tragedy

A man stands at the window of his flat looking across the courtyard at the opposite walls, not knowing what to do. As he emerges into clear view, we begin to lose track of the speculative voice that has summoned him into being. For some time, the voice has been speaking in the shadows, interrogating old myths while drawing closer. Now its meditative drift will flow through the man's mind, issuing into a narrative channel. The man is really all alone. But we sense that in its passing, the disappearing voice has swept open an imaginary hole at his back. In that empty space atoms fall endlessly, colliding and separating over and over again, always aslant and always downward.

The figure at the window is Tomas, the lead character in a group of four around whom Kundera builds his fifth novel, *The Unbearable Lightness of Being.*[1] He comes alive, fully formed, in the third chapter, out of the author's reflections on Nietzsche's myth of eternal return. "I have been thinking about Tomas for many years. But only in light of these reflections did I see him clearly," says the narrator (p. 6), in an aside that makes it plain that all the speculations in the two preceding chapters should be interpreted within Tomas's "magnetic field," as an approach to the "existential code" of his self.[2]

Tomas is a surgeon who experiences his profession as a mental imperative to explore the outermost limit of the human body, where its mechanism makes contact with something of a different order of being.[3] He is used to guiding his scalpel so as to cut into live human matter decisively, with precise, even strokes. Tomas's dilemma, as he stands at the window contemplating his own indecision, is that of a committed rationalist caught in a situation where reason is inoperative. Scientific rationality, after all, assumes the repeatability of the phenomena it seeks to hold in its grasp, whereas the experience that puzzles Tomas is escaping him into a stream whose flow is irreversible. We can never know what to do next, he reflects, because there is no valid basis for comparing the event we are in with those that came before. Moreover, the effects of our decisions never seem to match their intent. We grow older in our inexperience, playthings of a time whose "royal power" is that of "a child moving counters in a game."[4] If we cannot make sense of our ephemeral becoming, we might just as well not be at all. "*Einmal ist keinmal,*" says Tomas to himself (p. 8).

Tomas's perplexity at the window of his flat in Prague occurs three weeks after his meeting with Tereza, a young woman for whom he has begun to feel an inexplicable love. But this private moment, like everything that happens in Kundera's novels, also belongs to the flow of European history. Tomas's sense of a devalued time locates him at the tail end of the

Modern Era, long after the organic link between the living moment and the *arche* of divine creation was severed, but still proximate to the recent collapse of the secular teleology of Communism. Tomas's turn of mind inclines him to be skeptical of all symbolic systems of order, even while hankering after intelligibility. His thinking proceeds by negation, in a constant oscillation between the old question and a new doubt.

This pendulum swing of a mind moving through various hypotheses, from *interrogatio* to *dubitatio* and back again, had been at work in the opening meditation on the idea of eternal return. Tomas, we recall, owes his existence in the novel to that mental motion. The question raised by the disembodied voice is defined in Tomas's terms: "To think that everything recurs as we once experienced it, and that the recurrence itself recurs ad infinitum: What does this mad myth signify?" (p. 3).

Nietzsche himself presented his idea of eternal recurrence[5] as a "prophecy" linked to the "scientific" hypothesis of a mechanistic universe without beginning or end, apparently derived from the cosmological speculations of the pre-Socratics. This strange doctrine, whereby he welded his ecstatic affirmation of the power of the individual human will to the image of a self-generating cosmic dynamo, carried enormous consequence for Nietzsche. Kundera, noting its "mysterious" nature, points out that the myth "has often perplexed other philosophers" (p. 3). From everything Nietzsche has written on the subject, it emerges that for him its import was existential rather than theoretical. He wielded it as a functional myth out of whose imaginative matrix he hoped to bring forth an invigorating new discipline of mind and spirit. It was to be his "great cultivating idea"[6] for breeding fresh *virtù* in the tired blood of Europe. He staked his all on this passionate dream of health as his own life steadily progressed into mental darkness. Philosophically, Nietzsche was reacting to the culture of European nihilism, whose paralysis he diagnosed as stemming from the oppressive sense of a linear time that had gone dead once the Judeo-Christian idea finally retreated from it. The thought of duration without meaning or aim is a crushing burden for human consciousness. Unlike many of his contemporaries, Nietzsche did not look for relief in a secular substitute for a collapsed divine *telos.* Intent on creating being out of the transitory moment, he willed himself to think the burdensome thought of meaningless becoming in its most aggravated form. "Let us think this thought in its most terrible form: existence as it is, without meaning or aim, yet recurring inevitably without any finale of nothingness: '*the eternal return.*' "[7]

Taken by itself, as pure speculation, the myth remains opaque, like a mystery that eludes analysis. It becomes more tractable if approached as a metaphysical wager of sorts and a testing ground for the fierce individual spirit bound up with the mind that conceived it. Nietzsche, as we well know, was obsessed with the desire to overcome the merely human, a condition of being he experienced as pitiable weakness. The idea of eternal duration without meaning or aim and without reprieve was the weightiest challenge a nonhuman will could have thrown at his own humanity, and he bet everything he had to counter it. To take on the hypothesis of the eternal return was to be like Homer's Achilles in the act of lifting up the huge and splendid shield Hephaistos had forged for him, an immortal gift for the brief keeping of a man made for death. Now we can see Nietzsche's flaring eyes meeting the enormous pulsating image of the natural world, ringed all around by the endless flow of the Ocean River, and now he reads the scenes the divine artist has fashioned on the shield's surface. He has taken in the rhythm of our constant, restless passing to and fro, between marriage festivals and the sacking of cities, the vital pulse that holds us all to a common measure, men and beasts. And in the immanence of Nietzsche's transient self, a slumbering Achillean flame reawakens, a will rising up to a supreme lightness of being in its assent to the cosmic flow. Out of that instant of ecstatic identification was born the dark brilliance of the modern Dionysos, the transformational man-god whose image gradually came to dominate Nietzsche's imagination. In his last scribblings, the name Dionysos is often contrasted with "the Crucified." In that disqualifying noun, formed of the passive mode of the fateful verb, Nietzsche pins down his conception of the failed Christ forever caught in his derisive agony, no more a savior and not even a tragic hero, just a victim.

Imagine Nietzsche standing in the rarefied air of the Engadine Valley high in the Swiss Alps, where the thought of eternal recurrence first struck him,[8] and then flip back (or forward) to Tomas at the window of his flat in Prague. Kundera too treats the myth of eternal return as a metaphysical game plan to be tested in the crucible of individual human experience. Tomas's will is paralyzed because he understands, just as Nietzsche did before him, that he is being fooled by "duration in vain" and yet "lacks the power not to be fooled."[9] But the posture in which Kundera has frozen Tomas, at the window facing blank walls across an empty courtyard, offers an image of radical disassociation from being, the detachment of a fundamentally skeptical mind, pulling downward. This stasis is the polar opposite of Nietzsche's Dionysos about to enter the cosmic dance. Tomas's formula of negation, "*Einmal ist keinmal,*" expresses a mind that does not seem up to playing the royal game of time on an equal footing with the dizzy child who is its master, the one throwing the dice. If Tomas were to entertain a model of the cosmic "monster of energy,"[10] it would most likely be derived from Epicurus rather than coming straight out of the speculations of the pre-Socratics. The imaginary atoms I sense in the void at Tomas's back are falling, not rotating as they did for Democritus, who passed the circular motion on to Nietzsche.

However it may be construed, the cosmic scenario does not fall within Tomas's field of vision. Nor was it the prime focus for Epicurus, who adopted a modified version of the Democritean atomistic theory to create a mechanical backdrop of utter randomness for his meditation on man, conceived as an absolutely finite but composite creature with a mortal soul inside a mortal body. Democritus, who formulated the first cogent materialistic system in European philosophy, was an idealist by temper—matter was a grand idea to him.[11] For Epicurus, living in the mellow late afternoon of the Attic day in the sun—after the tragic masks and even Socrates had left the stage—matter was something much more intimate that he could touch and feel. Because he thought *through* his senses rather than *against* them, Epicurus taught that "we are born once and cannot be born twice, but for all time must be no more."[12] His mind, having disciplined the terror of the infinite in beholding the atomistic routine, being satisfied that no malignant deity was at work there, found itself at rest in contemplating human existence from the perspective of the finale of nothingness. That same perspective informs and livens Kundera's voice at Tomas's back, prompting this reader to invoke the gentle ghost of Epicurus as she moves through the pages of this mysterious novel.

Tomas's use of the German adage "*Einmal ist keinmal*" is his way of repeating the Epicurean teaching of human finality, but without heeding the lesson of serenity the old master had hidden there. His German formula harbors a double negation that feeds on itself, by leaping from an initial denial of cosmic repetition to an assertion about the meaninglessness of experiential human time.

Considered within the magnetic field of Tomas's mind, Nietzsche's myth is indeed a madman's dream, intelligible only in terms of what it appears to say *per negationem*. "Putting it negatively," argues the narrative voice in the first chapter, "the myth of eternal return states that a life which disappears once and for all, which does not return, is like a shadow, without weight, dead in advance, and whether it was horrible, beautiful, or sublime, its horror, sublimity, and beauty mean nothing" (p. 3). In other words, we should construe Nietzsche's metaphysical weight lifting as nothing more than an extravagant, cunning way of restating the proposition it was meant to overcome—that the human moment is irremediably doomed to nothingness. If that is so, then we were merely fooled in going along with Nietzsche's pathos, crediting with meaning a mental transaction that is really empty. In such an unmaking of our former reading, the modern Dionysos fares no better than the Crucified, whom he desired to supersede. All myths are mortal, after all, just like the men and women who invest their spirit in them. Kundera's meditation, filtered through Tomas's perplexity at the window, has nailed Nietzsche's Dionysos to the same cross of eternal futility as the Christ. "If every second of our lives recurs an infinite number of times, we are nailed to eternity as Jesus Christ was nailed to the cross," says the skeptical voice as it opens the second chapter. The added comment, "It is a terrifying prospect," casts the vision of the Engadine summits from the crest of its lightness back down into the unbearable heaviness of European nihilism. The notion of lightness receives consideration next, but only as an aesthetic effect of contrast to a discredited speculation. "If eternal return is the heaviest of burdens, then our lives can stand out against it in all their splendid lightness" (p. 5).

From this vantage point, the interrogation proceeds to examine the opposing values of heaviness and lightness brought forward in the assessment of Nietzsche's myth. The intellectual game is complicated by the introduction of Parmenides, a pre-Socratic philosopher whom classical tradition portrays with a smiling face, in contrast to the weeping Heraclitus: "[Parmenides] saw the world divided into pairs of opposites: light/darkness, fineness/coarseness, warmth/cold, being/nonbeing. One half of the opposition he called positive (light, fineness, warmth, being), the other negative" (p. 5). These antinomies prove elusive to the voice that reflects on them in the shadow cast by Tomas's existential stance. The categories of weight and lightness, in particular, keep exchanging qualities in a mutual process of conversion in which we recognize the perverse signature of the age of terminal paradoxes. It may be helpful to remember that *Parmenides* is the title of a mystifying Platonic dialogue in which Socrates finds himself acquiescing to notions that contradict his own established views. Long a riddle to scholars, this text is sometimes taken as an illustration of the pitfalls of purely metaphysical speculation. Rosalie Colie writes, "At its plainest, though, the *Parmenides* is clearly a demonstration of the axiom that paradox necessarily attends upon those men brave enough to travel to the limits of discourse."[13]

That same paradoxicality attends the restless meditation Kundera deploys in the shadows behind the standing Tomas. Here, Nietzsche's lightness collapses into the heaviness of eternal suffering without issue, and it is equally possible to reverse that process, changing the heavy back into the light, with equally damning results. On an earlier swing of the mental pendulum Kundera confronted the image of a wraithlike Hitler, whose enormous crimes became light as a feather when contemplated through the mitigating perspective of their transitoriness. The whorish forward motion of time that lets Hitler fade into a nostalgic haze of nonbeing is a scandal to the human mind, no less difficult to bear than the opposite scenario, which has Christ/Sisyphus eternally trapped inside an agony without redemption or release.

If Tomas's "*Einmal ist keinmal*" holds true, then the horror of history signifies nothing. "We need take no more note of it than of a war between two African kingdoms in the fourteenth century, a war that altered nothing in the destiny of the world, even if a hundred thousand blacks perished in excruciating torment" (p. 3). Hegel posited the category of "evil eternity," into which he could sweep vast chunks of human becoming—

indeed, whole societies whose life was characterized by the repeatability of events that had no impact on the progress of his Spirit of History in its march from East to West. Those forgettable events may or may not have been as bloody as the example chosen by Kundera—in any case, the thrust of Hegel's vision was to move above and beyond such horrors. Kundera cites the useless African war not to disparage that continent but to show that the crushing nightmare of evil eternity is matched, at the opposite extreme, by the unbearable lightness of malignant nothingness.

"Which one is positive, weight or lightness?" the narrator asks (p. 5), pondering the wondrous simplicity of Parmenides' vision, which led him to declare forthrightly that the *light* (i.e., the warm, the full, as of *being*) was positive, while the *heavy* (i.e., the cold, the dark, the empty, as of *nonbeing*) was negative. But here again, as with Nietzsche, Kundera gives us only the shadow of the Parmenidean world picture as it appears on the screen of Tomas's mind. Parmenides himself expounded his ontological system in a poem that begins with the poet's chariot ride to the Goddess who will make him see the truth of Being side by side with the deceptive beliefs of men. Divided into two distinct parts, the poem reflects the twofold nature of that revelation. The scheme of polar opposites Kundera invokes is lifted from the second part, where the deceptiveness of nonphilosophical thinking is exposed. Duality, for Parmenides, is an illusion embedded in our sense-based language. This defect can be corrected by the mind, since Parmenides holds that "thought is not different from Being; for it is only thought of Being."[14]

It is this triumphant monism that Nietzsche sought to reclaim by his metaphysical wager. For Parmenides, the *logos* of identity (*logos-ontos*) was a given, an inherent capacity of human thought. Nietzsche could only grasp it in the passion of his agonistic will, signified by his tragic *amor fati,* wherein the transient self merges with the permanence of being in a consummation of consciousness registered as pure immanence.

The Dionysiac experience, as Euripides shows in *The Bacchae,* is light to those who embrace it willingly and heavy to the resisting mind. Tomas, at his window, is a very reluctant lifter of metaphysical weights. When he says to himself, "*Einmal ist keinmal,*" he is not thinking of History or the nature of being, but of his love for Tereza. His hesitation to enter the stream of time defined by the red markers of love's signifiers reveals a fundamental dissociation between mind and will. He experiences the pull of Tereza's love as the pull of gravity, but the lightness he senses at his core when he tries to empty it of Tereza's presence comes to him as a depressing absence of beauty. Epicurus' exhortation, which stems from the thought of human finality ("for all time we must be no more"), applies to Tomas's situation: "But you, who are not masters of to-morrow, postpone your happiness; life is wasted in procrastination and each of us dies without allowing himself leisure."[15] In denying the possibility of eternal return,[16] Tomas appears to be in fundamental agreement with Epicurus' insistence on the grand finale of nothingness. But the content of his regret, when he contemplates the prospect of life without Tereza, addresses the loss of a magnitude of beauty rather than the waste of an opportunity for happiness.

Tereza, who enters Tomas's flat with *Anna Karenina* under her arm, and a heavy suitcase soon to follow, is a young woman of no particular outward distinction. Tomas had met her in a provincial town at the hotel restaurant where she was waitressing. The details given here of their first meeting are sparse and insignificant. They shared an hour together, and then she walked him to the railway station, staying until he boarded his train. Ten days later, responding to his casually dropped invitation, she appeared at his door in Prague. They made love almost instantly, and that night she came down with the flu, which kept her in Tomas's bed for a week.

Before Tereza, Tomas was an unencumbered man. Having long ago divorced his wife after two miserable years of marriage, he had refused to see the son she bore him, an act that estranged him from his disapproving parents. Once created, these external conditions of his freedom had become a must for him, providing the roomy privacy he needed to cultivate the intense variety of his erotic life. Tomas's libertinism had been a product of his reason as well as his instinct. Above all, it represented his calculated defense against the "aggression of love." He had even devised a "rule of threes" to discipline himself and his partners: "Either you see a woman three times in quick succession and then never again, or you maintain relations over the years but make sure that the rendezvous are at least three weeks apart" (p. 12).

Tereza, with her unexpected fever, violates Tomas's system by remaining with him for a whole week. "He smelled the delicate aroma of her fever and breathed it in, as if trying to glut himself with the intimacy of her body" (p. 7). The fever, which communicates itself to Tomas's imagination with the emotional force of the Tolstoyan "infection,"[17] is of course a metaphor for the conflagration caused by love.[18] Tereza's metaphoric fever pulls Tomas toward her like a magnetic force. His gestures of kneeling at her bedside while she sleeps and pressing his face into the pillow beside her head are those of a man wholly subdued by love, recalling Vronsky when he first dances with Anna in Moscow and his face, Kitty realizes, has "an expression which she had never seen before," of "submission and fear."[19]

"But was it love?" Tomas asks himself. His skeptical mind, resisting an imagination inflamed by beauty, seeks to undermine his new feeling with the suspicion that it might be a "little comedy" (p. 7) of simulation, staged by hysteria. And indeed, Tomas cuts a faintly comic figure as a lover with a paralyzed will, unable to decide whether to accept Tereza's offering of her life for his keeping. Buridan's ass, that model of scholastic abstraction, was immobilized between two equal appetites; Tomas is suspended between two qualitatively different options, two avenues of experience, each entailing the irretrievable loss of the other. Tereza's gift of love with its intense beauty, or his erotic disponibility with its adventure: the choice between heaviness and lightness appears to Tomas as an absolute either/or.

Yet was it really by his own choice that he took Tereza into his life, and was he moved to do so by love? "A single metaphor can give birth to love," observes the narrator (p. 11). As Tomas's mind oscillates from pole to pole, a mysterious image keeps surging to the surface of his consciousness whenever it touches on Tereza and their first week together: "She seemed a child to him, a child someone had put in a bulrush basket daubed with pitch and sent downstream for Tomas to fetch at the riverbank of his bed" (p. 6). This is the image of Moses' beginning, lifted out of the epic tale of Exodus,[20] which contains the Hebrew revelation of a new time made meaningful by the opening of the human to the divine. In the Hebrew messianic conception of history, which Christianity adopted,[21] the flow of human becoming is studded with moments of eternal significance that consecrate it by disclosing the situation of man in relation to God.

Reflecting on the image of Moses' predestination, which serves as the leitmotif of his love for Tereza, Tomas dwells on the gesture of intimate tenderness that launches the epic journey to the Promised Land. Later the narrator notes Tomas's attraction to the story of the infant Oedipus, the future tragic hero, who was also a child saved from death, taken in and nurtured by King Polybus of Corinth. In both stories the absolute helplessness of the child is a prelude to heroic action, and in both it is human co-feeling (in Czech, *soucit*) that throws open the ivory gates of our higher dreaming, that Moses and Oedipus may issue forth as something larger and more beautiful than what is known to us as the merely human.

Tomas's perplexity about the nature of his attraction to Tereza is not entirely groundless, for her metaphoric power over his imagination does not really stem from erotic love. Though their gestures may be similar, Tomas is very different from Vronsky, whose face reflects like a mirror the light emanating from Anna's eyes and the smile of pleasure that curves her lips as they dance together. Vronsky's fascination is a response to a luring, elemental force of sexuality, quite beyond Anna's control, in which a sharp edge of cruelty can be sensed. When Tomas lays his head on the pillow next to Tereza and imagines her dying, with a pang of grief that makes the thought of surviving her unbearable, the force that inclines him toward her sleeping, fragile figure is *soucit*. That commanding feeling of her vulnerability proves stronger than his reason.

Kundera's mini-essay on *soucit* occupies the ninth chapter of the first part, interrupting the narrative just at the point when Tomas, after two years of trying to balance his life between Tereza's love and his erotic system, is about to lurch into marriage. The phenomenological analysis of the notion of *soucit* begins with the etymology of the word. This time, Kundera's Czech is assisted by other European languages, which was not the case with his analysis of *lítost* in *The Book of Laughter and Forgetting*. The word *soucit* is derived from the noun that means "feeling" (*cit*) and the prefix "with" (*sou*), just like the Polish equivalent *współ-czucie*, the German *Mitgefühl*, the Swedish *med-känsla*. The etymology illumines the reach of an emotion that is free of the distancing admixture of "pity," which is embedded in the English word "compassion," and in all the other Romance derivatives of the Latin word for "suffering" (*passio*). Co-feeling is more expansive and generous than co-suffering, since it opens to the entire range of human emotions while remaining free of the contamination of duplicity that emanates from pity. "To love someone out of compassion means not really to love," says the narrator, speaking from within the magnetic field of Tomas's feeling for Tereza. Pity dwells below the high ground occupied by *soucit,* in that ambiguous undergrowth where *lítost* consorts with comic Eros. *Soucit,* which "signifies the maximal capacity of affective imagination," is defined as the supreme summit of the "hierarchy of sentiments" (p. 20).

In that extreme imaginative stretch and vault to the heights, Kundera's *soucit* evokes the coiling intensity of tragedy about to spring into action. It is *soucit* that provides the tragic momentum of Tomas's love for Tereza, and the initial gesture of consecration, which predestines all its future course, is inspired by a passion of tenderness rather than desire. Tomas's surrender to the emotional pull of Tereza is a Dionysiac experience as the young Nietzsche defined it when he wrote about the origin of tragedy. It effectively induces the collapse of the principle of individuation, so tenaciously guarded by Tomas's *ratio.* But unlike the assent to the cosmic will to power of the Engadine ecstasy, or for that matter, Vronsky's passion for Anna, which also involves an opening to the elementally nonhuman, Tomas's love-*soucit* is altogether and exclusively human. Tereza, whose feelings compel Tomas's will to shatter the form of his life, is a transient being whose power over his imagination stems from the absolute individuation of her mortal self.

Aristotle, whose model of tragedy is based on Sophoclean practice, maintains that the pathos on the stage must be distanced from the spectator in order to achieve the desired effect of catharsis. Kundera's sense of the tragic process is much more intimate. Writing long after Euripides, he can take for granted the elimination of the mediating chorus, and he can also dispense with the gods. Above all, his variation on tragedy cancels the collective spectator, since he is working in the novel form, whose affective power resonates in the meditative solitude of an individual mind rather than spending itself orgiastically in the instant communal response of the *theatron*. *The Unbearable Lightness of Being*, coming in the wake of the book of laughter, shows Kundera experimenting with the tragic mode of feeling and representation as a possibility of the novel in the age of terminal paradoxes.

Tragedy, both in its archetypal mythic form and in its modern illusionistic variety, speaks through the pages of Kundera's text in numerous intricate allusions to *Oedipus the King* and *Anna Karenina*. The tragic analogue controls the line of action that centers on Tomas and Tereza. These lovers, however, share the novel with two other major characters, Sabina and Franz, who remain at a distance from the lovers' tragic enclave but appear to us suffused by its aura, somewhat like Levin and Kitty in Tolstoy's novel, bathed in the afterglow of Anna and Vronsky's conflagration. Tomas is not quite a tragic hero but rather represents the tragic possibility of human existence as an option for his time.[22]

The four leading characters perform their parts in concert, like instruments in a musical quartet, each playing his or her existential code in strict relation to those of the others, often spatially separated but never imaginatively isolated in the reader's mind. Kundera's novelistic counterpoint is heard very distinctly in part 3 ("Words Misunderstood"), and even more aggressively in part 6 ("The Grand March"). Both these movements belong jointly to the antiphonal characters Sabina and Franz, developing their contradictory lines of action in the physical absence of Tomas and Tereza.

In the first movement, Tomas introduces the primary theme of lightness and weight with his motif of "*Einmal ist keinmal*," which is the initial formula of his existential code. By the end of the movement, his code of lightness has been converted into its opposite, signified by the "*Es muss sein*" motif from Beethoven's last quartet (Opus 135 in F Major), which speaks of the gravity of irresistible fate. The transformational nature of

Tomas's theme (theme A) is picked up in the novel's paradoxical title, *The Unbearable Lightness of Being*, which places the text under the composite sign of his existential dilemma, locking the two categories of lightness and weight in mysterious interpenetration. Theme B (Soul and body) belongs to Tereza. It emerges in the second movement, both as its title and in its development. Each of the two thematic titles is repeated twice within the sequence of the first five movements, thus creating a rhyme scheme based on repetition and reversal of order—part 1: theme A (Tomas); part 2: theme B (Tereza); part 3: "Words Misunderstood" (Sabina and Franz); part 4: theme B (Tereza); part 5: theme A (Tomas). This ring composition reflects a rhythmic heightening of the lovers' time within the enveloping closure of the tragic circle.

The Unbearable Lightness of Being, which works with a significantly reduced cast of characters, is marked by condensation and ellipsis. *The Book of Laughter and Forgetting* surrounds Tamina with a cast of minor players that keeps changing and multiplying, creating the illusion of an expansive form. That novel is built along the central axis of an inner journey, and for all its pathos, it retains something of the vital exuberance of a comic epic. Here, the central line of action describes a return rather than a progression. The lovers' time, which bends back on itself, flows rhythmically, like the time of Sophoclean tragedy. It can be argued that the entire novel, not just the parts devoted to Tomas and Tereza, is based on the two large themes they exemplify,[23] although these may fragment and recombine in a variety of new motifs when the action plays within the magnetic fields of Franz and Sabina.

When we left Tomas, he had long ago taken in the mysterious bulrush basket he found at the riverbank of his bed, but he is still pondering the irrationality of his act. To paraphrase Kundera's comment on Anna Karenina's suicide,[24] it is not Tomas who takes the decision but the decision that takes Tomas. Yet for all its impulsiveness, the *eventum* is pregnant with the meaning of Tomas's entire future with Tereza, just as Anna's leap under the moving train is an act that contains, in its tragic foreshortening, the full force of the gravitational pull into nonbeing she has followed throughout her affair with Vronsky. The seeing mind of Tolstoy knew the ending of his novel at its imaginative inception, when he viewed the crushed body of Anna Stepanovna Pirogova at the Yasenki station of the Moscow-Kursk railway in 1872.[25]

At the beginning of his relationship with Tereza, Tomas tries to achieve a formal balance between his commitment to her and his compulsive womanizing. But after two years of compromising with love, he marries Tereza and presents her with a puppy. The dog is a female of mixed breed, born of a German shepherd and a Saint Bernard bitch. Her identity problem is compounded by the male name Tomas gives her—Karenin—in spite of Tereza's objection that it may affect her sexuality. "It is entirely possible . . . that a female dog addressed continually by a male name will develop lesbian tendencies," he states mock-seriously (p. 24), as if to make light of the portentous allusion contained in the name.

The dog has a "funny face," like his namesake, who plays the comic part of cuckold in *Anna Karenina*. But the humiliated, vindictive husband reveals himself capable of a stunning transformation within the role to which the novel has consigned him. In an extraordinary moment of sincere tenderness and generosity, he suddenly vaults above the lovers emotionally, in the scene of Anna's near-death during childbirth. The dog Karenin, whose transformational power has yet to be revealed, enters Kundera's novel as an offering and emblem of love-*soucit*. It is the epiphany of that metasexual emotion that brings Anna and Karenin together for the space of the moment. But Karenin, by persisting in calling the event his "joy of forgiving," exposes himself to the intrusion of the zealous Countess Lydia, who is the personification of Kundera's category of kitsch transposed to the moral and emotional realm of Tolstoy's novel.

The human/inhuman dichotomy that plagues Tolstoy's Karenin[26] is also evident in Tomas's relation to Tereza. He seems doomed to inflict pain on her, only to soothe its impact with his inexhaustible tenderness. The other pole of Tomas's life, his libertinage, cannot remain hidden from Tereza for long. She suffers from a perpetual, tormenting jealousy that centers primarily on Tomas's longtime mistress and companion, the gifted painter Sabina. But Sabina, whose nature is fundamentally more libertine than Tomas's, recognizes his ambivalence. One day she catches him looking at his watch while making love to her, for which she punishes him by hiding one of his socks. Tomas is forced to return home with a net stocking of Sabina's on his foot. Thus appareled, he is the very image of the laughable fool of love.

As a painter, Sabina often uses the technique of "double exposure," which she defines by the formula "On the surface, an intelligible lie; underneath, the unintelligible truth" (p. 63). The technique was an accidental discovery, revealed to her one day in art school while she was playing with an imaginary crack that a trickle of red paint had suddenly opened in a canvas already filled with the compulsory socialist realist image of a steel factory under construction.[27] Sabina, the highly intellectual artist, who sees with the power of two, in mutual contradiction, describes Tomas as the embodiment of her aesthetic paradigm: "The meeting of two worlds. A double exposure. Showing through the outline of Tomas the libertine, incredibly, the face of a romantic lover. Or, the other way, through a Tristan, always thinking of his Tereza, I see the beautiful, betrayed world of the libertine" (p. 22). This brilliant definition reveals a Tomas conditioned by Sabina's own mentality. What she says is only provisionally true of him. In pursuing Tereza, Tomas will ultimately disappear from Sabina's field of vision altogether.

Tomas, the false libertine, inhabits his beloved's dreams as a figure of ruthless cruelty, whose recurrent image is that of a coldly willful executioner. The most terrifying of Tereza's repeated nightmares is one where she sees Tomas, his face shaded by a broad-brimmed hat, acting the part of macabre master of a drill in which she is ordered to march naked around a pool, doing kneebends, along with other naked women. The pool is full of the corpses of women Tomas has shot for poor performance. In another recurring dream, Tereza experiences the height of horror when she insists, on the strength of her need to pee, that she is still alive even though she is in a hearse, surrounded by corpses. The charnel house imagery is not a pure grotesque (which is just fantasy), since it carries an all too real odor of the Nazi concentration camp. Nature alone could not stage such horror without props from the special storehouse of evil that is human history.

The relation between Tomas and Tereza is based on complete inequality, and it is subject to a strange diurnal rhythm of cruelty and tenderness that bonds them together like a wedding ring. Tomas is the absolute master of Tereza's sleep. She dozes off, lulled by his reassuring words, only to sink into the sadoerotic nightmares he has inspired, from which she wakes in terror into his sheltering arms. From their first night as lovers, when he had remained at her side till morning, in violation of his erotic regimen that outlawed sleeping together after making love, Tomas knows that this shared sleep is the "corpus delicti" (p. 13) of their transgressing love. He finds his imagination held captive by Tereza's passionate dreaming, just as his hand was gripped in hers when he first woke up next to her and the image of the abandoned child in the bulrush basket surged up in his mind.

The crisis in the marriage is precipitated by the Soviet tanks that roll into Prague one night in August 1968. This hammerblow from history has the unexpected effect of momentarily freeing Tereza from the mental oppression of her jealousy. She experiences her temporary release as a holiday from her usual self, in tune with the carnival atmosphere in the streets of Prague during the first week of the occupation. Having become a professional photographer with Sabina's help, she now roams the roused city taking snapshots of tanks, raised fists, and Czech girls in miniskirts provocatively kissing random passersby under the eyes of the frustrated occupants of the tanks. But the euphoria of hatred soon collapses. Dubček, the kidnapped head of the Czech government, is returned to his post, but only to announce to his people that the proper relation has been restored between the firing power of tanks and the festive salvos of gaudy despair. His formal statement of national submission, heard over the radio, is spoken with a stutter and punctuated by excruciating pauses, as if a drowning man were gasping for air. Coming after all the wit of the week of joyous misrule, this broken voice signifies that the Czechs have been fooled by history once again. The incoherent speech with the painful syncopation of weakness will henceforth be the official language of the government. For Tereza, Dubček's abject broadcast causes a revulsion of shame. After her ephemeral week of empowerment, when, armed with her camera, she feared nothing, not even an officer with a pointed revolver, it seems unbearable to go on living in the altered city. She longs for a new setting, and even though she knows Sabina has emigrated to Geneva, she urges Tomas to accept the offer of a staff position at a Zurich hospital. Once they find themselves in Switzerland, in a bare flat, Tomas feels the vitality of a man of forty about to begin a new and interesting life.

Soon after, Sabina comes to Zurich, greeting Tomas at the door of her hotel room with a black bowler hat perched on her head, wearing nothing but her panties and bra. They hold their breath for a sharp instant of mutual recognition. Tomas is deeply stirred by Sabina's long-legged, incongruously hatted figure, like that of a virtuoso tightrope walker poised gracefully between erotic prospect and erotic memory. He congratulates himself on the reestablishment of his bipolar life, but then, after six or so months in Zurich, he finds the flat deserted. Tereza has left behind a letter explaining that she "lacked the strength to live abroad" (p. 28), and apologizing for taking Karenin with her to Prague.

Tomas's first reaction is to register the definitive quality of Tereza's move. Buoyed by that sense of finality, he contemplates the unexpected ending of his seven-year marriage through a pleasing haze of nostalgia. But his holiday from *soucit* lasts no more than one weekend. By Monday morning, the intoxication of lightness has collapsed into an oppressive burden. "There is nothing heavier than compassion. Not even one's own pain weighs so heavy as the pain one feels with someone, for someone, a pain intensified by the imagination and prolonged by a hundred echoes" (p. 31). Acting instantly on this conversion, Tomas tenders his resignation to the Swiss director, who seems shocked and even offended by the apparently motiveless decision.

In place of explanation, Tomas shrugs his shoulders and says, almost sheepishly, "*Es muss sein. Es muss sein.*" That twice-repeated assertion of necessity is the phrase to which Beethoven set a passage in the fourth movement of his last quartet, and the music-loving Swiss doctor immediately picks up on the allusion. Kundera provides us with the notation of the five bars of music that constitute the motif of grave but resisted destiny, which Beethoven characterizes as "*Der schwer gefasste Entschluss*"—"the difficult resolution" (p. 32). In the first bar the question "*Muss es sein?*" is sounded slowly (*grave*) but on an upraised note, while the answer sings out twice *allegro,* twice falling in a heavy cadence. The Swiss doctor, understanding the joke hidden inside the musical dialogue, smiles accordingly. Kundera, however, postpones his explanation until part 5, chapter 8, when Tomas hears his *amor fati* motif once again, this time in the context of a political decision. Here, we are provided with the private background of the musical passage,[28] which has puzzled the composer's interpreters. The reflective narrator points out that the famous motif began as Beethoven's little musical joke about his chronic need for money and ended as a metaphysical statement of tragic necessity. "It is an interesting tale of light going to heavy or, as Parmenides would have it, positive going to negative," he concludes (p. 195).

But inside Tomas's mind, the battering pendulum of skepticism swings into action once he is installed in the train that will return him to Prague. The narrator imagines him being sent off at the Swiss border by a tousled Beethoven conducting the local firemen's band in a brassy rendition of his "*Es muss sein*" motif. In this musical vignette, Beethoven, the lifter of metaphysical weights, parodies himself as the master of kitsch, turning Tomas's tragic *amor fati* into a flat-footed, aggressively sentimental marching song. Parmenides' polarities are recombined in the spirit of mockery to form an aesthetic perversion of the law of identity, whereby the heavy sound assumes the empty quality of voided meaning.

By the time Tomas reaches Prague, Tereza's love, whose resisted pull is heard in Beethoven's imaginary performance—"[The] allusion to Beethoven was actually Tomas's first step back to Tereza, because she was the one who had induced him to buy records of the Beethoven quartets and sonatas" (p. 32)—has grown cold, as if all tenderness had been left behind in Zurich. Their first embrace is relayed to Tomas's mind in an image of frigid estrangement: "He fancied himself standing opposite her in the midst of a snowy plain, the two of them shivering from the cold" (p. 34). Falling asleep at her side, he feels a pressure in his stomach that speaks to him of his bitter regret at having come back.

Tereza, who has occupied a privileged place in Tomas's imagination as the child in the bulrush basket sent down the river to be deposited in his bed, seems to have been deserted by her metaphoric powers. Without her mysterious latency she is once again the ordinary waitress he encountered in a provincial town. His mind, emptied of *soucit,* calculates that "it had taken six chance happenings to push Tomas towards Tereza, as if he had little inclination to go to her on his own" (p. 35). But by executing this deconstruction of the design of his fate, Tomas has only outwitted himself. Unrecognized by his imagination, Tereza, "that personification of absolute fortuity" (*ztělesnění absolutní náhody*), is still speaking to him through the dull pain in his gut. That physiological signal is a coded message containing the secret formula of her soul's entrapment within the lower body. "Tomas was born of the saying '*Einmal ist keinmal.*' Tereza was born of the rumbling of a stomach," declares the narrator at the outset of the second part ("Soul and Body," p. 39), which explores the novel's second major theme and in the process unveils Tereza's existential code.

The narrative line of part 2 traverses the same chronological segment already covered by Tomas, from the early sixties to 1969. Once again we review the lovers' first meeting in the provincial hotel restaurant, again we hear Tereza's night screams and see the couple reunited after Tomas's return from Zurich. But this time the events are illumined by the light Tereza's inner life sheds on them. In a formal sense, Tereza is the heroine of a twice-told tale, for as a character in the novel she is made to live the time of repetition. But her becoming, reflected in her own consciousness, has the singular beauty and density of significance that are the distinguishing mark of the "great time" of consecration. *Einmal ist doch nicht keinmal* within the magnetic field of Tereza, who experiences her love for Tomas as an opening to the radiance of true being. Once, during her brief stay in Switzerland, she hears herself called "anachronistic" by the editor of an illustrated magazine, who praises but declines to publish her photographs, shot in the streets of Prague during the invasion week. Perhaps the editor means to say that Tereza is out of date in deciding against a possible career as a fashion or garden photographer—"My husband is my life, not cactuses," Tereza objects (p. 71)—but she also senses that Tereza attaches a permanent significance to images whose market value consists in their relevance as news—pictures to be flashed on and off millions of televisions screens.

Tereza's "anachronistic" bent is a fundamental feature of her code. She lives *against* time conceived as Cronos, whose rule is based on a sequential, inexorably linear ordering of human experience. Cronos began his European career as a Titanic elder god who was in the habit of swallowing his own children until he was dethroned by his ambitious son Zeus. The ancient myth contains the seeds of future development. Cronos would get another chance for a royal ride, through the magnified space of modern Europe, proudly bearing his new secular name, History. And again his passage would signal the old message—that the future is always stronger and the dialectics of its perennial struggle to emerge on top bloody. For Tomas and those who share his mood of perplexity, History is no longer a meaningful process in whose inner logic one can read the shape of a distant *telos*. In part 5, chapter 15, we get a glimpse of Tomas in the act of thinking about history as he tries to figure out why he has refused to sign a statement of political protest with which he agrees. Once again the meaning of his decision escapes him into the dimension of the irrational. But history conceived as the flailing ground of irrational will cannot compel a sense of human significance. At best, it can be negotiated like a fast-moving escalator leading to nowhere in particular; that is how it might have felt in Switzerland, had Tomas thought about it there. But back in Prague after 1968, history feels like a trap, and it is difficult to escape its coiling reel.

Looking back on his love for Tereza through the dull pain in his stomach, Tomas is shocked to note the accidental, purely fortuitous course of its development. It seems to him that a course run by chance alone cannot have much significance. For Tereza, it is the exact opposite; chance appears to her not as a stumbling block but as a window of opportunity. From Tereza's perspective, the narrator observes, "Chance and chance alone has a message for us. Everything that occurs out of necessity, everything expected, repeated day in and day out, is mute. Only chance can speak to us" (p. 48). Intent on listening to her love, Tereza reads the initial situation with Tomas as a text full of mysterious signs written for her eyes only. She will always remember that when she first sighted Tomas at his table, he had an open book before him, and when he addressed her to ask for a glass of cognac, the radio was playing music she recognized as Beethoven's. That fortuitous concatenation of circumstance was the rousing instant of opportunity for Tereza's dormant soul, made keen by its long latency. Her soul responded by surging upward, armed with all its vital faculties. "Her nascent love inflamed her sense of beauty, and she would never forget that music. Whenever she heard it, she would be touched" (p. 51).

Kundera's depiction of the birth of Tereza's love for Tomas is mythopoetic rather than psychological. It also serves as the myth of origin that defines Tereza's soul, that mysterious entity whose existence is always subject to doubt and whose tendency to disappear into the pit of the lower body is the source of Tereza's deepest torment. We have just seen her soul becoming manifest in the epiphany of love. It is a revelation of pure creative energy, its power opening Tereza's senses to the unimpeded flow of metaphoric imagination. Beauty and love are the twin communicating vessels of that moment's alchemy, exchanging their mutual gifts—beauty issuing into love with its vital magnitude, and love passing back the intimate tenderness of its mnemonic speech.

"You're in room six and my shift ends at six," says Tereza (p. 50), thus raising the stakes of her initial dialogue with Tomas,[29] which begins with a banal exchange about paying the bill. The number six, which figures as a code for the merely accidental in Tomas's memory, is a seal of significance in Tereza's reading of the same happening. In both cases, the identical word, "chance" (*náhoda*), is used to designate two essentially divergent meanings. Within the conceptual frame of Tomas's debased *chronos, náhoda* is only the void of significance that serves as the necessary link between the contingency of past and future. For Tereza, who, living for love, lives the time of *kairos, náhoda* is a secret passageway into the radiance of being. When Tomas defines Tereza to himself as "the *embodiment* of absolute chance" (*ztělesnění absolutní náhody*),[30] he is virtually denying her body a soul, whereas she, using the same term, "absolute chance," interprets their encounter as the privileged instant of revelation.

The mystical allusion contained in Tereza's name is fully illumined by the contrast it presents to Tomas, whose namesake stands for evangelical doubt. This woman in love seems entirely molded from within, like Bernini's sculptured image of Saint Theresa in the Cornaro Chapel in Rome,[31] its finely modeled face with half-open mouth rising ecstatically from the heavily draped mass of the lower body, where we see a naked, dangling foot protrude. In Kundera's text, sacred and profane images of consecration proliferate around Tereza. She first appears to Tomas as little Moses in his cradle, the vulnerable bearer of a more than human destiny. In part 2 her moment of opportunity, when she seizes her *náhoda* by the forelock, is pictured in the repeated image of Saint Francis of Assisi with birds fluttering down to his shoulders. "If a love is to be unforgettable, fortuities must immediately start fluttering down to it like birds to Francis of Assisi's shoulders" (p. 49). The Franciscan motif, a portent of the miraculous, surprises and charms us with its apparent incongruity. It seems to hinge on nothing but pure air, but its latent meaning will come alive in the novel's last movement. Another recurring image for the mystical adventure of Tereza's soul rising out of its bodily entrapment is the worldly metaphor of a ship being outfitted for a journey of discovery. "It was a longing to be a body unlike other bodies, to find that the surface of her face reflected the crew of the soul charging up from below" (p. 47). Sacred and secular meanings resonate with each other through the transformational medium of Tereza's love, and two seemingly opposed value systems are fused in the singular locus of beauty.

Tereza, entering Tomas's Prague flat for the first time, feels herself humiliated by an inopportune rumble in her stomach. Commenting on the situation, which is Tereza's fictional genesis, the narrator states that it "brutally reveals the irreconcilable duality of body and soul, that fundamental human experience." By mechanizing the idea of the human body, modern thought has emptied our senses of their mysterious inner presence, their *anima,* for which the body was once considered a cage. "The face is nothing but an instrument panel registering all the body mechanisms: digestion, sight, hearing, respiration, thought." The physiological demystification of the soul, as Kundera presents it, has pushed the focal center of the body downward. The soul has been driven out of its ancient seat of honor somewhere inside the human breast, near the heart, whence it could issue from the lips, as in Bernini's image of Saint Theresa's upturned face with the parted mouth and the hooded eyes gazing inward. In Kundera's novel, what remains of the soul has pitched its precarious mansion in the lower body, the place where sexual love must consort with excrement. Tereza's being-in-love is the tangible evidence of the soul's existence. Proceeding *per negationem,* by denying "that lyrical illusion of the age of science" (p. 40) which would have us believe that the body feels all by itself, Kundera has revived the ancient theme of the discord between body and soul, translating it into the terms of our age of common denial.

Whenever Tereza looks at her body, she is shocked to recognize her mother's flesh. That is why she feels compelled to peer into the mirror, straining to catch in her face a glimmer of that unique illumination which bespeaks her soul's "I." For her, the discord between body and soul is a daily struggle to emerge into individual being from the Egyptian captivity of her body's prehistory within her mother's body. Tereza's life is bipolar, like Tomas's. Her mother represents the evil necessity of her body, while Tomas's love is her freedom.

Kundera tells the story of Tereza's mother's life in a grotesquely foreshortened tale about a beautiful body turned hideous by age. For Tereza's mother, her own likeness in the mirror represents nothing but the reflection of male desire, which shows her first as a capricious princess and then as a willful witch. The unrelenting pursuit of the underview of her beauty in men's eyes finally reduces her to flaunting her degraded body, emptied of its shame as it is forsaken by male desire. "Her behavior was but a single grand gesture, a casting off of youth and beauty" (p. 46). In Tereza's mother's radical immodesty, the reified body boasts of its victory over the last remnants of the soul in a language composed of the sounds of human digestion and excretion. Along with the humiliating legacy of such a body, Tereza receives from her mother the mental burden of guilt. That oppressive feeling, "as vague as original sin," is the demonic expression of her mother's carefully nurtured revenge on a child she blames for her first stumble on the road to fulfilling her body's narcissistic need. Whatever Tereza may do to placate her mother, she remains the unloved byproduct of an accidental pregnancy sealed by a botched marriage. "If a mother was Sacrifice personified, then a daughter was Guilt, with no possibility of redress" (p. 44).

In Tereza's life with Tomas, guilt finds permanent lodging inside her jealousy, working insidiously to undermine the soul of her love. Tomas's repeated infidelities are only the proximate cause of Tereza's torment, for her jealousy is the accompanying shadow of her love, her gray Frau Sorge. Tomas is not only the master of Tereza's sleep but commands the tenuous existence of her soul as well, since he wields the power to change her into a thing that suffers the indignity of sentient life under a pile of anonymous human bodies. Tereza's consciousness construes the power of Tomas's love as her own weakness. The pull of this weakness, with its paradoxical mix of gravity and lightness, is tantalizing to her will. The heavier the body, the greater the airy vacancy inside her head. It is the vertigo of weakness that she recognizes in Dubček's mutilated speech of surrender as something of her own. At the time, she felt strong after her week of exceptional freedom and could defy the fascination of falling; once in Zurich, with her jealousy back in place, she finds it impossible to resist. But her impulsive flight, whereby she consciously ranges herself with "the camp of the weak" (p. 73), has the unexpected effect of pulling Tomas after her.

Tereza's return to Prague is an expression of despair akin to an act of suicide. It has the same feel of irresistible momentum as Anna Karenina's last hours, which drive her relentlessly to that point of sudden resolve when she throws herself under the wheels of the approaching train. "Suddenly remembering the man who had been run over the day she first met Vronsky, she realized what she had to do," writes Tolstoy. Tereza's impulse carries the same keenness of recognition in an instant of mental rhyming when memory, in a single flash, unites the brightness of love's beginning and the reflection of the end. And Anna's plunge into death has the same mysterious combination of lightness and heaviness that characterizes Tereza's vertigo.[32]

Elsewhere in the same movement, the narrator speaks of the "dark beauty" of Tolstoy's rhythmic composition of Anna's tragedy. "Early in the novel that Tereza clutched under her arm when she went to visit Tomas, Anna meets Vronsky in curious circumstances: they are at the railway station when someone is run over by a train. At the end of the novel, Anna throws herself under a train" (p. 52). He goes on to say that Tolstoy's "symmetrical composition" is not merely a novelist's cunning device for shaping his narrative matter but something latently present in life, waiting to disclose its form. Our lives are composed like music, and if we listen well, they will speak to us in the heightened language of secret motifs, which are really the accidents of our becoming, transformed into significance by a roused imagination. This meditation throws light on Kundera's conception of the poetic capability of the novelistic form when it reaches beyond mimesis into epiphany. But Kundera, the novelist-*voyant,* is also a master of the reflective art of reading novels. His narrator's contemplation of *Anna Karenina* lights the path for Kundera's novel by examining the road traveled earlier by Tolstoy's imagination.

At the end of the second movement, Kundera deploys his variation on Tolstoy's "symmetrical composition" by linking the penultimate chapter to the last scene of the first part. The rhyming is based on contrast, highlighted by surface similarity. We recall that Tomas fancied himself standing opposite Tereza "in the midst of a snowy plain, the two of them shivering from the cold" (p. 34). In Tereza's movement, in the same scene, "they felt they were standing on a snow-covered plain, shivering with cold. Then they moved together like lovers who had never kissed before" (p. 77). Projected within Tomas's mind, the image shows a still life with two strangers confronting each other in an empty landscape. Tereza, for her part, experiences the moment as high drama and understands it as the resurrection of love. The incongruity of their experiences also contains a mutual reversal of roles as each assumes the other's theme. Tomas, with his pressure in the stomach, is enduring Tereza's condition of bodily necessity. He does not know, of course, that this is his *soucit,* taking refuge in the pit of his belly. Tereza, in turn, momentarily assumes Tomas's vital power as she feels for both of them that warmth and fullness which Parmenides designates as two attributes of real being.

The third narrative movement introduces another pair of lovers, Sabina and Franz, whose mutual interplay of strength/weakness runs counter to the model created by Tomas and

Tereza. Franz is a professor of literature at the University of Geneva, and as the first chapter of the sequence opens, he is on his way to visit his mistress Sabina in her studio. We are not told how their liaison was initiated, but we soon understand that Sabina provides the erotic spark while Franz holds up the idyllic, emotive end of the relationship. If we imagine the two pairs of lovers in this novel performing together, as in a string quartet, we may choose to assign the first and second violins to Tomas and Sabina, who share the same erotic timbre, but Franz's part would be lower strings—a bit heavy-footed, he sustains his melodic line with grave feeling, like a cello.

As a lover of women, Franz remains chained to the sentimental archetype of his mother. His imagination preserves the indelibly etched memory of an overpowering moment of a child's *soucit*. He can still see his mother walking through town with him, wearing a different shoe on each foot, suffering to the point of distraction under the sudden blow of her husband's desertion. Those mismatched shoes summon up the image of Tomas as the fool of love wearing mismatched socks. Franz's precocious *soucit* has predestined him to play the role of a comic Tristan, the grand fool of love, exposing himself to all manner of incongruity. Franz is so mesmerized by the value of erotic fidelity, a quality inculcated in him by a feeling of guilt no less pervasive than Tereza's, that he has managed to con himself into taking his wife Marie-Claude for a variation on his gentle maternal paradigm. In reality, Marie-Claude, an art dealer who has exhibited Sabina's work, is a brassy, selfish woman given to celebrating her own aggressiveness as if it were the key virtue of her innate vitality. Utterly devoid of tact and sensitivity, Marie-Claude and her daughter Marie-Anne, a budding replica of her mother, are the two truly unpleasant characters in a novel rich in empathy. Marie-Claude's existential code is the shallow optimism of the successful arriviste, which makes her the lucky twin of the Party sycophant Helena from *The Joke*. But unlike that unfortunate victim of her own bowels, Franz's wife has a knack for always coming out on top of any situation. Living for the externals of life, she only needs the plaudits of her cocktail party crowd, and in that company she always manages to have the last word.

In spite of Franz's eagerness to listen to the story of his mistress's life, he and Sabina are divided by an abyss of fundamental misunderstandings. Kundera documents their existential *quid pro quo* by compiling "A Short Dictionary of Misunderstood Words," in which he examines the antipodal meanings the two lovers attach to certain key words.[33] These segments of phenomenological analysis are interpolated between the narrative chapters, beginning in chapter 3, with entries on "Woman," "Fidelity and Betrayal," "Music," and "Light and Darkness." The dictionary resumes in chapters 5 and 7, thus occupying three of the eleven chapters in this part. This device contributes to the effect of a broken story line, in contrast to the fluidity of the two Tereza movements that frame it. We are meant to perceive the unfolding of Franz and Sabina's affair through the medium of disconnection, as a series of loosely attached situations. This fragmented, anecdotal form nevertheless embraces a long measure of chronological time, played out in an expansive and varied space.[34] During their affair, Sabina and Franz travel widely in Western Europe and even manage a foray into New York, a city whose "unintentional" beauty attracts Sabina while it unsettles and alienates Franz.

The jagged, suddenly interrupted form of Franz and Sabina's life together imitates the trail of betrayal that is Sabina's chosen path. Her name, considered in its Czech context, seems to allude to Karel Sabina, a minor nineteenth-century romantic poet who achieved memorable notoriety in the history of his nation as the paradigm of the political turncoat.[35] But if we apply Sabina's technique of "double exposure" to her compulsion to betray all her attachments, we see another likeness emerging from the background of her life.

Compare, for instance, Sabina's response to an old church in Amsterdam with Franz's. This Gothic cathedral, built to house the fervency of Catholic ritual, has been stripped down to the bare walls to suit the radically reformed religious taste of Calvinism. The huge vaulting space stands empty as a gymnasium, but at its center Sabina sees "several rows of chairs . . . arranged in a large square around a miniature podium for the minister." Her trained painterly eye immediately notes the inorganic intrusion of this rectangular form, and she is offended by its disdain for the spirit of Gothic architecture, bespeaking the callousness of the local winner in the historical dispute between two versions of the same faith. By now, of course, the church stands in unsought proximity to the famed Amsterdam red-light district, whose existential sign is the intense smell of urine in the streets. Franz is fascinated by the gaping evidence of the systematic process of obliteration by which History marches forward. "It's the emptiness of it that fascinates me," he says. "People collect altars, statues, paintings, chairs, carpets, and books, and then comes a time of joyful relief and they throw it all out like so much refuse from yesterday's dinner table. Can't you just picture Hercules' broom sweeping out this cathedral?" (p. 109).

As a lover, Franz has enshrined fidelity at the vital center of his emotions. But as a man of ideas, he aligns himself with the European left, whose basic marching order is always to go forward and spare no pity for the values of the past. The apparent duality resolves itself quite easily within Franz's basic code of fidelity: we are told that his commitment to the mood and mode of the left is an expression of loyalty to the atmosphere of his youth at the Sorbonne. Besides, the European left has itself become an expression of the psychic needs of its celebrants instead of an intellectual phalanx.

Franz was once dubbed "a pseudo-Socrates" (p. 102) by a reviewer, and he harbors a deep anxiety about the value of his scholarly writing, a suspicion, always ready to surface, that it may be no more than empty traffic in words. His fascination with the "Hercules' broom" of History on the march is also an attempt to find a heroic expression for his cultural fatigue. His love of History manifests itself as a desire to escape from History, which constitutes the substance of his emotional commitment to the myth of Revolution. Like other intellectual decadents, Franz is irresistibly drawn to the edge of his own annihilation, perhaps in hopes of being the first to sight the advancing barbarians. His thrill over the vacuum sweep of Cronos is the high of his ongoing flirtation with death.

Sabina, a refugee from Communist Czechoslovakia, is deeply conscious of being a survivor of a wave of cultural barbarism. From her vantage point, there is nothing liberating in the sight of a Gothic cathedral reduced to a hangar. She feels a poignant access of tenderness amidst that desecrated space, and suddenly, in a stunning flash of insight, she discovers her personal definition of beauty: "From that time on she had known that beauty is a world betrayed" (p. 110). This formula reveals the emotional underpinning of Sabina's aestheticism and is also the key to her existential code. Her compulsion to betray proceeds from her quest for the experience of beauty in an instant of tragic *soucit*. The path of unremitting escapism she traces is not that of an opportunist always running from the good to the better; behind the mask of Sabina the betrayer emerges the nostalgist of time lost, running in fear of being overtaken by kitsch.

Sabina and Franz practice two sharply divergent modes of creating meaning, rooted in two radically different ways of experiencing time. Sabina plays the royal game of caprice with a giddy lightness to match that of Heraclitus' child/grandmaster. Her consciousness is thrilled to the edge of vertigo when she feels the intensifying pace of the moving reel under her feet. Franz, for his part, needs to hold on to a fixed mental point. Moved by a secret nostalgia for a lost *arche* of being, he translates it into a compulsion to follow the European left's Grand March toward a disappearing *telos*. He experiences an orgiastic emptying of himself in the illusion of merging with something elemental, be it a marching crowd, rock music, or now, as Sabina's lover, the erotic power he senses within her. This intellectual is above all a lyricist of his own self-surrender, and that is what moves him to follow his dream of Revolution, even after the ideas that once teemed around it have grown exhausted.

Sabina has created for herself a rhythm of private meanings that keep changing their substance as they move on the restless current of her time. The old-fashioned black bowler hat she wore when receiving Tomas at the door of her Zurich hotel room is her secret metaphor for that process, as well as the magic object of her endless play. It is also the choice prop for her erotic improvisations, as she and Tomas had discovered quite accidentally in her Prague studio years earlier. The bowler had caught Tomas's eye as a relic of bygone bourgeois respectability, and he put it on his head, clowning in front of Sabina's large mirror. As they watched themselves in the mirror, Sabina began undressing and Tomas transferred the hat, now a Chaplinesque madcap, to her head. At first they laughed at the inspired mockery, but when she had stripped down to her underwear,

> . . . suddenly the comic became veiled by excitement: the bowler hat no longer signified a joke; it signified violence; violence against Sabina, against her dignity as a woman. She saw her bare legs and thin panties with her pubic triangle showing through. The lingerie enhanced the charm of her femininity, while the hard masculine hat denied it, violated and ridiculed it. (pp. 86–87)

This is Sabina's feeling, not Tomas's or the author's, sensed from within the erotic vertigo of a woman's thrilled response to the hard-edged excitement of male desire. Watching her image in the mirror, Sabina rises to the crest of her own sense of uniqueness as experiencing subject, teetering on the brink of a second wave of intensity that will pull her and Tomas down to the floor, as if she were "submitting of her own will to public rape" (p. 87). The experience is a privileged moment in Sabina's memory, and we watch her rehearsing it with renewed feeling just after the lovable Franz has left her studio. She now understands that Franz is impossible as her lover. When she tested the bowler hat on him, all he did was lift it gently from her head and hang it back on its rack, smiling indulgently all the while, "as though he were erasing the mustache a naughty child had drawn on a picture of the Virgin Mary" (p. 85). Despite his great physical strength, Franz is unable to conceive of sexual love as a medium of violence.

Under its erotic significance, the bowler hat harbors Sabina's reverence for her dead father, to whom she had failed to show any tenderness while he was alive, and who had killed himself out of grief the day after his wife's burial. Sabina had taken the hat, originally made for her grandfather, a small-town mayor, as the single physical token of her father's legacy. The transformational nature and the concealed emotional content of Sabina's magic hat assume the function of a motif in a musical composition, always recognizable but always renewed by contact with new configurations of tones.

> It returned again and again, each time with a different meaning, and all the meanings flowed through the bowler hat like water through a riverbed. I might call it Heraclitus' ("You can't step twice into the same river") riverbed: the bowler hat was a bed through which each time Sabina saw another river flow, another *semantic river.* (p. 88)

Long after all these events, walking through Montparnasse Cemetery in Paris with the news of Tomas and Tereza's accidental death running through her head, Sabina will still mourn her father in this fresh mourning for the man whom she knew as a fellow libertine, but who died like her father, the death of Tristan, the consecrated lover. We see Sabina at the conclusion of the third movement, leaning over a hole dug deep in French soil for an indifferent guest. "In Bohemia the graves were not so deep," she remembers (p. 123), dropping a flower into the pit. The warmth of her many-faceted grieving rises above the cold earth, a living reproach to the vanity of stone that surrounds her.

Sabina, the artist of betrayal, is at heart a musician of memory like Tamina. She keeps fleeing from present stasis with head averted, only to catch the beauty of her present in the act of becoming the past. The inevitable rupture of her liaison with Franz is staged by her as the grand gesture of betrayal. She leaves his life abruptly, having carefully erased all telltale signs of her future whereabouts, allowing him no parting view other than that of her empty studio. Shortly before, in Rome, they had made love with such passion that Sabina knew Franz would finally ask Marie-Claude for a divorce. This ultimate embrace is one of their great misunderstandings. Franz, thrashing on top of Sabina's body with eyes closed, feels "like a rider galloping off into a magnificent void" (p. 117). But to Sabina, he is like a gigantic child or a puppy trying to suckle at her breast. She can only overcome her inner revulsion at this imposition of an alien maternal code from the vantage point of her imminent betrayal.

The blow of Sabina's unexpected disappearance makes Franz dizzy at first, but he soon settles down to enjoy the side benefits. Sabina's moment of truth helps explode his myth of Marie-Claude's resemblance to his suffering mother. As it turns out, it is Marie-Claude who has the last laugh when his great love evaporates into thin air. Franz moves into a bachelor flat in old Geneva, and after some time, one of his students joins him to share his life and love. The absent Sabina, in the meanwhile, becomes a stellar presence at the far end of

Franz's mental horizon, whence she sheds her brilliant light on all his undertakings. Unwittingly, Franz has transformed Sabina into a cult memory whose monumental sentimentalism closely resembles the form of kitsch she hates most.

The next two movements belong to the lovers Tomas and Tereza, back together in Prague. The time span covered is about five years, from their return in 1969 to the eve of their retreat to the village. The city that staged a carnival of hate for one reckless week in August 1968 is now back in the yoke of its usual historical role as pliant victim. When they left for Zurich, Tereza had thought of Prague as the city of weakness. Now it will become the city of entrapment for both of them. In meditation on Kafka, Kundera has asked what possibilities remain open to human experience once the world we live in has become a trap."[36] Parts 4 and 5 of his novel can be read as a two-pronged experimental development of this inquiry. In a city whose labyrinthine workings once provided the stuff of Kafka's uncanny vision but have now settled into the everyday texture of the post-invasion "normalization," Tereza and Tomas both endure their unique form of the common ordeal. Tereza is caught in the noose created by her anxious love, whereas Tomas remains entangled within the perplexities of his mind.

The euphoria of love returning collapses quickly for Tereza as she finds her jealousy moving back in through the servants' entrance. Looking at herself in the mirror, she feels a revulsion for a useless body that "lacked the power to become the only body in Tomas's life" (p. 139). She is struck by the ugliness of Prague, whose civic life seems to imitate the degradation of the country's political style. The rigidifying conditions around them are ill-suited to their need for autonomy, and they both give up on their chosen professions, retreating to the obscure periphery of their society. Tomas is now an itinerant window washer, and Tereza waits tables again, officiating from behind the bar of a seamy suburban hotel, where the reception desk is manned by a former ambassador. (He still keeps an autographed photo of JFK above his cot.) Karenin, who follows Tereza everywhere, finds refuge behind the counter at her feet.

This bar becomes the setting for Tereza's entrapment into an act of sexual betrayal that shakes the structure of her love for Tomas to its foundations. Tereza has always known that her assigned role in Tomas's life is to play the faithful one, thus upholding the other end of his prerogative of infidelity. "Their love was an oddly asymmetrical construction: it was supported by the absolute certainty of her fidelity like a gigantic edifice supported by a single column" (p. 160). The inequality of their lots does not offend her, but now, in the nausea of her body's impotence, she begins to read a whispering invitation "to dismiss her body as one dismisses a servant: to stay on with Tomas only as a soul and send her body into the world to behave as other female bodies behave with male bodies" (p. 139). Accordingly, she has been going to the outer edge of sexual flirtation with some of her male customers, who keep harassing her with more or less explicit propositions. Tereza experiences the temptation of sexual infidelity as a script governed by her existential code: she wants to try the supreme gamble to unlink her loving soul from its humiliating bondage to a devalued body.

Tereza's risky sexual event is viewed through a double-barreled narrative focus. The description of Tereza's real-life scene with an unknown engineer in a half-empty flat is appended to a dream sequence of her mock execution, another variation on her familiar nightmares. The imaginary reel runs from chapter 11 to chapter 15, merging smoothly, almost imperceptibly, into the raw of Tereza's experience, just at the point when she stands ready to enter the stranger's place in a working-class district of Prague. The dark-hued, mysterious fabric of Tereza's dream, which is set on Petřín Hill above Prague, in a landscape dotted with trees, is woven into the rough texture of the experience of violation she undergoes. It is as if a merciful veil of beauty had been prepared for the occasion, only to be ripped off during the odium of the bad moment. The language of counterpoint between the two levels of the narrative delivers the message of Tereza's despair: her act of sexual betrayal is a suicidal gesture of exhaustion dictated to her by what she conceives to be the imperative of her love for Tomas.

In both sequences, we witness Tereza's mesmerized soul watching her body advance in slow motion toward the moment of the kill. Tereza's inward sense that her executioner on Petřín Hill and the engineer in the borrowed flat are both acting at the behest of Tomas, whose unseen presence looms gigantic over the event, is strengthened when she sees *Oedipus* staring at her from the bookshelf. "One of the books caught her eye at once. It was a translation of Sophocles' *Oedipus*. How odd to find it here! Years ago, Tomas had given it to her, and after she had read it he went on and on about it. Then he sent his reflections to a newspaper, and the article turned their life upside down" (p. 153). Tereza, intent on reading private messages from her beloved, does not suspect that the book alludes to her ignorance of the true meaning of what she is about to do, in the prophetic code of the darkly scheming Apollo, who is preparing the knot for her noose.

Tereza's mind, lacking all experience of the tricky slope of sexual adventurism she has stumbled onto, goes on rehearsing the irrefutable logic of her dream. "Hadn't [Tomas] told her time and again that love and sexuality had nothing in common?" Up there on Petřín Hill, she retains the option to stop the man with the rifle by simply uttering the magic words "It wasn't my choice" (p. 152). But here inside the closed room, the situation is reversed in the moment of truth, when all the revulsion welling up inside her lacks the power to stay the orgasmic momentum of her body once it is yoked to the pitiless mechanism of the stranger's sexual command.

Throughout the event Tereza's soul, refusing to be unlinked

from its body, watches perversely what the body is doing. "For what made the soul so excited was that the body was acting against its will; the body was betraying it, and the soul was looking on" (p. 155). Having pushed its curious companion back into the pit where it belongs, the body goes about its business in shameless glee. But the soul, retreating inch by inch, still manages to implant its seal of individuation on the body in the form of a birthmark just above the pubic triangle. That mark of her body's uniqueness entrances Tereza just at the instant when that selfsame body is being invaded by the stranger's sexual will. She feels the rising wave of an unwanted orgasm flooding her, "flowing through her veins like a shot of morphine" (p. 156).

Next we see her sitting on the toilet bowl, enduring her body's necessity, while her consciousness registers bitter acquiescence to her mother's dictum that the body "was good for nothing but digesting and excreting" (p. 157). Once, swayed by the magic of rhythmic speech, Yeats heard his Crazy Jane cry out to the Bishop that "Love has pitched his mansion in / The place of excrement."[37] Tereza's mute, humiliated figure, utterly deserted by beauty, images a Crazy Jane—a woman "on love intent"—in the distorting mirror of Jonathan Swift. But no, it is not so, and this forbidden upside-down look at Bernini's Tereza as her soul issues out from below is not blasphemy, for Kundera has illumined his Tereza's despair with his *soucit*.

As if to confirm this merciful reading, the next episode, placed back to back with her misery, shows Tereza in the act of manifesting her own *soucit* for a creature trapped in misery. Walking home with Karenin one morning, she chances to see a crow's head lying on the cold dirt of a barren plot, bobbing helplessly and emitting mournful sounds. The bird has been buried alive by two boys who flee as Tereza approaches their victim. She digs the crow carefully out of its grave and carries it home wrapped in her red scarf. In spite of all the tender nurture Tereza lavishes on it—"She could have been keeping vigil over a dying sister"—the maimed bird dies in her bathroom. Tereza's display of supreme affective power, which transforms a dying bird into "my sister," expands the Franciscan motif that imparted its gentle, miraculous aura to her nascent love for Tomas. Is it Tomas's love-*soucit* calling her back to him through the crow's beak? In the forgiving light of her sisterly vigil, Tereza finds a new insight into the tormenting relation between sex and love, which keeps dividing her from Tomas. "Tereza knew what happens during the moment love is born: the woman cannot resist the voice calling forth her terrified soul; the man cannot resist the woman whose soul thus responds to his voice. Tomas had no defense against the lure of love, and Tereza feared for him every minute of every hour" (p. 160). Tereza's compassionate revision of her situation with Tomas does not lessen the pain inflicted by his womanizing, but some of the humiliation is assuaged in this sudden awareness of their common vulnerability.

Soon afterward, Tereza is told by the former ambassador that the strange engineer may be working for the secret police. She quickly figures out the dismal implications—her chance rendezvous may have been a predetermined scenario, a trap set for purposes of future blackmail by the ubiquitous, darkly scheming government. "They need to trap people," explains the ambassador (p. 163). It is an explanation that goes to the root of the situation, even though it appears to beg the question. There is no reason to know the purpose behind this exercise of a hidden power, for the will to exercise power down to the level of utmost banality is not just the form but the ultimate meaning of its fundamental irrationality. Now Tereza understands that *Oedipus* on the bookshelf was a sham sign. Tomas was not the unseen presence behind her executioner but more likely the intended victim of the whole show. Tereza trembles in fear of what her act of betrayal, now duly recorded in the police files, may do to Tomas and their relationship.

During a weekend trip to a spa, Tereza and Tomas meet a farm worker who had been Tomas's patient. He praises the quiet life of his village, where he serves as the elected chairman of the agricultural collective. The man's sincere friendliness immediately wins Tereza over, evoking for her a submerged poetic echo of the village idyll that she, like most Czechs, remembers from her country's literary tradition.[38] As they drive back to Prague, she wants to tell Tomas of her dream of settling down to the quiet life, but she can't bring herself to speak. We only learn of their decision to leave Prague at the end of the fifth movement.

In the last scene of this narrative segment, Tereza is shown experiencing her "great farewell" to Prague. She is leaning casually against a balustrade, watching the river Vltava flow by. She is at the town's periphery, nowhere near the glamorous spot where the waters reflect the photogenic image of Hradčany Castle. Suddenly Tereza sights a strange red object floating downstream, and then another and another. The improbable apparition is a flowing cortege of Prague park benches, which some unseen hand has loosed from their usual moorings and abandoned to the stream. No one but Tereza sees what she sees in this surrealistic epiphany of farewell, which deploys its polyphonic image of a forever disappearing Prague before the eyes of a *voyante*. Tereza, in this magic moment, stands in for all the walkers of Prague who have now departed the scene—for Apollinaire and Nezval and Kafka, for Kundera himself and for Tomas, who will soon be leaving for the village with her. And of course what Tereza also sees in the Heraclitean flux of transience, the river of time studded with the red markers of her love's significance, is her own death, transfigured by beauty.

When Tomas finally acquiesces to Tereza's desire to live in the village, it seems that he is adopting her idyllic image of nature. But it is not quite so. Tomas's retreat from Prague means that he is ready to give up an almost infinite variety of erotic opportunities to be alone with Tereza. That move is the last in a series of actions induced by the momentum of his love-*soucit*. But his decision is also the result of a sequence of external events and circumstances to which he finds himself responding, each time, with a gesture of disengagement. The fifth narrative segment presents Tomas's five years in Prague as a protracted act of turning his back on history.

Tomas's backward journey, which begins with his return from Zurich, is in essence a return to the autonomy of the self from the labyrinth of the world. The ready-made classical/Christian reading of his course of action shows it to be a quest for true freedom, which can only be found within, in the light of individual consciousness/conscience. But Tomas's skeptical temper is inimical to the rhetoric of heroism, even when couched in the language of philosophy. He tends to question his motives to the point of perplexity, and his finely tuned sense of the ridiculous restrains him from performing grand gestures for the eyes of others, just as modesty restrains a woman from undressing in public. Within the formal scheme of the novel, Tomas's obscure path presents a stark contrast to the clamorous Grand March Franz joins one last time in the sixth movement. For Tomas, politics has long ceased to be a matter of substance, and it would be excessive to describe his turning away from history as a renunciation, since he harbors no illusions about the quality of the stage history offers for human action.

Tomas is acutely aware that the tall, stooped editor who is asking him to sign a clever petition of protest against the regime has been reduced to "displaying [his] wit before hidden microphones" (p. 221). The secret police, who command the ubiquitous recording system, also have the power to stop the public circulation of documents, such as the editor's demand for the release of all political prisoners. The thought that a personal expression of moral conviction and courage may be immortalized in the form of a bureaucratic file is profoundly distasteful to Tomas, in spite of the intense empathy he feels for the quixotic editor. The man is accompanied by Tomas's estranged son, now grown. This is a surprise at first, since Tomas knows the boy's mother to be an orthodox Communist. But it does not take long for Tomas to discern that the young man's stammer, coupled with his strident advocacy of the dissident cause, is a veiled appeal for recognition from his absentee father. The half-aggressive, half-supplicatory fervency he reads on the young face that wears the mask of his own flesh has the effect of alienating Tomas. He dislikes being squeezed between two imperatives that have little to do with what he is in himself. Tomas refuses to sign the petition on a distinctly antiheroic impulse, which he himself understands as a gesture of giving up a game he cannot win.

This is the second time Tomas finds himself saying no to a demand requiring a clear-cut choice though rooted in tangling contingencies and contradictory emotions. A year or so after coming back to Prague, he is visited by a man from the Ministry of the Interior, who tries to pressure and cajole him into retracting his article on *Oedipus,* now being interpreted as an attack on the legitimacy of the government. Tomas has already declined to write a much milder version of the retraction, which the friendly chief surgeon of his hospital had urged him to do as a career-saving preventive measure. Everyone is busily retracting thoughts and deeds of the recent past, and Tomas's colleagues cannot understand why he should go against the norm of behavior dictated by the times. In a second meeting with the government agent, Tomas stalls for time, having understood that the purpose of the cat-and-mouse game is to get him to name names. Then, abruptly preempting the inevitable chain of events, he resigns his medical post, becomes a window washer, and starts roaming Prague with bucket and brush in hand.

Having given up his cherished profession for reasons he finds difficult to formulate in the language of moral principle, Tomas experiences his new, footloose situation as a wonderful opportunity to resume the adventure of his "epic womanizing."[39] The narrator explains that considered within Tomas's existential code, the adventure is cognitive rather than purely sensual. Tomas is driven by the desire to know and possess the world in the variety of infinitesimal differences that distinguish one woman from another at the instant of sexual abandon. The categorical imperative of his sexual libertinism is another expression of the need that made him choose surgery as a vocation. "Even with his mistresses, he could never quite put down the imaginary scalpel. Since he longed to take possession of something deep inside them, he needed to slit them open" (p. 200). Having divested himself of the socially sanctioned practice of his quest for that kind of knowledge, Tomas indulges it in the unlicensed form of epic womanizing, for which the picaresque life of the itinerant window washer is ideally suited.

In essence, Tomas's refusal to sign the retraction represents a move out from under the sway of his "*Es muss sein*" into the lightness of freedom, experienced as erotic disponibility. But to the outside world, his renunciation of a brilliant career makes him a hero/martyr for the times,[40] a reputation that causes him to be courted by the tall, stooped editor and by his own son. Such is the paradoxical path of Tomas's inner autonomy. We see him, once again frozen at the window of his flat, contemplating the impenetrable irrationality of his decision not to sign a statement he agrees with. "Alone in his flat, he stared across the courtyard at the dirty walls of the building opposite" (p. 221). Tomas considers the loss of the existential possibility embodied by the quixotic editor while on the wall that blocks his view into a larger world, history, "that smudge on time's pure surface,"[41] paints its gray over the grime. As his old motif "*Einmal ist keinmal*" jingles with derisory lightness inside his brain, Tomas meditates on the history of his nation within the larger frame of European events. What emerges is "a pair of sketches from the pen of mankind's fateful inexperience" (p. 223). He reflects that in 1618 the Czech estates acted boldly, even recklessly, in their rebellion against Habsburg encroachments upon their religious and civic freedoms. The effect of the Prague defenestration was the Czech defeat at White Mountain, followed by the near destruction of the nation in the course of an expanded all-European war that lasted thirty years. By contrast, the signing of the Munich agreement in 1938, a display of cowardice, nevertheless failed to stave off Hitler's occupation of the country and paved the way for the Second World War. Czech historical destiny traces a line of action that in its paradoxical relation between intent and outcome closely resembles the course of Tomas's two linked decisions. (The fatal repetition of the terminal numeral 8 in 1618, 1938, 1948, 1968, creates a rhyming, just like the repetition of Tomas's "no.")

In the light of his historical reflections, Tomas's two acts of disengagement make tragic sense together, as a single gesture of stepping out of history in favor of something intangible, which for lack of a better term we may call the irreducibly human. Perhaps it is the same mysterious quality of being human, in spite of the odds, that draws Tomas to the "dark beauty" of Sophocles' play. "Then tell me, Doctor, do you really think that Communists should put out their eyes?" the man from the Ministry of the Interior had pressed (p. 186). Apart from the gross provocation, the question also strikes at the gist of Tomas's article, which we can reconstruct from the brief summary given in the first chapter of this movement. The relevant sentence is: "When Oedipus realized that he himself was the cause of their suffering, he put out his own eyes and wandered blind away from Thebes" (p. 176).

Whatever else one may read into the tragedy, Oedipus' gesture of self-mutilation is the culmination of a rising tide of horror. But it is also a multifaceted symbolic act of self-definition that reveals Oedipus' spirit at the moment of exercising a residual option for freedom, a self-branding that marks him off to live the rest of his life outside Thebes, with the terrible imprint of human significance on his face.

Tomas's elliptical restatement of Oedipus' story deliberately leaves out the suprahuman dimension of the Apollonian prophecy. He eliminates the speculations of the chorus about the possibility of a divine origin for the mysterious foundling of Mount Cythaeron, whose groves are sacred to Dionysos: "Who was it bore you, child? One of / the long lived nymphs who lay with Pan—the father who treads the hills?" (Soon after, the chorus comes down to earth, to contemplate Oedipus as the paradigm of human nothingness: "O generations of men, how I / count you as equal with those who live / not at all! . . . Oedipus, you are / my pattern of this / Oedipus, you and your fate!") Tomas's summary of the tragedy also dispenses with the hypothesis of a malignant Apollo pulling strings in the background, which Oedipus himself entertains in an agonizing moment of doubt before the light of truth strikes him: "Would not one rightly judge and say that on me / these things were sent by some malignant God?"[42]

The metaphysical framework of Tomas's interpretation of Oedipus appears stripped down to Jocasta's view, when she says that "chance is all in all / and man can clearly foreknow nothing." In the play, Jocasta herself cannot sustain the burden of her advice to Oedipus that it is "best to live lightly,"[43] without trying to match the external shape of our acts with our darkest intuitions about them. Soon after uttering these words, Jocasta is seen bringing garlands in a fearful attempt to appease Apollo, whose oracles she does not believe in. The queen's existential code of "lightness" does not hold up to the dreadful revelation of the scheming Apollo at work behind the mask of Tyche. She hangs herself in the darkness of her bedchamber even before Oedipus has performed his last stab at the violent truth.

It is for Oedipus to enact the ritualistic gesture of self-indictment, by which he acknowledges as his own the actions he committed in ignorance. "It was Apollo, friend, Apollo, / that brought this bitter bitterness, / my sorrows to completion. / But the hand that struck me / was none but my own."[44] As he speaks these words, Oedipus is showing the citizens of Thebes the bloody mask of a man who has just gouged out his eyes. The moment of excruciating pain is also a triumph of human significance over the malignant tangle of necessity and chance that a scheming god has devised as a trap for Oedipus. The act of self-mutilation contains the affirmation of a residual freedom attainable at the crest of the tragic agon, in an illumination of spirit that transforms the heaviest of fates into the ecstatic lightness of true being.

It is this pivotal moment of recognition, duly marked by Tomas's article, that the Ministry of the Interior finds so threatening. Kundera's narrative voice, expanding on the implications of Tomas's essay, takes issue with the intellectuals of his generation who, acting in ignorance, propelled Communism into power in 1948 and then, twenty years later, sought in vain to take back their deed, whose consequences had escaped their control. "We didn't know! We were deceived! We were true believers! Deep in our hearts we are innocent!" (p. 176). On "the planet of inexperience" (p. 224), where all humans are compelled to act in darkness, the plea of presumptive innocence amounts to a cop-out from humanity.

Tomas, having experienced his carnival of erotic freedom for several years, finds himself suddenly assailed by anxiety, signaled by the pressure in his stomach. "Prague has grown so ugly lately," Tereza says to him (p. 233). Under his coaxing she confesses that her revulsion is caused by the telltale odor of female genitals that emanates from his hair. The intensity of Tereza's misery explodes the beautiful balloon of Tomas's sexual adventurism. He tells himself that his compulsive womanizing may be, after all, the last vestige of his "*Es muss sein,*" an imperative that enslaves him. His love-*soucit* speaks to him in the irresistible language of a death metaphor from

Tereza's dream: "I was buried," she tells him. "I'd been buried for a long time. You came to see me every week. Each time you knocked at the grave, and I came out. My eyes were full of dirt" (p. 227). Not long before, Tereza had brought the maimed crow home in her red scarf, and the combined power of the two images of death and compassion overwhelms Tomas. One night he dreams of an "enormous naked woman" whose image makes him experience his sexual excitement as a mechanical reflex of his body, contemplated by an alienated mind. Out of that dream vision, Tomas constructs his new theory of sex and love, which unlinks the two by reducing male sexual desire to the act in which it finds its basic expression. "If excitement is a mechanism our Creator uses for His own amusement, love is something that belongs to us alone and enables us to flee the Creator. Love is our freedom. Love lies beyond '*Es muss sein!*' " (p. 236). Tomas reasons like a newly confirmed fool of love, trying to justify a decision that has nothing to do with his reason. He will go with Tereza to the village, having created his own utopia about a love that can be detached from the "clockwork of sex" (p. 237). In that vehicle of intellectual convenience he can steer his mind's passage into Tereza's idyllic world.

After the closing of the lovers' tragic circle, the novel explores the finale of nothingness in two contrasting, antiphonal visions of human mortality. The penultimate movement, "The Grand March," is sharply lit and noisy, casting its action on a vast spatial and temporal scale as it explores the problematics of history. Part 7, which follows, sketches a single fluid line of action in an atmosphere suffused by an indefinable quietude. Its title, "Karenin's Smile," draws attention to the mysterious transformational nature of Tereza's dog, thus indicating that the movement will center on the problematics of nature. The lovers' isolation in an unnamed Czech village, with Karenin as companion, gains in significance by being played against the global dimensions of "The Grand March," which begins in Germany during World War II and reaches from the Cambodian border to California in the early eighties. Kundera has explained to us in musical terms the emotional effect he sought by this final contrast.[45] The *fortissimo* of the penultimate movement, followed by the *adagio pianissimo* of the novel's ending, reverses the harsh terminal dissonance we heard in *The Book of Laughter and Forgetting* in favor of a gentler resonance.

In the interplay between the two parts, the actual sequence of fictional events is deliberately violated by the anachronistic order of presentation. Franz's march on Cambodia and Sabina's ultimate flight to California occur several years after the lovers' death in the village, which is made known to us at the end of part 3. Detached from the proper sequential spot in the causal chain that History weaves for itself, "The Grand March" is like a window in the facade of a half-ruined building. Looking through it, we see bits and pieces of fragmented, almost phantasmagoric action that seems like a parody of what History was meant to be.

The section opens with a digression on kitsch,[46] around which all the subsequent episodes are organized. Unlike the meditation on Nietzsche and Parmenides, these reflections are not attached to the existential code of a single character. Rather, they speak for the novel as a whole, defining "kitsch" as an aesthetic category with a vast metaphysical dimension. The phenomenological analysis of the concept is supported by a narrative background that centers on three deaths. "Kitsch is a folding screen set up to curtain off death," says the narrator (p. 253), thus exposing the blinding, illusionistic function of the device. To understand how kitsch operates, we might borrow terms already familiar to us from Sabina's description of her technique of "double exposure." Kitsch always serves up the "intelligible lie," whose particular stylization differs depending on time and place. Instead of the heroic socialist realist image of a steel factory under construction, we may get the kitsch of American happiness represented by a big car full of kids, but the aim and effect are the same: to please the eye and heart in accordance with a conventional set of expectations.

Kitsch, which is endowed with a tireless capacity to swallow up reality and churn it out as something plastic, seems to have a special appetite for death. But that craving for death is also the expression of an equally strong compulsion at the heart of kitsch, which is to evade shit. Kundera's digression situates the problematics of kitsch at these two extreme margins of our being.

The relation of death to shit is illustrated by the opening vignette about Yakov Stalin's suicide in a German prison camp during World War II. Kundera makes clear that he treats this story as fact: "Not until 1980 were we able to read in the *Sunday Times* how Stalin's son, Yakov, died" (p. 243). Yakov habitually left a mess after himself in the camp latrine. Some British officers who shared the facility complained, and Yakov demanded a hearing with the German commander, who brushed the issue off as unworthy of his attention. Unable to bear the humiliation, Yakov threw himself into the electrified barbed-wire fence of the camp. Kundera calls his gesture "the sole metaphysical death" (p. 245) in a war that mass-produced death.

Kitsch, as Kundera understands it, cannot be explained as a simple absence of beauty, and even less as its opposite, ugliness. Parmenides' scheme of polarities fails to account for a category of human expression that is the aesthetic equivalent of the theological notion of sin. Kitsch is a perversion of beauty, just as sin (the Christian term for evil) is much more than a transgression of law, being in essence a perversion of the natural love of God. Yakov Stalin, the unclean son of a deified father, is a man who experiences his personal physical being as a metaphysical scandal. It seems to me that he figures here as Kundera's variation on Ivan Karamazov, a character whose inner pain also proceeds from a tormenting relation to a monstrous father. Kundera hints at such a reading when he writes, "Shit is a more onerous theological problem than is evil. Since God gave man freedom, we can, if need be, accept the idea that He is not responsible for man's crimes. The responsibility for shit, however, rests entirely with Him, the Creator of man" (p. 246).

Here the question of shit, or to be more precise, the exposure of its existence as a stumbling block to the human mind, is couched in terms of a judgment of God, bringing to mind Ivan Karamazov's treatment of the question of evil in history. Ivan, the rebellious son, stages an imaginary trial of the idea of God the Father inside the laboratory of his Euclidean mind. His advocacy of human innocence culminates in a rhetorical gesture of withering contempt for the impeached Creator, who stands indicted as either a tyrannical sadist or an impotent: "It's not God that I don't accept, Alyosha, only I most respectfully return Him the ticket."[47] But Ivan, the Russian radical intellectual, is really a sham rationalist. His weapon, which he calls reason, is the emotional logic of indignation, adapted from his French ancestor, Fouquier-Tinville. Yakov Stalin's existential category is shame—a silent, hidden torment that ill bears disclosure. When the uncleanliness of his body is revealed in the eyes of strangers, he hurls the offending part of himself against the electrified fence.

Yakov, who is trapped by the kitsch image of his deified father, cannot play the avenger, pointing the accusing finger of scandal outward. His act of self-immolation is a judgment against himself, inspired by a paroxysm of reverence. Yakov Stalin's body pinned to the deadly fence seems a grotesque parody of the futile Christ pinned forever to his unredemptive cross. But it also calls to mind another image from this novel, that of Tereza seated on the toilet bowl, enduring the scandal of the human body in the absence of the beautifying screen of kitsch. Our civilization, as Kundera glimpses it through Tereza's moment of truth, seems an insubstantial superstructure thrown over the basic matter of our accumulating excrement. "We are happily ignorant of the invisible Venice of shit underlying our bathrooms, bedrooms, dance halls, and parliaments" (p. 156). This damning upside-down view of civilization demystifies the Venice of our creativity, and all our other strivings, as varnish on the face of nature, a labor that produces kitsch.

The accidental death of Franz in Thailand occurs decades after Yakov Stalin's suicide, and in another geographical zone. Having survived the anticlimactic protest march to the Cambodian border, which is planted with Vietnamese mines, Franz succumbs ignominiously to a blow on the head delivered by an unknown Bangkok thug, apparently for no other reason than the theft of his wallet. The entire event of the "Grand March" appears as a mockery of the act of consciousness it was meant to dramatize. The chief organizers are European, mostly French intellectuals, joined by an American contingent. Their aim is to demonstrate solidarity with the plight of Cambodia and demand that a team of doctors be allowed to treat the people of that small country, whose fatal affliction seems to be its geographical location. The recent historical misfortunes of Cambodia make it a perfect Third World analogue to Kundera's Czechoslovakia. For European consciousness at the time, Cambodia had the advantage of being above, or better, under, the binary crunch of cold war partisanship. In 1970 the Americans unseated Sihanouk and put Lon Nol in power, the better to prosecute their brutal, losing war in Vietnam; their military withdrawal led to the toppling of Lon Nol by Pol Pot's Khmer Rouge guerrillas, whose brutalities led to the military intervention of their former allies, the North Vietnamese, who installed the puppet government of Heng Samrin, in charge at the time of Franz's march.

The happenings during and around the protest event, which is followed doggedly by a huge caravan of media people, seem no less confusing and absurd than the acts that led to the situation being protested. An internal quarrel develops, pitting the French linguistic phalanx against the American actress, who, as a true daughter of Hollywood, insists that celebrity should take the lead over mere intellectuals. In the midst of the squabble, a photographer steps on a mine and is ripped apart under the eyes of the TV cameras. At the border of Cambodia, which is formed by a small river, the march halts at the line of death across which Thai sharpshooters exchange fire with the Vietnamese forces stationed on the Cambodian side. Using a bullhorn and a Khmer interpreter, the European intellectuals broadcast their appeal to be allowed to enter with medical supplies. Their cry is countered by an impenetrable silence.

Within that silence, Kundera has encapsulated the great finale of nothingness he senses engulfing European history. Paris, once the holy city of the secular West, can still issue invitations to such global political events as this march, and Franz, the last European of the great tradition of the left, may still join the call. But the power axis of contemporary world significance no longer turns around Paris. Kundera's vision of a reduced Europe as a tiny stage where people gesture to each other, unable to engage anyone outside a confined audience, elicits a sudden upsurge of tenderness[48] that recalls Jakub's last look at Bohemia in *The Farewell Party.* But here we are saying goodbye not only to Europe but also to an idea of History that has been one of Europe's major inventions, and perhaps also its root disease.

Meanwhile, in the New World, the view of California from inside Sabina's head shows an abstract place that seems to stand for the ultimate border, where the extremity of the Western adventure falls into the Pacific Ocean, which is, after all, an Oriental sea. Sabina, we are told, is fearful of "sinking into American earth" (p. 273). She has drafted a will requesting that her dead body be cremated and her ashes thrown to the winds. The narrator draws attention to the contrast between Sabina's airy death option and the fate of the two lovers, Tomas and Tereza, who die crushed under the weight of their overturned, hurtling truck. Their distant accident is the third violent death this section forces us to confront, even though the accident is now only a memory in the mind of Sabina, vaguely contemplating her own impending death. She keeps receiving letters from Tomas's son Simon, who has become a practicing Catholic, lives in a Czech village, and, we learn, had one last meeting with his father, which was friendly. The reconciliation between the young man, who bears the Hebrew name of the founder of the Church, and his father, whose name signifies evangelical doubt, must have taken place shortly before the fatality, since we hear Tereza, in the next section, urging Tomas to meet with his son, just before the end.

Death speaks its unique counterpoint of the banal with the meaningful in the epistolary communication from a solemn young man to the casually aging woman somewhere in California. But the last word of "The Grand March" belongs to the noisy Marie-Claude. Having repossessed her straying husband in death, she has managed to impose herself on his memory with the self-serving aggressiveness that is her code. "A Return After Long Wanderings" is the inscription she orders carved into Franz's tombstone, in a verbal gesture that unites kitsch with the vanity of stone Sabina had noted among the tombs of Montparnasse. "Kitsch is the stopover between being and oblivion" (p. 278).

That judgment-definition, with which the section closes, is a bitterly ironic answer to the question "What remains?" "What remains of the dying population of Cambodia? . . . of Tomas? . . . of Beethoven? . . . of Franz?" (pp. 277–278)—whereby Kundera redirects our attention from the grave sadness of the *Ubi sunt?* theme to a grotesque vision of the survival characteristics of the intelligible lie.

The seventh movement, which shows the lovers descending to their death preceded by Karenin, rehearses the finale of nothingness in the truer light of nature, heightened by the incandescent glow of tragedy. Since Tomas and Tereza's passing is already firmly embedded in our consciousness, we read everything that happens in this segment through the melancholy mood of a prolonged mourning.[49] Death is the unseen, animating presence in the brief idyll lived by Tomas and Tereza, who, as we already know, experience it through divergent sensibilities. Tereza, who follows the living clock of cyclical time Karenin has come to embody for her, is happy enough under the "sweet law of repetition" (p. 299), her closest approximation to the timelessness of Paradise. We see her, with Karenin at her side, sitting on a hillside reading a book, intermittently minding her grazing cattle and looking into the open landscape. The image has the humble grace of the Czech pastoral.

The friendly chairman of the local farm collective is an easy boss, walking around the village with his pet pig Mefisto, who behaves like a dog and looks like "a heavy-thighed woman in high heels" (p. 283). Mefisto's name reminds us of that most historical of all devil figures, who accompanied Faust in all his erratic temporal undertakings. No, we are not in Eden, which comes before the beginning of mortal time, but somewhere much later, inside an interval of calm created in a small place after the great noise of history has passed it by.

The death of Karenin is the major unrehearsed event in this movement. He develops cancer, and in spite of Tomas's successful surgery the tumor grows back. Karenin must be put to sleep with a lethal injection Tomas administers. The description of Karenin's dying, as experienced by his two loving master/companions, has a sustained pathos of beauty to match the intensity of the scene in *The Book of Laughter and Forgetting* where Kundera records his father's death. The futile medical gestures show all the fragility of human loving, agonizingly poised between hope and desperation. Tomas's medical skill is at least effective in releasing Karenin into a painless death. After the injection, Tomas and Tereza carry Karenin's body to the garden and set him in his grave between two apple trees. The man and the woman, in muddy boots, appear to us like the primordial Adam and Eve, already fallen, inventing for all time to come the tender rituals of their newfound mortality.

The dog Karenin, Tereza's closest friend and Tomas's sole remaining playfellow, is the ruling presence in this movement, where Kundera seeks to reclaim nature from the devastation man has inflicted on it. During the interval of hope when Karenin is recovering from surgery, Tereza and Tomas read a smile on his face, interpreting it as a sign that he is happy and wants to go on living. We can never know if Karenin's facial language is anything but the reflection of human *soucit,* but it figures here as the locus of mystery through which the dog's *anima* issues out into the world as something tenderly human. The narrator points out that the Modern Era of European history, which unleashed an intensified human violence against nature, can be roughly dated from the time when Descartes proclaimed man to be sole master and proprietor ("*maître et propriétaire*") of nature (p. 288). Simultaneously, Descartes reduced all other living creatures to the condition of *machina animata* by denying them a soul. In the late twentieth century, nature is rapidly retreating under our depredations, and we are dangerously close to being left in possession of a dead mass of matter hurtling through endless space.

By placing his meditations on "what remains" of nature under the mysterious sign of Karenin's smile, Kundera tries to restore the balance, setting the dog up as the ultimate measure of what it means to be human. It is in this light that we should see the coming together of Nietzsche and the Franciscan motif of the miraculous as Kundera contemplates his image of Tereza, the woman who talks in human language not only to

Karenin but also to her cows. Now we see Nietzsche emerging from Tereza's shadow, as he was on the day he went mad on a street in Turin in the winter of 1889. He stood for a long while weeping into the neck of a horse still quivering from the coachman's whip. "I feel his gesture has broad implications," says the narrator. "Nietzsche was trying to apologize to the horse for Descartes" (p. 290).

After the wrenching pain of Karenin's death and burial, and the reverberating echo of Nietzsche's tragic *peripeteia,* the last scenes flow through a more temperate emotional zone. Tomas and Tereza will be taken by death at the crest of a wave of bounty, when love is on the mend. Tereza, who knows she has been neglecting Tomas because of Karenin, decides to make amends by prettying up for a special evening together. She has just stepped out into the front room, freshly bathed and dressed, when Tomas bursts in with the chairman and a young farmhand who is wincing with pain. Tomas has just set his dislocated shoulder back in its socket with one decisive motion of his skilled hands. A short while before, watching Tomas change a tire on his truck, Tereza had seen a man no longer young, whose roughened hand could never again hold the surgeon's scalpel. But now, in the generous mood of the moment, surrounded by friends, he looks animated and happy. "Let's all go and dance," proposes Tereza (p. 311), and they soon set out, all four of them, for a nearby town where the hotel bar has a dance floor.

Holding each other as they circle the floor, Tomas and Tereza talk a little, and Tereza voices her self-incriminating thoughts. "Haven't you noticed I've been happy here, Tereza?" Tomas says, adding, "And it's a terrific relief to realize you're free, free of all missions" (p. 313). We suddenly know that all this time we have been in the garden of Epicurus, where the revelation of happiness comes gently shaded by the reflection of mortality.

It is getting late, and the chapter holds yet another revelation. It comes in the same narrative breath, but with a deeper, darker hue that betokens inspired dreaming. We see the lovers entering their sleeping place: it is a room with two beds pushed together, and when they switch on the light, a nocturnal butterfly escapes from under the lampshade and begins circling in the air. In the preceding chapter, the same butterfly had appeared in Tereza's dream, and she was already standing inside this room. The lampshade was also the same, but the butterfly was still perched precariously on outstretched wings.

The effect of the rhythmic repetition of this image suggests the vital step of beauty about to enter, breaking through the partition of reality that keeps it hidden. The circling butterfly, which was once a larva, traces the mystery of the final transformation into the transparent medium of absolute transience. The lovers can still hear the strains of the piano and violin rising from below, but their death is already on the wing.

7

Immortality

OR

Midnight on Prague's Astrological Clock

In a novel in which reflection proceeds from metaphor, a singular dream image has the power to unlock the meaning encoded in the author's larger narrative gesture. That instance occurs in part 2 of *Immortality*,[1] in the skit Kundera attaches to the story of Bettina von Arnim and Goethe. The grotesquely attired Goethe, a veteran immortal in the 156th year of his existence in the hereafter, recounts his last dream to his companion, the more recently dead Hemingway.

In the dream (part 2, chapter 16), Goethe saw himself standing behind the scene of a puppet show, directing the performance of *Faust*, when suddenly he became aware that the theater was empty. Instead of watching the play, the audience was behind him, watching his every motion. Retreating in terror, he woke up covered in sweat, hiding in a corner of his room with a bedsheet pulled over his face.

Goethe's flight from the myriad-eyed monster of publicity exemplifies the desire to withdraw from a world of debased values that serves as a thematic link for the multiple time frames of the novel's fractured action. Narrative time, released from the compulsion of forward motion, follows its own capricious course. It meanders back and forth in self-reflection, often letting go of the story altogether, always improvising its own gesture of escape from the tyranny of the straight line. So it must wait until part 4, chapter 17, for Goethe to remind Hemingway that both of them are nothing but a frivolous fantasy in another author's fiction. Their puppeteer is playing the theme of immortality as a farce, unleashing a wave of laughter to rock the Pantheon. Goethe seems to appreciate the irony of his situation. "Man doesn't know how to be mortal. And when he dies, he doesn't even know how to be dead" (p. 215). He admits that a residual vanity made him choose to appear that day in the youthful, virile aspect of his Sturm und Drang period. That is the image he wants to leave Hemingway with, as he proceeds to disappear into the finale of nothingness, having shed even the desire to survive within the pages of his books. "Those books exist in the world without me," he says (p. 214). "I have decided to make use of my death at last and, if I can express it with such an imprecise term, to go to sleep. To enjoy the delights of total nonexistence, which my great enemy Novalis used to say has a bluish color" (p. 216). Goethe's exit metaphor and the ironic, sensuous voice that delivers it awaken the reader to the game of the living author standing behind the puppet stage.

The meditation on Goethe's immortality links together parts 2 and 4 in a comedy of misunderstanding whose heavy historic import descends into Olympian levity. Kundera's ironic, analytical voice is heard insistently throughout the story of Bettina's duel with Goethe, alternately prompting and dissecting the combination of images that make up the action. But in the enveloping outer movements that frame the historic couple, part 1 and its resolution within the dominant fifth step on the scale of seven, Kundera joins the mortal game of his contemporary characters by seeking refuge within the magic circle of novelistic possibilities.

The question of illusion, its meaning and value in confrontation with the face of the world of reality, is paramount in part 1 ("The face"). The curtain rises on the narrator, whom we recognize as Milan Kundera long before he names himself, in a casual phrase dropped by the manager of a Montparnasse café as he hands Avenarius a paperback copy of *Life Is Elsewhere*: "Mr. Kundera stopped by here. He said he would be late . . ." (p. 152). This is the message that links the present novel to the one Kundera wrote twenty years earlier, while still living in Prague. But now we see him lounging at the poolside of a supermodern health club in the penthouse of a high-rise building with a panoramic view of Paris. This setting evokes a host of echoes, recalling the observatory in Rennes, from which Kundera first recorded the sounds and sights of Western Europe in *The Book of Laughter and Forgetting*. From a greater distance, we hear Dr. Havel's whistle summoning all the impossible Don Juans from their old hunting grounds in the spa towns of Bohemia. The calendar shows it is already 1988,[2] and the narrator has a rendezvous with a man whose name and title smack of the ponderous pedant. Professor Avenarius, too, will be late. His entrance is postponed until the middle of part 3. In his absence the narrator relaxes into the posture of an idle observer.

"The woman might have been sixty or sixty-five"—the novel's first sentence—captures the moment of perception when an object first flows into the eye. Looking on, the narrator sees the woman standing in the pool waist-deep in water, listening intently to the instructions of a young lifeguard. She is practicing deep breathing, which the narrator, suddenly moved, compares to the puffing sound of the locomotive of his childhood. The sound speaks to him with the timeless magic of an idyll, whose pathos is vulnerable to the ravages of time, as is the body of the aging woman herself. To the lifeguard the woman's puffing is merely comical.

The lesson is over and the woman suddenly turns back toward the lifeguard. Smiling, she raises her hand in farewell. The graceful lightness of her gesture stuns the narrator with its beauty, as if a playful feminine hand had just thrown a multicolored ball to a lover. The gesture opens a kaleidoscopic world of meaning the instant it enters the narrator's field of vision. Illumined by male desire, the woman's body comes into focus, in an erotic epiphany ignited by the crossing of the live wires of memory and *soucit*. The instant her hand flew up in the air, the woman forgot her age, momentarily shedding the mask of aging flesh time had pressed on her features. In creating the illusion of being-beyond-time, the gesture allowed her submerged self to surge into expression, imaging a face and body far more faithful to her essence than her actual likeness. This is the hide-and-seek game of remembering/forgetting (*vzpomínání/zapomínání*) whereby the body's *anima* manifests its presence. It is also a manifestation of the desire for immortality that keeps vigil in our mortal bodies, always ready to take wing.

For the observer, the anachronistic gesture has the effect of shifting the realm of erotic significance into the past. Whether in the libertine mode of Don Juan's unfinished list of 1,003 conquests, or in the mode of high feeling that prompted Stendhal to define beauty as the promise of happiness, the erotic instance opens up time as a prospect of possibility. But in this retrospective novel, eroticism remains trapped under the hard surfaces and the harder sounds of a world that resembles Kundera's health club, lined with wall-to-wall mirrors that multiply ad infinitum the physical sameness of well-toned bodies. In pursuit of the latest rejuvenation technique, they enact the contemporary variation of the human desire for immortality. Exiled from the world of actuality, Eros takes refuge in memory, staking a claim on a domain that rises above the plane of physical possibility. The narrator's nostalgia for an impossible object of desire finds articulation in two syllables of a single word. "I was strangely moved. And the word Agnes entered my mind. Agnes. I had never known a woman by that name" (p. 4).

Agnes, whose name emerges from the older woman's gesture like a flame rising out of water, is initially apprehended within a metaphor that negates the conditions and causal relations of the given world. Summoned into being by a single word that transforms a snapshot of reality into the stuff dreams are made of, she is a privileged player in a polyhistorical cast of characters. The narrator calls her "the heroine of my novel" (p. 7) when he first visualizes her, naked, stepping out of her empty marital bed, about to confront a world whose negation is encoded within her name.

The process of Agnes's fictional incarnation, as described in the second chapter, doubles as a meditation on her existential code. Whereas Tomas, in *The Unbearable Lightness of Being*, was conceived in the pendulum swing of interrogative cogitation, Agnes's image as a woman with her own body, face, and personal history originates in a more secret chamber of the narrator's mind. He is lying in bed, in early-morning half-slumber, sinking in and out of dreaming. The transistor radio on his pillow pours the unpurged noises of reality into his ears, which his imagination, oscillating between wakefulness and dreaming, instantly transforms into a parade of operatic clowns singing about the weather. The parodistic motif is followed by the narrator's confession that this swinging state between waking and sleeping is splendid enough to dispel his regret at having been born. And yet that unexpected flourish in a composition whose canon sings the dark melody of disengagement from living sounds strangely beautiful. It suggests the vitality of that other generative pendulum, whose pulsations inscribe the parabola of male desire upon the map of a real woman's body. The narrator's delight in the early-morning hour recalls Bartleff, the lone holy fool stranded in the age of terminal paradoxes, who compared its leisure to "a beautiful sculpture-lined bridge across which I stroll from dream into reality. During those hours how I long for a miracle!"[3]

Kundera's bedroom may be located in Paris, but at the start of a hot summer day in 1988, when the radio announces a storm, his imagination abolishes time and space by wiring Montparnasse to Charles Bridge in Prague. He walks in the direction of the Castle, nearing the spot where Jaromil Xavier entered the open window with the silhouette of a woman half concealed by a rococo bird cage. The window is closed now, and the Prague stroller turns back, slowly recrossing the road lined by Baroque statues, whose insistent, pathos-laden, upward-pointing gestures he questions.

The expressive power of a gesture rides on the illusion of authenticity it projects upon the observer, making it a transparent messenger between two selves suddenly individualized in the act of communication. The narrator initially read the gesture of the woman in the pool as the unveiling of her feminine essence. But in the second chapter, the woman has vanished and the gesture has come to inhabit Agnes. This discovery leads to the maxim "many people, few gestures" (p. 7), which points out that some demographic norm of human individuation has been exceeded.

The motif of a woman turning back toward a man with a smile as her hand flies up in the air traverses the whole novel like a semantic river. It keeps changing in value as it is adopted by various characters at different moments in time. When it first surfaces in part 1, the gesture has the transparency of a mountain stream that is, however, flowing downward. It eventually disappears in the muddy delta of confusion. In part 7, its feminine essence is lost to parody. Kundera's phenomenology of gestures is permeated by the feeling of human helplessness before time, whose medium of manifestation is nonfreedom. We are trapped in bodies we did not choose and whose degradation we cannot prevent. Our visible bodies—crowned by faces in which lovers, in the first blush of desire, read the expression of the self's uniqueness—are mere instruments programmed to reproduce motions whose origin and intent are moot. Repetition, not originality, is the operative mode of that pantomime charged with the pathos of lost significance.

The pessimism of these reflections drifts unimpeded from the narrator's mind into Agnes's. "When I wake up, at almost eight-thirty, I try to picture Agnes. She is lying, like me, in a wide bed. The right side of the bed is empty" (p. 6). But even while identifying with Agnes, the narrator simultaneously strips her of the privilege of unexamined individuation which is every heroine's invisible aura. Agnes experiences the phenomenon as a radical estrangement from her own face, a sensation most virulent whenever she is exposed to the unwanted scrutiny of looks or lenses.

Agnes is an attractive woman in her mid-forties. She lives in Paris with her loving husband, Paul, and a teenaged daughter, Brigitte, both of whom she loves. She works in some mathematical capacity at a small office. The scantiness of these data only highlights the singularity of Agnes's inner world. The Saturday morning when we see her stepping out of bed, walking noiselessly past Brigitte's bedroom, has a special significance; it is the fifth anniversary of her father's death. She guards the privacy of that remembrance even from her nearest ones; her anxiety about disclosure defines her, body and soul. We recall that sensing the narrator's eyes upon her body, she fled to get dressed, in a gesture of feminine modesty.

Agnes's bond to her father is the key to the spiritual order of her being; this key is unavailable to those who share in her everyday life. Agnes herself understood the depth of her love for her father only during the three days she spent alone with him after her mother's death. In that brief interlude, they renewed the magic companionship of her childhood when he used to take her walking through the woods. After his death, she discovered that he had deposited a considerable sum in her Swiss account. At first, she thought of sharing the legacy with Laura, her sister eight years her junior, for whom she feels a nagging sense of responsibility. In the end she decides to keep the gift a secret, having decoded it as a sign meant for her alone, an invitation to seek freedom by withdrawing into solitude.

Educated in Paris and teaching in Switzerland, Agnes's father, a distinguished mathematician, comes from a German family originally from Hungary but now dispersed throughout the world. The status of expatriate cosmopolitan intellectual with roots in Central Europe ties Agnes's father to Milan Kundera, as the author appears both in and out of this fictional circle. Though educated at a French lycée in a small Swiss town located on the linguistic border between the French and German cantons, Agnes shares her father's attachment to German, the language of a great culture tainted by its recent history. In the recesses of Agnes's memory, insulated from the noises of contemporary Paris, the father's voice speaks a German idiom that resonates with both the appeal of speculative reason and the beauty of pure poetry.

Once, when as a child Agnes asked him if he believed in God, her father replied: "I believe in the Creator's computer" (p. 11), confining the idea of God to his sole function as engineer. By bracketing off the question about God's ontological essence, the statement sheds a sharp light on God as he appears to humans within the magnetic field of their consciousness. Neither a personal credo nor a theological definition, the father's reticent, intellectually ascetic observation yields the root metaphor of our contemporary world wherein we function, reduced to opaque instrumentality. It is a world where the creative and normative powers once attributed to God have been usurped by the computer and television, the two magic boxes of *techne*. Like all things of power, these instruments of our nonfreedom speak to us from behind a curtain, a screen of double intent, revealing and concealing a ruthless will to dominate by appealing to our facile need for convenience. In the age of mass democracies, which translate the banner values of freedom, equality, and the pursuit of happiness into transactions of consumerism, the user-friendly interface of a computer operates according to a law of inequality. So the maximal complexity of a system programmed by scientific intelligence generates the simplest possible signs even a child can read. In a parallel action on our TV screens, the talking heads process the world by reducing the plethora of camera-made images into sound bites. In the age of terminal paradoxes, the highest capabilities of an individual intelligence are drafted into collusion with the tentacular spread of universal ignorance. In a sorry parody of the creative act, intellect engineers the conditions of its own demise.

To Agnes's second question, whether he ever prayed, her father replied with impeccable logic that the idea of addressing a God who hides behind a computer is tantamount to praying to Edison whenever an electric bulb is switched on. The father's parable about a God concealed behind a mechanical screen offers an up-to-date variation of the *deus absconditus* theme, which, as Kundera told us,[4] is inscribed in the genetic code of the modern era of European history. *Immortality*'s images of contemporary Parisian life are all informed by the implicit argument that the creative thrust of that meaningful time sequence is over, and all the residual cultural activities designated by the prefix "post" (as in "postmodernist" and "posthistorical") belong to the redundant time of epilogues.

In philosophical terms, Ivan Karamazov's saying that he has given up trying to figure out whether it was God who invented man or vice versa is now a proposition without sting, a convention of contemporary theological discourse. The drama of man's revolt against the idea of God has been played out in a variety of ideological scripts that bore us. Into that vast yawn of exhausted humanism, the specter of the *ci-devant* majesty returns to haunt us in the guise of tribalism. For the post-ideological age of mass consumerism is also a pseudo-theological age. Its ubiquitous camera lenses fixed on the most private secrets of our existence simulate the benevolent eye of Divine Providence. Kundera's transistor had caught the proposal to monitor the safety of health delivery by installing photographic gear above the surgeon's operating table. And as I write this, TV screens show generals who describe the operations of smart bombs equipped with high-precision cameras, instantly recording the efficiency of a programmed kill.

Agnes, reflecting on the implications of her father's words, imagines a cosmic creator whose engineering capabilities extend to a multiplicity of computers turning out a variety of simultaneous programs of existence in a corresponding plurality of worlds. "That God created the world and then left it to a forsaken humanity trying to address him in an echoless void—this idea isn't new," she notes (p. 11). Her own hypothesis, which substitutes a series of computers for a single, personalized image of God, truly demystifies the residual self-centeredness lurking behind the complaint about an unresponsive God.

At the beginning of the modern era, Pascal articulated the human need for a divine presence spanning the abyss of infinite space, in the form of a negative proof of faith, akin to the pedestal for the upward soar of the Baroque theological gesture. By contrast, Agnes's hypothesis seems an update of Democritus's cosmic vision of a space swept clean of all theological ghosts. Its vastness is animated by the atomistic routine that Epicurus used as the backdrop for his moral serenity. Like the endless fall of atoms, Agnes's multiple computers purge the human mind of arrogance and the terrors that stalk in its wake. But the price of this release is the abandonment of the illusion of freedom, a prime philosophical value that is now reduced to the purposeless indeterminism of chance. Within Agnes's technological scheme, human individuation suffers the same collapse. The cosmic intelligence that programmed the human specimen as one of its numerous ontological projects may or may not have access to some Platonic *arche* of Being. Evident to Agnes is the fact that the human creature is thus a mere derivative of the original prototype, "giving rise to a large number of specimens that are based on the original model and haven't any individual essence. Just like a Renault car, its essence is deposited outside, in the archives of the central engineering office. Individual cars differ only in their serial numbers. The serial number of a human specimen is the face, that accidental and unrepeatable combination of features" (p. 12). In his despair at the sight of his father's malicious face, Ivan Karamazov had seen the mask of a mocking devil forging the act of creation to produce the pitiful human specimen. Agnes, interpreting her father's intellectual legacy, comes up with the whimsical image of an absentminded engineer busy at many projects, one of which is humanity and turns out to be an Edsel. What a comedown from Michelangelo's fresco of the creation of Adam, which displays face-to-face divine filiation, at that precise moment when Time uncoils at the touch of God's finger upon Man's outstretched hand! Contemporary restorers of the Sistine Chapel have uncovered the outline of a human brain in the convolutions of a cloudlike divine garment. No one has yet detected such a structural likeness in the intricate operations of artificial intelligence. A computer can outdo a genius in the volume of its memory and the speed with which it can manipulate symbols. But only the human brain can attach meaning to these functions.

Yet in the computerized world of mass-produced humanity the creation of meaning has retreated before the aggressive intensity of ego assertion. During her morning session at the health club, Agnes observes a woman who seems to pick on any subject introduced to discharge a violent, rapid-fire tirade of indignation. "No, no! You know perfectly well you're in the right!" she harangues her milder interlocutor in a voice that instantly climbs by an octave (p. 10). As she speaks, her head shakes rapidly, bobbing from side to side, and her eyebrows are raised high to match her voice. Agnes recognizes this as the gesture of protest against the violation of human rights. Her daughter, Brigitte, uses it often.

Viewed in the light of Agnes's ontological reflections, the militant angel's gesture of protest confirms the law of substitution that seems to convert all our acts and expressions into sham repetitions of some long-forgotten intent and purpose. "Many people, few gestures" the narrator had said. Agnes could add that there seem to be even fewer individual faces. The hysteria she senses in such expressions of ego assertion is the negative of a desire to reclaim the illusion of individuation from the emptiness of vanishing being.

But what about life after death, Agnes asks. What existential model has been programmed for us by the divine computer? She entertains two hypotheses. If the cosmic engineer is confined to a single computer operating solely on our planet, eternity could at best be only a variation on the form of existence we already know. The ensuing image of an infinity of time to be endured within the same accidental specimen of a face, to be looked at indefinitely by other faces, like those of the cackling women in the sauna, is a nightmare. Alternatively, in the pluralistic scenario of many computers operating in different worlds, it is possible to postulate a hierarchy of programs and with it the hope of rising above our current earthly level of existence. Agnes, we recall, is a daughter of fire, conceived of the seemingly impossible movement of a flame rising out of water. Her imagination responds to the vertical appeal of transcendence by summoning the image of a mysterious stranger as a messenger from an alternative higher world. He has already visited her once, and she knows that he will return to ask certain questions. The stranger, who does not seem to recognize the Eiffel Tower, knows however her innermost desire to step outside the conditions of earthly existence. He is the angel of her death, and his expected second visit on this anniversary renews the appeal of beauty wherein she reads the ultimate meaning of her father's legacy.

Agnes remembers the poem by Goethe that her father used to recite to her when she was about eight years old during their walks in the forest.

> Über allen Gipfeln
> Ist Ruh,
> In allen Wipfeln
> Spürest du
> Kaum einen Hauch;
> Die Vögelein schweigen im Walde.
> Warte nur, balde
> Ruhest du auch.

Kundera quotes it twice in chapter 6 (pp. 26 and 27), first in translation and then in the original German. The text is accompanied by a commentary that defines poetry as the dazzling effect achieved by the transformation of an instant of being into an object of memory, worthy of inspiring an unbearable nostalgia. The melody heard in Goethe's lyric stasis has the ineffable charm of musical silence, recalling the beauty/death motif associated with the sound of a golden ring falling into a silver basin. Tamina received that motif from Thomas Mann, and Agnes inherits a kindred beauty in a lyric image that fuses the powers of hearing and seeing at the summit of poetic intelligence. The experience of the poem stills all motion. It inhibits the forward flow of ideas in Agnes's consciousness, much like the rapture that held Dante and Virgil captive, listening to Casella's song at the foot of Mount Purgatory.[5] Kundera intervenes with a brief formal analysis of

Goethe's poem, tapping the pulse of its subtle melody at the point of asymmetric linkage between the first line and the fifth. This grammatical enjambment leaps over the border of two seemingly symmetrical four-line strophes in an effect that the design of this novel will reproduce more than once by vaulting a motif across the delimitation of the seven constituent parts.

Agnes remembers how her father read Goethe's poem to her one last time two or three days before dying. She understood it then as a sign of his impending death, a coded message delivered from the summit of his love. In her imagination the voice of her father's death calls to her "like a hunter's horn sounding from the depths of a forest" (p. 28). The flawless melody lures her—an invitation to a voyage into freedom and beauty, with the promise of adventure to match the immensity of her desire. In Paris, Agnes is virtually an expatriate, a daughter exiled from the father's magic forest in a lost Transylvania whose mythic charm remains irreducible, since it can no longer be located on the map of Central Europe.

After releasing Agnes from the sauna, the narrator throws her into the battle zone of a noisy Parisian thoroughfare, recognizable as the rue de Rennes. Once an unremarkable, relatively quiet street one strolled down on the way to St.-Germain-des-Prés, it is now an artery for the waves of commuters that keep spewing out of the huge Montparnasse Métro station. Agnes, walking against the traffic, tries to weave her way in and out of the ambulatory flow of humanity, pedestrian or mechanized. The motorcycles and the cars keep encroaching on the sidewalks, as if to lend their wheels to the advancing juggernaut from which Agnes cannot find refuge.

In the fast-food establishment to which she repairs for a bite, the aggressive ugliness pursues her in the image of open mouths, chomping, shouting, yawning with shameless abandon. A wave of revulsion washes over her as she takes in the primitive blood beat of a humanity marching nothingness. She experiences the terror of loss of being, then a wave of aggression. Back outside she finds herself passionately wanting the death of a dark-haired, helmeted girl riding a motorcycle from which the muffler has been deliberately removed. "Suddenly frightened by her hatred, she said to herself: the world is at some sort of border, if it is crossed, everything will turn to madness: people will walk the streets holding forget-me-nots or kill one another on sight. . . . There is a certain quantitative border that must not be crossed, yet no one stands guard over it and perhaps no one even realizes that it exists" (p. 22). Agnes knows that the instant she yielded to the gravitational tug of her murderous wish, she crossed into the world of insane terror. Her retreat from the borderline is a clue to the existential choice she envisages when she imagines herself walking through the streets of Paris with a single forget-me-not held in front of her face, ". . . staring at it tenaciously so as to see only that single beautiful blue point, to see it as the last thing she wanted to preserve for herself from a world she had ceased to love" (p. 21).

The blue flower, a metaphor born of the play of naming with seeming, anticipates the sensuous oblivion of Goethe's final sleep. By holding the obliterating wand before her face like a screen, Agnes performs a gesture that unveils her by veiling; her face is now screened from the looks of others. Kundera's imagination, schooled in the semantic music of Czech speech, implicates the duality of meaning signified by the two words[6] available in his native lexicon for the single word *visage* (face) that figures at the head of Agnes's initial movement. *Tvář* and the etymologically linked word *tvar* (form) relate to the verb *tvořiti* (to create), thus connecting Agnes's visible face to the expressive power of the unseen inner self that inhabits it. In Kundera's dictionary, the word *tvář* is a prime erotic category. We recall Jaromil's stab of desire when he saw Magda's sorrowful face (her *smutek/krásná tvář*) floating above the water.

Back at home after her rue de Rennes *psychomachia*, Agnes

has another insight while leafing through the pages of an illustrated magazine. She counts ninety-two different photographs of different people, all of them variations of one single specimen face. When she confides this observation to Paul, he responds by taking her into his arms and saying, "Agnes. Your face does not resemble any other" (p. 33).

The pathos of individuation is the fundamental illusion that sustains the play of Eros not only in Kundera's fiction but in the history of European romance that begins with the *fin'amor* game of courtly love. Agnes, who feels herself trapped in a face (*obličej*) of accidental necessity and whose spirit is in retreat from the borderline terror of existence, asks the messenger if people have faces on his planet. He replies that faces exist only here. On his planet, "They're all their own creations. Everybody, so to speak, thinks himself up" (p. 41). With her mathematical mind, Agnes understands that the logic of her radical disengagement demands that she step outside the illusion of her love for Paul, thus breaking the grave spell they have both cherished over many years. "We prefer never to meet again," she declares to the angel of her death (p. 42), who has offered her the possibility of staying together with Paul on the other planet. This refusal snaps in two the melodic line of the love-beyond-death song that was heard with such beauty in the recessional of Tamina's memory.

Agnes's death option, which brings the first part to an abrupt closure, leaves the stage bare for another pair of lovers. Enter Bettina, née Brentano, aged twenty-six, newly married to the Romantic poet Achim von Arnim, and in hot pursuit of Goethe. The great man of letters at sixty-two still has another twenty-one years to live inside a face and body that are a ruin of those he sported in the days of *Werther* and in the sensual fullness of the Campagna afternoon. A councillor at the Court of Weimar, he is not only toothless but encumbered by a prosaic wife, the forty-nine-year-old Christiane.

None of this matters to Bettina, whose real object is not

Goethe's love but his immortality. The chase after immortality, as Bettina stages it in the theater of European history, is a game of masked values, best played in the vicinity of death. Kundera explains: ". . . for death and immortality are an indissoluble pair of lovers, and the person whose face merges in our mind with the faces of the dead is already immortal while still alive" (p. 49).

This defining statement attaches to a vignette of François Mitterrand. Leaving a crowd of supporters and journalists, the newly elected President of France climbed the steps of the Panthéon with three roses in his hand, which he would deposit on the tombs of three immortals whose glory he wished to emulate. This homage could only be accomplished alone, behind closed doors. "He was like a surveyor, planting the three roses like three markers into the immense building site of eternity, to stake out a triangle in the center of which was to be erected the palace of his immortality" (p. 49).

Mitterrand, the geometer of eternity who wishes to inaugurate his advent of political power by a solitary communion with the great dead of France, is a child of modern history just like Bettina, possibly the last of that series. But Kundera's irony notes that he was "followed in his thoughtful solitude only by the eyes of the camera, the film crew, and several million Frenchmen, watching their screens from which thundered Beethoven's Ninth" (p. 49). Invaded by the camera eye of actuality, Mitterrand's gesture of desire for immortality loses its anachronistic serenity to become merely ridiculous.

Jimmy Carter, for whom Kundera professes a liking, is seen defenseless against the accidental cruelty of the lenses that fixed him forever in a stumble during jogging, with his face contorted by pain; a photo opportunity converted into an image of laughable immortality.[7] Whether rehearsed or unrehearsed, the game of immortality requires the artifice of a stage for the pair of lovers—death and immortality—to disport on, in gestures and acts whose choreography varies with the genre chosen. Kundera suggests some possible variations: ". . . for as I said, death and immortality form an inseparable pair more perfect than Marx and Engels, Romeo and Juliet, Laurel and Hardy" (p. 52).

From the outset of the Bettina/Goethe story, Kundera makes it plain that the form of immortality at stake between them has nothing in common with the immortality of the soul. The origins of that dream about an eternal life beyond the portals of death are lost to us in the vastness of prehistoric time. The arcane desire may indeed be inscribed in the genetic code that defines us as humans, the only animals capable of thinking their own death. The human wish for eternal life is a metaphysical quiver containing many arrows that can be aimed from several postures and in several directions. The Egyptians, who were the greatest geometers of material immortality, constructed their gesture from the ground up in the form of a triangular solid tent standing on a square base. The Greeks surely loved this earth with no less passion. They thought the earth eternal and felt it coming alive at the touch of the mortal heel. Still, they aimed the arrow of immortal desire at the sky, reserving the privilege of stellar apotheosis for the rarest heroes.

The Middle Ages placed Earth and Man at the center of a divinely created universe, which Dante compared to an open book filled with signs God intended us to decipher. The individualized Christian conception of immortality is a state of being that completes the self's history in a perfected form wherein human memory is redeemed rather than abolished. Dante dramatizes this idea in the dynamic image of two lovers traveling together through the circles of Paradise, the degree of their ascent measured by the increasing radiance on the woman's transparent face.[8] The Renaissance contemplates the divinely formed circularity as the perfect form of being in the microcosmic sphere of human *physis*, now augmented by its extended global outreach. Michelangelo's image of Adam's creation traces the macrocosmic and theological vision of immortality in the act of filiation. More intimately, a humanist father, Gargantua, urges his princely son Pantagruel to marry, to partake of the "visible form of the divine process of human immortality in the act of seminal propagation."[9]

Goethe's moment in European history, as Kundera defines it, is at the center of the Modern Era, halfway between Rabelais and Mitterrand:

> Now, perhaps, when the end of our century provides us with the proper perspective, we can allow ourselves to say: Goethe is a figure placed precisely in the center of European history. Goethe: the great center. Not the center in the sense of a timid point that carefully avoids extremes, no, a firm center that holds both extremes in a remarkable balance which Europe will never know again. As a young man Goethe studied alchemy, and later became one of the first modern scientists. Goethe was the greatest German of all, and at the same time an antipatriot and a European. Goethe was a cosmopolitan, and yet throughout his life he hardly stirred out of his province, his little Weimar. Goethe was a man of nature, yet also a man of history. In love, he was a libertine as well as a romantic (p. 75).

Born in a Protestant family during the Enlightenment, Goethe is not easily pinned down on matters of religion. But about secular immortality, there can be no doubt as to his attitude. He considers it a prime value to be tended to with the delicate care of a skilled gardener working in the garden of genius. Kundera refers us (p. 48) to a passage from *Dichtung und Wahrheit*,[10] in which Goethe shows himself as a youth of nineteen, seated in the newly built theater of Leipzig, avidly scanning the image of the Temple of Fame, painted on the stage curtain, of all the great dramatists. Shakespeare alone stands out, a figure seen from the back, striding toward the literary pantheon, seemingly indifferent to all the others. This view of creative genius as a titanic spirit of absolute originality reflects the Sturm und Drang aspirations of Goethe as a nineteen-year-old hopeful of his future greatness. The mature man of genius, who was in a position to write this fictional autobiography, cross-fertilized the ideal of originality with the solid classical model of a humanistic transmission of cultural achievements, in a continuum that links the present to a noble past. The question of Shakespeare's genesis, whether or not he was the pampered, fatherless child of creative Nature, recedes before reverence, in the profoundly knowledgeable act of appraisal by young Goethe. He alone can give full significance to the figure of a man in a light cloak, visible only from the back. The image of immortality sought by the mature Goethe presumes the continuous flow of cultural values into a virtually timeless pool of world literature. Nothing else signifies for Goethe. That is why he finds it useless to enter into a contest with *Homo politicus*. He prefers to hold him at a polite distance—as he did Napoleon, in a celebrated historic meeting at Erfurt. In chapter 4, Kundera gives a parodistic update of that encounter, placing it under the anachronistic glare of photographers.

Whether romantic or classical, the European conception of secular immortality is not egalitarian. It stages a contest under the banner value of strenuous individuation, for a prize to be won in an effort combining heroic emulation and antagonistic strife. Bettina, whose entry into this novel has a precise date—September 13, 1811—exemplifies the generational mode of confrontation that will become the trademark of all the modernist movements issued from the great matrix of Young Germany. Her self-assertiveness identifies her as a member of the Romantic vanguard no less than do the dark glasses she wears to the irritation of Christiane.

Goethe's simple-minded wife was quite right when she sent Bettina's spectacles flying to the ground in an angry gesture of pent-up humiliation (p. 46). Bettina had targeted her as the prime recipient of a generationally based insult, when she quarreled with her taste in art, even though Christiane was dutifully echoing her husband's opinions. "And we know what people are trying to say by their proud and ostentatious identification with the younger generation: that they will still be alive when their elders (in Bettina's case, Christiane and Goethe) have long been ludicrously pushing up daisies" (p. 46). Unlike the toothless Goethe, whose nearness to death affects Bettina's imagination like an aphrodisiac of fame, Christiane is merely old. Bettina compounds the scandal of the broken glasses by gossiping about it in the drawing rooms of Weimar.

Bettina's indiscretion is not a momentary lapse of judgment, but an essential part of her existential outlook. She refuses on principle to draw the line between the private and public. Her ideal of *Geselligkeit*, which involves publicizing the private and personalizing the public events, shows her a fellow traveler of the age that produced Marx, a son of Young Germany whose advocacy of the historical mode of being-in-the-world would engender the Kafkaesque nightmare of the twentieth century. Goethe, whose roots are in a distinctly pre-Marxian soil, takes his wife's side in the public quarrel and breaks off all relations with Bettina.

The rupture scene, involving Bettina and Christiane as a proxy for Goethe, is placed at the head of a series of five encounters in which Bettina faces Goethe directly. Though Goethe is absent, the outbreak of hostility between the two women is nevertheless the defining moment of the protracted duel in which Bettina plays the masked aggressor, calling out the writer of genius across a huge generational gap. It was Bettina who set the terms of the challenge with her first visit to Goethe in 1807. And in spite of the bitter reverses she suffered later, it was she who wrestled him to the ground by publishing the doctored version of their correspondence three years after his death. Kundera explains Bettina's gesture of rewriting the record of her relations with Goethe in terms of the great love that he systematically rebuffed, as a method combining artful addition with subtraction: ". . . she rewrote her own letters even more radically. No, she didn't alter the tone, the tone was just right. But she altered, for example, their dates (to erase the long pauses in their correspondence, which might deny the constancy of their passion) . . . she added other passages, dramatized various situations . . ." (p. 74). The charter of human rights makes no provisions for the dead, and even the greatest among them are open to the aggression of the living. The manipulation of human memory can alternately take the form of enforced forgetting and the equally onerous imposition of enforced remembering. Bettina wields both of these weapons, a *sine qua non* of all those who would control the Future.

In Bettina's politicized lexicon, "love" is a fighting word. When she first met Goethe in the spring of 1807 at Weimar, she brandished love from under the shield of childhood; an inspired posture that ensnared Goethe into careless sympathy when she unceremoniously jumped into his lap and fell asleep, blissfully nestled on his breast. In her book, *Goethe's Correspondence with a Child*, she gives no less than three renditions of that scene, addressing the first to Goethe's mother, the second to Goethe himself, and the third, presumably to herself, in the "Diary" section of the chronicle.[11] All three versions preserve the essentials of that astounding gesture. Kundera draws attention to the multifaceted sexual ambiguity of the posture struck by Bettina in her masked assault on Goethe. In chapter 5 he explains that in his youth, Goethe had a brief and sentimental romance with Bettina's mother, Maximiliane La Roche, a fact well known to Bettina from childhood on. Bettina, moreover, is a familiar of Goethe's own mother, Frau Rat Goethe, who literally passes the child to her son from her own lap. In 1807, Bettina is exactly the same age as Goethe when he courted Maximiliane. By reenacting his act of courtship, Bettina implicitly feminizes Goethe, which is another way of disarming his masculinity. The gender reversal game has the edge of lesbian excitement. This submerged, probably unconscious motif in Bettina's life reflects the invincible innocence that Romantic ideology attaches to the myth of childhood. It may also reflect the profound narcissism of the phase of psychic development Lacan calls "the stage of the mirror,"[12] when the child's self first takes stock of the body it inhabits. However that may be, it is clear that Bettina's seduction of Goethe is undertaken under the double sanction of the maternal seal, cast into the sacred mold of the Madonna and Child icon, which Goethe himself revitalized in his image of Gretchen.

Eroticism is notably suppressed in Bettina's rhetorical stylization of her love for Goethe. Kundera effects a stunning reversal of values when he assumes Goethe's point of view in order to describe the evening scene at Teplitz, late in August 1810, shortly after Bettina had confided to Goethe that she was going to marry von Arnim. They were standing in the window niche at dusk when Goethe, his eyes fixed on Bettina's reddening face, placed his hand on her disrobed, girlish bosom, asking: "Has anyone ever touched your breast?" (p. 63). She said no, in a voice strangely altered by an emotion that is conspicuously missing in her book. Kundera comments: "This is approximately how Bettina herself recorded the scene,[13] which probably had no sequel and remained in the midst of their story, more rhetorical than erotic, the sole exquisite jewel of sexual arousal" (p. 63).

In chapter 8, Kundera creates a sequel for the Teplitz blush in the telescope scene, set in Weimar in September 1811, a few days before the incident with Christiane. Bettina and her new husband are houseguests of Goethe, who has switched back to his paternalistic mode. Bettina talks to him about the soul in her lofty manner, and he patiently redirects her attention to the real sky above them, which is so clear that night. He points out that Mercury is perfectly visible in the telescope he has trained on the heavens. Bettina, who prefers to view Nature through the subjective lenses of pathetic fallacy, resents this distancing device. Protesting that she can see nothing, she leaves the room in a huff. Bettina's nearsightedness, which is real, also figures metaphorically as the obverse of Goethe's cosmic focus. Her inability to see what Goethe delights in is also a fundamental defect of her Romantic self-centeredness, which no pair of spectacles can correct.

In 1823, Bettina sends Goethe the sketch of a statue she is planning in his honor.[14] It is a design showing him seated, monumentally, as the poet enthroned, with a laurel wreath around his head, while she herself is at his feet, in the figure of a tiny Psyche. Goethe, who has just begun writing his *Dichtung und Wahrheit* and has invited Eckermann to his house as the chronicler of his timeless self, is instantly vulnerable to Bettina's flattery. He is touched to the point of overlooking the ominous sign of encroachment in the child/woman figure at his feet, who is returning in her imperious mode, now masked as his Muse about to claim an eternal share of his portion of immortality.

The grotesque kneeling scene that follows in 1824 shows that the duel is on again. Kundera, who describes it in his ninth chapter, notes that Bettina, in a letter to her niece, did not fail to draw attention to the fact that Goethe had wine on his breath when he came out to meet her.[15] Her aggression assumes the extreme form of self-abasement, clearly a trap prepared for his immortal image. She attempts to bar Goethe's exit from the room by throwing herself on her knees at the threshold, offering him the challenge of trampling upon her monumental love. Goethe, who evidently has overcome his brief lapse in vigilance, is on to her ploy. He bypasses her provocation by walking around her kneeling figure, "because you are too wily and it's better to stay on good terms with you!" Kundera cites from Bettina's letter (p. 69), interpreting

Goethe's circumspection as tantamount to suing for a truce. Yet the same Goethe, who can be so acutely wary of Bettina's poisoned pen, apparently loses all control over himself two years later. In a letter addressed to Charles August,[16] he explodes in anger against Bettina, calling her "that annoying gadfly" (p. 70); he has inherited from his mother words of uncharacteristic intemperance destined to blemish his immortal image. Bettina, his self-appointed executrix, will exact her symbolic revenge for this insult.

In attempting to explain Goethe's seemingly irrational switch, Kundera delivers a meditation on the nature of individual human time in a brief passage whose imaginative resonance soars above the essentially comic level of discourse that predominates in part 2. "It is necessary to understand the dial of life," he writes (p. 70), employing a metaphor of circularity that will emerge to full view in part 6. Retrospectively, this image aligns with Agnes's problematic notion of her face as the screen of aging, signaling time as a process of degradation that cuts deeper than the skin. For Goethe, as Kundera sees him at the end of a lifetime of contemplating his immortality, an intimation of freedom stirs at the mysterious core of the temporal circle, no longer sensed as a trap of limitation but as the defining form of individuation.

Kundera divides the circle of individual human time into three portions. The first belongs to youth, when death is distant, almost invisible. In the second phase, during middle age, we dwell in the nearness of our own death, which has by now invaded our field of vision. This is the stage when death's dialectical twin, having jumped out of the box, fools and diverts us with all manner of trickery. This happened to Goethe in 1823, when he succumbed to the image of the monument Bettina had sketched for him. The third phase is the briefest and the most secret. It comes when "death is so close that looking at it has already become boring" (p. 71). It is signaled by a great lassitude of being, whose paradoxical effect is to restore us to the primal state once known when death was still invisible. "A weary man looks out of the window, sees the tops of trees, and silently recites their names: chestnut, poplar, maple. And those names are as beautiful as being itself. The poplar is tall and looks like an athlete raising his arm to the sky. Or it looks like a flame that has soared into the air and petrified. Poplar, oh poplar. Immortality is a ridiculous illusion, an empty word, a butterfly net chasing the wind, if we compare it to the beauty of the poplar that the weary man watches through the window. Immortality no longer interests the weary old man at all" (p. 71).

The beauty of the world of nature, seized in the quick of the instance when individualized forms of natural *physis*, purged of the accumulated impurities of language, flow into a seeing intelligence, is an epiphany of being molded within the frame of philosophical *ataraxia*. Epicurus learned that discipline from the Stoics and taught it in his garden as the lesson of freedom that obtains only in the illumination of death and within a human self voided of all worldly ambition. Kundera teaches it as the phenomenological recovery of being that repairs the gap between appearance and essence in a language restored to its original power.

After this high point, the dissection of Goethe and Bettina's story resumes for another two chapters, beyond which we transit into the fantastic world of Goethe's immortality, where he graciously consorts with Hemingway. Why Hemingway? Precisely because he is neither Schiller nor Christiane nor, *a fortiori*, Bettina, but a perfect stranger with no part whatsoever in Goethe's earthly history. As an American man of letters who was also a first-rate journalist before the massive debasement of that art, Hemingway declares his mortal self innocent of any desire for immortality. All he cared about, before putting an end to his life with a shotgun, was to write his books so well as to preclude the deletion of a single word (p. 81). Thus the American *Homo faber* underlines the fact that the secular myth of immortality remains primarily a European cultural construct. In the comic skit that forms the epilogue to Bettina and Goethe's duel, the myth they fought over is staged as an amusing costume play, a balloon of hot air that Goethe and Hemingway, the two Olympian clowns, happily puncture with a volley of laughter.

Part 3, encased between the double frame of mortality/immortality, as represented by the two Bettina movements, ringed around by Agnes's journey into death, is the longest section in the novel. Fragmented into twenty-one distinct segments, each with its own defining title, it is also the most crowded, with the largest cast of characters. Agnes returns with Paul and Brigitte, and most notably with her sister Laura, who trails an invisible, shadowy Bettina in her wake. Two unseen players from part 1 join the action—Bernard Bertrand, the media personality whose voice the narrator heard on his radio; and the mysterious Professor Avenarius, so far notable by his absence. These main players and a few others at the margins interact in the bustling world of contemporary Paris, whose characteristics are already known to us from part 1.

We are at the dead center of the novel's narrative possibilities. The narrator who throws us in the middle of the city's everyday life seems disillusioned with the act of storytelling, being either unwilling or unable to prevent the constant breakdown of his plots. The upstaging of action by intellection mocks the title and theme ("Fighting") that Kundera has chosen for this section. He writes: ". . . the word 'fight' [in Czech, *boj*] was repeated at least five times, and this immediately reminded me of my native land of Prague, of banners, posters, the fight for peace, the fight for happiness, the fight for justice, the fight for the future, the fight for peace; a fight for peace that ends with the destruction of everybody by everybody, the Czech people wisely add" (p. 89). The passage is an ironic jibe at Bertrand Bertrand, a politician who advocates banning beer commercials in a crusade to eradicate the carnage of automobile accidents on French highways. But it is also a distancing device aimed at the larger picture of society. The man from Prague, who will soon name himself as the author of *Life Is Elsewhere*, observes Paris through a lens that aligns Bertrand Bertrand's constituency with Jaromil's Prague. The effect is to open the narrative moment to the "enigma of collective time, the time of Europe looking back on its own past, weighing up its history like an old man seeing his whole life in a single moment."[17]

Immortality is Opus No. 7 in Kundera's continuous meditation on the enigma of human time. It may be his most ambitious and most hermetic variation on that theme, playing out in multiple, subtly interlocking temporal codes. Written in 1988, the novel was published in 1990. On the official dial of French history, this time frame centers upon the Bicentennial of the French Revolution that Mitterrand staged in Paris in the form of the Pan-European festival of human rights. Even though Kundera does not refer to this event, he implicates its message in the irony of his commentary on contemporary French life. The initial thrust fell in part 1, when the narrator, switching frequencies on his transistor, kept hearing a multitude of voices talking almost simultaneously, but always of the same things. "A harmonious combination of uniformity and freedom—what more could mankind ask?" he exclaimed (p. 6). In this ironic formula of civic bliss, the banner values of the French Revolution are collapsed into a travesty of happiness that mates freedom with loss of individuation. In 1989, on Bastille Day, Mitterrand staked his claim on the future of United Europe by projecting the magnified doctored image of the French democratic past in the authoritative manner of an encyclical proclamation *urbi et orbi*. Having built an opera house for the people on the spot baptized with blood, he proceeded to televise his show to the whole world. This grand gesture, which infuriated Thatcher, reenacts Bettina's publicist impulse in the style appropriate to the decade that witnessed the victory of imagology over ideology.

Kundera coins the term "imagology" in order to define what he considers to be the key category of human existence in the world of posthistorical Europe. His meditation on the phenomenon, in a mini-essay placed in the middle of a description of the transactions prevailing between the media and their public ("Imagology," pp. 113–17), makes it plain that he holds the triumph of image-makers over politicians to be anything but a victory for human liberty. "The politician is dependent on the journalist. But on whom are the journalists dependent? They are dependent on those who pay them" (p. 113). A relation of hidden dependence, concealed under the cover of the all-purpose kitschified value of freedom of the press, fosters the ideal conditions for the uncontrollable expansion of arbitrary power. The image-makers who have so boldly stepped to center stage in public life, usurping the political levers of society, are merely the technicians, not the masters, of the media power system they serve. The anchorman of any TV station, whether state-owned or private, with his whole crew of cameramen and writers, is first and foremost an image on the screen of the magic box, a creature of the medium that imposes its stamp on his gestures and prompts his formulaic false speech.

There are no winners in the victory of imagology. Ideology finally lost its grip on human consciousness because, writes Kundera, "Reality was stronger than ideology. And it is in this sense that imagology surpassed it: imagology is stronger than reality, which has anyway long ceased to be what it was for my grandmother, who lived in a Moravian village and still knew everything through her own experience" (pp. 114–15). Reality, understood as hands-on, intelligible experience, has become *terra incognita* for minds ruled by opinion polls and statistics, those quantifying abstractions that constitute the new scholasticism of our age. The "truth" derived from an opinion poll is nothing but a statistical snapshot of a momentary *doxa* hypostatized in the form of objective authority. Yet, the normative value of the information it contains is the result of a serial questioning that predetermines the format and partially the content of the answer by pitching the question to what Kundera calls "the lowest ontological floor" (p. 111) of truth.[18] The media, whose power rests on these artifacts of imagology, are the newest purveyors of the "forgetting of being,"[19] a phenomenon Husserl deplored in 1935. The authority of the media establishment, based on the methodology of opinion polls and automatically responsive to their command, appears to be the most democratically constituted form of tyranny ever visited upon the human mind. That is why Kundera despairs of the possibility of its overthrow: ". . . and although I know that everything human is mortal, I cannot imagine anything that could break this power" (p. 115).

The instant consensus of majoritarian opinion is virtually impervious to the law of dialectical opposition. The notion of change itself no longer means the same as it did for Vico, Hegel, or Marx, who defined it as a new phase in the historical development of reality. In the new Europe, Hegel's category of "end of History" takes on the semblance of the changeability of fashion, a phenomenon ruled by the permanence of change devoid of purpose. Fashions can be as tyrannical as ideas, and frivolity becomes a compelling category of human need in an existence where nothing else signifies. Pascal talked of this *misère* in one of his most celebrated meditations, attributing its violent restlessness to the magnitude of the loss sustained by the disappearance of God from center stage. For his part, Kundera argues that the entertainment industry, having swallowed culture, has begun to impose its standards on all other forms of expression, from politics to sex. This part of the essay, though intrinsically linked to the theme of imagology, is filtered through the mind of Paul.

Agnes's husband, Paul, a lawyer by profession, has been hosting a Saturday-morning radio talk show titled *Rights and the Law.* He has just been informed by his station director, a genial fellow called the Bear, that the program is being canceled. While the Bear rails against the "ad-agency swindlers" (p. 118) for having shot down quality, Paul finds his reasons for accepting his dismissal in good grace: "In Paul's words: ideology belonged to history, while the reign of imagology begins where history ends" (p. 116). Paul is an intellectual, a well-educated, witty man, whose nimble mind is adept at paradoxes. By temperament a man of the Left, he is formed, as Franz was, by the values of the revolt at the Sorbonne in 1968, in whose festival he participated. Paul still marches to the slogan "One must be absolutely modern," which his generation took from Rimbaud, even if it means that he must collaborate with those forces that aim to destroy his essentially intellectual nature. This is what irritates the Bear, who dubs Paul "the brilliant ally of your own gravediggers" (p. 122). Paul's attitude is a remnant of revolutionary lyricism that, having undone Jaromil, appears to have survived the demise of ideology. Unlike Camus's penitent-judge, Jean-Baptiste Clamance,[20] Paul lacks the vocation of summits. Instead, he prefers to exercise the judicial dignity on the horizontal level of defense. "I am not a lawyer, I am the poet of the defense," he likes to say (p. 124).

The retreat from the act of judgment is the defining posture of an intellectual in the age that has denounced culture, with its hierarchical scale of values, for the sake of the democratic principle of leveling. In the chapter "To be absolutely modern" (pp. 137–41), Kundera says of Paul: "He merges in my mind with the figure of Jaromil from a novel that I finished exactly twenty years ago, which, in a forthcoming chapter of this book, I shall leave for Professor Avenarius to find in a bistro on the Boulevard Montparnasse" (p. 137). Paul too subscribes to the Shigalovism of the age of the masses. He reasons as follows: "War and culture, those are the two poles of Europe, her heaven and hell, her glory and shame, and they cannot be separated from each other" (p. 122). Having fashioned this conundrum of necessity, he bows his head low before its logic that dictates the imperative of deconstructing all the summits of human achievement. "Do you realize what is the eternal precondition of tragedy? The existence of ideals that are considered more valuable than human life," he charges (p. 120).

Paul, the brilliant ally of his gravediggers, acts out the terminal gestures of Faust as Goethe depicted him in act 5 of the second part of the tragicomedy. A man blinded by his struggle against Care, unable to distinguish between his desire to build on and on for the future and the actual work of the Lemurs, who are digging a hole in the ground for his soon-to-be-dead body. That is what living for the Future really means. "Fixed upon futurity/ [He] can never come to be" was the gray song Care murmured into Faust's ears.[21] Kundera sums up with the definition "to be absolutely modern means to be the ally of one's gravediggers" (p. 141).

In Paul's life, it is his daughter, Brigitte, who owns the privileged space of the Future. A grown-up child, she likes to sit on his knees, but she also exercises the right to sleep with her boyfriend in her parents' apartment. She is comfortable with the ways of the contemporary world of mass consumerism, where wishes and needs are immediately stated as rights and entitlements. Contrary to her father, who instinctively assumes the role of the defender in any dispute, Brigitte is a perpetual claimant. One day she happened to witness a demonstration by the unemployed in front of Fauchon, a luxury food store near the Madeleine. She pushed her way through the crowd of protesters and police, and once inside the shop, loudly demanded to be served. Returning to her illegally-parked car with a wine bottle in hand like a trophy, she redirected her defiance at two traffic cops who had ticketed her car. At home that evening she told her story in a high-pitched voice, accompanied by the head-shaking gesture, exactly like the militant angel Agnes had noticed in the sauna. The charter of human rights, for whose sake men like Havel sat in prison, has been converted into a mass phenomenon of self-serving aggressivity. Paul, who gladly faces up to any form of authority, is unable to resist Brigitte, not only because he is a doting father, but because, like Jaromil and Éluard, he is mesmerized by the irrational need to stand with her at the cutting edge of the Future.

Although part 3 hinges on the act of cogitation, it nevertheless contains the embryo of a main narrative event, or more exactly, nonevent—Laura's sham suicide. It is that narrative motif that pulls together all the gestures of bustling futility that add up to the portrait of contemporary Parisian life. The opening chapter shows Kundera listening to the news being announced by Bernard Bertrand. He is reporting a major road catastrophe: ". . . last night a girl sat down on a highway, with her back to the oncoming traffic. Three cars, one after the other, managed to swerve aside at the last moment and ended up in the ditch, all smashed up, with a number of dead and injured. The suicidal girl herself, when she realized her lack of success, slipped from the scene, and only the mutually consistent testimony of the injured bore witness to her existence" (p. 90). This image of accidental death on the highway strikes the narrator with a note of terror that leaves him temporarily unable to continue writing his novel. The suicidal gesture of an unknown, vanishing girl, converting a private desire for self-annihilation into a multiple public killing, is far more alarming to him than Bertrand Bertrand's statistical cumulation of road deaths. The narrator's dread, at once suggestive and opaque, recalls Agnes's "border terror" on rue de Rennes, a linkage highlighted by the following comment: "I had to force myself to get rid of this image in order to be able to continue with my novel, which if you remember began with my waiting at the swimming pool for Professor Avenarius and seeing an unknown woman wave to the lifeguard" (p. 90).

Having wound up his narrative thread, the episodic storyteller recounts how little Laura discovered the feminine charm of the hand gesture by secretly spying on her older sister at the moment of saying goodbye to her boyfriend at the gate of their childhood home in Switzerland. Agnes's gesture, observed from behind the barrier of sexual immaturity, tantalizes Laura with the vague idea of love as something immense, blown beyond measure by the feeling of dispossession that overwhelms her in the presence of her more experienced and, she believes, favored sister. But we already know that the gesture does not belong to Agnes, nor to the woman at the pool. Agnes herself had discovered it, standing at the same spot as Laura, but quite by chance. One afternoon as her father's secretary was leaving the house—Agnes remembers the sunburst on the sandy garden path—she used the gesture to wave goodbye, and Agnes suddenly understood that a bond of tenderness linked her father to this forty-year-old woman, the stranger whose visits always sparked off the mother's ill humor.

Many people, few gestures. The winged gesture of greeting passes from hand to hand in this novel, charging its large, cyclical structure with the electric current of a mysterious femininity. Akin to a musical cell in a Mahler symphony, the motif animates the surface texture of the composition with a pattern of recognizable repetition, while its variations play out more subtly on several hierarchical levels of time and meaning. It is in Agnes's hand that the gesture generates its highest and richest semantic value, by fusing the playful motif of erotic possibility with the deeper tonality of love's tenderness. Agnes's improbable, strangely unearthly harmony is another legacy from a dead father that the loving daughter preserves against the flow of time. And just like Sabina's bowler hat, it became Agnes's erotic signature in the days of her youthful flirtations, until she became disenchanted with it, having seen herself copied by an eleven-year-old Laura. Many years later, the gesture returned to her with the poignant stab of unrehearsed memory, when she was parting from her father after a visit to the Swiss villa (p. 38). She happened to stand at the same spot near the garden gate where the other woman had stood, and this accidental, anachronistic crossing of two such diverse affections jolted Agnes. "The thought passed through her head that those two women might have been the only ones he had ever loved" (p. 38).

Unlike Agnes, whose spirit is forged in the intelligence of love, Laura is a woman of excess whose emotions, clouded by self-pity, predispose her to think of herself as a victim of love. While Agnes lets go of her favorite gesture the moment she understands that her little sister has appropriated it, Laura clutches on to it precisely because it is a token of Agnes's envied charisma. Because Agnes likes to screen her eyes with dark glasses, Laura puts on a pair and wears them with a flourish of self-dramatization. The sibling relation is not one of choice, and Agnes endures its necessity like a recurrent bad dream in which she vainly tries to escape from Laura's pursuit. While Agnes defines her selfhood by means of subtraction, manifested in her repeated gestures of casting off attributes of things and people once held dear, Laura proceeds by the opposite method of symbolic addition. Her militant identification with everything that touches her body, be it her sunglasses, her Siamese cat, or her lovers, is an expression of her radically dispossessed self, luxuriating in the pathos of imitation. Laura consciously imitates Agnes; but on a subliminal level, she simulates Bettina von Arnim's often disappointed quest for the great love.

Laura's existential moment comes at the tail end of the historical sequence of masked values, inaugurated by Bettina and her fellow Romantics. Bettina, "the nymph of history, the priestess of history" (p. 162), had the pick of two vessels of genius, Goethe and Beethoven, for her voyage into immortality. Laura is a childless divorcée on the wrong side of thirty, living in the Paris of imagology from which the God of History has finally retreated. She is confined to desiring the "little immortality" of the private sphere. "Bettina, who aspires to grand immortality, wishes to say: I refuse to die with this day and its cares, I wish to transcend myself, to be a part of history, because history is eternal memory. Laura, though she only aspires to small immortality, wants the same: to transcend herself and the unhappy moment in which she lives to do 'something' to make everyone who has known her remember her" (p. 164). When she tells Agnes about her ache, Laura tilts her head back just a little, touches the hollow of her bosom with her fingertips, and then throws her arms forward, fully extended before her (p. 159). Laura knows nothing, wishes to know nothing, about Bettina, who used this same gesture whenever her friends reproached her with neglect of her family for the sake of her public causes. Laura has no cause but herself and her female body, the only vehicle she can summon for her journey beyond. Agnes understands that when her sister alludes to suicide, she is projecting her act of dying as the ultimate erotic gesture, the fullest offering of her body to her lover. This embrace of her sexual body in a narcissism quite impervious to the physical horror of death is alien to Agnes, who experiences her body as an ordeal of necessity, redeemable only at rare moments of erotic excitement, which lend it a brief transparency. Laura's body is always fully sexual, and she delights in feeling its weight augmented by the burden of a male lover, an opaque presence to be possessed rather than known.

Laura's current lover is eight years younger than she. Sensing his passion flagging, she makes the desperate bid of asking him to marry her. He is Bernard Bertrand, descendant of two generations of politicians, a media personality who stars at the station run by the Bear, which has just eliminated Paul's program. Bernard is a good friend of Paul's, and it was his voice we heard on the narrator's transistor radio. Bernard shares Paul's belief in the media's mission to demystify political power. More than anything else, Bernard desires the glory of Woodward and Bernstein. Bernard is a master of the forensic interview, a format that treats the art of conversation as a police interrogation of the sinister kind, in which the suspect has no right to remain silent about the most intimate details of his life.

To Laura's misfortune, she assaults Bernard with a demand for marriage just as he finds himself in the unaccustomed position of a quarry, an inculpated man with no recourse against his accuser. The situation, as he recounts it to Paul, is bizarre. "A stranger came to see me, a man taller than me by a head, with an enormous belly. He introduced himself, smiled in an alarmingly affable manner, and told me: 'I have the honor of presenting you with this diploma.' Then he handed me a big cardboard tube and insisted that I open it in his presence. It contained a diploma. In color. In beautiful script. I read: 'Bernard Bertrand is hereby declared a Complete Ass' " (p. 125).

In spite of his sympathy for the victim, Paul cannot restrain his laughter, in a burst of comic cruelty that convinces Bernard of his humiliation. His vulnerability is amplified by the newly launched publicity campaign that forces him to confront the ignominy of his own image blown to billboard size all over Paris. The delivery of a deadly insult wrapped in ceremonial politeness is a long-forgotten gesture straight out of the code of dueling. That arcane ritual of manliness, which Dumas played as a swashbuckling novelistic game of brilliant intrigue in *The Three Musketeers*, seems now to have lost its enchantment even in Hollywood. Being a child of actuality, Bernard first suspects his visitor of carrying a bomb, in a misinterpretation that carries the metaphoric essence of the incident. The stranger's message works like a hidden time bomb in Bernard and Laura's affair, finally detonating in the sham, hysterical explosion of Laura's suicide gesture.

Bernard's visitor, soon to be unmasked as Professor Avenarius, acts as a comic playmaker who sets off a chain of events he is unable to control or even predict. His seemingly capricious intervention in Bernard's life inscribes the text with the motif of laughter stalling in the track of its consequences, a device familiar to us from Kundera's earliest story, "Nobody Will Laugh." In his first novel, *The Joke*, its narrative possibilities are developed to the fullest. Almost all the French reviewers of *Immortality* have commented on the denial of the storytelling impulse, laid bare in part 5 during the narrator's extended conversation with Avenarius. The Czech novelist Ivan Klíma, in his review, puts the matter into perspective by reminding us that Kundera is a brilliant storyteller, second to none in the artful ways of setting up a narrative event.[22] The waning of fabulation in this novel must be understood as a device of choice, deployed by a discursive narrator intent on subverting the narrative art. Professor Avenarius, whose original mention in the first scene of part 1 casts him in the role of the interlocutor, proves himself unwilling to be confined within the mode of colloquy. Here, in part 3, he jumps out of the novel's box like the personification of that childish practical joke, and having delivered a certificate of asininity to Bernard, lets himself loose in the streets of Paris.

Professor Avenarius, the episodic mischief maker, materializes from below, in the subway passage underneath the Montparnasse tower, a spot that combines the function of Métro station and shopping mall. When he appears, the faces of the inanimate mannequins in the display windows of the Galeries Lafayette instantly strike an expression of entrancement, like women petrified in the mimickry of sacred horror. Avenarius reads this stunning effect as a tribute to the superb erection of his gigantic phallus, distinguishable from the ordinary male generative member by the head of a horned devil that crowns it. This fantastic feature, linking the joker to the devil, is to be expected in Kundera's Paris, cast in the image of the terminal act of Faust's history. Moreover, the linkage throws us back to the parable about the origin of laughter in *The Book of Laughter and Forgetting*. But in present conditions, under the Montparnasse tower, the devil's assumption of the scepter of royal dignity seems most precarious. Avenarius's demonic status is easily reducible to that of the all-too-human rogue Panurge, a carnival figure boasting a decorative codpiece, whose generative magic was demonstrated in the miraculous raising of Epistemon from the dead. But Avenarius, in spite of his hyperbolic erection, is not quite free of the pathos of imitation that afflicts Laura, whom he is about to meet and who is the only woman he comes close to possessing in the pages of this novel. The professor's assimilation to the devil is a synecdochal secondhand trick, a figural relation that bespeaks the *modus operandi* of the age of imagology.

Taken at face value, the name Avenarius, thrown in as the rogue's calling card on the novel's first page, represents a now obscured nineteenth-century philosopher, Richard Heinrich Ludwig Avenarius (1843–99), an extreme positivist notable for his pedantic manner of exposition and for his debate with Marx. In a book entitled *The Critique of Pure Experience* (1888–90), Avenarius argued that the difference between mental objects (images) and real objects rests solely on their consequences (e.g., real fire has the effect of burning our hands). Mind and matter are made of the same stuff, he held, thus sidestepping the vexing problems inherent in philosophical dualism. Avenarius caused a stir by postulating the category of *introjection*,[23] which he defined as the psychological mechanism that misleads us into believing that what we directly apprehend is always an "image" and never an independently existing object. Thus decoded, Kundera's professorial picaro also figures as the demonic doctor of the age of imagology. A realist of illusionism, he projects the effects of his scholastic doctrine into a world where philosophizing is reduced to wordplay. His own philosophical mandate is a sham, capable at best of covering the characters and their gestures with a somewhat threadbare replica of Mephisto's magic cape. Avenarius's command of the magic of novelistic incarnation is not absolute. He flits in and out of the fictional circle, his absences as notable as his appearances. He is out of Goethe's privileged moment in parts 2 and 4, nor heard from in part 6. But in part 3 he consorts with the main characters, most notably with Laura. Agnes, the creation of the narrator's high dream, remains a stranger to his world, unattainable within his orbit.

Philippe Sollers, who ingeniously derives Avenarius's demonic essence from the etymology of the word *avoine* (oats), which alludes to the devil's legendary proximity to horse markets, may have overstated his power to make things happen by saying that he "leads the dance."[24] He does that, in a manner of speaking, in the incident with Laura that is about to follow, but only as a part of a sequence of parodistic gestures. Avenarius merely shadows bits of action with his mockery, as in the case of his provocative counterdemonstration on the boulevard, whereby he derides the futility of an attempt to rouse the sympathy of Parisians for the cause of the persecuted Turkish minority in Bulgaria.

When Avenarius detects Laura, she is stationed in the busy subway passage in the operatic posture of a beggar, soliciting contributions for African lepers. There is a moment of recognition between them, as he appraises her well-dressed, still attractive physique, reckoning her to be about forty years old. The poor woman, with her appetizingly expressive derrière, seems to appeal for his help against the drunken bums who are encircling her menacingly. Stepping forward, Avenarius plays the role of protector in his own parodistic fashion. Lifting his legs high in a mimickry of a ribald cancan, Avenarius emboldens one of Laura's assailants to bawdily imitate him. While the humiliated woman is forced to dance in full view of the gawking public, one of the drunks tugs up her skirt, to disclose her remarkable behind clothed in green panties. Avenarius's instigation of this perverse peep show recalls the cruel trick Panurge played on the devout Parisian lady inside a church.[25] Both incidents aim at deflating the pretense of high values that some women are apt to use as a cloak for their sexual appetites. Laura's performance as the noble beggar was motivated by her vague desire to "do something" that might retrieve the compromised dignity of her love for Bernard. This scene is the immediate sequel to the chapter "Fighting," which describes the desperate lovemaking Laura imposes on Bernard in terms of the "struggle for Life" kitsch first associated with Bertrand Bertrand's legislative crusade. In her attempt to overpower the younger Bertrand with her superior sexual dexterity, Laura had turned her erotic organ into a frenzied war machine. In that context, Avenarius's profanation of Laura's body seems a reassertion of the male claim over a woman's body as a thing to be had for the taking. This resembles the style of revenge Ludvik Jahn imposed on Helena, a cruel bedroom joke with unexpected scatological results. Here the pattern is reversed: Avenarius will soon take pity on Laura's body by enclosing it in his protective embrace.

Even in the absence of Avenarius, Laura is doomed to exemplify the *trompe l'oeil* quality of a world of simulated acts, where parody limns the paradigm. In the penultimate chapter of part 3, "Suicide," she acts out the histrionics of shooting herself, simulating a gesture that ended Hemingway's life with matter-of-fact dignity. Laura is a mistress of masked values. And her suicide trip to Martinique, where she proposes to kill herself in the family villa of the Bertrands, is not intended to be an exit scene, but rather the fulfillment of her desire for self-perpetuation in her lover's memory. Paul and Agnes, who fear the worst, are made to endure the agony of a late-night telephone call in which Laura seeks instructions on how to load her revolver. The death threat dissipates into bathos as Laura returns to Paris, teary-eyed but more vital than ever. The last scene, "Dark glasses," is a retake of Bettina's rupture scene, with Agnes assuming the role of Christiane. Paul stands as a powerless witness to the verbal duel between the two sisters. Its violence even exceeds their quarrel after their mother's death, when Agnes defended her father, who had destroyed all the photographs showing him with his wife. This time, the fighting word between the sisters is "love," which each of them defines within her personal code. Laura identifies love with her subjective feeling, whereas Agnes insists that it is the beloved who matters most. Their exchange redirects Laura's emotional focus from Bernard to Paul, suddenly unveiled as the predestined target of her love. In a precisely choreographed dumb show, Laura keeps advancing toward Paul's frozen figure, until she finds herself leaning with her back against him. Agnes, separated from the newly formed couple by a distance that grows by the minute, drops and shatters the sunglasses Laura has left on the mantelpiece.

Laura's metaphor of her love as "a pair of wings beating in her heart" (p. 180), driving her to act in a manner Agnes considers unreasonable, leads straight into the argument of part 4, effecting a thematic enjambment of the borderline separating the private quarrel of two sisters and the historical debate about Bettina's love for Goethe. In this leap, the novel achieves a con-fusion of two different epochs of European history. Within the formal design, part 4 rhymes with part 2 by returning Goethe and Bettina center stage. "Homo sentimentalis" is an extended digression from all action, executed in the discursive mode of a polyhistorical essay. Kundera meditates on the relation between the rise of subjective sentiment as a cultural value and the expansive development of music in the Modern Era of Europe. The voice is that of his fictive self as we know it within the novel's magic circle. In part 1, the man from Prague identified himself with the transcendent point of view of Agnes, his heroine. Here he seems to be speaking over Bettina's head, in the manner of Jaromil's narrator in *Life Is Elsewhere*.

We recall that Laura insulted Agnes by charging her with being "beyond the border of love" (p. 180). The same accusation is leveled at Goethe by the cultural legatees of Bettina's myth of her great love. The prominence of Bettina's partisans in the twentieth century and the stridency of their advocacy have succeeded in changing the poet's immortality into something approaching the character of an eternal trial. In the last chapter of "Homo sentimentalis," we hear an Olympian Goethe expressing his supreme contempt for this eternal inculpation. He says to Hemingway: "You know I did not say one single word at the eternal trial. Out of contempt. But I couldn't keep myself from going there and listening to the proceedings. Now I regret it" (p. 213). These words are said in the posthistorical epilogue, not long before Goethe exits into his finale of nothingness. By contrast, Kundera's essay, which attempts to dispel the Kafkaesque nightmare of Goethe's eternal trial by analytical reason, belongs to the agonistic mode of history in which no one can have the last word.

Nobody can predict the meaning that might be assumed by Beethoven's immortal hat within the semantic river of human time. Kundera says this (p. 80) apropos of the anecdote about Goethe and Beethoven when they met the Empress during a promenade in Teplitz (p. 77). The scene,[26] described by Bettina in a letter to Hermann von Pückler-Muskau, shows Goethe as the courtier, lifting his hat respectfully before the embodiment of established power. By contrast, a revolutionary Beethoven pushes past the Empress, his hat pulled down to the eyebrows over his leonine crown. Kundera expresses doubt about the veracity of the image Bettina claims to have culled from Beethoven himself in 1812, exactly a year after the quarrel with Christiane. True or false, Bettina's allegory is aimed at Goethe, who has violated the code of behavior Young Germany prescribed for men of genius. Some 150 pages after citing this anecdote, Kundera turns it around by interpreting Goethe's gesture as the ironic politesse of a man who knows full well that creativity represents a higher value than power, but finds it useless to assert it as a lesson to the temporal masters of this world (p. 208). That lesson, he remarks, was easily forgotten by the twentieth-century heirs of Bettina's revolutionary flame, who found themselves faced with Stalin, a man whose power, unlike that of the Empress at Teplitz, bore the stamp of terror. The dunce's cap of laughable immortality can be clamped down on the least suspecting head, for, as Kundera wrote elsewhere, "the future is always mightier than the present. It will pass judgment on us, of course. And without any competence."[27] His revisionist essay on the eternal trial takes on the *ad hominem* level of discourse favored by Goethe's detractors only to redirect it into the panoramic realm of ideas. Much more than an advocacy of defense, his commentary is above all a meditation on cultural values.

Kundera initiates the debate by citing the writings of three twentieth-century men of letters, whose partisanship of Bettina's spurned love constitutes the bare knuckles of the case against Goethe. Romain Rolland, the grand old man of European socialism, a belated Romantic who wrote a worshipful biography of Beethoven, focuses on the trio, Bettina, Goethe, Beethoven. In his essay "Goethe and Beethoven" (1930) he sympathizes with Bettina's contempt for Christiane's nullity and, while remaining respectful of Goethe the great poet, appears deeply embarrassed by what he construes as his human coldness.

Paul Éluard, in *Les Sentiers et les routes de la poésie* (1949), speaks in the peremptory voice of the avant-garde still exultant in the hot embrace of Revolution. Like a Saint-Just waving the banner of *amour-poésie*, he is harsh on Goethe: "The distinguished poet, author of *Werther*, gave domestic peace precedence over the active deliriums of passion" (p. 188).

Rilke's commentary on the case in *The Notebooks of Malte Laurids Brigge* (1910) is less an indictment of Goethe than an agonistic meditation on the meaning of the lyric experience. "That lover was bestowed upon him," quotes Kundera, immediately proceeding to ask the crucial question: "What does this passive construction mean? In other words: *who* bestowed her upon him?" (p. 188). That question defines Kundera's antilyrical attitude, in contrast to Rilke's unquestioning assumption that Bettina's imperious challenge to Goethe is like any angel's trumpet call, a message from the summits of sacred dread, most terrifying when left unanswered. In Rilke's eyes, Goethe's failure to respond to Bettina leaves him tragically unfulfilled as a poet, depriving his passage into death of all mythic resonance. Kundera translates these reflections into the comic mode by imagining Goethe as a "Falstaff of love" (p. 189), a figure as incongruous as that of Simon had he remained fishing on lake Tiberius instead of following Christ's appeal.

In spite of significant differences in tone and temper, the three writers agree in according a privileged status to Bettina's self-proclaimed feeling of winged love, whose essence as a heavenly gift is deemed impervious to analysis. If one were to put a class label on this value, one should conclude that in the cultural ripeness of bourgeois Europe, the old aristocratic myth of courtly, adulterous love has beaten out the middle-class cult of domesticity, uniting two men of the Left and a profoundly nonpolitical poet in the dismissal of Christiane's virtue as a loyal wife of impeccable democratic pedigree.

But Kundera is pursuing bigger game. He argues that European civilization, presumed to be founded on reason, is also the matrix of the category of consciousness he classifies under the prototype of *Homo sentimentalis*, characterized by the hypertrophy of subjective emotion. Bettina, true to type, is no more interested in knowing the beloved than Laura is in understanding Bernard. Kundera derives the rise of subjectivity as a cultural value from its deep roots in the moral revolution initiated by Christ's evangelical appeal to love as opposed to the objectivity of Judaic law. He overhears the echo of Saint Augustine's imperative, "Love God and do as thou wilt," in Bettina's contention that love can free us of all earthly constraint and make us innocent again.

In an earlier essay, Kundera followed Husserl in the argument about the progressive encroachment of objectifying reason (*ratio*) upon the concrete world of human living.[28] Here he sheds light on the other side of the conundrum. The scientific age of Galileo is also the age that witnessed the dominion of the Baroque style over all art forms, in an explosion of feeling that shattered the geometric order of the Renaissance. Kundera takes a page from his favorite novel to show us the image of Don Quixote's penance, when he is acting out the contorted, self-lacerating gestures of a mad lover in the crags of Sierra Morena, under the scandalized eyes of Sancho Panza. Sancho protests in vain that the Lady Dulcinea has given the knight no cause for such despair. "That is the point," replies Don Quixote, "and in that lies the beauty of my plan. . . . The thing is to do it without cause. . . ."[29]

This statement asserts the quintessentially Baroque desire to recapture the persuasion of faith, already tainted by doubt, in the ostentatious illusionism of a magnificent gesture. We recall that Don Quixote is conscious of having a choice between two literary models: should he imitate the fury of Orlando, as Ariosto described him, laying waste the countryside in jealous rage over Angelica's betrayal, or should he follow the example of the chaste and melancholy love that Amadis bears for his incomparable Lady? Don Quixote's decision in favor of Amadis reveals his nostalgia for the medieval purity of the courtly love that Ariosto, that great Renaissance skeptic, parodied in all the psychological and social forms of its manifestations. Cervantes's incongruous knight, whom Kundera saw as the vanguard explorer of the adventure of the high road, at the dawn of the Modern Era, is now revisited as the great vessel of nostalgia. An anachronistic courtly lover, he is stranded in "this detestable age of iron," seeking to restore the paradigm of a high dream conceived in the twelfth century. Don Quixote is also a splendid example of *Homo sentimentalis*, in his propensity for hysteria as he strives to simulate a feeling whose spontaneity eludes him.

By superimposing the image of Don Quixote upon the mental image we retain of Bettina and Laura, Kundera deliberately con-fuses three distinct phases of modern European history. The result of this experiment is to show up subjectivism as the genetic marker of the cultural code. The inflation of sentiment into value travels from the Baroque to the Romantic period, the two great ages exploding in the diapason of music. In the present epilogue, subjectivism assumes the terminal forms of imagology. Unlike the statues on Charles Bridge, whose gesticulation imitates the persuasion of transcendence, the religious posturing that appears on our TV screens seems to pull downward, pursuing the meaning of the sacred archetype in the murky depth of blood and ethnicity. The music issuing from those chasms has the orgasmic hysteria of a rock beat, endlessly celebrating the release of rhythm from its old fealty to melodic line and rich harmonic texture, the twin dignities developed over a thousand years of European music. Kundera points out that this history was nurtured in the same cradle as *Homo sentimentalis*.

While seeking to redress the balance between Beethoven's romantic revolt and Goethe's classical respect for formality, Kundera also pays tribute to the genius of Romantic music, whose pathos still retains the power to unite all Europe on grand public occasions. When Chopin's *Marche Funèbre* or Beethoven's *Eroica* are played, Hitler and Stalin, de Gaulle and Mussolini are filled with "identical fraternal emotion" (p. 205) that seeks something ineffably lofty, beyond all ideologies.

Paul, through whom these reflections are filtered, would be happy to dispense with that historic noise, but finds himself confronted by the ultimatum Laura gives him in the early days of their marriage: either Mahler or rock. Laura's talent for music is genuine, though misdirected from piano to voice. She adores Mahler, who, Kundera points out, is the last great European composer to speak directly to *Homo sentimentalis* (p. 204). In the generational conflict that pits Laura against her stepdaughter, Brigitte, Kundera clearly prefers the older woman, whose quest for the singular great love represents the neo-Baroque equivalent of Don Quixote's attempt to whip up long-dead meaning in the conventions of courtly love.

The announcement of Agnes's death drops casually into the essay near the end of its meandering course. Kundera has just been considering Goethe's recoil from a flicker of narcissistic emotion sparked by Bettina's monumental sketch. Then, without warning, he shifts temporal and emotional gears to write: "About a week after the horrible death of Agnes, Laura visited a despondent Paul" (p. 202). The last glimpse we had of Agnes showed her standing dry-eyed at some distance from the newly formed couple. Her tearless eyes are the motif wherein the narrative careens off the essay, providing the link between Goethe's embarrassment at being seduced by Bettina's offering of immortal memory and Paul's tearful surrender to Laura's embrace. The lovemaking that follows, uniting Agnes's bereaved husband with her equally bereaved sister, is literally bathed in tears. The couple, submerged by the tidal wave of grief spiked with the taste of a transgression that approximates incest, draws on a deep pool of emotional ambiguity to rise to the crest of sexual arousal. We recall that excitement was notably missing in the virtuosity of Laura's performance with Bernard. Paul, on the other hand, is overwhelmed by Laura's passion, the oceanic power of which opens the floodgates of erotic lyricism within his soul.

In his reflections on the history of European sentiment,

Kundera draws on the novel to show that the highest hierarchical value is attached to the passion that preserves the poetry of desire by excluding sexual consummation. Roaming randomly across the cultural territory that is bounded in the West by France, the land of form, and in the East by Russia, stretching out ad infinitum in the uncoiling of emotion, Kundera makes his case by citing examples of lovers from the landmark novels. From Don Quixote to the Princess of Clèves, through Werther to Fromentin's Dominique and Dostoevsky's Prince Myshkin, the heroes and the sole heroine among them articulate the power of sexual love in the coded language of sexual denial, inventing a variety of gestures that range from the ridiculous to the sublime and back again. The twentieth century, which boasts of having liberated sexuality from the bondage of romantic sentiment, has failed to create a new meaning for the notion of love, and "this is one of its debacles," remarks Kundera (p. 197), in a devastating parenthetical diagnosis of our time.

The land of enchantment where Laura leads Paul with her transgressional lovemaking retains the residual magic of the lyricism of love, an anachronistic experience that is *terra incognita* for Brigitte and her generation. In chapter 16 of part 4, just before raising the curtain on the comic skit of Goethe with Hemingway, Kundera takes final leave of Bettina by redefining the gesture of longing for immortality in terms that fit perfectly with the subjectivism of Laura's love. Bettina always began by touching her breast at the presumed place of her heart and then flinging her arms forward, in a dynamic movement that projected the immensity of her feeling of self into the immensity of the world, apprehended through the open gate of the Future. The horizontal line described by Bettina's gesture is the preferred expression of the ancient desire for immortality in an age that deified History, thus confusing the future with eternity and self-projection with transcendence.

Part 5 reveals the mystery of Agnes's path to transcendence in the course of a narrative event that centers on her accidental death in a highway crash. In his essay on Broch,[30] Kundera asks why the slaughter on our highways, a form of death that combines banality with horror, fails to dumbfound us. Is it because, unlike death by AIDS or cancer, a car accident is viewed as the handiwork of man's choice, rather than the product of dumb necessity? "No, it does not dumbfound us, because like Pasenow, we have a poor sense of the real." And thus, as the argument went in part 1, we can only access reality at second hand, on the screen of symbols whose meaning has become opaque to us.

Agnes's accident, told in syncopated synchronization with an extended dialogue between Avenarius and the narrator about the problematics of novelistic form, is a stunning event. Though intricately set up by the lucid artificer who lets us watch the scaffolding of his narrative project being erected, the incident that kills Agnes leads us paradoxically into the living heart of the real, unveiling the beauty smoldering in the ashes of a world gone gray. In Kundera's usage, the Czech word *Náhoda* (translated into French as "Le Hasard" and into English as "Chance"), which he chose as the section's title, is a philosophical category that summons to mind the restless variety of contingency at the antipodes of a world ruled by necessity. *Náhoda* achieves its full poetic resonance when it is conceived as the launching moment of the surrealistic epiphany, a time of *kairos*, as Tereza seized it in the quick of her fortuitous meeting with Tomas. The etymological pun concealed in the Czech word is darkened by the paranomasial association of *náhoda/nehoda* (chance as happenstance vs. chance as mishap), which redirects the heightened meaning of the event back to its literal level as a catastrophe, a disastrous throw of the dice by Agnes. In the common Czech expression *automobilová nehoda* (an automobile accident), we hear the depressing base tone of the mechanical world of reified instrumentality, which creates a profound ambivalence around the meaning of Agnes's road to death, wherein her existential theme of death/freedom is about to undergo its final transformation.

We see Agnes at the countryside Swiss hotel, in retreat from Paris, with a volume of Rimbaud's poems in her hand. She had always associated Rimbaud with the time of Paul's courtship, when he used to take her riding on his motorcycle. She is surprised to discover that the adventure of Rimbaud's poetry, which Paul defines in terms of the imperative of modernity, speaks to her instead with the beauty of pristine nature, as it was in the days of his inspired *vagabondage*, unsullied by mechanized traffic. "*Depuis huit jours, j'avais déchiré mes bottines/aux cailloux des chemins . . .*"[31] Agnes reads, and feels a profound nostalgia for the landscape of her childhood, when she walked with her father along the footpaths that wound around meadows and led deep into the heart of the forest. Unlike Paul, who sees nature as a hostile, predatory force and responds to its appeal only when it assumes the elemental aspect of the ocean, demanding total surrender, Agnes loves nature more than she loves human beings. Her spirit responds to the call of the high Alps and her heart is at home in the landscape of the European pastoral, with its wooden benches perched at choice vantage spots. Its beauty speaks to her with the tender memory of her father. Here Kundera weaves in with a digression on the semantic contrast between the footpath (in Czech, *cesta*), which is an invitation to pay tribute to nature and the highway (*silnice*), a line of force cutting straight across an abstract space, leading quickly to the foreseen goal in an arrogant devaluation of the surrounding countryside. As Kundera reflects on Agnes's nostalgia, we sense the rounding of her time, the turning away from Paul toward her childhood in a retrospective curve that traces the journey of return to her essential self, just like her father's retreat after the death of his wife. Agnes has decided to withdraw to Switzerland from Paris, and she must tell Paul and Brigitte.

At the precise moment when Agnes slips her key into the door of her car to begin her return trip to Paris, Professor Avenarius at last catches up with the narrator at the poolside of the penthouse health club. This magic trick of novelistic synchronization, joining together two moments of existential time that we know to be far apart on the calendar of calculable time, instantly abolishes sequence in favor of poetic association, displacing the logic of causality by the metaphoric magic of contiguity. We recognize the *ars poetica* of Surrealism, the alchemy of vision that guided Jaromil's journey of wakeful dreaming from image to image as he walked the streets of Prague. Twenty years after creating Jaromil, the narrator of this fiction takes time off from the burden of storytelling in order to meditate on the art of the novel. The novel he is writing has grafted the lyric power of metaphor on the ancient stem of the narrative form. The storytelling impulse, no longer mindful of the obligation to develop a plot, veers in the chance direction offered to it by the improvisational possibilities of coincidence.

The narrator explains to Avenarius that he plans to write a treatise on the theory of chance. He has already isolated four different categories of coincidence, classifying them in hierarchical order according to the value of poetic resonance they evoke. He then turns to Avenarius for help in pinning down a fifth category—the story-producing coincidence (p. 226). He wants to know what happened with Laura after Avenarius took her in his arms. It seems that Avenarius, whose favorite novel is *The Three Musketeers*, an intricately plotted sequence of adventures, holds the key to the possibility of action. Being capricious, the designated picaro demurs, temporarily resisting this diversion. The dialogue runs on in high philosophical gear, developing as an inquiry into the great theme of human time. The discourse, led by the theoretical narrator, proceeds in orderly fashion, in an analytical display that seems inapposite to the matter at hand. The narrator's search for what he calls "existential mathematics" meets with Avenarius's approval. The discipline is in need of the resources inherent in generative paradox, a capability denied to it by the seeker, who says wistfully: "Unfortunately, no existential mathematics exists as yet" (p. 227).

So far, the theoretician of chance has been able to distinguish three types of human time, a classification that recalls Goethe's mysterious circle of death and immortality. Avenarius intervenes to redirect the talk to the concrete level of incidental action. He insists that his act of certifying Bernard as a complete ass was not a chance incident but an event guided by necessity. Avenarius will not give an inch on this, even after the narrator proves that he has confused the two Bertrands, delivering to the son a certificate of shame intended for his politician father. It turns out the causal chain that led Laura to the verge of suicide, and incidentally surrendered her body into Avenarius's arms, had sprung from an error. The argument of mistaken identity does not faze Avenarius. He retorts that his cuckolding of Bernard, far from being grounded in a mistake, is a necessity predetermined by his physical attraction to Laura, whom he had seen near the radio station while stalking Bernard. By deriving the force of objective necessity from the caprice of sexual appetite, this *post hoc ergo propter hoc* thesis, which turns logic on its head, is well suited for the rogue of Montparnasse. But in this dialogue he dons his philosophical cap and uses his professorial privilege to drop the weighty name of Marx into the half-told story of his sexual adventure: "No coincidence was involved. It was simple necessity. Not even the iron laws of history described by Marx involve greater necessity than this title" (p. 227). We understand that Professor Avenarius is a subversive joker whose mockery operates on the large intellectual scale of Dr. Skreta in *The Farewell Party.*

But Avenarius is a much sadder lord of misrule. Though he alludes to his revolutionary past, he is thoroughly disillusioned about the viability of the act of revolt in his time, in a world ruled by the mysterious and tentacular entity he calls Diabolum. On this topic he will have more to say in chapter 11 of part 5. For now let it be noted that even though he exhorts the narrator to give up writing novels for the sake of direct action, the dynamics of his own praxis appear confined to staging petty provocations for the incidental gain of a furtive embrace. Avenarius is a radically reduced devil, a Mephisto shorn of the vital power of contradiction.

As the dialogue adjourns, Agnes returns to view during the next three chapters (part 5, chapters 6, 7, 8) and two extra paragraphs in chapter 9. We hear her rehearsing the theme of chance/necessity within the intimate sphere of her family circle. Agnes has never been able to identify with her mother's dictum that maternal love is stronger than conjugal love. She values her relation to Paul because it is grounded in a choice, unlike her sibling bond to Laura, the little sister always at her heel like an insistent, aggressive beggar. She dreams of eluding Laura's pursuit once and for all by performing some existential version of the castling movement in chess. She has decided to seize upon the opportunity offered her by a new position her firm is establishing in Bern. She will spare her family's feelings by using her career as an excuse to move from Paris to Switzerland, preferably somewhere in the Alps.

The account of Agnes's return trip to Paris moves by fits and starts in a fragmented narrative that intermittently yields to the ongoing dialogue between the two male companions. A pattern of three is established: Agnes's three chapters are followed by three more of the colloquy, in which we accompany the two interlocutors into a restaurant, for a meal of roast goose with wine, whose succulence matches the pleasures of their wit. It is here that Avenarius reveals more fully the secret of his attraction to Laura. He draws two arrows of unequal length, joined at the base and aiming in opposite directions, up and down, in a sign of ambivalence that pulls downward, since the lower arrow is thicker and larger. The drawing is the semantic abstract of Laura's inner contradiction, the signature of her sexual ambiguity, which so excites Avenarius. He explains: "That's Laura: full of dreams, her head looks up at heaven, and her body is drawn to earth: her behind and her breasts, also rather heavy, look downward" (p. 242). The narrator counters with a design for Agnes, which reverses the arrows. "Her sister Agnes: her body rises like a flame. And her head is always slightly bowed: a skeptical head looking at the ground" (p. 242). Agnes's formula, coined by the narrator, is rooted in a metaphor of transcendence, her native element, in contrast to the physiological concreteness of Laura's sensuality. This bit of dialogue codifies and condenses Kundera's great theme of body and soul, a *psychomachia* of major imaginative tension that animates all his great sex scenes. Avenarius declares his preference for Laura, but keeps mum about their putative lovemaking, even though the narrator goads him with the image of a passionate coitus showing Laura, drenched in tears and urine, melting inside her protector's arms. Appreciating his friend's fantasy for what it is, Avenarius remains noncommittal, veering the talk away from Laura to his favorite topic, the nocturnal raid.

The adventure, as Avenarius tells it with the urgency of persuasion by which he hopes to rope the narrator in, is a nightly escapade of raids on parked cars. The careful strategy requires the cover of darkness for the systematic slashing of tires by means of a carefully concealed knife. He opens his coat to show his friend the knife dangling below his belly in an elaborate contraption like a horse's harness. Avenarius's urban guerrilla warfare is a comic invention with multiple meanings.

A man appareled as a horse attacks cars in the darkened streets of Paris, using a knife stolen from his wife's kitchen. It is a parody of adventure as such, laughing at itself by deflating all private and public schemes of direct action. Avenarius's well-chosen target is the automobile, once known to us as the vehicle of libertinage when Martin and his companion drove it along the roads of Bohemia, in pursuit of a forever receding golden apple of desire. Now it stands condemned in the streets of Paris and elsewhere in Europe as the polluter of nature and destroyer of cityscapes. In puncturing the tires, the equine avenger, who is also a satyr, attacks the erotic potency of the Don Juan myth, armed with its Castilian blade. Avenarius's mimicry is a game that delights with the variety of its poetic resonances. An exercise in formal perfection, it is nevertheless a futile gesture in Avenarius's ongoing struggle against Diabolum.

That mysterious power, whose name usurps the *ci-devant* majesty of the laughing devil, seems to have mastered the art of co-option to such a degree that it turns every protest against itself into an act of complicity. Diabolum's protocol of conversion bears the telltale signature of the age of terminal paradoxes. Avenarius gives anecdotal evidence to that effect by describing a demonstration by German ecologists he once attended. They had assembled in a forest to protest against the building of a nuclear power plant and, having had their say, departed in various directions on their motorcycles, leaving behind a landscape littered with their refuse. Avenarius himself is not immune from such contamination. For all his hatred of automobiles, he drives an impressive Mercedes.

Though innocent of all illusion about the effectiveness of his subversive game, Avenarius persists in it, moved by a nostalgia for an impossible adventure that seems to have a will of its own. For his part the narrator, speaking as a novelist in the process of writing a new fiction, acknowledges that the appeal of adventure, still available to Dumas in his brilliant potboiler *The Three Musketeers*, is now truly exhausted. His current praxis deliberately eschews all the old ploys and devices that once worked so well to advance the drama of action. His novelistic code denounces the causal chain of a well-made plot, with its predictable and obligatory effect of dramatic tension. ". . . I regret that almost all novels ever written are much too obedient to the rules of unity of action. What I mean to say is that at their core is one single chain of causally related acts and events. These novels are like a narrow street along which someone drives his characters with a whip. Dramatic tension is the real curse of the novel, because it transforms everything, even the most beautiful pages, even the most surprising scenes and observations, merely into steps leading to the final resolution, in which the meaning of everything that preceded is concentrated. The novel is consumed in the fire of its own tension, like a bale of straw" (p. 238).

Many reviewers of *Immortality* have cited this passage as a key to their reading of the novel, emphasizing the rejection of storytelling as its essential gesture. Kundera makes his code as explicit as he can by stating a program for the contemporary novelist who wishes to protect his art—he must write in a way that makes it impossible to recount his story on film (p. 238).

And yet, the momentum of the event that will soon pull Agnes to her death keeps pace with the interest created by the art of conversation. In chapter 9 of part 5, which denounces the art of storytelling, the narrator confides to Avenarius the alarming story of the suicidal girl who caused a deadly triple car crash on the highway, only to vanish into thin air. When Avenarius asks him to speculate about her motives, the narrator offers a theory of irrational causation derived from the etymology of the Latin word for reason. He explains that *ratio*, in its primary sense, denotes the faculty of reflection as such. It is this capacity that gave rise to the secondary connotation of the word as the function of relating cause and effect, which is how we now commonly understand the concept of reason. But the attempt to limit reason to the mental instrumentation of the formula of logical necessity may be a cultural convention, a bias perpetuated by the Cartesian tradition of thought. In German, he points out, the word for reason is *Grund*, i.e., the soil or the bottom of a phenomenon.

The narrator's organic interpretation of the verbal sign for causation yields the key to his creation of character. Each experimental self in this novel has his or her *Grund*, a genetic code that circumscribes the character's acts and gestures within its operative limits. The uniqueness of each program, with its restless interplay between innate necessity and random chance, is best apprehended by metaphor, which appears to be a higher category of reflection, subtler at unraveling the complexities of human existence than logic. The metaphoric method eliminates the tyranny of final causes that drives Hegelian Reason in History and that also bogs down psychologists in asking about the purpose of a particular act or gesture, a form of questioning that has a way of returning upon the questioner in the guise of a causal answer. Rather than inquiring about the causes of the girl's suicidal gesture, the narrator contemplates her existential code. Her deadly move is inscribed in the code of her radical alienation from the world. She lives in the feeling of incurable disconnection from the pain of others, a dysfunction of *soucit* that reflects upon her own being as an inner sense of utter devaluation. A self that is voided of all human empathy becomes a gaping invitation to all the destructive energies emanating from the opaque and inert space that surrounds it.

Agnes experienced the phenomenon of radical alienation in the flash of "border terror" on rue de Rennes. When we see her in chapter 12 of part 5, she is driving her car on the road to Paris, looking for a place to eat. We revisit her moment of "border terror" in the palpable aggressivity of the speeding and blaring traffic. Agnes takes all this in marginally, while her mind actively rehearses the old ache of shame in living inside a body experienced as a thing not of her choosing, caught in the whiplash of chance and necessity. But in this moment of repetition we know that Agnes's death is already advancing to meet her, in the shape of the anonymous girl whose minus ego dictates that she should wish to discard her body somewhere, to be crushed by something heavy.

Two separate narrative strains, each filled with the flow of a woman's inner time, once released from the matrix of metaphor, will surely converge in a coincidental crossing of major significance. The novelist alternates between them, intermittently disrupting the momentous time flow by shifting to the ongoing dialogue of the two male companions, who are now in the street, walking toward Avenarius's Mercedes. The narrator supplies us with the concrete details of the inarticulate girl's history (chapter 14). She is a saleswoman at a department store in a provincial town somewhere between Paris and Switzerland. Alternately ignored and harassed by all who come in contact with her, she is unable to raise the thin reed of her voice to the tone of anger. One late afternoon, instead of returning home from work, she begins walking out of town. "She wasn't aware of anything around her, she didn't know whether it was summer or winter, whether she was walking along a beach or a factory wall; after all, for a long time now she had no longer been living in the world; her only world was her soul" (p. 254). This evocation of existential emptiness is eloquent with the verbal echo of Rimbaud's cry "*Nous ne sommes pas au monde*,"[32] whose expressive magic is denied in the girl's muteness. Much later, when it is fully dark, she veers off the main highway to Dijon into the same secondary road (p. 256) that Agnes chose two chapters before (p. 251) in an attempt to avoid the heaviest traffic.

It is either love or the convent, Agnes muses, contemplating her own variation of the *contemptus mundi* theme, in which the world is defined as the spiderweb spun for humans by a cruelly indifferent Creator (p. 257). A sentence flows into her memory: "*Il se retira à la Chartreuse de Parme*," the mysterious conclusion of Stendhal's novel, which presents Fabrice's love for Clélia, a woman seen through the bars of his prison tower, as the summit of erotic feeling. But Agnes is suddenly aware that for her, the summit of feeling does not belong to Paul or sexual love as such, but to the tenderness she attaches to her father. Her private version of monastic utopia, in her dream of retreating to Switzerland, is a repeat of her father's recoil from conjugal love into contemplative solitude.

As Agnes journeys into death, the poetry of renunciation she reads in the last sentence of *The Charterhouse of Parma* commingles with the memory of a moment of surpassing happiness she experienced that same day, in late afternoon, during a walk through the Swiss countryside. She lay down on the grassy meadow and remained still for a long time, feeling a cleansing flow passing through her mind and body, carrying away the stain of the familiar self that used to inhabit her. And into that inner space of freedom, created by her self-forgetting, the world of nature poured in with a beauty she had never known before. Her mind, registering the gurgling of a nearby brook, recognized the steady song of that mysterious current within her; it was the *cantus firmus* of pure being, the voice of time running with its own sweet measure; time uncoupled from the metronome of human consciousness was within her now; she could see it moving in the blue sky above her, knowing that nothing would ever match its beauty.

Agnes's merging with nature, an ecstatic experience to which Kundera attaches the emblematic eighteenth-century word *le bonheur* (. . . *et là il y avait le bonheur*),[33] suggests a comparison with the moment of communion with nature that Rousseau evokes in the fifth "*Promenade*" of *Les Rêveries du promeneur solitaire* (1782). He describes the state of happiness he experienced on the island of Saint-Pierre in Switzerland, lying on his back inside an idly floating boat, gently cradled by the barely perceptible rhythm of the lapping waters underneath his sensitive body. "*Le sentiment de l'existence depouillé de toute affection est par lui-même un sentiment precieux de contentement et de paix* . . ."[34] writes Rousseau, comparing that fullness of self to something akin to a divine level of existence ("*. . . on se suffit à soi-même, comme Dieu*,"). Agnes's self-divestment has the opposite effect: "Living, there is no happiness in that. Living, carrying one's painful self through the world. But being, being is happiness. Being: becoming a fountain, a fountain on which the universe falls like warm rain" (p. 259). In Rousseau's epiphany, the self grows immense as God himself, whereas it disappears altogether in Agnes's ecstasy. Rousseau's pantheism, which dissipates God's essence into sensual nature, retains the old Christian notion of the self as the vital center of *physis*. His rediscovery of Nature is another flowering of the seed of subjectivism planted deep in the soul of *Homo sentimentalis*. By contrast, Agnes's happiness in being, which returns to Nature the sense of sacredness humans have appropriated for themselves, is authentically pagan. Her desire for a metamorphosis outside the form of humanity resonates back to Ovid and beyond that, to the astral sensibility that permeates the cosmological system of the Vedas and the Upanishads. The aesthetic dimension of Agnes's moment of fullness likens it to the beautiful image of Goethe in his third age, contemplating the poplar. But Agnes's experience is more participatory than contemplative, drawing on the capabilities of her spirit to transcend the gap intellection cuts between the seeing eye and its object.

The fatal car crash, envisioned within the magnetic field of the girl who causes it to happen, occurs in chapter 17 of part 5. This places the event virtually back to back with Agnes's epiphany of being. The accident comes to the reader voided of all elements of suspense, having been rehearsed in forebodings, foretold and forethought. The girl's death-dealing gesture is described in physical detail by the narrator, as he and his companion reach the Mercedes: "And she longed to die like a beetle crushed by a sudden fist. It was almost a physical longing to be crushed, like the need to press one's palm against the part of the body that hurts" (p. 253).

Yet, the moment when the girl's desire turns into an act, the effect upon the reader is one of stunning surprise. Her posture, folded upon herself in the middle of the crowded road, her eyes closed, the crushing noise of the heavy impact of metallic masses colliding, even the piercing shriek of pain from the victims, were all predictable. But nothing could have prepared us for the terrible beauty of the instant when the exultant cry of the world's terror suddenly awakens an answer within the mute voice of the empty girl. "At that point, the scream that was in her throat finally came to life" (p. 261). The world, illuminated by the explosion of primal terror, where creation consorts with destruction, suddenly grows real and colossal within her consciousness. "I am become Death, the shatterer of worlds." These words spoken by Krishna in the *Bhagavad Gita*, when he manifests himself to Arjuna as *visvarupa*, were quoted by Robert Oppenheimer, one of the scientists who created the atom bomb, as he watched it explode in the Nevada desert a few weeks before its impact on Hiroshima.

Like the crossroads where Oedipus meets Laius, the accident on this highway becomes a vortex of meaning, drawing into itself all the disparate jetsam of devalued action with which this novel is strewn. The deadly, excruciating clash of two feminine selves on a crowded highway, one woman filled with pure being, the other with nothingness, is the overarching metaphor of this novel, conceivable alternately as its semantic apex or abyss. The instant has the effective power of pulling everything into itself, like a black hole pulling at the density of matter. Even Avenarius finds himself swept by its cataclysmic force. Later that same night, he is arrested on the street, in the middle of his raid, and charged with the intent of committing assault upon a terrified girl whose shrieks have alerted a patrolling policeman. Another catastrophic woman, anonymous to us just as is the would-be suicide, stands before Avenarius in the ambiguity of her status as victim/victimizer.

Appearing from nowhere, the girl confronts Avenarius, her putative rapist, with an expression of petrified terror that is replicated on the accused man's face. Regaining his composure, Avenarius smiles and asks her, in all innocence: "What time is it?" (p. 263). Coincidentally, just as the policeman is about to discover Avenarius's incriminating knife, a man appears in the street, emerging from a nearby house in the unsteady gait of a sleepwalker. Having sighted the agent of public order in the act of arresting a citizen, the man mechanically hands Avenarius his professional card; it is Paul, awakened by the telephone call announcing Agnes's accident. Distraught by anguish, he absurdly performs the rote gesture of his vocation as the poet of defense. While Avenarius is being led away, Paul sinks to the pavement next to his car, shaken by sobs at the discovery of the slashed tire.

The time wasted in searching for another form of locomotion robs Paul of the chance of finding Agnes alive. He races to the hospital, consumed by the desire for one parting kiss "with which he might catch her face, as in a skein, before it vanished and left him with merely a memory" (p. 266).

The pathos of Agnes's death vibrates within the frame of her loving husband's life. Projected inside its own inner space, the image of Agnes's act of dying has the essential dignity of tragic experience as Sophocles captures it at the turning point of the *agon*, when the scapegoat emerges as hero or heroine by commanding the meaning of the event that destroys it. It was for the sake of this great finale that Agnes was conceived, rising like a flame out of the waters of Kundera's imagination. We recall that he endowed her with a name unlike those of the real women he had known. Agnes, Agnes. Repeated, the name, pronounced in the Czech way with a stress on the long open A, suggests the effect of a trochaic dirge. I hear it in a poem by František Halas written as an occasional tribute to an actress whose interpretation of a tragic role had moved him.[35] In the real world of Prague under Nazi occupation when this poem was written, death was stamping around in the terrifying mask of banality. But in the magic confines of a lyrical drama, an actress's voice and flamelike stance had summoned the concealed meaning of death, "in darkness where being flows into grand finale," as the last great adventure, beautiful as the call of a hunting horn heard in the depth of the night forest.

When Paul finally catches up with Agnes, she lies in her hospital bed, her eyes closed to the world. A nurse explains that she has been dead for fifteen minutes. Her pale, beautiful face will forever deny the claims his love brought to bear upon it. But in the last reel of Agnes's living time, a less forbidding image of death surges into view. The figure of the demented girl, the angel of her death, flits before her inner eye, and Agnes sees it "as if a ballerina were pulling the curtain across at the end of a show" (p. 268). Paul, leaning over the deathbed, sees a smile on Agnes's face. Meaningless to the world of the living, it is the expression of a spirit at last face to face (*tváří v tvář*) with the divine form of Being whose intelligibility does not require a human semblance.

Part 6 throws us back into the flux of life. Formally, this section functions exactly like part 6 of *Life Is Elsewhere*, "The Middle-Aged Man," described by the author as relating to the rest of the novel "as does a small guesthouse to a country manor."[36] But in this novel, there are many guests scattered in its many paths and no single lord or lady to command the venues of the main action. Viewed within the poetic spectrum of values, part 6 of *Immortality*, "The dial" (*Ciferník*, in Czech), burns darkly like a patch of crimson next to the lone brilliance of the fugitive moment of erotic excitement in the scene of Goethe and Bettina at the window in Teplitz.

The tonal pitch for the sixth movement was set by the narrator in part 5, when he announced to Avenarius: "I am really looking forward to Part Six. A completely new character will enter the novel. And at the end of that part he will disappear without a trace. He causes nothing and leaves no effects. That is precisely what I like about him. Part Six will be a novel within a novel, as well as the saddest erotic story I have ever written" (p. 238). The new character, hero of a story presumed useless, who makes nothing happen, lends a major poetic resonance to a novel that is a meditation on human time. His digression develops the melancholy counterpoint of a double theme of decline, combining the story of the waning of Eros in a singular male consciousness with that of the waning of European painting in the late decades of the twentieth century. The new experimental self belongs to the category of *Homo eroticus*, stalled in his tracks by a terminal condition of a sexuality decoupled from love. His story opens "a secret window through the novel's wall,"[37] allowing us to fathom the outline of Agnes's hitherto concealed sexual self.

The name of Agnes's episodic lover is Rubens. His erotic career, contemplated from its inception in the cradle down to its abrupt cessation in late middle age, occupies approximately the same number of pages as the single day of Agnes's life when she journeys into death. These two narratives move at the same tempo, in violation of the law of chronometric proportion this novel has abolished, along with the tyranny of a linear plot. Rubens's time is conceived in the holistic form of roundness, made intelligible by existential mathematics. Its metaphor, as imaged in the section's title, "The dial," shows the face or screen of an old-fashioned round clock. Its circumference is divided into twelve equal sections, whose numbers run the progressive sequence of 1 to 12 in the paradoxical form of circularity, joining the highest sign with the lowest. In our computer-driven era, such dials are yielding to the digital clock, the image of a time of instant gratification, flashing ahead of itself with precise monotony. The meaning of Rubens's time is best viewed in retrospect, from the finite perspective aging imposes. "When someone is young, he is not capable of conceiving of time as a circle, but thinks of it as a road leading forward to ever-new horizons; he does not yet sense that his life contains just a single theme; he will come to realize it only when his life begins to enact its first variations" (p. 275).

The same law of aging prevails in the macrosphere of human culture. Accordingly, the reflections about European painting that emerge from Rubens's private life show us "Europe looking back on its own past, weighing up its history like an old man seeing his whole life in a single moment."[38] Rubens acquired his nickname when he was a student at the *lycée* in his Swiss hometown. He was then at the height of his glory as a painter, universally admired for his witty caricatures of teachers. He holds on to this mask even after deserting his artistic vocation. He made that choice at age twenty-four, by marrying a beautiful girl who seemed to him the embodiment of ineffable happiness, in a gesture he interpreted as the renunciation of ambition for the sake of life itself.

Given what we are told about the young man's budding art, the nickname seems incongruous, chosen at random. But then we note: Peter Paul Rubens (1577–1640), the master colorist of the Flemish School, excelled at depicting the vitality of the human body in motion, both in and out of the natural landscape, which he would endow with the same superabundant joy of life. An immensely successful painter, he became rich by selling his canvases not only to the Church, but also to wealthy patrons of the new bourgeoisie who, at this time, also engaged in humanistic learning. With such buyers, Rubens consorted on a footing of cultural equality and friendship. Positioned at the beginning of Europe's Modern Era, Rubens occupies the privileged midpoint in the history of his art form: when the painter is an individual of significance rather than an obscure craftsman. He himself set the value of his creation, which was not yet reduced to a token of financial speculation. Thus viewed, the Flemish master is the appropriate starting point for the lesser Rubens's meditation on the terminal condition of the art of painting in his time.

Instead of being a painter, Rubens becomes an art dealer. Once, many years into his business career, he makes a startling discovery during a visit to the Museum of Modern Art in New York. On the first floor, devoted to the twentieth-century avant-garde, represented by the generation of Matisse, Braque, Picasso, Miró, Dalí, Ernst, etc., he is stunned by the vitality that speaks through the enormous variety of styles and mediums. Paintings, collages, drawings—all are animated by the same exuberance of attack, transforming the artist's encounter with reality into a duel, as violent as a bullfight and pleasurable as sex (pp. 290–91). By contrast, the contemporary art exhibited on the second floor seems petrified by a secret fear of reality, either evading it altogether in the ready-made formulae of abstraction or caving in to its opaque appearances in the slavery of imitation called pop art. Observing Rubens, Kundera asks himself what happens to a man born with a talent for a medium of activity whose clock has already struck midnight (p. 291). Or, alternatively, if the first hour has yet to sound, Rubens would never know whether his talent for painting was genuine. But he now understands that his abandonment of artistic vocation for the business of art, an activity he does not respect, may have been grounded in the subversive morality of uselessness, just like Rimbaud's gesture of giving up poetry at nineteen for the African slave trade. The category of painting that lingers on after the circle of its legitimate history has closed is marked by the sham illusionism of the age of the instant snapshot, when the mimicry of life's movement can be obtained on TV screens with push-button efficiency.

Reflecting on the great tradition of European painting, Rubens notes that all expressions of human mirth, with the sole exception of the archaic smile, were relegated to the lower register of semantic dignity. On a hierarchical scale that privileges the beauty of stasis, the expression of open-mouthed laughter was codified as the sign of perversity, representing either something wholly evil or at best the convulsive, suffering mask of vice. The examples cited are Poussin's *Le Massacre des Innocents* and Correggio's *Allegory of the Vices*. The Dutch painters were the first to show the innocence of laughter, as in Franz Hals's *Clown* or his *Gypsy* (p. 323). Looking at those portraits, Rubens notes that they prefigure the advent of photography, with its democratic revolution in the beauty/ugliness code. In our time, laughter is considered the most democratic of all facial expressions. It has become the obligatory mask of a politician under the public lens. One day, examining an old illustrated magazine, Rubens happened to note that it contained some fifty different color photographs of President Kennedy, all laughing. He was able to verify the aesthetic law of degradation that imposed the convulsive mask of a frozen rictus upon the debonair, witty face of the living JFK. In the absence of metaphoric reflectivity, the photographic reproduction of human emotion is as painfully inadequate to its subject as the image of her own face was to Agnes's *tvář* when she read it mirrored in anonymous, staring faces. The thought about Kennedy's unnaturally stilled smile occurs to Rubens in chapter 21 of part 6, near the end of his story, when the image of a dead Agnes begins to haunt his actual lovemaking. It is a major point of intersection between the two thematic lines of development.

Rubens's erotic nature, as Kundera defines it in the first three chapters of this digression, brings to mind the poetic emblem of the great painter in the first stanza of Baudelaire's poem "Les Phares":[39]

Rubens, fleuve d'oubli, jardin de la paresse,
Oreiller de chair fraîche où l'on ne peut aimer,
Mais où la vie afflue et s'agite sans cesse,
Comme l'air dans le ciel et la mer dans la mer.

The second line, in particular, offers a key to Rubens's erotic contradictions, by setting up a negative tension between an apparently simple, generic verb of action—*aimer*—and its complex object. *Aimer* is an ambiguous word that designates both the physical act of lovemaking and the emotion of loving, in its dual aspect as love-feeling and love-relation. Rubens is a man of innate sexual vitality, predestined from the cradle to a life of erotic hedonism. But in his youth, under the penumbra of his betrayed artistic vocation, he erects as his supreme value the ideal of the singular great love, imagining himself called to the summit of feeling. On the eve of his marriage, he is nevertheless surprised by the sudden stab of nostalgia he feels for his latest mistress, a woman never loved and happily discarded. The bubble of his marriage, filled not only with "love" but also with the potential for laughable disaster, eventually collapses in the ordeal of the conjugal bed. During their first honeymoon night, Rubens addresses his bride with the discarded mistress's name. The divorce, not long in coming, releases Rubens from the oppression of monogamous ecstasy.

After the shipwreck of his marriage Rubens, still in his first youth, is free to devote himself to the arts of sexual libertinage that represent his vital theme, inscribed in his natal chart at the moment of his emergence into the world. The astrological metaphor Kundera deploys at the inception of Rubens's story rehearses the theme of chance/necessity, first articulated in Agnes's fable about the Creator's computer. But in this naturalistic variation, the function of the vaguely anthropocentric Creator is transferred to the astral belt of the Zodiac. With this transposition, the semantic focus is redirected from the idea of blind necessity to the subtler notion of human limits as the sphere of creative possibilities. Astrology is often condemned as the school of fatalism. Not so, says Kundera. ". . . [I]n my view, astrology (please understand, astrology as a metaphor of life) says something far more subtle: you won't escape your life's *theme*" (p. 275).

An individual's natal chart with its particular planetary configuration remains fixed forever, expressing the precise but inherently accidental relation between his moment of birth and the map of the heavens above his head. As time keeps advancing on the finite dial of one's life, its circle intersects with the constant, even rotation of the Zodiac, creating a shifting pattern of coincidences that plays itself out in multiple variations of the basic theme. Thus conceived, the metaphor of the astrological clock can easily be translated into the language of musical composition that seems to govern the complex, circular art of this novel. "And that's life: it does not resemble a picaresque novel in which from one chapter to the next the hero is continually being surprised by new events that have no common denominator. It resembles a composition that musicians call a *theme with variations*" (p. 275).

Astrology, with its arcane numerological system of correspondence between the microcosmic human and the macrocosmic astral spheres of being, is the school of limits that allows full play to the diversity of human individuation. In his conversation with Avenarius, the narrator spoke of his desire to codify the human relation to time in terms of existential mathematics. We recall that he came up with four types of human coincidence and three stages of time consciousness in a single life. Here the mathematical game picks up again, in the form of the heavenly algebra contained in the number twelve, a multiple of four and three. Just like the dial of an ordinary clock, the heavenly clock of the Zodiac is divided into twelve sections, each represented by its astrological sign.

Within this circle are inscribed the seven planets and their twin companions, the sun and the moon, making nine, the perfect combined number of circularity, three times three.

These observations, like everything else in this digression, are enclosed within the orbit of an experimental self whose *theme* defines him as *Homo eroticus*, accidentally born in the posthistorical moment of European culture when sexual love lacks a meaningful content. Turning to the individual clock of Rubens's erotic life, the narrator divides it into five phases. The initial period of silent athleticism belongs to raw youth, soon to be upstaged by the more inventive phase of metaphors when the collector of women becomes a collector of words, to use Dr. Havel's formula. In the third, the phase of obscene truths, the libertine reaches his maturity, which coincides with the loss of erotic solitude. In the game of "Telephone" that Rubens learns from his friend M, sex is a comic invention played by a team of male friends sharing the same pool of mistresses, signaling to each other by whispering sophisticated obscenities into a feminine ear in a rotation of many separate moments of lovemaking. It occurs to Rubens that a whole nation could be thus connected by a shared pool of verbal obscenity. In the fifth, most enigmatic stage, Rubens feels that obscenity is like a river of oblivion, running deep under the superficial layer of individual consciousness, uniting all men and women in its mystical, impersonal flow.

The erotic adventure that brings Rubens face to face with Agnes, in a pattern of intermittent encounters separated by long gaps, spans the whole arc of his erotic maturity. The episodic affair occurs within the territory of erotic pluralism that Rubens had discovered by wandering into the overgrown, neglected backyard behind the Palace of Love. In this zone of sexual freedom only one rule obtains—the injunction against the single great love. Though experienced within this territory, Rubens's erotic image of Agnes has the enchantment of a dream figure, forever mixing memory with desire.

She enters Rubens's story in chapter 9 of part 6, in a scene unlike any other in this novel, charged with the highest voltage of sexual excitement while preserving an absolute chastity of gesture. The chance encounter in the park of the Villa Borghese above Rome, bringing together a nameless young woman in dark glasses and a mature man suddenly startled from his ruminations as if struck by a vision, is an instant of mutual recognition. Its sexual significance is endowed with the charm of high romance, as if the setting had enclosed them within its intrinsic magic. They walk together on the same footpath where Stendhal, wearing the mask of Henry Brulard, traced the initial letters of his great loves into the sand.[40] Briefly, they sit down at a café table in the park of the Villa Borghese, in the landscape where Goethe conceived the phantasmagoric images of sexual vitality that would renew Faust's capacity for desire.[41] She tells him that she is in Rome with her husband and disposes of no more than an hour of time. Having lifted the dark glasses from her face, he renames her with the musical name "the lute player," which she will carry throughout his story.

The timbre of Agnes's voice, heard in internal monologue, had a lucid, intellectual quality barely distinguishable from the narrator's voice at her shoulder. Rubens's name for Agnes evokes the delicate musical line of the courtly love song and the articulate elegance of the Renaissance art of polyphony. A bit later, Rubens reminds her how they first met about fifteen years earlier, on the dance floor in a Swiss town, when she was only seventeen years old and he ten years older. He likens her to another artistic image. "Women in Gothic paintings walk with their bellies sticking out. And with their heads bowed toward the ground. Your walk is that of a Gothic maiden. A lute player in an angelic orchestra. Your breasts are turned toward heaven, your belly is turned toward heaven, but your head, which realizes the vanity of everything, looks into the dust" (p. 301). The lover's act of naming informs the narrator's abstract of Agnes by the resonance of two subtly intertwined metaphors of sight and hearing.

The lute player enters Rubens's life at the turning point when erotic retrospection begins to deepen the hues of his desire with the melancholic touch of nostalgia. The rumination from which the sight of her woke him turned around the regret of having wasted all his opportunities: ". . . all the women he had ever known filed past his eyes, and it seemed that he had missed them all, that he had experienced much less than he could have or should have" (p. 294). The grace of intimate individuation had eluded him throughout his richly varied erotic practice. The memory of a shy young girl on a dance floor, shielding her figure from his eyes by strangely appealing hand gestures, suddenly recovered in the lute player's darkly masked face, addresses him with the potent charm of individual uniqueness. He treasures the moment when he had placed his hand on her breast in a daring gesture while dancing, followed by the question "Has anyone ever touched your breast?" and the trembling answer "No" (p. 296).

A week after their Rome encounter, he repeats his gesture and his question as a prologue to their first lovemaking in a Paris hotel. Yes, she remembers the question, not knowing that it links her across an even deeper time chasm to Bettina, standing in the window niche with Goethe. The gestures of their lovemaking are veiled in the mystery of a language that aims at describing their hidden, more powerful meanings. "Eagerly, they let themselves be carried away by that stream that flows through all women and all men, that mystic stream of obscene images where every woman resembles every other woman and yet a different face gives the same images and words a different power and enchantment" (p. 303).

Though the essence of the lute player's charm for Rubens resides in her ability to command his memory, the verbal mode of their sexual communication employs the future tense, the mode of a desire as yet to be fulfilled. The basis of Rubens's eroticism is excitement, and it thrives on ambiguity. The highest value of his sexual code attaches to the equivocal situation of two men making love to a single woman, a game that opens the intimate couple to the intrusion of a stranger, who participates in the dual capacity of observer/participant. With the lute player the erotic mystery of the triangle within the sexual circle remains forever suspended between promise and fulfillment. One day in Paris, Rubens had invited his friend M to join him at the appointed time. Having disrobed the lute player in the hotel room, the two men led her in front of a large mirror. She stood silently between them, covering her naked breasts with her hands, oblivious of their looks upon her, gazing straight ahead, as if hypnotized by her own reflected image. Rubens himself disrupted the sequence at this point by signaling for M to withdraw, thus changing the erotic instance back to unfulfilled promise. Soon after, he lost track of M and his meetings with the lute player, already rare, dwindled to a stop.

Several years later, Rubens begins an affair with a beautiful young Australian student of the semiotics of painting at a Swiss university. She always wears a pair of sneakers that appear enormous to Rubens. Their silent sex scenes are a puzzle to him, a routine of strenuous gestures whose meaning he cannot decode. She belongs to the generation of women who grew up unacquainted with the delicate shame that once bore the name of modesty. Rubens was already forty when women took off their bras on European beaches. His erotic sensibility, trained to read his own arousal in a woman's blush, finds no resonance in his antipodal mistress. He decides to put an end to their opaque love bouts, but just at the moment when he watches her lithe figure turning the corner of the street after their parting, his forsworn desire for her turns upon him with a violence of nostalgia that shocks him like the onslaught of a sudden illness. "He slowly began to realize what it was about. The hand on the dial had touched a new number. He heard the clock strike, saw a little window open, and thanks to the mysterious medieval mechanism, a woman in huge tennis shoes came out" (p. 310).

This passage delivers the completed form of the metaphor introduced earlier, in chapter 2 of part 6, when the narrator invited us to imagine the erotic clock of Rubens's life as "some great medieval clock, like the one in Old Town Square in Prague, which I passed regularly for some twenty years" (p. 276). The twice-repeated image grafting the time of Kundera's experience onto Rubens's time signals a moment of major symbolic congruence.

Erected in the fifteenth century, the astrological clock on the facade of Old Town Hall, with its complicated scheme of interlocking times, is one of the wonders of Prague.[42] It displays two circular dials, each divided into twelve sections, whose interaction images the narrator's conceit of life's *theme*. The large, numbered circle remains stable even as the smaller gyrating zodiacal sphere travels on its inside, rotating the signs over and over, but never losing contact with the circumference of diurnal time. On the wall above the clock are two windows, framing a Gothic angel in high relief. At the strike of the hour the windows open on a puppet show of twelve apostles, parading around in a Christian allegory of human time laden with death and redemption. The angel presides over the dance, a messenger of double meaning, and when the processional counts down to twelve, the cock crows as a grinning skeleton turns over the hourglass, rattling the sands.

The Australian appears in the window of Rubens's erotic clock that began ticking when he was fourteen and a little girl half his age accosted him to ask the time of day (pp. 275–76). Her sneaker-shod entry signals the hour of erotic repetition, presaging desire's ebb. "He realized that from now on great excitements were to be found only behind him, and if he wanted to find new excitements, he would have to turn to his past" (p. 310). In a flash of insight, Rubens reclassifies his erotic career from five to three phases: in the dark, eyes closed; in full light, eyes open; in full light, eyes closed (p. 311). Within this circular system, the mysterious number three no longer signifies the highest intensity of erotic tension, but the terminal condition of his desire, when he can make love to his present mistress only by interposing images from a distant past. It is here that he starts collecting his erotic snapshots and finds himself envying Casanova's incomparable memory (p. 313). Out of his own impressive number and variety of conquests, Rubens can only dredge out seven erotic snapshots, three of which record the lute player's gesture of modesty. He remembers her dancing, with hands moving in an effort to conceal her face, then his hand on her breast as she speaks to him with a trembling voice. The third, most powerful image shows her between two men, her hands on her naked breasts, gazing into the distance.

After a gap of eight years, Rubens renews the sporadic meetings in the Paris hotel. The lute player retains the same unmistakable nobility of feature, but her skin has lost its freshness. None of this matters to Rubens, since the living woman has already disappeared behind the image in his memory. And it is that image he desires to bring back into play by the magic of sensual contact. His lovemaking nowadays requires a third spectral presence to animate its illusion, whether he is with G, his current mistress, or with the lute player herself, repossessing his past. A few years are spent in this fashion, but one day, the lute player puts off their meetings indefinitely.

The culmination of Rubens's ultimate sexual episode comes to him in the form of a Gothic Crucifixion scene. During a visit to a Roman museum, he stands a long time before a painting showing the agonized Christ on the cross between two thieves, exposed to the derision of a motley crowd. Gazing in, he begins to superimpose the lute player's face and figure over the icon of the Savior's Passion. He sees her hoisted up, her hands on her naked breasts. Two men, one on each side of her, are pulling her arms apart to form a cross with her body, while her face remains fixed upon a mirror lost in the distance. She is oblivious to the howling crowd below her. Enthralled by this transgressional image of erotic transcendence, he calls it *Rubens's Vision in Rome*, as if to underline the mystical meaning it conveys from the borderline where the sacred meets with blasphemy. For the reader, the image also reads as a retrospective view of Agnes's death agony, rehearsed in the pathos of her lover's imagination. Alternately, it is also a premonition for Rubens, who is about to hear that Agnes is dead (p. 326) when he calls the lute player's Paris number from Rome in a desperate effort to break the four-year silence. Another meaning of the scene rises from the root word "passion," conceived as suffering. It reveals the intimate essence of Agnes's eroticism on the rack of the body/soul contradiction, between concealment and surrender.

Rubens's vision marks the summit of his erotic history, when desire, overcome by *soucit*, consumes its flame beyond the limits of bodily gesture in the transparency of love's intelligence. After hearing of Agnes's death, he continues his appointments with G, not yet understanding that he has crossed into the posthistorical phase of erotic uselessness. He has noticed, however, that his young mistress's convulsive, feverish spasms in bed, a routine she uses to rush him toward orgasm, are frightfully reminiscent of death throes. But he persists, relying more and more on his technical dexterity to compensate for his declining desire. But on one occasion, about two or three years after Agnes's death, when he calls on his favorite snapshot of her standing at the mirror, the lute player comes to him with the fleshless grinning face of death. He sees her body, topped by an empty cranium, rearing up in the fire of the crematorium furnace. These flames, rising above the great sea of sex ("*où la vie afflue et s'agite sans cesse*"), lick him dry of all desire, body and soul. He excuses himself with G, knowing that the postponement of their pleasures will be indefinite.

Immortality's seventh movement is short and noisy. The circularity of the novel's form throws us back into the initial setting at the poolside where Agnes's image was ignited in the narrator's imagination. The penthouse spa has added more mirrors to the decor, no doubt responding to its clientele's infantile narcissism. In contrast to the spaciousness of Rubens's playground, the dimension of this locale represents a drastic narrowing down. In the novel's terminal movement ("The celebration") we are confined to a corner at the edge of the pool, where the narrator and Avenarius occupy a table, sharing a bottle of wine and conversation. One senses the bare, wooden board of a stage under their feet, as the text proceeds to assemble the surviving characters for their exit scene.

Avenarius tries gamely to revive the comic spirit by engaging the topic of womanizing. The question at issue is the relative value of vanity vis-à-vis the physical pleasure of sexual possession, framed in the hypothetical choice between a Bardot on one's arm, to be paraded in public view, and a Bardot possessed in the privacy of one's bed. Avenarius argues for vanity but muddles himself up with statistics in an attempt to demonstrate the objectivity of his thesis. The old exuberance has gone out of both companions, and laughter seems in short supply.

The strain of conversation is relieved by the arrival of Paul at their table. Avenarius introduces him to his creator, identified as the author of *Life Is Elsewhere*. More wine is ordered, and henceforth the quickening pace of the farce will be measured by the rapidity with which Paul gets drunk. His voice, rising to a high pitch over the even-toned voices of the two companions, becomes the sound projector of the European post-cultural age, when great ideas and values are doomed to survive in the form of kitsch. There is an implicit argument running through this novel, which holds that the crossing of Lethe into true death is a fate more merciful than sham survival. Paul, who has survived his grief over Agnes's death, is still the great leveler. He is about to demonstrate how easily the defender's passion can turn accusatory. With the vehemence of Saint-Just, Paul denounces "the terror of the immortals" (p. 336). The artistic perfection of Mahler's Seventh Symphony is a special provocation. He calls it arrogant and inhuman, since no listener can fully comprehend it. Mahler, he confides, is his wife's favorite composer, and she has explained to him that Mahler locked himself up in a hotel room in Prague on the eve of the Seventh Symphony's first performance in 1908, reworking its orchestration so as to achieve the subtle effect of harmony he could hear in his inner ear. "He was convinced that his whole work would be ruined if the melody were played by a clarinet instead of an oboe during the second movement" (p. 335). The narrator seizes the occasion to drop in a giveaway phrase: "That's precisely so," he says, thinking of his novel.[43]

Paul, the metaphysical tribune of democracy, toasts the end of an epoch. But the death of European culture seems to inaugurate the age of his own dotage. A woman in a swimsuit approaches; she is about forty years old and still attractive, with an expressive derrière that pulls slightly downward. It is Laura, the new repository of Paul's happiness, firmly married and mother of a three-month-old daughter. Paul explains that he lives in the intimacy of four women: his wife and child, as well as Brigitte, who has returned to him husbandless, with an infant daughter in her arms. Paul suddenly seems to grow very old, his face assuming the mask of an old woman, his mother. He cites Aragon's winged words "Woman is the future of man," and suddenly his face begins to merge with that of the lyricist of Revolution—he is Aragon, just as he was in 1968 when Kundera met him. Proclaiming his solidarity with "the *Ewigweibliche*, the eternally feminine" (p. 339), Paul/ Aragon rolls down the slope of his lyrical rhetoric. But *sotto voce* he confides his terror of women, who are relentless once they begin to fight. If they were in charge of war, he whispers, no one would survive.

At this precise moment, Laura steps center stage. Approaching the table, she makes the gesture with her hand that seems to the male trio as if "a golden ball had risen from her fingertips" (p. 340). The narrator having decoded the sign as a greeting meant for Avenarius, rather than her drunken husband, we suspect Paul is about to be promoted to the rank of complete ass. As it is, he aggravates his case by confiding to the two companions that he has been practicing an imitation of Laura's gesture. He associates it with the enchanting moment when she waved at him in parting as she entered the maternity ward. In this absurdist gender reversal of the sign, the paradigm disappears behind the parody, wherein the memory of Agnes is revived in travesty.

Paul exits through an imaginary gate above which shines the golden balloon, leaving the two companions alone, sitting in the afterglow (p. 342). Whatever else he may be, Avenarius is a loyal rogue. He is grateful to Paul for having defended him against the false accusation of rape. But, as he explains the case to his friend, he swears that nothing, not even the threat of prison, could have compelled him to reveal the secret of the kitchen knife. In a flash of illumination, the narrator suddenly captures the ground metaphor of Avenarius's being, which has eluded him so far. The formula "You play with the world like a melancholy child who has no little brother" (p. 344) paradoxically derives the ludic spirit from loneliness and need. Linking laughter and desire, the defining image also contains a clue to the enigmatic meaning of Diabolum. That tentacular entity of power Avenarius has to contend with is finally unmasked as nothing more or less than a trademark of a children's game, diabolo; a yo-yo in the guise of an hourglass, with the figurine of a tiny devil rotating around a tightly stretched string. Diabolum serves as the metaphor of a world that reduces time to a flash on the digital screen and sex to the repetition of a pendulum swing.

This is also a moment that seems an echo of Rimbaud's *Le Bateau ivre:*

> Si je désire une eau d'Europe, c'est la flache
> Noire et froide où vers le crépuscule embaumé
> Un enfant accroupi plein de tristesses, lâche
> Un bateau frêle comme un papillon de mai.[44]

The image of the melancholy child playing with a tiny boat inside a dark, cold puddle comes in the penultimate stanza of the poem, at the crest of the wave of nostalgia initiated within the line *"Je regrette l'Europe aux anciens parapets!"* Placed on the edge of the two preceding strophes, the exclamation marks the turning point where the imaginative trip of a reckless adventure of discovery recoils on itself, as if responding to the sudden stab of regret and desire for landscapes left far behind.

The terminal scene of the novel separates the two companions in the street, where they have descended together from their penthouse perch. Avenarius walks toward his Mercedes. The narrator takes the opposite direction, breaking out of the limits of his magic circle, now fully rounded. It is two years since he first saw the image of Agnes, and the celebration at the poolside was meant to be a tribute to his novel's completion. Agnes returns to his mind as he walks in her footsteps, holding before his eyes her talismanic flower, the forget-me-not, whose name and color mix and confuse death with memory. He is disappearing from our sight beyond Montparnasse, entering Prague's Old Town Square by way of the Town Hall, where the astrological clock has just sounded midnight.

NOTES

Page citations to Kundera's fiction are given parenthetically in the text. The abbreviation *AN* stands for Kundera's collection of essays, *The Art of the Novel,* translated from the French by Linda Asher (New York: Grove Press, 1988).

Introduction

1. Kundera received the Jerusalem Prize in the spring of 1985. His address was first published in English in *New York Review of Books,* June 13, 1985, under the title "Man Thinks, God Laughs." I quote from "Jerusalem Address: The Novel and Europe," *AN*, p. 158.
2. "The Depreciated Legacy of Cervantes," *AN*, p. 13.
3. "Jerusalem Address," *AN*, p. 158.
4. François Rabelais, *The Histories of Gargantua and Pantagruel,*

trans. J. M. Cohen (New York: Penguin Books, 1955), bk. 5, ch. 4, p. 704.

5. Rosalie L. Colie, *Paradoxia Epidemica: The Renaissance Tradition of Paradox* (Princeton: Princeton University Press, 1966), p. 10.
6. Antonín J. Liehm, *The Politics of Culture*, trans. Peter Kussi (New York: Grove Press, 1973), p. 138.
7. "A Kidnapped West; or, Culture Bows Out," *Granta*, no. 11 (1984): 114.
8. Ibid., p. 118.
9. The essay originated as a lecture delivered at the University of Pittsburgh in 1983. It was published in France that same year, in *Le Nouvel Observateur,* under the title "Et si le roman nous abandonne?" In *L'art du roman* (Paris: Gallimard, 1986) it figures as "L'héritage décrié de Cervantes."
10. "The Depreciated Legacy of Cervantes," *AN*, p. 6.
11. "TEMPS MODERNES (Modern Era). The coming of *les Temps modernes*. The key moment of European history. In the seventeenth century, God becomes *Deus absconditus* and man the ground of all things. European individualism is born, and with it a new situation for art, for culture, for science. I run into problems with this term in the United States. The literal translation, 'modern times' (and even the more comprehensive 'Modern Era'), an American takes to mean the contemporary moment, our century. The absence in America of the notion of *les Temps modernes* reveals the great chasm between the two continents. In Europe, we are living the end of the Modern Era: the end of individualism; the end of art conceived as an irreplaceable expression of personal originality; the end that heralds an era of unparalleled uniformity. This sense of ending America does not feel, for America did not live through the birth of the Modern Era and has only come along lately to inherit it. America has other criteria for beginnings and endings" ("Sixty-three Words," *AN*, pp. 149–50).
12. "The Depreciated Legacy of Cervantes," *AN*, p. 4.
13. Ibid.
14. "The more he advanced in knowledge, the less clearly could he

see either the world as a whole or his own self, and he plunged further into what Husserl's pupil Heidegger called, in a beautiful and almost magical phrase, 'the forgetting of being' " (ibid., pp. 3–4).

15. "CENTRAL EUROPE. . . . The destruction of the Hapsburg empire, and then, after 1945, Austria's cultural marginality and the political nonexistence of the other countries, make Central Europe a premonitory mirror showing the possible fate of all Europe. Central Europe: a laboratory of twilight" ("Sixty-three Words," *AN*, p. 125).
16. "The Depreciated Legacy of Cervantes," *AN*, p. 4.
17. Colie, p. 37. Colie describes Renaissance paradoxes as follows: "They are, because of the formulation of their impossible affirmations, all 'nothings': but 'nothing' is also precisely what they are not, since they are so generative."
18. "MODERN (modern art; modern world). There is the modern art that, in *lyrical* ecstasy, identifies with the modern world. Apollinaire. Glorification of the technical, fascination with the future. Along with and after him: Mayakovsky, Léger, the Futurists, the various avant-gardes. But opposite Apollinaire is Kafka: the modern world seen as a labyrinth where man loses his way. The modernism that is *antilyrical*, antiromantic, skeptical, critical. With Kafka and after him: Musil, Broch, Gombrowicz, Beckett, Ionesco, Fellini. . . . The further we advance into the future, the greater becomes this legacy of 'antimodern modernism.' " ("Sixty-three Words," *AN*, pp. 140–41; ellipsis in original).

1: *The Joke*

1. Kundera finished writing *Žert* (*The Joke*) in December 1965. The first notebook of *Směšné lásky* (*Laughable Loves*) appeared in 1963, *Druhý sešit směšných lásek* (*The Second Notebook of Laughable Loves*), in 1965. For the full publication history of *Laughable Loves*, see ch. 2, nn. 2, 3.
2. "Author's Preface," *The Joke*, translated from the Czech by Michael Henry Heim (New York: Harper & Row, 1982), p. viii.

All English quotations from *The Joke* in this chapter are from this version of Kundera's text.

3. Philip Roth calls it "a direct and realistic book, . . . something like a cross between Dos Passos and Camus"; see "Introducing Milan Kundera," in *Laughable Loves,* translated from the Czech by Suzanne Rappaport (New York: Alfred A. Knopf, 1974), p. vii. See also Sylvie Richterová, "I romanzi di Kundera e i problemi della communicazione," *Strumenti critici,* no. 45 (June 1981): "Il primo dei tre romanzi, *Lo scherzo,* può essere, senza imbarazzo, definito realista, nel senso che esso riflette una delle situazioni tipiche della storia cecoslovacca del dopoguerra" (p. 310). I suggest that the definition *básnivý realistický román* (mythopoetic realistic novel), which Kundera used to characterize the mature novels of the Czech avant-garde writer Vladislav Vančura, applies here; see Milan Kundera, *Umění románu, Cesta Vladislava Vančury za velkou epikou* (Prague: Československý spisovatel, 1960), p. 133.
4. See Josef Škvorecký, *All the Bright Young Men and Women: A Personal History of the Czech Cinema,* trans. Michael Schonberg (Toronto: Peter Marlin Associates, 1971). Škvorecký describes the making of the film, *The Joke* (1969), under the direction of Jaromil Jireš, with Kundera's direct participation in the preparation of the script. "The shooting was interrupted by the invasion, but despite that the film was completed and with tremendous success distributed in Czechoslovakia, where they knew what it was about" (p. 189). *The Joke* was the second film to be based on a Kundera scenario. In 1965, the director Hynek Bočan made a film from the short story "Nobody Will Laugh," which is in the 1963 cycle of *Laughable Loves* (ibid., p. 205).
5. The most notable of such works was Ludvík Vaculík's *Sekyra* (*The Axe*), published in 1966. The novel depicts the complicated relationship between a Party official who led the collectivization effort and his son, a journalist, who begins to question his father's values and methods. Finally the son opts out of the system his father helped create. The conflict of generations was a popular theme in Czech drama in the late fifties, especially after the 1956 thaw; see Paul I. Trensky, *Czech Drama Since*

World War II (New York: Columbia Slavic Studies, 1978): "The motif of children as touchstones of their parents' moral fiber becomes a virtual stereotype in this period and can be found in plays by authors of such varied artistic persuasions as Kohout, Blažek, Hrubín, Březovský, Topol, Pavlíček, and others" (p. 17).

6. *La plaisanterie,* translated from the Czech by Marcel Aymonin (Paris: Gallimard, 1968). Kundera issued a revised translation of this text in 1980, and in 1985 the definitive French translation appeared, in Aymonin's text as thoroughly revised by Kundera himself and Claude Courtot. This authoritative edition is without Aragon's preface. Instead it has a postscript, "Note de l'auteur" (pp. 397–401), dated May 1985, which explains the textual corrections and asserts the nonpolitical character of the novel.
7. See n. 2.
8. "I was appalled by the British edition. The number of chapters was different; the order of chapters was different; a number of passages were omitted. I published a letter of protest in *The Times Literary Supplement* requesting readers not to accept the English version of *The Joke* as my novel; the publisher apologized and authorized a paperback edition which restored the order of the chapters. At about the same time, the British translation was published in New York—but even more simplified, more mutilated!" ("Author's Preface," p. xi).
9. My translation. The original reads, "I personaggi del romanzo poi si dimenano in un vortice dove tutto può essere invertito" (Richterová, p. 315).
10. Květoslav Chvatík, "Romány Milana Kundery a krize lidské existence v moderním světě," *Proměny* 22, no. 2 (1985): 55–67.
11. L. Doležel, "Narrative Symposium in Milan Kundera's *The Joke,*" *Narrative Modes in Czech Literature* (Toronto: University of Toronto Press, 1973), p. 112. See also Chvatík, p. 57.
12. "Dialogue on the Art of Composition," *AN,* p. 80.
13. "Somewhere Behind," *AN,* p. 112.
14. Richterová, p. 313.
15. The word *agélaste* is a neologism coined by Rabelais. According to Kundera, "It means a man who does not laugh, who has no sense of humor" ("Jerusalem Address," *AN,* p. 159).

16. My translation. The Czech original, as quoted by Kosík, reads: "Jeden teolog mi řekl, že vše je pro mne dobré a dovoleno, jen když se podrobím koncilu a dodal: kdyby koncil prohlásil, že máš toliko jedno oko, třeba máš dvě, bylo by tvou povinností vyznati s koncilem, že tomu tak jest. Odpověděl jsem mu: I kdyby mi to tvrdil celý svět, já, maje rozum, jaký nyní mám, nemohl bych to připustiti bez odporu svědomí." See *Svědectví* (*Témoignage*), no. 32 (Paris, Fall 1967): 511. The full text of Kosík's and other addresses to the congress (June 27–29, 1967), including Milan Kundera's speech, can be found in English translation in the appendix to Dušan Hamšík's *Writers Against Rulers,* trans. D. Orpington (London: Hutchinson Press, 1971).
17. "Somewhere Behind," *AN*, p. 102.
18. Chvatík, p. 57.
19. Richterová, p. 310.
20. Ibid., p. 318.
21. František Halas (1901–1950), a Moravian lyric poet of great originality and power, belonged to the avant-garde of the twenties and thirties. Despite his proletarian origin and lifelong dedication to Party work, he was attacked by Party-line critics in the official press in 1949, charged with encouraging pessimism and a morbid preoccupation with death among the youth of the victorious working class. Halas's reputation nevertheless continued to grow, and he was posthumously rehabilitated in the late fifties.
22. In an essay on Hermann Broch, "The Legacy of *The Sleepwalkers,*" *Partisan Review* 55 (1984): 724–28. Kundera describes the world of Broch's novel as "a world in which there are no values, in which values have lost their *arche*" (p. 726). Kundera's reflections on Broch also figure as chapter 3 of *The Art of the Novel,* "Notes Inspired by 'The Sleepwalkers.' "
23. *Žert* (Prague: Československý spisovatel, 1967), p. 199.
24. "Dialogue on the Art of Composition," *AN*, p. 85.
25. Curiously, this debate between two fictional characters anticipates the main line of the disagreement between Kundera and the Russian poet in exile Joseph Brodsky, which flared into print in 1985. See Milan Kundera, "An Introduction to a Varia-

tion," and Joseph Brodsky, "Why Milan Kundera Is Wrong About Dostoyevsky," *New York Times Book Review,* January 6 and February 17, 1985, respectively. Kundera's essay serves as the introduction to his *Jacques and His Master,* translated from the French by Michael Henry Heim (New York: Harper & Row, Colophon Books, 1985).

26. Rabelais, bk. 2, ch. 22, "How Panurge Played a Trick on the Parisian Lady Which Was Not All to Her Advantage," pp. 242–44.
27. *Žert,* p. 289; my translation.
28. Rabelais, bk. 1, ch. 13, "How Grandgousier Realized Gargantua's Marvellous Intelligence by His Invention of an Arse-Wipe," pp. 66–69.
29. W. L. Webb, in his introduction to Hamšík's *Writers Against Rulers,* describes Pavel Kohout as he saw him during the wave of enthusiasm that swept Prague in the early summer of 1968, when petitions of protest were being signed in public. "Kohout, something of an actor, as well as a playwright, was hopping about on tiptoe, like a boxer, shaking hands with both fists, carrying on four conversations at once, exalted and fulfilled. . . . he had gone into the streets in February 1948 to cheer on the communist takeover of power in Czechoslovakia. More romantic than opportunist always, to him what had been happening in 1968 was indeed *obroda,* the rebirth of revolution" (pp. 9, 11). Born in Prague in 1928, Kohout began his literary career as a poet and a devotee of the cultural policies of the Soviet Union. He was cultural attaché in Moscow in 1949, at the age of twenty-one. From 1954, Kohout wrote plays that were increasingly critical of the Czech situation. He was among the most active propagators of "Communism with a human face," and after the Soviet invasion in August 1968, which he resolutely condemned, his works were banned. He now lives in Vienna.

2. *Laughable Loves*

1. Milan Kundera, *Laughable Loves,* translated from the Czech by Suzanne Rappaport, with an introduction by Philip Roth (New York: Alfred A. Knopf, 1974).

2. The first installment (*Směšné lásky,* 1963, subtitled "Melancholy Anecdotes") contained three stories: "Já, truchlivý Buh" ("I, a Mournful God"), "Sestřičko mých sestřiček" ("Sister of My Sisters"), and "Nikdo se nebude smát" ("Nobody Will Laugh"). Only the third exists in English translation. *Druhý sešit směšných lásek (The Second Notebook of Laughable Loves,* 1965) contained "Zlaté jablko věčné touhy" ("The Golden Apple of Eternal Desire"), "Zvěstovatel" ("The Precursor"), and "Falešný Autostop" ("The Hitchhiking Game"). "Zvěstovatel" has not been translated into English. *Třetí sešit směšných lásek* (*The Third Notebook of Laughable Loves,* 1969) included four stories: "Ať ustoupí staří mrtví mladým mrtvým" ("Let the Old Dead Make Room for the Young Dead"), "Symposium," "Eduard a Buh" ("Edward and God"), and "Doktor Havel po deseti letech" ("Dr. Havel After Ten Years"). Kundera tells me that the last of these stories was completed about a week before the August 1968 invasion.
3. In 1970, Kundera collected eight of the stories in a single volume, *Směšné lásky* (Prague: Československý spisovatel). "Sister of My Sisters" and "The Precursor" were eliminated. The same year, preparing the French edition for Gallimard, Kundera set aside "I, a Mournful God" and changed the order of presentation of the remaining seven stories as follows: (1) "Nobody Will Laugh"; (2) "The Golden Apple of Eternal Desire"; (3) "The Hitchhiking Game"; (4) "Symposium"; (5) "Let the Old Dead Make Room for the Young Dead"; (6) "Dr. Havel After Ten Years"; (7) "Edward and God." The sequence in the first American edition (1974) was different, but the only authoritative arrangement is the one just given, which also prevails in the definitive Czech edition (Toronto: Sixty-Eight Publishers, 1981), the revised French edition, *Risibles amours,* translated from the Czech by François Kérel (Paris: Gallimard, 1986), and the definitive English text revised by the author, *Laughable Loves,* translated from the Czech by Suzanne Rappaport (New York: Penguin Books, 1987). All English quotations from *Laughable Loves* in this chapter are from the 1987 Penguin edition.

4. In a dialogue with Kundera, Christian Salmon summed up the two basic "archetype-forms" in Kundera's novels as: "(1) polyphonic composition that brings heterogeneous elements together within an architecture based on the number seven; (2) farcical, homogeneous, theatrical composition that verges on the improbable" ("Dialogue on the Art of Composition," *AN*, p. 96). One can say that the structure of *Laughable Loves* as a whole conforms to the first archetype-form, while a single story within it, "Symposium," anticipates the five-act structure of the second archetype, which finds its fullest expression in Kundera's novel *The Farewell Party.*
5. "Dialogue on the Art of Composition," *AN*, p. 83.
6. "IRONY. . . . the novel is, by definition, the ironic art: its 'truth' is concealed, undeclared, undeclarable. . . . It is futile to try and make a novel 'difficult' through stylistic affectation; any novel worth the name, however limpid it may be, is difficult enough by reason of its consubstantial irony" ("Sixty-three Words," *AN*, p. 134).
7. "LAUGHTER (European). For Rabelais, the merry and the comic were still one and the same. In the eighteenth century, the humor of Sterne and Diderot is an affectionate, nostalgic recollection of Rabelaisian merriment. In the nineteenth century, Gogol is a melancholy humorist: 'The longer and more carefully we look at a funny story, the sadder it becomes,' said he. Europe has looked for such a long time at the funny story of its own existence that in the twentieth century, Rabelais' merry epic has turned into the despairing comedy of Ionesco, who says, 'There's only a thin line between the horrible and the comic.' The European history of laughter comes to an end" ("Sixty-three Words," *AN*, p. 136). Kundera wrote this reflection in light of his awareness that he and the European novel were experiencing the age of "terminal paradoxes." But its applicability to his earliest prose experiments confirms him in his insistence that such intellectual formulations are the result of, not the blueprint for, his practice of the art of the novel.
8. "Introducing Milan Kundera," *Laughable Loves* (1974), p. xii.
9. Ibid., p. xiv.

10. Søren Kierkegaard, "The Immediate Stages of the Erotic or the Musical Erotic" (1843), *Either/Or,* vol. 1, trans. David F. Swenson (Princeton: Princeton University Press, 1944), p. 102.
11. Ibid., p. 133.
12. Ibid., p. 129.
13. Ibid., p. 131.
14. Ibid., p. 101.
15. Ibid., p. 124.
16. *Směšné lásky* (1981), p. 51.
17. "Introducing Milan Kundera," *Laughable Loves* (1974), p. xv.
18. Blaise Pascal, Pensée 139, section 2, "Misère de l'homme sans Dieu," *Pensées* (New York: Doubleday and Co., Collection Internationale, 1961), p. 41.
19. Plato, *The Symposium,* trans. W. Hamilton (New York: Penguin Books, 1951), 206b, p. 86.
20. Explaining the genesis of his stage adaptation of Diderot's novel *Jacques le fataliste,* Kundera wrote about his experiences after the Soviet invasion of Czechoslovakia in 1968: "Faced with the eternity of the Russian night, I had experienced in Prague the violent end of Western culture such as it was conceived at the dawn of the modern age, based on the individual and his reason, on pluralism of thought and on tolerance. In a small Western country I experienced the end of the West. That was the grand farewell" ("An Introduction to a Variation," *The New York Times Book Review,* January 6, 1985, p. 28).
21. See Tirso de Molina, *The Playboy of Seville; or, Supper with a Statue,* in *Three Classic Don Juan Plays,* ed. Oscar Mandel (Lincoln: University of Nebraska Press, 1963). Don Juan's speech in the final confrontation with the statue reads, "I'm burning, let my hand go! (*Don Juan draws his dagger with his free hand.*) I'll stab you to death. . . . Useless! I'm stabbing the empty air" (act 3, scene 7, p. 51).
22. Ibid.
23. Molière, *Don John; or, The Libertine,* in *Three Classic Don Juan Plays,* act 3, scene 1, p. 78.
24. The original title of the story, as published in Czechoslovakia in 1969 (see n. 2), was "Dr. Havel After Ten Years." A decade later,

while preparing the 1979 Gallimard edition, Kundera aged his Don Juan by ten years, changing the title to "Dr. Havel After Twenty Years." The first American edition (1974) retains the original title; in the definitive English text (1987), the title is "Dr. Havel After Twenty Years."

25. Kierkegaard, pp. 106–7.
26. Alexander Pushkin, *The Stone Guest,* in *The Works of Alexander Pushkin,* (New York: Random House, 1936), scene 3, p. 450.
27. Ibid., scene 4, p. 461.
28. Ibid., p. 462.

3. *Life Is Elsewhere*

1. The novel first appeared in France: *La vie est ailleurs,* translated from the Czech by François Kérel (Paris: Gallimard, 1973). It won the Prix Médicis as the best foreign novel published in France that year. It has never been published in Czechoslovakia, but an authoritative Czech edition is available in the West: *Život je jinde* (Toronto: Sixty-Eight Publishers, 1979). In 1985, and again in 1987, Kundera issued a revised edition of the French text with a postface by François Ricard, also published by Gallimard. The first American edition, translated from the Czech by Peter Kussi, was published by Alfred A. Knopf in 1974. Kundera and Kussi collaborated on a revision for the 1986 Penguin paperback, which is the definitive English text; all quotations from *Life Is Elsewhere* in this chapter are from this edition.
2. Milan Kundera, "Paris or Prague?" *Granta,* no. 13 (Autumn 1984): 13. This article was originally written in French to serve as the preface to the French edition of Josef Škvorecký's novel *Miracle.*
3. Josef Škvorecký, *The Engineer of Human Souls,* trans. by Paul Wilson (New York: Alfred A. Knopf, 1984), p. 533.
4. Kundera, "Paris or Prague?," p. 14.
5. Ian McEwan, "An Interview with Milan Kundera," *Granta,* no. 11 (Spring 1984): 33.
6. Ibid., p. 23.
7. Jean-Michel Rabaté, "Le sourire du somnambule: de Broch à

Kundera," *Critique,* no. 433–34 (June–July 1983): 516. "Kundera ne se borne pas à liquider son passé lyrique de 'jeune Communiste' et de 'jeune poète' dans les années 1948–50. Il l'intègre à une vision plus large qui exige le cadre formel du roman et le langage de la prose, déterminé par l'ironie." Rabaté goes on to say, "Le référence à Rimbaud n'est pas fortuite, car elle permet de mesurer la force du lyrisme et de la révolte adolescente face aux pouvoirs que s'arroge le roman dans son désir propre, la totalisation des valeurs d'une époque et leur mise en question. . . . Mais ce que Jaromil représente, en plus de la veulerie de l'arriviste en poésie dans une période révolutionnaire, n'est pas seulement la parodie du 'cas Rimbaud' dans notre siècle, mais le même rabattement du désir du sujet que pour Joachim von Pasenow" (p. 515). The substance of this article consists in a comparison between Kundera's first three novels, centered on Bohemia and Moravia, with Hermann Broch's trilogy *The Sleepwalkers* (1931), centered on Germany. Rabaté sees Broch and Kundera as two masters of the postmodern Central European novel, which practices a systematic deconstruction, by means of laughter, of reigning cultural values and ideologies.

8. Claude Roy, "Jeu de massacres sur grandes figures," *Le Nouvel Observateur,* Fall 1983. Shortened and translated into Czech, this article serves as an introduction to the Sixty-Eight Publishers edition of the novel (pp. 7–10).
9. François Ricard, "Le point de vue de Satan," in *La littérature contre elle-même,* preface by Milan Kundera (Montréal: Boréal Express, 1985), p. 63: "Car l'objet de la critique (de la subversion) ici, n'est pas la 'mauvaise poésie,' mais bel et bien–il faut se le dire—*toute* poésie, toute forme de lyrisme, quelle qu'elle soit." Kundera chose this essay for the postface to the 1987 French edition of *Life Is Elsewhere.*
10. Pierre Gascar, *Rimbaud et la Commune* (Paris: Gallimard, 1971), p. 67: "La Révolution est un movement historique agrandi à un rêve d'enfance." Gascar's discourse on the phenomenon of a Parisian revolution carries a distinct verbal echo of the most famous slogan of the May 1968 student rebellion at

the Sorbonne and Nanterre, "*L'imagination au pouvoir!*" Gascar further discloses his debt to the politics of surrealism by choosing his epigraph from André Breton's *Second Manifesto of Surrealism* (1929–30): "Transformer le monde, a dit Marx. Changer la vie, a dit Rimbaud. Ces deux mots d'ordre, pour nous, n'en font qu'un." For the full text of Breton's second manifesto, see André Breton, *Manifestes du Surréalisme,* (Paris: J. J. Pauvert, 1963), pp. 154–221. For more on the relations between French surrealism and left-wing politics between the two world wars, see Maurice Nadeau, *Histoire du Surréalisme* (Paris: Editions du Seuil, 1945).

11. It is now firmly established (as even Gascar agrees) that whatever may have happened in April, Rimbaud was not in Paris during the bloody May days of 1871; see "Chronologie," in Arthur Rimbaud, *Oeuvres complètes* (Paris: Gallimard, Bibliothèque de la Pléiade, 1972), p. xlii. The legend of Rimbaud's participation in the Commune as a volunteer sharpshooter comes from his Charleville schoolmate E. Delahaye, who believed that Rimbaud returned to Paris in April 1871. In *Arthur Rimbaud* (New York: W. W. Norton, 1939) Enid Starkie dates Rimbaud's stay in Paris that winter from February 26, 1871, to mid-March. He had run off to Paris from Charleville in February, but he was definitely back at home on May 13, when he wrote the letter to Georges Izambard. In part 4 of *Life Is Elsewhere,* Kundera sums up his version of the "case of Rimbaud" thus: "Life was so much harder for Rimbaud, who dreamed about the barricades of the Paris commune but was unable to leave Charleville" (p. 175).
12. *Oeuvres complètes,* p. 248; my translation. The original reads, "Les colères folles me poussent vers la bataille de Paris,—où tant de travailleurs meurent tandis que je vous écris! Travailler maintenant, jamais, jamais, jamais, je suis en grève."
13. Ibid., p. 249.
14. "La Poésie ne rhythmera plus l'action; elle sera *en avant*" ("Poetry will no longer serve to give rhythm to action; it will be *ahead* of it"; my translation; ibid., p. 252). For the full text of *Lettre du voyant,* see "Rimbaud à Paul Demeny" (Charleville, May 15,

1871), *Oeuvres complètes,* pp. 249–54. In this famous letter, the seventeen-year-old poet describes with lapidary brilliance his conception of poetry as the magic gnosis of the unknown and his method of poetic initiation. "The unknown" (*l'inconnu*) is Rimbaud's term for a higher reality that the everyday realness of the world conceals and denies. By practicing a radical and disciplined negation of all control over his senses, the poet transforms himself into a seer ("Le poète se fait *voyant* par un long, immense, et déraisonné *dérèglement de tous les sens*"). For Rimbaud, the seer (*le voyant*) is the supreme man of knowledge ("le suprême savant!—Car il arrive à *l'inconnu!*") and the Promethean bearer of the gift of true freedom and true reality, not only for all of humanity, but even for the realm of nature and the animals ("Donc le poète est vraiment voleur de feu. Il est chargé de l'humanité des *animaux* même"). In this doctrine, the *words* of the initiated poet (*paroles du voyant*) are charged not only with the *vision* of the future but with the *power* to make it real.

15. The phrase "la cité sainte assise à l'Occident" denotes Paris in Rimbaud's poem "L'orgie parisienne," written in late May 1871 (*Oeuvres complètes,* pp. 81–83). With violent invective and passionate scorn, Rimbaud addresses the French bourgeoisie as it returns to repossess Paris in the wake of MacMahon's Versailles troops, which had just crushed the last remnants of communard resistance.
16. Kundera, "Paris or Prague?" p. 15.
17. *The Marx-Engels Reader,* ed. Robert C. Tucker (New York: W. W. Norton, 1978), p. 594.
18. Klement Gottwald (1896–1953), who also figures memorably in *The Book of Laughter and Forgetting,* was born in Moravia. A faithful member of the Moscow-dominated Czechoslovak Communist Party from 1925 on, he became Party chairman in 1945. President Beneš named him premier in 1946, and after the coup on February 24, 1948, he succeeded Beneš as president, a post he held until his death.
19. Breton, *Manifestes du Surréalisme,* p. 63; my translation. The original reads: "Cet été les roses sont bleues; le bois c'est du verre. La terre drapée dans sa verdure me fait aussi peu d'effet

qu'un revenant. C'est vivre et cesser de vivre qui sont des solutions imaginaires. L'existence est ailleurs."

20. Rimbaud, *Oeuvres complètes,* p. 103; my translation. The statement ("Quelle vie! La vraie vie est ailleurs. Nous ne sommes pas au monde") figures in "Délires I" of *Une saison en enfer* (1873).
21. For more on Wolker (1900–1924), see the chapter "The Proletarian Phase," in Alfred French, *The Poets of Prague: Czech Poetry Between the Wars* (New York: Oxford University Press, 1969), pp. 8–28.
22. Zdena Wolkerová, *Jiří Wolker ve vzpomínkách své matky* (Prague: Václav Petr, 1937).
23. Jaroslav Seifert, "Dosti Wolkra," *Všecky krásy světa* (Prague: Československý spisovatel, 1982), pp. 265–71.
24. Renato Poggioli, *The Theory of the Avant-Garde,* trans. Gerald Fitzgerald (Cambridge: Harvard University Press, 1968), p. 46. Poggioli also points out that the term "avant-garde," in its application to art and literature, is of Parisian origin and was used for the first time by the Fourieriste Gabriel-Désiré Laverdant in *De la mission de l'art et du rôle des artistes* (1845), which argues that art should serve as an instrument of social reform and revolutionary propaganda. "The avant-garde image originally remained subordinate, even within the sphere of art, to the ideals of a radicalism which was not cultural but political" (p. 9).
25. The phrasing of this categorical formula recalls the definition of beauty offered by André Breton in *L'amour fou* (Paris: Gallimard, Collection Métamorphoses, 1937): "La beauté sera violente ou elle ne sera point." It also echoes the implied violence of Vítězslav Nezval's dictum "Křečovitá krása" (spasmodic beauty), which is at the core of his aesthetic credo.

    The Moravian poet Nezval (1900–1958) was the founder of a Czech surrealist group that included the poet Konstantín Biebl and the painters Toyen and Štýrský. See French, "Interval for Surrealism," pp. 91–108. In 1934 Nezval issued his own manifesto of surrealism, *Surrealismus v ČSR,* and in 1935 he organized an international gathering of surrealists in Prague, which was attended by Breton and Éluard.

26. *Oeuvres complètes d'Isidore Ducasse, Comte de Lautréamont* (Paris: Librairie José Corti, 1956), p. 327. The phrase figures in the dream sequence of the sixth canto of *Les chants de Maldoror,* where the dreamer/narrator meets an English youth, sixteen years and four months of age, at the corner of Rue Colbert and Rue Vivienne in the Montmartre section of Paris. The boy's beauty sets in motion a series of violent images that play with the sadomasochistic ambiguity of a predatory chase, perceived simultaneously from within the consciousness of predator and victim.

The French poet Isidore Lucien Ducasse (1846–1870), who wrote under the pseudonym Lautréamont, was born in Montevideo, Uruguay, and died of tuberculosis in Paris shortly before the outbreak of the Franco-Prussian War. The surrealists enthroned him in their pantheon as a twin brother of Rimbaud and a visionary of cruelty. *Les chants de Maldoror* (1869), his famous cycle of prose poems (and the only known collection of poems he wrote), associates the idea of evil (*mal*) with gold (*or*) and pain (*douleur*). Maldoror, who practices a willed regimen of cruelty in order to explore the nature of God, mates violently and triumphantly with a female shark in a scene (canto 2) that was admired by the surrealists for its savage beauty and for linking the act of love to its most primitive aspect of torture. Maldoror, the poet-seer who experiences the erotic act as a sadistic sufferer, commands a unique place in the ranks of living creatures, midway between the purely physical realm of brutality and the absolute spirituality of the being he calls God. See Wallace Fowlie, *The Age of Surrealism* (Bloomington: Indiana University Press, 1960), pp. 28–44.

27. "Sorrow-lovely face" is the last line of "À peine défigurée," from Éluard's *La vie immédiate* (1932); see Paul Éluard, *Poèmes* (Paris: Gallimard, 1951), pp. 121–22. The full text reads:

> Adieu tristesse
> Bonjour tristesse
> Tu es inscrite dans les lignes du plafond
> Tu es inscrite dans les yeux que j'aime

Tu n'es pas tout à fait la misère
Car les lèvres les plus pauvres te dénoncent
Par un sourire
Bonjour tristesse
Amour des corps aimables
Puissance de l'amour
Dont l'amabilité surgit
Comme un monstre sans corps
Tête désappointée
Tristesse beau visage.

Here, as in Jaromil's poem, the sexual magnetism of the beloved woman resides in her face, in its expression of sadness at being severed from its erotic body.

28. See Maria Němcová Banerjee, "*Prague with Fingers of Rain:* A Surrealistic Image," *Slavic and East European Journal* 23, no. 4 (1979): 505–14.
29. Breton, "Position politique du Surréalisme," *Manifestes du Surréalisme,* p. 252; my translation.
30. I use the term *clinamen* in the same way as Harold Bloom in his *Yeats* (New York: Oxford University Press, 1970), to denote a poet's "swerving away from his precursors" (p. 7) in order to overcome what Bloom has called the "anxiety of influence." The Greek word *clinamen* comes from Lucretius, who used it to describe the swerving, sloping movement of atoms in their free fall through space.
31. I am reminded here of Jindřich Chalupecký's description of a poetry evening in the Lucerna hall in Prague shortly after 1948. Chalupecký recalls that almost all the famous representatives of the Czech literary left were present. To mark the solemnity of the occasion, most of the poets on the podium wore dark formal suits, with the exception of František Halas, a longtime Communist and a bold avant-gardist in poetry, who wore his customary casual gray. Zdeněk Nejedlý, the new minister of culture, spoke as usual against modern art. Chalupecký writes, "I shall never forget with what ostentatious servility Nezval applauded. And I shall also not forget that the only one whose hands did not

move was Halas" ("Poezie a politika," *Proměny* 22, no. 4 [1985]: 25; my translation).

32. "Dialogue on the Art of Composition," *AN*, p. 85.
33. "Sixty-three Words," *AN*, p. 129, under FATE.
34. André Breton, *Entretiens, 1913–1952* (Paris: Gallimard, 1952), p. 222; my translation.
35. *See Život je jinde*, pp. 307–33.
36. Jan Masaryk (1886–1948) was the son of Thomas Garrigue Masaryk (1850–1937), the founding president of the Czechoslovak Republic. Jan Masaryk was minister of foreign affairs in Beneš' cabinet and was the only minister to remain in office under Gottwald. His defenestration, officially declared a suicide, is widely believed to have been the work of the KGB.

4. *The Farewell Party*

1. "Dialogue on the Act of Composition," *AN*, 95.
2. The only published Czech text of the novel is *Valčík na rozloučenou* (Toronto: Sixty-Eight Publishers, 1979), carrying the postscript "Completed in Bohemia in 1972." An earlier draft of the novel dates from 1970 and bears the title, *Epilog, román;* a photocopy of the manuscript can be found in the Houghton Library of Harvard University. The French publication of the novel, *La valse aux adieux,* translated from the Czech by François Kérel (Paris: Gallimard, 1976), was followed in quick succession by other European editions. The Italian translation received the Premio Mondello for best novel published in Italy in 1976. In 1986 Kundera issued a revised French edition. In the United States, the novel was first published by Alfred A. Knopf in 1976, in a translation by Peter Kussi; I quote from the paperback edition, *The Farewell Party,* translated from the Czech by Peter Kussi, with an introduction by Elizabeth Pochoda (New York: Penguin Books, 1983).
3. François Rabelais, *The Histories of Gargantua and Pantagruel,* trans. J. M. Cohen (New York: Penguin Books, 1955), bk. 2, ch. 19, pp. 234, 237.
4. Ibid., ch. 20, p. 239.

5. "Dialogue on the Art of Composition," *AN*, p. 95.
6. "*The Farewell Party,* the novel I completed at approximately the same time, was to have been my last novel," he wrote in Paris in 1981 ("Introduction to a Variation," *Jacques and His Master: An Homage to Diderot in Three Acts,* translated from the French by Michael Henry Heim [New York: Harper & Row, Colophon Books, 1985], p. 11). This play was completed in Prague in July 1971. The introduction was first published in the French edition: "Introduction à une variation," *Jacques et son maître: Hommage à Denis Diderot en trois actes* (Paris: Gallimard, 1981).
7. "In the years that followed the 1968 Russian invasion of Czechoslovakia, the reign of terror against the public was preceded by officially organized massacres of dogs. An episode totally forgotten and without importance for a historian, for a political scientist, but of the utmost anthropological significance! By this one episode alone I suggested the historical climate of *The Farewell Party*" ("Dialogue on the Art of the Novel," *AN,* p. 37).
8. "Introduction to a Variation," p. 11.
9. "Dialogue on the Art of Composition," *AN*, pp. 93–94. The affinities between "The Symposium" and *The Farewell Party* are thematic as well as formal. In both pieces, the pivotal event is the death or near-death of a female nurse, resulting from an inscrutable accident that is interpreted as a suicide.
10. "Sixty-three Words," *AN*, p. 136.
11. The entire sequence of the thought is as follows: "The great European novel started out as entertainment, and all real novelists are nostalgic for it! And besides, entertainment doesn't preclude seriousness. *The Farewell Party* asks: Does man deserve to live on this earth, shouldn't the 'planet be freed from man's clutches'? To bring together the extreme gravity of the question and the extreme lightness of the form—that has always been my ambition. And it's not a matter of purely artistic ambition. The union of a frivolous form and a serious subject lays bare . . ." ("Dialogue on the Art of Composition," *AN*, pp. 95–96).
12. Fyodor Dostoyevsky, *The Idiot,* trans. David Magarshack (New York: Penguin Books, 1955), p. 38.

13. "Introduction to a Variation," p. 1.
14. Rabelais, bk. 3, ch. 26, p. 362.
15. Honoré de Balzac, *Old Goriot,* trans. Marion Ayton Crawford (London: Penguin Books, 1951), p. 157. Balzac's attribution of the idea of such a moral test to Rousseau is an error (he had already used the same example in 1824, in *Annette et le criminel*). The real source of the idea is Chateaubriand, in *Le Génie du christianisme* (1802). See the notes on this subject in *Année balzacienne* (1968) by A. Coimbra Martins and P. Ronai, pp. 520–23.
16. In František Halas, *Básně* (Prague: Československý spisovatel, 1957), pp. 246–49.
17. Later (p. 97) Bartleff compares the regimen of Christian saints to the training routine of athletes. He also declares that contrary to accepted modern opinion, saintly ascetics were not motivated by a desire to feel pain but by a desire for the greatest possible human pleasure, which he defines as the pleasure of "being admired."
18. Simeon Stylites (from the Greek *stylos,* column), also called Simeon the Elder, was born circa 390 in Cilicia and died in 459 in Telanissus, Syria. He was the founder of the tradition of pillar hermits—the stylites—ascetics known for their independence from Church authority. While the tradition never took root in the West, it was practiced as late as the nineteenth century in Russia, by Seraphim of Sarov. Simeon began as a shepherd, entered a monastic community, but was expelled because of the excessive severity of his way of life. He then became a hermit, but his reputed miracle working generated such popular veneration that he took up his pillar life northwest of Aleppo to escape his fame. His first column was six feet high; later he extended it to fifty feet.

    Bartleff puts his own paradoxical twist on Simeon's *vita* when he asserts that the saint was motivated by an "enormous thirst for admiration," a quality he deems admirable since it implies that in spite of his isolation, the hermit was "communing with all mankind" in his imagination. Bartleff concludes, "It is a great example of love for mankind and love for life" (pp. 98–99).

In *Jacques and His Master,* Kundera puts words of admiration for the saint into the mouth of the Marquis, who uses them as a ploy to get the attention of the beautiful young woman he is courting, whom he believes to be a marvel of chastity and religious devotion. In response to the girl's question, "Didn't Saint Simeon suffer from vertigo?," the Marquis explains that "he who looks upward is forever free of vertigo" (act 2, scene 7, p. 59).

19. Feodor Dostoevsky, *Crime and Punishment,* trans. Jessie Coulson, ed. George Gibian (New York: W. W. Norton, 1964), pt. 5, ch. 4, p. 402.
20. The Balzacian scheme for getting rich is indeed a component of Raskolnikov's idea, but in Dostoevsky's variation, it is raised to the level of humanitarian ideology. On the eve of the crime Raskolnikov recalls a conversation he overheard between a student and an officer in a tavern about six weeks earlier, when the germ of the idea of the murder was already growing inside his own brain. The student proposed to kill and rob the noxious Alëna Ivanovna, with the object of using her ill-gotten money to serve the "common good." "One death and a hundred lives in exchange—why, it's simple arithmetics!" the student exclaimed (ibid., part 1, ch. 6, p. 62).

    Georg Lukács noted the presence of the Balzacian motif in *Crime and Punishment* in his study *Der Russische Realismus in der Weltliteratur* (Berlin: Aufbau-Verlag, 1949), p. 178. Philip Rahv, in "Dostoevsky in *Crime and Punishment,*" *Partisan Review* 27, no. 3 (Summer 1960): 393–425, called the Balzacian motif "germinal" to the plot of *Crime and Punishment*.
21. André Gide, *Les caves du Vatican* (Paris: Gallimard, 1944), p. 48; all translations from this novel are mine. The words "Lafcadio Wluiki a présentement dix-neuf ans. Sujet roumain. Orphelin" appear in the postscript of a letter from Lafcadio's father, the former diplomat Juste-Agénor de Baraglioul, to his legitimate son Julius, whom he is sending to find out about Lafcadio, his character and his manner of life.
22. "Maintenant, Lafcadio, écoutez-moi: Aucun acte civil, aucun papier ne témoigne de votre identité" (ibid., p. 74).

23. Lafcadio, sitting calmly opposite his unsuspecting prey in the night train between Rome and Naples, visualizes the details of the action he is about to launch: "Un crime immotivé, continuait Lafcadio: quel embarras pour la police! Au demeurant, sur ce sacré talus, n'importe qui peut, d'un compartiment voisin, remarquer qu'une portière s'ouvre, et voir l'ombre du Chinois cabrioler. Du moins les rideaux du couloir sont tirés . . ." (ibid., p. 207). Lafcadio's offhand reference to his victim as "le Chinois" carries an allusion to the Balzacian motif of the killing of the mandarin. A few pages earlier, when Amédée Fleurissoire—a middle-aged Frenchman from the south, who has been told that the Freemasons have captured the Pope and are holding him prisoner in the caves of the Sant'Angelo Castle, and who fancies himself to be investigating this mysterious plot—enters the compartment, Lafcadio says to himself, "Entre ce sale magot et moi—quoi de commun?" (p. 202). The expression *sale magot* (*sale* meaning "dirty," a *magot* being a Barbary ape, a paunchy fellow, or a Chinese porcelain figurine) implies the same contempt for his victim as Raskolnikov's term "louse" for the pawnbroker.
24. Gide characterizes the genre of his novel in his subtitle, "Sotie." *Soties,* popular farces with overtones of political satire, were common in fifteenth- and sixteenth-century France. The plays may have originated in the clowning of the *fête des fous,* as the term *sotie* (from *sot,* foolish) seems to indicate. Pierre Gringoire (1475–1538), the most famous author of *soties,* gained the favor of King Louis XII with *Le jeu du Prince des Sots* (1512), which satirized Pope Julius II, thus lending support to the king's anti-Vatican policy.

    In *Lafcadio's Adventures,* Gide also satirizes the politics of religion by portraying the Catholic Church and its archenemy, the Masonic brotherhood, as two rival conspiracies whose means and ends mirror each other. The plot turns on a criminal conspiracy masterminded by the superman outlaw Protos with the object of defrauding rich Catholic devotees. Protos sponsors a fantastic "crusade" to free the Pope from the hands of the Masons, who, he suggests, have managed to abduct him and replace him with their puppet. Amédée Fleurissoire, a provincial French innocent, becomes the first martyr of this phony crusade when he dies at Lafcadio's hands, having traveled to Italy as an undercover scout for the holy cause.

Protos is a Vautrin-like character who shadows Lafcadio. It is he who picks up the telltale hat from the scene of the crime. His bid to subjugate Lafcadio to his will fails, and he is arrested. Lafcadio, however, confesses his guilt to his half-brother Julius, who counsels him to embrace the Church while allowing Protos to pay for his action. At the end of the novel, Lafcadio is in the arms of Julius's gentle daughter Geneviève, who advises him to submit and repent his crime.

5. *The Book of Laughter and Forgetting*

1. The novel was first published in France as *Le livre du rire et de l'oubli,* translated from the Czech by François Kérel (Paris: Gallimard, 1979); in 1985 Kundera issued a revised French edition. I quote from the English translation by Michael Henry Heim, *The Book of Laughter and Forgetting* (New York: Penguin Books, 1981), first published by Alfred A. Knopf in 1980. The Czech text, copyrighted in 1978, first appeared in Canada: *Kniha smíchu a zapomnění* (Toronto: Sixty-Eight Publishers, 1981).
2. The question of the book's genre has preoccupied many critics. In an interview with the author, published as an afterword to the Penguin edition, Philip Roth asks, "Your latest book is not called a novel, and yet in the text you declare: This book is a novel in the form of variations. So then—is it a novel or not?" Kundera replies, "As far as my own quite personal esthetic judgment goes, it really is a novel, but I have no wish to force this opinion on anyone" (pp. 231–32). Kundera reaffirms the same opinion in "Dialogue on the Art of Composition": "In *The Book of Laughter and Forgetting,* the coherence of the whole is created *solely* by the unity of a few themes (and motifs), which are developed in variations. Is it a novel? Yes, to my mind. The novel is a meditation on existence as seen through the medium of imaginary characters" (*AN*, p. 83).

Herbert Eagle, in "Genre and Paradigm in Milan Kundera's *The Book of Laughter and Forgetting,*" argues that "within each of the novel's seven parts (one might call them movements, adopting a musical metaphor of which Kundera himself is fond), the genres (as instruments) play their lines individually and also in concert, as Kundera frequently allows one genre to 'slide' into another, producing hybrid transitional forms." Eagle considers that the "dominant genre" that "organizes and situates" all the others in this "hybrid novel" is the essay. Eagle's essay appears in *Language and Literary Theory: In Honor of Ladislav Matějka*, ed. Benjamin Stolz, I. R. Titunik, and Lubomir Doležel, Papers in Slavic Philology, vol. 5 (Ann Arbor: University of Michigan Press, 1984), pp. 251–84 (quotation from p. 252).

3. Miguel de Cervantes Saavedra, *The Adventures of Don Quixote*, trans. J. M. Cohen (New York: Penguin Books, 1950), p. 940.
4. The lover's polynomia proceeds from the desire to express the infinite variety he perceives in the beloved's being. But there is another more sinister variation on that practice, on which Kundera will comment in part 6: "The street Tamina was born on was called Schwerin. That was during the war, and Prague was occupied by the Germans. Her father was born on Cernokostelecka Avenue—the Avenue of the Black Church. That was during the Austro-Hungarian Monarchy. When her mother married her father and moved there, it bore the name of Marshal Foch. That was after World War I. Tamina spent her childhood on Stalin Avenue, and when her husband came to take her away, he went to Vinohrady—that is, Vineyards—Avenue. And all the time it was the same street; they just kept changing its name, trying to lobotomize it" (p. 158). This type of polynomia is the nadir of the phenomenon of which the lover's practice is the apex, since it aims at reducing the identity of the thing named to an adjunct of the power that names it.
5. In the English text Tamina's husband also bears the name Mirek. It is dropped casually during a telephone conversation between Tamina and her mother-in-law in Prague: " 'There's a favor I'd like to ask you. When we left the country, we left

behind a small package.' 'Package?' 'Yes. You and Mirek locked it in his father's desk' " (p. 81). Kundera explained to me that this identity of names between two very different characters (Tamina's deceased husband and the dissident intellectual of part 1) is an error. In the Czech text, the husband's name is Petr (p. 91); in the definitive, fully revised French edition of 1985, it is Pavel (p. 121). Tamina's husband's name has no particular significance for the meaning of the novel.

Herbert Eagle reads particular significance into Kundera's choice of the name Mirek for the character in part 1: "Thus we feel from the outset that Mirek is a *privileged* character (privileged by the author with certain understandings which are very close to the author's own). This is further augmented by a play on Kundera's own name (Mirek=Milan Kundera)" (p. 257). It seems to me that it is not Mirek but the narrator who draws attention to the irony of Mirek's attempt to wipe Zdena from his past. And again, it is the narrator who links the telltale letters in Zdena's hands with the incriminating cap on Gottwald's head. Mirek retires to prison as if he were entering the "splendidly illuminated theater of history" (p. 24), blissfully unaware of being caught in Kundera's irony.

6. See Thomas Mann, "Der Kleider-Schrank: Eine Geschichte voller Rätsel" (1899), in *Erzählungen* (Frankfurt: S. Fischer Verlag, 1959), pp. 152–61. The German text reads, "Während er durch das vordere Zimmer ging, glaubte er, zwischen dem Geräusch seiner Schritte, nebenan, in jenen Klang zu hören, einen leisen, hellen metallischen Ton, . . . aber es ist ganz unsicher, ob es nicht Tauschung war. Wie wenn ein goldener Ring in ein silbernes Becken fällt, dachte er, . . ." (p. 158).
7. Kundera coins the formula *smrt-krása* (Czech text, p. 113) to characterize the lyrical attitude toward death. In the original Czech, the two words are both feminine nouns and their order, "*death-beauty,*" is the reverse of the English translation. This is an instance of a definition by lyric decree, in the manner of the surrealists. By the sole magic of metaphoric utterance, the material aspects of death are abolished and "beauty" emerges as the single attribute of "death."

8. The opera was commissioned by Emanuel Schikaneder for his popular suburban Viennese theater. Schikaneder, like Mozart, belonged to a Masonic lodge. This was, after all, the third year of the French Revolution, and the fancy mythological costume drama concealed an allegory about the ideological quest leading away from conventional knowledge and into the freedom of true enlightenment, as symbolized by the maligned figure of Sarastro. See *The Magic Flute,* English version by Edward J. Dent (New York: Oxford University Press, 1937). In Kundera's variation, the mask of Sarastro belongs to Death. Kundera has assured me that he was not thinking of Mozart's opera when he invented Tamina's name, which he chose purely for its phonetic value. My reading of a "variation on Mozart" here is my own interpretation.
9. Heim's translation says, "When she was finally naked, Hugo, excited by what he took to be her excitement, was stupefied to discover that Tamina's *genitals* were dry" (p. 109, my emphasis). The original Czech text uses *luno* ("A pak už byla docela nahá a Hugo, vzrušen jejím domnělým vzrušením, byl najednou ohromen, když zjistil, že Taminino luno je suché," p. 119), a word that lacks the physiological concreteness of "genitals." It sounds faintly archaic to the Czech ear, accustomed to hearing it used metaphorically, to denote the core, or the center (womb) of being. It seems to me that Kundera's usage deliberately raises the scene from the descriptive to the philosophical level. Emotionally, the word *luno* is merciful toward Tamina's person, thus creating an effect of powerful tension between body and soul within the obvious cruelty of the event. Kérel's French translation has *le ventre* (p. 129) in the 1979 edition, and *le sexe* (p. 160) in the revised 1985 edition.
10. Leo Tolstoy, *War and Peace,* Maude translation, ed. George Gibian (New York, W. W. Norton, 1966), p. 785.
11. Kundera's original Czech text says, "Smích, který je k smíchu, to je debakl" (p. 70). The word *debakl* suggests a disastrous happening that is also a disgrace. Heim has translated, "Laughable laughter is cataclysmic" (p. 62), which leaves out the tinge of scandal overheard in Czech.

12. Herbert Eagle has noted the binary pattern of organization at work in this novel. "In *Laughter and Forgetting* Kundera presents his concerns in the form of two major and opposed sets of images (paradigms): memory–forgetting, and demonic laughter–angelic laughter" (p. 253).
13. Eugène Ionesco, Author's Preface to the First Edition (1959), *Rhinocéros*, 2nd ed. (New York: Holt, Rinehart & Winston, 1976), pp. xi–xii.
14. The situation is a fiction created by Kundera, but the poetry is authentic, as indicated by Kundera himself at the end of part 3 (p. 76), where he gives the titles of the three works quoted in that narrative section: Annie Leclerc, *Parole de femme* (1976); Paul Éluard, *Le visage de la paix* (1951); and Eugène Ionesco, *Rhinocéros* (1959). Éluard's *Le visage de la paix* is a slim pamphlet that was published with twenty-nine illustrations by Picasso to commemorate the Congress of Partisans of Peace, held in Vienna under Communist auspices in 1950. It consists of twenty-nine short poems, some of them no more than two lines, written in a hortatory, prophetic style befitting a solemn message addressed *urbi et orbi*. Éluard's poem-proclamations have the same lyrical imperiousness ("ce qui est dit, sera") as the slogans Jaromil, Éluard's disciple, devised for Prague's May Day banners in 1949, before he was countermanded by Party hacks.
15. Here (part 6, "The Angels") Kundera is speaking of the "terrifying burden of buoyancy" that Tamina experiences after spending some time on the island of children, where the weight of remembering has been lifted from her.
16. *Parole de femme* is a heretical sermon written by a militant feminist angel. *Parole,* the word as *logos,* signals the solemn, authoritative thrust of Leclerc's discourse about female empowerment, which simultaneously seeks to deauthorize the prevailing male *logos* in our culture.
17. "To take, with Cervantes, the world as ambiguity, to be obliged to face not a single absolute truth but a welter of contradictory truths (truths embodied in *imaginary selves* called characters), to have as one's only certainty the *wisdom of uncertainty,* requires . . . courage" ("The Depreciated Legacy of Cervantes," *AN*, p. 6).

18. Leclerc writes, "Don Juan ne se tire de la mort que par l'aventure nouvelle qu'à son tour l'abandonne. Son culte de l'instant lorgne l'éternité. Mais tragiquement, il repète. Sa mort a vraiment le goût horrible du néant" (p. 73).
19. "*Laughable Loves* began as ten stories. When I was putting it in final form, I eliminated three of them and the whole thing became very coherent, in a way that prefigured *The Book of Laughter and Forgetting:* the same themes (especially the hoax) make a single entity out of seven narratives, the fourth and sixth of which are further linked by having the same protagonist, Dr. Havel. In *The Book of Laughter and Forgetting,* too, the fourth and sixth parts are linked by the same character: Tamina" ("Dialogue on the Art of Composition," *AN,* p. 85).
20. *Kniha smíchu a zapomnění,* p. 35; my emphasis.
21. "Lítost" is the title of the lead poem in František Halas's lyrical sequence "Kohout plaší smrt" ("A Cock's Crow Dispels Death," 1930). The full text of the poem (translated by Ron D. K. Banerjee) reads:

    Denně podléhaje kráse prvotného hříchu
    unavíš stráž ráje spustí meč
    zustávajíc netečnou a v tichu

    S žalem hledáš cestu zpáteční
    bloudě v širé rovině svých skutku
    naříkáš si na své zrození

    Zrazen krví zkažená je
    hruzou v nocích třeseš se
    jediného nervu nezapomínaje

    Svět tak známý až je cizí
    leží na tvém snu
    Plž skrytý v ruži

    (Daily prone with the beauty of original sin
    you tire out Eden's sentinel to down the sword
    stand indifferent and dumb

In grief you seek the trail of return
errant in the flats of your deeds
rail at your birth

Betrayed by blood gone bad
you shake with nightly terrors
aware of every nerve end

The world known grows alien
presses down on your dreaming
a slug lurking in the rose)

22. In the revised French text of 1985, Kundera pares down the definition: "*Litost* est un mot tchèque intraduisible en d'autres langues. Sa première syllable, qui se prononce longue et accentuée, rappelle la plainte d'un chien abandonné" (p. 174).
23. Plato, *The Symposium*, trans. W. Hamilton (New York: Penguin Books, 1951), p. 60.
24. Ibid., p. 113.
25. *Kniha smíchu a zapomnění*, p. 173.
26. "What is the connection between my father and Tamina undergoing her torment at the hands of the children? To invoke the Lautréamont phrase that the Surrealists loved, it is 'the encounter of a sewing machine and an umbrella on the dissecting table' of the same theme. Polyphony in the novel is much more poetry than it is technique" ("Dialogue on the Art of Composition," *AN*, p. 76).
27. "[Kafka's] novels are that seamless fusion of dream and reality. His novels: that supremely lucid gaze set on the modern world, along with the most unfettered imagination" (ibid., p. 81).
28. Leclerc, p. 157; my free translation. The original reads, "Horreur et fascination, la mort les a hantés, ces fanatiques du désir. . . . Cette mort qui les occupe tant, qui les assiège, franchement, qu'est-ce qu'ils en savent? Ils ne connaissent de la mort que les cadavres."
29. In "The Tragedy of Central Europe," Kundera has defined the region as "a small arch-European Europe, a reduced model of Europe made up of nations conceived according to one rule: max-

imum variety within minimum space" (*New York Review of Books*, April 26, 1984, pp. 33–38).

Nina Gladziuk's interesting essay "Sixteen Measures of Infinity," which I have read in typescript, argues that the "novel of variation" is the organic expression of Kundera's "metaphysics of small being." Gladziuk notes that this metaphysical view permeates all of Kundera's novels as well as his cultural meditations. She singles out three categories of thought and sensibility as characteristic of the "metaphysics of small being": "lightness" (bred of a sharp sense of the finite and mortal nature of all human things), "irony," and "interrogation."

30. "Dialogue on the Art of Composition," *AN*, pp. 89–90.
31. Kundera names no specific geographical location, leaving the seashore setting deliberately vague and open to a variety of imaginative associations. My reading of the scene suggests the presence of the Atlantic Ocean, with America beyond. If we imagine the beach to be somewhere in French Brittany, at the western limit of continental Europe, the Mediterranean allusion to Daphnis and Chloe assumes the dimension of a dream.

6. *The Unbearable Lightness of Being*

1. The novel first appeared in the French translation by François Kérel, *L'Insoutenable légèreté de l'être*, (Paris: Gallimard, 1984). In 1987 Kundera issued a revised edition of the French text. I quote from the English text, *The Unbearable Lightness of Being*, translated from the Czech by Michael Henry Heim (New York: Harper & Row, 1984). The Czech text, to which I also refer, is *Nesnesitelná lehkost bytí* (Toronto: Sixty-Eight Publishers, 1985).
2. Kundera has defined the novel as "the great prose form in which an author thoroughly explores, by means of experimental selves (characters), some great themes of existence" ("Sixty-three Words," *AN*, p. 142). Elsewhere he says, "To apprehend the self in my novels means to grasp the essence of its existential problem. To grasp its *existential code*" ("Dialogue on the Art of the Novel," *AN*, p. 29).
3. "Surgery takes the basic imperative of the medical profession

[i.e., to spend one's entire life involved with human bodies and all that they entail] to its outermost border, where the human makes contact with the divine" (p. 193).

4. Heraclitus, fragment 24: "Time is a child moving counters in a game; the royal power is a child's" (in Philip Wheelwright, *Heraclitus* [New York: Atheneum, 1964], p. 29).
5. See *The Will to Power,* trans. Walter Kaufmann and R. J. Hollingdale (New York: Vintage Books, 1968). In book 4 ("Discipline and Breeding"), section 3 ("The Eternal Recurrence") of this work, which is composed of his notes from 1883 to 1888, the year before he went mad in Turin, Nietzsche laid down a plan for a book on the subject ("*The Eternal Recurrence.* A prophecy," fragment 1057, 1883–88, pp. 544–45):

   1. Presentation of the doctrine and its *theoretical* presuppositions and consequences.
   2. Proof of the doctrine.
   3. Probable consequences of its being *believed* (it makes everything *break open*).
      a. Means of enduring it;
      b. Means of disposing of it.
   4. Its place in history as a *mid-point.*
      Period of greatest danger.
      Foundation of an oligarchy *above* peoples and their interests: education to a universally human politics.
      Counterpart of jesuitism.

   In book 1 ("European Nihilism," fragment 55, June 10, 1887, p. 36) he writes, "This is the most extreme form of nihilism: the nothing (the meaningless), eternally! The European form of Buddhism: the energy of knowledge and strength compels this belief. It is the most *scientific* of all possible hypotheses. We deny end goals; if existence had one, it would have to have been reached."
6. "I want to teach the idea that gives many the right to erase themselves—the great *cultivating* idea" (*The Will to Power,* fragment 1056, 1884, p. 544).
7. Ibid., fragment 55, June 10, 1887, p. 35.
8. In his autobiographical sketch "Ecce Homo," written in the

autumn of 1888, Nietzsche says, "The fundamental idea of my work—namely, the Eternal Recurrence of all things—this highest of all possible formulae of a Yea-saying philosophy, first occurred to me in August, 1881. I made a note of the thought on a sheet of paper, with the postscript: 6,000 feet beyond men and time! That day I happened to be wandering through the woods alongside of the lake of Silvaplana, and I halted beside a huge, pyramidal and towering rock not far from Surlei. It was then that the thought struck me. Looking back now, I find that exactly two months previous to this inspiration, I had had an omen of its coming in the form of a sudden and decisive alteration in my tastes—more particularly in music. It would even be possible to consider all 'Zarathustra' as a musical composition. At all events, a very necessary condition in its production was a renaissance in myself of the art of hearing. In a small mountain resort (Recoaro) near Vicenza, where I spent the spring of 1881, I and my friend and Maëstro, Peter Gast—also one who had been born again—discovered that the phoenix music that hovered over us, wore lighter and brighter plumes than it had done theretofore" (quoted in Elizabeth Förster-Nietzsche, "How Zarathustra Came into Being," in *The Philosophy of Nietzsche* [New York: Modern Library, 1954], p. xxiv).

9. *The Will to Power,* fragment 55, June 10, 1887, p. 35: "Duration 'in vain,' without end or aim, is the most paralyzing idea, particularly when one understands that one is being fooled and yet lacks the power not to be fooled."
10. The term "monster of energy" is the first of a series of metaphors Nietzsche uses to evoke his sense of cosmic *physis* as sheer will (*The Will to Power,* fragment 1067, 1885, pp. 549–50): "And do you know what 'the world' is to me? Shall I show it to you in my mirror? This world: a monster of energy, without beginning, without end; a firm, iron magnitude of force that does not grow bigger or smaller, that does not extend itself but only transforms itself; as a whole, of unalterable size, a household without expenses or losses, but likewise without increase or income; enclosed by 'nothingness' as by a boundary . . ." The passage runs on like a litany composed of metaphors and defini-

tions riding each other ("a sea of forces flowing and rushing together, . . . out of the play of contradictions back to the joy of concord . . ."), and all the while transforming the game of enumeration into a paean to what Nietzsche finally apostrophizes as "my *Dionysian* world of the eternally creating, my 'beyond good and evil,' without goal, unless the joy of the circle is itself a goal, without will, unless a ring feels good will toward itself." Finally, at the climactic end of the verbal projection of his act of *Wagnis* (metaphysical daring), Nietzsche delivers the secret formula of his metaphysical game plan by coupling the definition of cosmic being, as eternally pulsating nonhuman will, with a command addressed to his fellow humans, conceived in the absolute transience of their ephemeral selves: "*This world is the will to power—and nothing besides!* And you yourselves are also this will to power—and nothing besides!" That ecstatic affirmation of identity is the fundamental formula of Nietzsche's new Dionysian *logos*. It is the distillation of the tragic agon of "*Übergang*" (overcoming of the merely human), whereby Nietzsche has recaptured (unconsciously, by way of his unique blending of Heraclitus with Parmenides) the spirit of the Upanishadic *logos* in whose triumphant monism the Indo-Aryan speculative adventure finds its original impetus.

11. See Eduard Zeller, *Outlines of the History of Greek Philosophy* (New York: Meridian Books, 1960), pp. 81–82: "By temperament one of the greatest idealists of all time, this materialist [Democritus] devoted his whole life to research and thought it a greater gain to discover a causal connection than to receive the crown of Persia."
12. "Epicurus' Exhortation," fragment 14, in Cyril Bailey's *Epicurus: The Extant Remains* (Oxford: Clarendon Press, 1926), p. 107.
13. Rosalie L. Colie, *Paradoxia Epidemica* (Princeton: Princeton University Press, 1966), p. 23.
14. Fragments 8–34ff, in H. Diels, *Die Fragmente der Vorsokratiker* (1922), quoted in Zeller, p. 65.
15. Bailey, pp. 107–9.
16. Kundera is explicit on this point. Tomas's fundamental problem,

he says, is "the lightness of existence in a world where there is no eternal return" ("Dialogue on the Art of the Novel," *AN*, p. 29).

17. Tolstoy, in *What Is Art?*, uses the term *zaraza* (infection) to describe the powerful affective immediacy that distinguishes art from all other forms of human communication. Tolstoy introduces this subjective, emotional definition of art after dismissing the major aesthetic theories of the modern European tradition, all of which turn on the definition of beauty. In defining art in terms of its effect, Tolstoy turns away from the question "What is Art?" to the question "What is it that art does to us?"
18. See *Anna Karenina*, Maude translation, ed. George Gibian (New York: W. W. Norton, 1970), pt. 1, ch. 29. Here it is Anna herself, rather than Vronsky, who experiences such a metaphoric fever during her famous train ride back to Petersburg from Moscow, where she had been exposed to the "infection" of Vronsky's passion. "She passed her paper-knife over the window-pane, then pressed its cold smooth surface against her cheek and almost laughed aloud, suddenly overcome with unreasoning joy. She felt that her nerves were being stretched like strings drawn tighter and tighter round pegs" (p. 92). I wish to thank Michael Henry Heim for letting me see the text of his unpublished lecture "The *Anna Karenina* Subtext in Kundera's *The Unbearable Lightness of Being*," which he read at Harvard University in 1986. Heim sees Kundera's novel as a playful attempt to turn *Anna Karenina* on its head; he points out that Kundera reverses all the Tolstoyan signs, as in his realignment of the two couples: "Anna and Vronsky are lovers, Levin and Kitty man and wife; Tomas and Tereza are man and wife, Sabina and Franz lovers. Anna predominates over Vronsky, Tomas over Tereza; Levin predominates over Kitty, Sabina over Franz" (p. 5).
19. "Every time he spoke to Anna the joyful light kindled in her eyes and a smile of pleasure curved her rosy lips. She seemed to make efforts to restrain these signs of joy, but they appeared on her face of their own accord. 'But what of him?' Kitty looked at him and was filled with horror. What she saw so distinctly in the mirror of Anna's face, she saw in him. What had become of his usually quiet and firm manner and the carelessly calm expres-

sion of his face? Every time he turned toward Anna he slightly bowed his head as if he wished to fall down before her, and in his eyes there was an expression of submission and fear. 'I do not wish to offend,' his every look seemed to say, 'I only wish to save myself, but I do not know how.' His face had an expression which she had never seen before" (*Anna Karenina*, pt. 1, ch. 23, p. 74).

20. "And when she could not longer hide him, she took for him an ark of bulrushes, and daubed it with slime and with pitch, and put the child therein; and she laid it in the flags by the river's brink. And his sister stood afar off, to wit what would be done to him. And the daughter of Pharaoh came down to wash herself at the river; and her maidens walked along by the river's side; and when she saw the ark among the flags, she sent her maid to fetch it. And when she had opened it, she saw the child: and, behold, the babe wept. And she had compassion on him, and said, This is one of the Hebrews' children" (Exodus 2:3–6, King James Version).
21. Mircea Eliade, in *The Myth of the Eternal Return; or, Cosmos and History,* trans. Willard Trask (Princeton: Princeton University Press, 1954), argues that the Judeo-Christian conception of sacred time differs from the "great time" notion available to other archaic cultures, where the passage from the temporal to the eternal is accomplished through the ritual of repetition that opens the window on a sacred event or gesture located in a distant, mythical past. In the Judeo-Christian prophetic tradition, the locus of eternal significance has shifted to a distant, mythical future where all profane time will be canceled, or redeemed. In the messianic conception of time, "the future will regenerate time, that is, will restore its original purity and integrity. Thus, *in illo tempore* is situated not only at the beginning of time but also at its end" (p. 106), writes Eliade in the chapter "Misfortune and History."
22. In a privileged moment of authorial self-awareness, reflecting on Tomas's decision not to sign a petition of protest against the post-invasion Czech government, Kundera repeats the image of Tomas's indecision at the window, which was his moment of genesis in the novel. "This is the image from which he was born. . . . I have known all these situations, I have experienced them

myself, yet none of them has given rise to the person my curriculum vitae and I represent. The characters in my novels are my own unrealized possibilities. That is why I am equally fond of them all and equally horrified by them. Each one has crossed a border that I myself have circumvented. It is that crossed border (the border beyond which my own 'I' ends) which attracts me most. For beyond that border begins the secret the novel asks about. The novel is not the author's confession; it is an investigation of human life in the trap the world has become" (p. 221).

23. In "Dialogue on the Art of Composition," Kundera reveals that his best musical composition, created in his youth before he became a writer, mysteriously prefigures the architecture of his yet unwritten novels. He cites his Composition for Four Instruments (piano, viola, clarinet, percussion), which is divided into seven parts and consists of heterogeneous musical forms (jazz, fugue, chorale, etc.). Yet in spite of its formal diversity, it is a composition based exclusively on two themes elaborated from beginning to end. Though the composition in seven parts is a formal design that holds for all his novels (as well as his final version of *Laughable Loves*), Kundera says that it is not a deliberate ploy but "an unconscious drive, an obsession" (*AN*, pp. 90–91). This compositional dominance of two large themes holds true in *The Unbearable Lightness of Being*.

24. "She throws herself beneath the train without having taken the decision to do so. It is rather the decision that takes Anna." Kundera praises Tolstoy for having illuminated "the causeless, incalculable, even mysterious aspect of human action" ("Notes Inspired by 'The Sleepwalkers,' " *AN*, pp. 58, 57).

25. "On the 4th of January, at 7 o'clock at night, an unknown young woman, very well dressed, having arrived at the station Yasenki of the Moscow-Kursk railway, in Krapivensk Uyezd, went up to the rails, and when freight train no. 7 was passing, she made the sign of the cross and threw herself on the rails under the train, which cut her in two. An inquiry is being conducted into the incident." This notice, which appeared in *Tulskie Gubernskie Vedomosti* the day after the event, is reprinted in the section "Extracts from Letters, Diaries, and Newspapers," following

the text of *Anna Karenina* (p. 745). The editor's note on the same page informs us that Tolstoy, who had known the young woman suicide as the common-law wife of a neighboring landowner, went to see the autopsy carried out in the barracks at Yasenki.

26. Whenever Karenin is viewed in the light of Anna's alienating passion for Vronsky, he appears as a vindictive husband, a bureaucratic machine, and a monster of social propriety. But Tolstoy as narrator intervenes to correct Anna's optical defect, pointing to the hidden softness inside the man, a vulnerability to emotion that Anna once knew was there, even though she is now pretending to forget it. "None but those who knew Karenin most intimately knew that this apparently cold and sober-minded man had one weakness, quite inconsistent with the general trend of his character. Karenin could not with equanimity hear or see a child or a woman weeping. The sight of tears upset him and made him quite incapable of reasoning" (*Anna Karenina,* pt. 3, ch. 13, p. 253).
27. Sabina's technique, as she explains it to Tereza, is strikingly reminiscent of Tolstoy's description of the painter Mikhaylov at work on his picture of Christ before Pilate (*Anna Karenina,* pt. 5, ch. 10, p. 427). In both instances, it is an accidental occurrence—the trickle of red paint on Sabina's canvas and the spot of candle grease on Mikhaylov's—that acts as a window of opportunity, allowing the imagination to slip in and effect a visual transformation of the conventional painting in the process of being completed. And in both cases, the "technique" is not an end in itself but serves as a vehicle for the release of the transforming power of creative seeing, which unveils the latent beauty hidden under the lifeless surface of conventional forms.
28. "This is how it goes: A certain Dembscher owed Beethoven fifty florins, and when the composer, who was chronically short of funds, reminded him of the debt, Dembscher heaved a mournful sigh and said, '*Muss es sein?*' To which Beethoven replied, with a hearty laugh, '*Es muss sein!*' and immediately jotted down these words and their melody. On this realistic motif he then composed a canon for four voices: three voices sing '*Es muss sein, es muss sein, ja, ja, ja, ja!*' (It must be, it must be, yes, yes,

yes, yes!), and the fourth voice chimes in with *'Heraus mit dem Beutel!'* (Out with the purse!).

"A year later, the same motif showed up as the basis for the fourth movement of the last quartet, Opus 135. By that time, Beethoven had forgotten about Dembscher's purse. The words *'Es muss sein!'* had acquired a much more solemn ring; they seemed to issue directly from the lips of Fate. In Kant's language, even 'Good morning,' suitably pronounced, can take the shape of a metaphysical thesis. German is a language of *heavy* words. *'Es muss sein!'* was no longer a joke; it had become *'der schwer gefasste Entschluss'* (the difficult or weighty resolution).

"So Beethoven turned a frivolous inspiration into a serious quartet, a joke into metaphysical truth" (p. 195).

29. I hear a subtle echo here of the scene in *Anna Karenina* (pt. 1, ch. 18) where Anna meets Vronsky for the first time on the platform of the Moscow railway station. In Tolstoy's novel, it is Vronsky rather than Anna who transforms a purely social exchange into a coded invitation to love. Michael Heim, in the unpublished lecture already cited, has drawn attention to the gender switch Kundera performs in his intertextual dialogue with *Anna Karenina*. Vronsky comes to the station as a dutiful son meeting his unloved mother, who is arriving on the same Petersburg train as Anna. Instead of his shriveled mother, Vronsky sights Anna descending from the train carriage. Instantly, he is enveloped by the vital charm and grace emanating from Anna's figure. Her charm communicates itself to him through the lightness of her step and the casual but tender look she bestows on him, almost by mistake, as she searches for her brother Stiva in the waiting crowd on the platform. Soon after, Vronsky sees his mother, who introduces him to Anna formally, identifying her as her chance traveling companion. This is the launching of the first dialogue between Vronsky and Anna:

> "Anna Arkadyevna Karenina has a son who, I think, is eight years old," explained the Countess [Vronsky], "and she has never before been separated from him and so she is worried at having left him."

"Yes, the Countess and I have talked all the time—I about my son and she about hers," said Mrs. Karenina, and a smile brightened her face, a kind smile on his account.

"I expect you got very weary of it," he said, quickly seizing in its flight the ball of coquetry she had thrown at him. (pp. 57–58)

Vronsky, seizing his opportunity just like Tereza, translates Anna's code of maternal affection into the heady, adventurous code of erotic courtship. He is, of course, quite unaware that his flirtatious banter opens their nascent romance at the delicate spot where it will eventually rupture—the sore spot of the as yet unrevealed tension within Anna's mind and heart, between the contradictory pull of sexual and maternal love.

30. *Nesnesitelná lehkost bytí,* p. 37; my translation, my emphasis. The English translator, Michael Heim, occasionally substitutes a variant for the word *náhoda:* "It had taken six chance happenings to push Tomas towards Tereza. . . . And that woman, that personification of absolute *fortuity,* . . ." (p. 35, my emphasis). In the Czech original, Kundera deliberately repeats *náhoda:* "A ta žena, to ztělesnění absolutní náhody, . . ." (p. 37). The repetition is a significant device in this formula of definition that encapsulates Tomas's sense of Tereza. The word *náhoda* resounds six times in the paragraph that summarizes Tomas's retrospective vision of his first meeting with Tereza, and then it reverberates in the reflective commentary that follows, first in the adjectival form, *o lásku tak nahodilou. Nahodilá láska* (a love made up of chance) is an expression that reveals the etymological link of the adjective to the verb *nahoditi. Hoditi* means "to throw" and carries the suggestion of dice thrown at random, which makes Tomas's love for Tereza akin to something strewn across Tomas's path. On the other hand, *se hodilo* (past reflexive of the verb *hoditi*) connotes a sense of being "just right" for the situation, thus opening up the notion of the accidental to the notion of latent opportunity.

The interpretation of the word *náhoda* in all its complex

connotations as the instant of imaginative opportunity is central to the poetic theory and practice of Vítězslav Nezval (1900–1958), the great Czech surrealist poet, whom Kundera admires. In Nezval's theoretical lexicon, *náhoda* figures as the code word for the launching moment of surrealistic epiphany.

31. See Robert T. Petersson, *The Art of Ecstasy: Tereza, Bernini and Crashaw,* (New York: Atheneum, 1970). "Bernini gives us the figure of a woman uniquely posed, neither sitting nor lying down. The tendency for the weight of her body to make her fall is weaker than the tendency for her cloud-borne figure to rise. The highest folds of her habit are more buoyant than air. The ecstasy is a troubled state of transition between existence on earth and existence above. While her exterior nature occupies space and time, very little of her interior nature, the secret scene of her experience, is still in the world" (p. 95).
32. As Tolstoy describes Anna's inner experience at the moment of plunging under the wheels of the moving train, it is as if she were reliving the feeling of diving into water, which she had enjoyed when she went swimming as a young girl: ". . . and drawing her head down between her shoulders [she] threw herself forward on her hands under the truck, and with a light movement as if preparing to rise again, immediately dropped on her knees" (*Anna Karenina* pt. 7, ch. 31, p. 695).
33. "In the part called 'Words Misunderstood,' I examine the existential codes of Franz and Sabina by analyzing a number of words: woman, fidelity, betrayal, music, darkness, light, parades, beauty, country, cemetery, strength. Each of these words has a different meaning in the other person's existential code. Of course, the existential code is not examined *in abstracto;* it reveals itself progressively in the action, in the situations" ("Dialogue on the Art of the Novel," *AN*, pp. 29–30).
34. Part 3 opens not long after Sabina's arrival in Geneva, that is, not long after August 1968. It is more difficult to pin down the time of her flight from Geneva, but at the conclusion of the third part we see her in Paris, on the eve of her departure for America, when she has just received the news of Tomas and Tereza's accidental death. We know that Tomas and Tereza

stayed in Prague for five years (part 5), before withdrawing to the village. There the lovers lived the circular, evenly revolving time of nature's seasons for at least a couple of revolutions of the solar clock. We can therefore reckon that the elapsed time between the beginning and the end of the third narrative movement (which covers the chronological stretch of the action described in parts 5 and 7) is seven to eight years, which places Sabina's flight across the Atlantic somewhere around 1975.

35. In 1848 Sabina (1813–1877) was a radical and participated in Bakunin's ill-fated Prague uprising. Arrested in 1849, he saw his death sentence commuted to eighteen years of incarceration. By 1859 he had made a deal with the Austrian secret police, becoming a regular informer on radical activities in Prague. In 1872 Sabina's role was uncovered by his literary colleagues at a stormy meeting, and since then the reputation of infamy has stuck to his name like glue. Sabina wrote the libretto of Smetana's comic opera *The Bartered Bride* (*Prodaná nevěsta,* 1863), whose plot turns on the felicitous invention of a pseudo-betrayal by the young hero Jeník, which successfully resolves the threat to his true love for Mařenka. Some critics have seen a coded allusion to his own life in Sabina's text. See Antonín Měštan, *Česká literatura, 1785–1985* (Toronto: Sixty-Eight Publishers, 1987), p. 83. Kundera, in conversation with me, has disclaimed any intent to allude to Karel Sabina. The association is my own, an effect created by *náhoda*.
36. He raises this question in the context of Kafka's significance in the history of the European novel. "That life is a trap we've always known: we are born without having asked to be, locked in a body we never chose, and destined to die. On the other hand, the wideness of the world used to provide a constant possibility of escape. A soldier could desert from the army and start another life in a neighboring country. Suddenly, in our century, the world is closing around us. The decisive event in that transformation of the world into a trap was surely the 1914 war" ("Dialogue on the Art of the Novel," *AN*, pp. 26–27).
37. *The Collected Poems of W. B. Yeats,* (New York: Macmillan, 1966), p. 255. The poem, "Crazy Jane Talks with the Bishop,"

is the sixth in the cycle "Words for Music Perhaps." The last of its three stanzas reads:

> A woman can be proud and stiff
> When on love intent;
> But Love has pitched his mansion in
> The place of excrement;
> For nothing can be sole or whole
> That has not been rent.

38. In defining the concept of the idyll, Kundera notes its importance to Central European culture: "IDYLL. A word rarely used in France, but a concept important to Hegel, Goethe, Schiller: the condition of the world before the first conflict; or beyond conflicts. . . . The desire to reconcile erotic adventure and idyll is the very essence of hedonism—and the reason why it is impossible" ("Sixty-three Words," *AN*, p. 132).

    In Czech literature, the enduring model of the village idyll was fixed by Božena Němcová (1820–1862) in her pastoral novel *Babička* (1855). Her images of the Czech village helped nourish a rich strain in Czech lyrical poetry (see also p. 41 above). František Hrubín (1910–1971), the poet whose funeral is alluded to briefly in *The Unbearable Lightness of Being* (p. 229), was one of the last great poets of the Czech village idyll.
39. In part 5, chapter 10, Kundera distinguishes two varieties of the male compulsion to pursue an endless number of women. He defines the "lyric" womanizer as one who obsessively seeks his own "subjective and unchanging dream of a woman in all women." The Don Juan of Mozart's opera is the paradigm of this type of lover. The "epic" womanizer is "prompted by a desire to possess the endless variety of the objective female world" (p. 201).
40. "But many also died without being directly subjected to persecution; the hopelessness pervading the entire country penetrated the soul to the body, shattering the latter. Some ran desperately from the favor of a regime that wanted to endow them with the honor of displaying them side by side with its new leaders. That is how the poet Frantisek Hrubin died—

fleeing from the love of the Party. The Minister of Culture, from whom the poet did everything possible to hide, did not catch up with Hrubin until his funeral, when he made a speech over the grave about the poet's love for the Soviet Union" (p. 229).

41. In "Notes Inspired by 'The Sleepwalkers,' " Kundera calls History "that European oddity, that smudge on time's pure surface" (*AN*, p. 56).
42. Sophocles, *Oedipus the King,* trans. David Grene (Chicago: University of Chicago Press, 1954), ll. 1088–1107, 1188–1223, 828–30.
43. Ibid., ll. 977–79.
44. Ibid., ll. 1329–32.
45. "Contrasts in tempi are enormously important to me. . . . There [in *The Unbearable Lightness of Being*], from the moment the writing began, I knew that the last part should be *pianissimo* and *adagio* ('Karenin's Smile': a calm, melancholy mood, with few events) and that it would be preceded by one that was *fortissimo, prestissimo* ('The Grand March': a rough, cynical mood, full of events)" ("Dialogue on the Art of Composition," *AN*, pp. 89–90).
46. "Digression means: abandoning the story for a moment. All of the reflection on kitsch in *The Unbearable Lightness of Being,* for example, is a digression: I leave off telling the novel's story to go at my theme (kitsch) *directly*" (ibid., p. 84).
47. Fyodor Dostoevsky, *The Brothers Karamazov,* trans. Constance Garnett, rev. Ralph E. Matlaw (New York: W. W. Norton, 1976), pt. 2, bk. 5, ch. 9, p. 226.
48. In "Notes Inspired by 'The Sleepwalkers,' " Kundera says that History, "that European oddity, . . . looks finished already, abandoned, lonely, and suddenly as humble, as touching as some little personal story we'll forget by tomorrow" (*AN,* p. 56).
49. "Because of that dislocation, the last part, despite its idyllic quality, is flooded with a melancholy that comes from our knowledge of what is to happen" ("Dialogue on the Art of Composition," *AN*, p. 77).

7. *Immortality*

1. *Immortality* was first published in France as *L'immortalité*, translated from the Czech by Eva Bloch (Paris: Gallimard, 1990), in a definitive text approved by the author. All quotes here are taken from the first American hardcover edition, translated from the Czech by Peter Kussi (New York: Grove Weidenfeld, 1991).
2. Kundera has left a number of clues to help us calculate the time of the novel's composition. In part 4, chapter 17, Goethe gives his postmortem age as 156; added to the year of his death, 1832, this pinpoints the year 1988. In part 7 we learn that the narrator took exactly two years to complete the act of writing *Immortality*.
3. *The Farewell Party*, p. 22.
4. "The Depreciated Legacy of Cervantes," *AN*, p. 6.
5. *Purgatorio by Dante*, trans. by John Ciardi (New York: New American Library, A Mentor Book, 1961).
   "Purgatorio II," lines 112–115:

   > *"Love that speaks its reasons in my heart,"*
   > he sang then, and such grace flowed on the air
   > that even now I hear that music start.
   > My Guide and I and all those souls of his
   > stood tranced in song: . . .

6. The other word for "face" is *obličej*. Etymologically linked to the Slavic root word *lik*, the word can be associated to the Russian word for "mask," *lichina*.
7. Carter's case follows the paradigm established in the novel by Tycho Brahe, the sixteenth-century astronomer whose name remains forever linked to the incident Kundera describes on p. 50. During a dinner at the Prague Castle, in the presence of the emperor, Tycho was too ashamed to show that he needed to relieve himself. His bladder burst, turning him into a "martyr to shame and urine."
8. *Paradiso* (Dante), trans. by John Ciardi (New York: New American Library, A Mentor Book, 1961).

"Paradiso I," line 86:

> And she, who saw my every thought as well as I
> (Ed'ella, che vedea me sí com'io)

9. François Rabelais, *The Histories of Gargantua and Pantagruel*, trans. J. M. Cohen (New York: Penguin Books, 1955), *Pantagruel*, ch. 8, p. 193.
10. *Dichtung und Wahrheit*, part 2, book 8.
11. Bettina von Arnim, *Goethes Briefwechsel mit einem Kinde* (Frankfurt am Main: Insel Verlag, 1984). The first description is in Bettina's letter to Goethe's mother, dated May 16, 1807 (pp. 38–39), the second in a letter to Goethe, dated May 15, 1897 (pp. 106–7), and the third in *Tagebuch*, pp. 541–42.
12. Kundera refers to Lacan's theory in part 3, "Fighting," where he cites the example of a young Czech woman who returned to Bohemia from Paris in 1969, armed with Lacanian techniques. He takes this opportunity to describe "the stage of the mirror": "meaning that before we become aware of our parents' bodies we become aware of our own" (p. 166).
13. In Bettina's book, the eroticism of Goethe's hand gesture is diluted—Goethe is playing with Bettina's curls. Letter to Goethe, dated October 18, 1897, p. 408. Kundera draws on the original text of Bettina's letter, which was discovered only in 1929, when the family archives were opened to the public. I found an English translation in Arthur Helps and Elizabeth Jane Howard, *Bettina: A Portrait* (New York: Reynal, nd), p. 120.
14. Von Arnim, letter to Goethe dated January 12, 1824, pp. 463–69.
15. This letter is cited in Helps and Howard, p. 155.
16. *Goethes Briefe*, Band IV (Hamburg: Christian Wegner Verlag, 1967), letter dated September 13, 1826, p. 201.
17. "The Depreciated Legacy of Cervantes," *AN*, p. 16.
18. The expression occurs during a discussion of the interviewing technique that treats the person interviewed as a guilty party, forcing him to reveal the most intimate or petty facts of his life.
19. See "The Depreciated Legacy of Cervantes," *AN*, p. 3. The formulation "the forgetting of being" has its origins with Heidegger.

20. Jean-Baptiste Clamance, described as the penitent-judge, is the voice of Albert Camus's novel *La Chute* (1956).
21. I cite from Louis MacNeice's translation of Goethe's *Faust* (New York: Oxford, 1960), part 2, act 5, "Midnight," p. 283.
22. Ivan Klíma, "Kunderova Nesmrtelnost," *Přítomnost*, c. 3, 26 (September 1990).
23. See the references to Avenarius in John Passmore, *A Hundred Years of Philosophy* (London: Gerald Duckworth, 1957). Passmore discusses Avenarius's theory of introjection in relation to William James, *Essays in Radical Empiricism* (1912).
24. Philippe Sollers, "Le diable mène la danse," *Nouvel Observateur*, 1/11.90.
25. Rabelais, *Pantagruel*, ch. 22, "How Panurge Played a Trick on the Parisian Lady Which Was Not at All to Her Advantage," pp. 242–46.
26. Kundera first discusses the scene in part 2, chapter 13.
27. "The Depreciated Legacy of Cervantes," *AN*, p. 19.
28. Ibid., p. 4.
29. Miguel de Cervantes Saavedra, *The Adventures of Don Quixote*, trans. J. M. Cohen (New York: Penguin Books, 1950), p. 203.
30. "Notes Inspired by *The Sleepwalkers*," *AN*, pp. 62–63.
31. The line comes from Rimbaud, " 'Au Cabaret-Vert,' Cinq heures du soir," in *Oeuvres de Arthur Rimbaud* (Paris: Mercure de France, 1952), "Poésies," p. 54. It is dated October 1870.
32. Rimbaud, "Délires," *Une Saison en enfer*, in *Oeuvres*, p. 176. This utterance follows immediately after "*La vraie vie est absente*," the sentence Kundera refers to in *Life Is Elsewhere*.
33. This reference to *le bonheur* appears in the French edition on p. 258; in the American edition *le bonheur* has been translated as "happiness," see p. 308.
34. Jean-Jacques Rousseau, *Les Rêveries du promeneur solitaire* (New York: Doubleday, Collection Internationale, 1961), p. 122.
35. František Halas, *Básně* (Prague: Československý Spisovatel, 1957). The poem figures in the cycle *Ladění* ("Tuning"), 1937–41. It is inscribed to the actress Marie Burešová. Here is an English translation by Ron D. K. Banerjee.

The Pied Piper

Agnes Agnes from the land of seven castles
Where do you then lure us on
Calling death's bird oh god when I'll tiptoe in
Into the anointed land of seven castles
Discovered by your voiced chanson

Agnes Agnes the Lethean stream sings
Tragedy flares in your brow's flambeau
In darkness where being flows into grand finale
Leading your voice and a dirge takes wings
That path of death to greatness turning

36. *Life Is Elsewhere*, p. 271.
37. "Dialogue on the Art of Composition," *AN*, p. 85.
38. "The Depreciated Legacy of Cervantes," *AN*, p. 16.
39. Charles Baudelaire, *Les fleurs du mal* (Paris: Classiques Garnier, 1952). "Les Phares," from the "Spleen et idéal" section, p. 17.
40. Stendhal, *Vie de Henry Brulard*, ch. 2, in *Oeuvres intimes de Stendhal* (Paris: Bibliothèque de la Pléiade, 1961). On p. 15, Beyle/Stendhal, in a nostalgic review of his erotic life, lists and meditates on six women.
41. Goethe wrote the Witch's Kitchen scene of *Faust*, part 1, in the garden of the Villa Borghese during his stay in Rome, in early spring of 1788. The information comes to us from Goethe's conversation with Eckermann more than forty years later (April 10, 1829). See *Faust*, edited by Cyrus Hamlin (New York: Norton, 1976), "Interpretive Notes," p. 317.
42. The astrological clock was constructed in 1410 by Master Mikuláš. Its complicated mechanism shows four different times simultaneously: the normal Central European time; the so-called Old Czech time, counted from sunset on; the astral time, indicated by the angle of the meridian and the vernal equinox; and the so-called *temporalis*, indicated by the movement of the zodiacal belt. The clock divides night and day evenly, regardless of seasonal differences.

During the period of national revival in the nineteenth century, the city commissioned the painter Josef Mánes to paint the twelve months of the year in the form of a rotating calendar. Mánes's "Czech clock" (*český orloj*), with its twelve images of village life conceived in the genre of a pan-Slavic stylization, was inaugurated in August 1866, under the eyes of the Prussian general who was then occupying Prague. This *český orloj*, showing the idyllic time of the village, is placed under the two main time dials, thus counterpointing from below the spiritual allegory of Christian time with its earthbound myth of a nurturing, cyclical Nature.

For the description of the clock I have drawn on Jiří Horák, *Kniha o staré Praze* (Prague: Práce, 1989), "O Staroměstském orloji," pp. 324–28.

43. Gustav Mahler was born in Moravia in 1860 and died in Vienna in 1911. Mahler's Seventh Symphony, like *Immortality*, is a vast cyclical composition notable for its avoidance of a programmatic content. It is constructed around the concept of two large-scale outer movements framing a middle part. "There are no programmatic clues to the Seventh, but if the signs and images in the slow introduction to the first movement are read correctly, then a good case can be made out for the symphony as a whole having been consciously built around the poetic idea of nocturnal nature, progressing through various shades of darkness" (*The New Grove Dictionary of Music and Musicians*, edited by Stanley Sadie [London: Macmillan, 1980], vol. 2, pp. 521–23).

Another common feature of Kundera's novel and Mahler's symphony is a design based on sudden discontinuity and a final display of cyclic conjuring tricks. For sheer listening immediacy, the most powerful Mahlerian resonance in this novel is captured in the metaphor of the father's magic hunting horn heard from the depth of a darkened forest, which is linked to the *Wunderhorn* echo in the nocturne passage of the symphony.

44. Rimbaud, *Le Bateau ivre*, in *Oeuvres*, pp. 110–14.